A Theory of Human Need

A Theory of Human Need

Len Doyal and Ian Gough

MACMILLAN

First published 1991 by
THE MACMILLAN PRESS LTD
Houndmills, Basingstoke, Hampshire RG21 2XS
and London
Companies and representatives
throughout the world

ISBN 0–333–38324–9 (hardcover)
ISBN 0–333–38325–7 (paperback)

A catalogue record for this book is available
from the British Library.

Printed in Hong Kong

Reprinted 1992

'The absurd is born of this confrontation between human need and the unreasonable silence of the world'.—**Albert Camus**

Contents

List of Tables

List of Figures

Preface

Talking in front of a coal fire in 1982, we discovered that we both had strong views about the existence of universal human needs and the inconsistencies of those who didn't. Although we come from different academic backgrounds – philosophy and political economy – we both believed that without a coherent theory of human need to back them up, many of the political causes to which we were committed made little sense. This belief was underlined by the political successes of the New Right in the early 1980s which fed upon the theoretical confusion of its opponents.

Our initial attempt at clarification was in an article with the same title as this book which was published in *Critical Social Policy* in 1984. Expanding these ideas has taken much longer than we and many others hoped and expected. This has been because of the enormity of the topic itself, the pressures of busy professional lives and the difficulties of academic collaboration over long distances. In some ways we regret the delay. For example, many of the changes which we argued in early drafts would have to come in the Eastern Bloc and Russia have actually occurred. Indeed, this change has occurred with such a vengeance that we have postponed plans for a second volume on the political economy of needs until the dust settles.

Yet the long gestation of our work has had two important advantages. First, we have been able to benefit from some fine research on human needs published since 1984 and have had time properly to contemplate the work of earlier writers. We have tried in all cases to give credit where credit is due but in a work of this size and complexity we may have left someone out. If so, we apologise in advance.

Second, the years have also led to the primary joy of our work – the evolution of our friendship and that of our families. A project of this duration is inevitably a burden for the partners. The simple fact is that our book could not have been completed without the labour and love of Lesley Doyal and Margaret Jones. Lesley edited two drafts of the entire book and made invaluable suggestions on both substance and style. Margaret also provided consistent intellectual support. Both gave emotional and material help on many weekends of intense – and sometimes pretty obscure – discussion and writing. Most important of all, in constant dialogue and debate, they both kept us honest with ourselves and with the ideals which the four of us share. We dedicate it to them both with our love and thanks.

There are so many other colleagues and friends who have joined in our effort and who merit our public thanks that we hardly know where to begin. At Middlesex Polytechnic and Manchester University, Jonathan Powers and Paul Wilding have been staunch in their support, though they must often have doubted at times whether anything would result from it. It is no longer straightforward to write a book, let alone one as ludicrously ambitious as this, at a British institution of higher learning, but thanks to Jonathan, Paul and members of the School of Philosophy and Religious Studies at Middlesex and the Department of Social Policy and Social Work at Manchester, it has not proved impossible. Ian Gough is grateful, too, to the ESRC for the relief offered by a two-month personal research grant way back in the winter of 1984–5.

We are especially indebted to Roger Harris, Harry Lesser, Ian Miles, Raymond Plant, Jonathan Powers, David Purdy, Laurent van der Maesen and Grenville Wall, who read and commented on earlier drafts of the entire book, and to Meghnad Desai who did the same for the almost-final version. Warm thanks also to Paul Cammack, Roy Carr-Hill, Pat Devine, Diane Elson, Ian Forbes, Caroline Glendinning, Geoff Hodgson, Phil Leeson, Elena Lieven, Peter Osborne, Rosemary Pringle, Sophie Watson and Daniel Wilsher – all of whom have assiduously read and criticised various parts of the book. We have also benefited from the comments of no fewer than six anonymous readers commissioned by our publishers. It is safe to say that no one agreed with all of what they read. We learned a lot from their help, but of course bear sole responsibility for what remains.

We are grateful to Martin Baldwin-Edwards, who gave invaluable research assistance in compiling and computing the data in Chapters 12 and 13, to Sarah Jane Evans, who meticulously copy-edited the typescript, to Jackie Butterley, who prepared the index, and to Ben Jones, who did an excellent job checking the bibliography.

Finally, there is one other person whose encouragement and patience has been indispensable in our finally delivering the goods – to him! Steve Kennedy has been a pillar of strength and enlightened editing. We will always be grateful to him for his friendship and his concern about our basic needs.

LEN DOYAL
IAN GOUGH

Acknowledgements

The authors and publishers wish to acknowledge the following for permission to reproduce copyright material:

Figure 8.1 from Peter Warr, *Work, Unemployment and Mental Health*, Oxford University Press, 1987, p. 10, figure 1.1.

Figure 9.2 from U205 Course Team, *The Health of Nations*, Open University Press, 1985, p. 19, figure 3.3.

Figure 10.1 from G. W. Brown and T. Harris, *Social Origins of Depression*, Tavistock Publications, 1978, p. 46.

Figure 13.1 from Frances Stewart, *Planning to Meet Basic Needs*, Macmillan, 1985, p. 61, figure 4.2.

Table 12.2 from Howard Jones, *Social Welfare in Third World Development*, Macmillan, 1990, p. 110, table 5.3.

Introduction

The idea of human need is widely used. Sometimes it is employed in attempts to justify social policies (e.g. 'The frail elderly need more sheltered housing') and to criticise them (e.g. 'British schooling does not meet the needs of its children'). So general is this use that it is hard to imagine how we could function without it. Are not decisions inevitable which prioritise some things and not others on the basis of need? Yet the idea of need has also been widely abused. On the grounds of their expertise about the satisfaction of human need, planners have justified and implemented disastrous social policies. Examples are unpopular public housing or the sometimes officious and meddling managers of welfare benefits. This abuse was most notable in the Eastern bloc system, labelled in a recent book 'a dictatorship over needs' (Feher *et al.*, 1983). Indeed, such perceived abuses have become so extensive that many have rejected the existence of common human needs, the satisfaction of which can be planned for in a uniform and successful way.

This rejection has gone hand in hand with a more general scepticism about the coherence of conceptions of rationality or reality which purport to be universal and objective. Stressing the impact of differences in language and culture on the way in which the world is theorised and perceived, such critics have either denied or minimised the importance of theories which contend that the needs of all humans are fundamentally the same. Economists, sociologists, philosophers, liberals, libertarians, Marxists, socialists, feminists, anti-racists and other social critics have increasingly regarded human need as a subjective and culturally relative concept, a credo which has contributed to the intellectual dominance of the New Right in the 1980s. For if the notion of objective need is

1

groundless, then what alternative is there but to believe that individuals know what is best for themselves and to encourage them to pursue their own subjective goals or preferences? And what better mechanism is there to achieve this than the market?

One thing is clear. A wide range of concepts concerning the evaluation of the human condition seems inextricably linked to the view that universal and objective human needs do exist. For example, it is difficult to see how political movements which espouse the improvement of human welfare can fail to endorse the following related beliefs:

1. Humans can be *seriously harmed* by alterable social circumstances, which can give rise to *profound suffering*.
2. Social *justice* exists in inverse proportion to serious harm and suffering.
3. When social change designed to minimise serious harm is accomplished in a sustained way then social *progress* can be said to have occurred.
4. When the minimisation of serious harm is not achieved then the resulting social circumstances are in conflict with the *objective interests* of those harmed.

Of course, the concept of serious harm is not the only place we could begin. Theory and practice which are critical of the political and moral status quo could equally well start with the more positive image of fundamental human *flourishing* and refer to the different sorts of social environments which encourage and sustain this process.

Either way, the most significant arguments supporting social *equality* focus on the extent to which humans have the same *potential* to be harmed or to flourish. Assuming that such potential exists, it is often argued that it is *unjust* and therefore wrong to favour one individual or group to the arbitrary disadvantage of any other. The history of socialist, reformist, anti-capitalist and anti-communist writing is, of course, full of both negative and positive images. The main point is that the theory and practice which they articulate are essentially *critical* and embody a range of *standards* with which morally to assess human affairs.

So the clarity of the preceding inter-related concepts presupposes that it *is* possible to identify objective and universal human goals which individuals must somehow achieve if they are to be able to optimise their life chances – that all humans have basic human needs in these terms. Similarly, when people express outrage at injustice, somewhere in the background is the belief that basic human needs exist which should have been satisfied but were not. It is the belief that the satisfaction of basic needs has normative *precedence* over the satisfaction of wants that generates condemnation when such needs are not satisfied. Generally speaking, we are morally more concerned when what we believe to be basic needs rather than wants go unsatisfied – free speech rather than free sweets. Yet without the concept of objective human need and the moral work of which it alone seems capable, this move from 'is' to 'ought' would not be possible.

We might therefore expect considerable agreement, at least among critics of the status quo, about what basic human needs are and how they should be satisfied. Yet as we have said, this is not the case. We are thus faced with the paradox that an idea which is still regularly used in the practice of social policy and in much political discourse is regularly rejected in the domain of theory. The result can only be confusion for providers of welfare and for those who are committed to the political struggle for the increased provision of welfare.

In order to correct this situation, we believe that a coherent, rigorous theory of human need must be developed to resurrect an acceptable vision of social progress and to provide a credible alternative to the neo-liberalism and political conservativism which have caused serious harm to so many within the capitalist world. However, such a theory must be informed by the mistakes – some terrible, some foolish – of welfare state paternalism, Stalinist collectivism and other political practices which have been premised on the existence of common needs. A credible and morally attractive theory of human need must draw upon both liberal and socialist thought. It will need to chart a third way forward which rejects both market individualism and state collectivism. We hope that this book will provide such a theory and will suggest how it should be applied in practice.

In general, we shall argue that basic human needs can be shown to exist, that individuals have a right to the optimal satisfaction of these needs and that all human liberation should be measured by assessing the degree to which such satisfaction has occurred. Yet in extolling the plausibility and importance of the concept of basic human need, we will not forget how its use has sometimes caused serious harm. Any acceptable concept of need must be designed so that it cannot be used in authoritarian and paternalistic ways. Welfare states must somehow combine the individual right to need-satisfaction with the right to participate in deciding how such satisfaction is to occur in practice. It is for this reason that the problems of welfare provision and effective democracy are inextricably linked. A successful theory of human need must show why and how. In other words, in developing such a theory and demonstrating its use in practice, our approach will be both *substantive* and *procedural*.

Part I introduces the issue of individual and cultural relativity through examining and rejecting arguments that human needs are reducible to individual or collective preferences. In doing so, we explore the grammar of 'need' in ordinary discourse, illustrating its relationship to more general arguments about relativism.

Part II argues that 'health' and 'autonomy' constitute the most basic human needs which are the same for everyone. It is further argued that all humans have a right to optimum need-satisfaction. For this to occur, it will be shown that that certain societal preconditions – political, economic and ecological – must be fulfilled.

The theory of need that emerges is then operationalised in Part III. The distinction between universal needs and culturally-relative satisfiers is clarified. Indicators of basic and 'intermediate' needs are identified and used to chart human welfare in the First, Second and Third Worlds.

Human needs, we argue, are neither subjective preferences best understood by each individual, nor static essences best understood by planners or party officials. They are universal and knowable, but our knowledge of them, and of the satisfiers necessary to meet them, is dynamic and open-ended. We conclude the book in Part IV by endorsing recent proposals for a mixed economy which also combines elements of both central planning and democratic decision-making – a 'dual strategy' for the optimisation of need satisfaction.

In exploring these ideas, we face a dilemma with regard to the significance of the individual in the politics of human need. When the moral importance of the needs of individuals is politically minimised, it is sometimes argued that the collective will benefit as a result – through, for example, a forced redistribution of wealth and income. Yet at the same time, if individual liberty and privacy are too much ignored in the name of the collective then we risk discarding what is valuable with what is not. Without understood and secure parameters of individual self expression and personal ownership, the raison d'être for redistribution – the maximum development of the individual as a person – becomes lost.

In articulating the theory of human need which follows we cannot be satisfied with just highlighting this tension; it will be necessary somehow to resolve it. In attempting to do so, we hope to add our voices to those who argue that the long-accepted antipathy between many of the classical principles of socialism and liberalism are illusory. As the continuing collapse of state socialism has revealed, without respect for the rights of the individual socialist principles become dangerous abstractions. Yet as the plight of the exploited and deprived throughout the Western world also shows, formal guarantees of political and economic freedom which ignore the material preconditions for their individual expression can undermine the principles of liberalism in a similar way.

I

Relativism and the Problem of Human Need

1

Who Needs Human Needs?

Abuses of the concept of objective and universal human need have led to disillusionment and scepticism. This has contributed to the collapse of confidence in the prospect of successful socialist politics, the threat to welfare citizenship rights, the fragmentation of political struggle against varied forms of oppression, and, gaining strength from all of this, the intellectual influence of the New Right. Many argue that it is morally safer and intellectually more coherent to equate needs with subjective preferences – that only individuals or selected groups of individuals can decide the goals to which they are going to attach enough priority to deem them needs. The aim of this book – the demonstration that we all have the same needs – is obviously inconsistent with such relativism. Therefore, we must begin by exploring some of its more representative forms.

Orthodox economics: needs are preferences

For the orthodox economist, the 'objectivity' of need is suspect. Against the background of disagreement among consumers and producers about who needs what, 'preferences' and 'demand' are regarded as sufficient for the purposes of much positive and normative economic theory. So just because a majority might rank their preference for food higher than, say, that for fashion does not mean that a clothes-conscious minority might not legitimately make the opposite choice. Such choices have the same ontological and moral status – they are consumer demands which either can or cannot be acted upon through the expenditure of income. The idea of need signifies no more than a preference shared by many people which they persuade the government requires special attention. 'Social needs are demands which have been defined by society as sufficiently important to qualify for social recognition as goods or services which should be met by government intervention' (Nevitt, 1977, p. 115; cf. Williams, 1974).

Orthodox welfare economics thus enunciates two fundamental principles. The first is the subjective conception of interests: the premise that individuals (or, frequently, households) are the only authorities on the correctness of their interests, or more narrowly, their wants. Following from this, the second is the principle of private sovereignty: that what is to be produced, how it is to be produced, and how it is to be distributed should be determined by the private consumption and work preferences of individuals (Penz, 1986, pp. 55; cf. p. 40). While numerous criticisms have been made of both principles over the last century, they still form the normative basis for the inattention paid to the concept of need by neo-classical economics.

A variety of approaches have been adopted to translate the first principle into an operational method of evaluating well-being. Early theories relied on utilitarian thinking and the contribution of objects to an assumed equal capacity for subjective pleasure or happiness[1]. Later this was modified to assess desire-fulfilment as indicated by choice expressed in market situations. From here it is but a short step to the direct equation of well-being with opulence or the real income of people as measured by the vector of commodities they consume (Sen, 1985, ch. 3; 1987, pp. 5–17). In this way it is claimed that subjective want satisfaction can be measured scientifically and thus be used to evaluate states of affairs or policies. Despite the differences between these approaches they all have in common the implicit rejection of an objective and universal notion of need.

The New Right: needs are dangerous

Related to this implicit equation of needs with preferences is the argument of recent conservative political theorists that once it is accepted that some have a right to legislate for others about what they need then the slippery slope to authoritarianism does seem more likely. If the voice of the people is regarded by government as damaged goods to begin with – blemished either by ignorance or self-interest – then it is hardly surprising that abuses of power and intrusions into individual liberty will follow. These can range from the relatively minor, like small increases in taxation for purposes which have not been democratically approved, to the major, like substantial restrictions on political freedoms in the name of meeting the real needs of the the public (Flew, 1977, pp. 213–28; cf. McInnes, 1977, pp. 229–43). Writers of the New Right all argue that it is the market rather than extensive state welfare to which we should turn to avoid these problems, maintaining that it is a *morally* superior as well as a more efficient method of allocating resources and defining goals (Green, 1987, Part I).

A major consequence of accepting this argument is that there is no basis for collective agreement on principles of justice, no consensual norms which would allow us to identify one pattern of the distribution of wealth, say, as the correct one. Conservative theorists like Hayek and Nozick argue, for example, that at the end of the day welfare must take the form of charity if it is to be morally justified. Individuals must, more or less or in toto, be left to choose what they need and what they should spend on what they perceive others as needing. Gray, another representative of the New Right, underlines this argument: 'The objectivity of basic needs is equally delusive. Needs can be given no plausible cross-cultural content but instead are seen to vary across different moral traditions...One of the chief functions of the contemporary ideology of social justice may be, as Hayek intimates, to generate an illusion of moral agreement, where in fact there are profound divergencies of values' (Gray, 1983, p. 182). In other words, basic human needs are nothing but a dangerous and dogmatic metaphysical fantasy.

To the extent that the preferences of the well-off are seen as carrying with them the same moral legitimacy as those of the poor, then this will reinforce a social system which encourages individual capital accumulation. For the utilitarians of the Right, it is the wealth and consumer power of the majority which has moral priority. For libertarian followers of Nozick, moral power translates into the right of individuals to dispose of their property in any way they like, even if this leads to widespread poverty and suffering. However, for both, what humans do and do not need is something that can only be determined by themselves.

Marxism: needs are historical

It is not surprising that those who support an unbridled capitalism should endorse such views. What is more surprising is that some socialists could embrace the cultural relativism which follows from them. To explore this paradox, we must begin with Marx. On the one hand, there seems no question but that he believed in the existence of objective human needs. Marx railed eloquently about the costs to working people of providing the labour power for the development of capitalism via the industrial revolution: 'oppression', 'degradation of personal dignity', 'accumulation of misery', 'physical and mental degradation', 'shameless direct and brutal exploitation', 'modern slavery', 'subjugation', the 'horrors', 'torture' and 'brutality' of overwork, the 'murderous' search for economy in the production process, capital's 'laying waste and squandering' labour power, 'exacting ceaseless human sacrifices' (Lukes, 1985, p. 11). The same can be said of those who further laid the foundations of revolutionary Marxism in the twentieth century. Ostensibly, such denunciations of capitalism cut little moral ice without the belief that there are some requirements which all humans have in common and which lead to unacceptable levels of individual impairment when they are not met.

Yet on the other hand, Marx was equally convinced that attempts to limit human nature to the dictates of either biology or culture were both misconceived and politically dangerous. Anticipating a range of contemporary philosophical and sociological approaches to the same question, he argued that the formation of individuality was inexorably linked to language and to the way in which we learn a wide range of normative rules and mental and manual skills (Doyal and Harris, 1986, pp. 80–8; Elster, 1985, pp. 62–4). It is from the social application of these that self-consciousness and individual identity evolve. For Marx, the economic aspects of the social environment were by far the most important in shaping human identity. If such conditions differ, then so will the individual conception of self – what is natural or unnatural, possible or impossible, harmful or beneficial, good or bad, normal or abnormal. This will mean that individual perceptions of need will also differ in the most profound ways for the same reasons.

The attractiveness of such a position for Marx and all socialists is understandable. To fix the boundaries of human nature biologically or anthropologically seems unnecessarily to freeze human consciousness at particular points of time and culture. In other words, if human needs are reified – imbued with a thing-like, static or physical quality – then individuals are arbitrarily constrained in changing those aspects of their physical, personal and social environment which inhibit their self-exploration. Prioritising alterations in the 'economic base' of society as the central dynamic of such change opens the way to radical changes in the superstructure of the entire spectrum of human expectation and imagination, especially in what humans believe that they need and have a right to demand. Marx thought that the social relations of capitalism are uniquely constituted to lead to a veritable explosion in human productivity and material expectation, bringing in their train a 'constantly enriched system of needs'.[2] These new needs are not only testimony to the creativity of the human spirit. In the midst of large-scale poverty and exploitation, they also sow the seeds of revolt through underlining *what might be* – the prospect of abundance and the injustice of a social system where the needs of those who produce the wealth remain unmet.

Heller has taken this scepticism about universal human needs to its logical extreme. She argues that precisely because of the holistic impact of society on human consciousness and on the formulation of what is and is not a basic need, it is impossible to compare cultures with respect to their progress in maximising need-satisfaction: 'The structure of needs in capitalist society belongs therefore exclusively to capitalist society. It cannot be used to judge any other society in general and least of all that of the "associated producers"' (Heller, 1976, pp. 96–7; cf. Springborg, 1981, pp. 198–213). In short, human needs are socially relative and stipulate only what some groups of humans prefer over others. Attempts by those in one culture or social formation to impose their conception of basic needs onto any other is no more than cultural imperialism – the pursuit of specific group interests.

Critiques of cultural imperialism: needs are group specific

This concern about cultural imperialism is both understandable and widespread in a variety of forms. Its popularity reflects an acute sensitivity to the fact that those in positions of power can always legitimate its arbitrary exercise through arguing that they know what is in the best interests of the powerless. That is to say, the preferences of the dominated are downgraded as inferior to their 'real' needs as defined by those in authority. Indeed, such arguments have constituted one of the ideological means by which capitalism has frequently ravaged the traditional societies which it has economically and culturally colonised. Colonialists have legitimated their economic domination through encouraging a sense of inferiority and helplessness in the face of Western 'progress'. The rejection of the concept of universal needs is also part of the background to more contemporary struggles against oppression. Here, human liberation is equated with reclaiming the right of oppressed groups to determine what preferences *they* will designate as needs. Against this background, it is sometimes argued, the concept of *universal* needs inevitably favours the dictatorial oppressor (Rist, 1980, pp. 233–53).

The argument shifts from an equation of need with the sovereign preferences of the individual to an acceptance that objective needs exist but of a sort which can only be determined by specific oppressed *groups*. Truth claims are made about human need but truth is perceived as varying from group to group. It is but a short step to identify group preferences with group need. What on the face of it appears as an endorsement of the objective need of specific groups collapses into subjectivism of a collective rather than individual variety. This collapse can be illustrated by three further examples of the politics of need: versions of radical anti-racism, anti-sexism and anti-scientism.

Beginning with anti-racism, the basic message is clear. Black people from many different backgrounds are discriminated against in a host of well-documented ways. The classic examples of racism are well known and do not require further description here. Yet in abhorring all of these manifestations of racism, some contemporary writers – both black and white – go much further and appear to reject any common foundation of human need between all races and nationalities. This is suggested by Shah when she writes: 'Whenever white people ... have attempted assessments of black people they have come out with a distorted analysis. Because black people's ways are different, and white people cannot be bothered to work at a proper understanding, black experience is distorted and dismissed' (Shah, 1989, p. 183; cf. Smith and Smith, 1983, p. 113).

The blanket of inescapable cultural/biological determination does not just affect those who we all knew were racists by their overt actions. It contaminates all whites – even those who might ostensibly seem to be allies. For example, many feminists criticise some cultural practices such as arranged marriages, purdah and female circumcision as oppressive and objectively harmful to the black women involved. Such arguments have been attacked by some radical anti-racists, however, as ethnocentric and damaging to the dignity of both the black women and the black men whose life styles are seen to be under attack. Implicitly or explicitly, it is said to be the 'whiteness' of these critics which lies behind their adoption of such prejudiced views and the basic needs to which they implicitly refer are really no more than their own cultural preferences. Such arguments suggest but one conclusion: only blacks can ever know what they need in a white-dominated world.[3]

With some 'radical feminist' arguments against sexism, we have a similar picture. There is no doubt that throughout history and in a variety of cultures, women have been exploited and abused by men. In struggling against all of these inequities, some feminists have argued that men are naturally agressive and prone to violence, domination and exploitation. Such tendencies are explained in different ways depending on the theorist. Contenders for primary causation are biology and the patriarchal cultures within which male consciousness is formed. This combination of cultural determination and psycho/socio-biology is said to account for what is regarded as the universality of patriarchy and the apparent inability of men to behave otherwise.

Dworkin (1980, p. 288) takes this to its logical extreme in arguing that: 'One can know everything and still at bottom, refuse to accept that the annihilation of women is the source of meaning and identity for men'. Daly (1984, p. 363) is equally pessimistic in claiming that in the 'phallocracy' in which men and women live, the former are 'radically separated from the natural harmony of the universe' and motivated by 'the dynamics of demonic possession'. The argument has even been carried so far as to suggest that there is a female 'rationality' and a 'feminist methodology' which must be used instead of traditional approaches to scientific inquiry which are also contaminated by their patriarchal background. Stanley and Wise (1983, p. 117) maintain, for example, that 'women's experiences constitute a different view of reality, an entirely different ontology or way of going about making sense of the world'. If these arguments are accepted, then, as in the case of anti-racism, 'group relativism' is the result, this time parading in the guise of an essentialism geared to gender. Only women can ever know what they need in a male-dominated world.[4]

Indeed, scientific knowledge itself can be viewed as just another manifestation of culture – no more than a reflection of the 'social relations' within which it evolves. This would mean that all attempts scientifically to determine the nature of human need also fall into this category. Aronowitz, for example, has argued that 'the constitution of the scientific object of knowledge is linked to the prevailing social and technical division of labour' which means that 'since the relations of science, magic, and religion are internal to each other because they all purport to offer adequate explanations for natural and social phenomena, it is rank ethnocentrism to claim that one may be privileged over the other without specifying the social-historical setting which under capitalism tends to subsume all discourse under its system of rational-purpose action' (Aronowitz, 1988, pp. 320, 340–1; cf. Young, 1977, pp. 65–118).

In short, the horrendous uses to which modern science and technology are put are said to be no accident. For implicit in their structure and content *are* the destructive and exploitative relations of capitalism. We no longer have universal science; we have 'bourgeois', 'white' and 'male' science. That science might be capable of articulating how best to identify and satisfy human need is seen, therefore, as a gigantic ideological con. The 'radical needs' – as Heller calls them – of individuals can only be properly understood *after* society has undergone a radical transformation which can then produce the radical science necessary for the task (Heller, 1976, chs 4–5; cf. Lebowitz, 1979, pp. 349–55). On this view, it seems that, under capitalism at least, *no one* ever really knows what they need!

Radical democrats: needs are discursive

The idea that only individuals or particular social groupings can ultimately define the extent and substance of their 'needs' extends further still. While rejecting the radical individualism of the former and the various determinisms of the latter, some contemporary social critics – Walzer, Laclau and Mouffe and Keane, for example – seem more interested in radical democratic reform. They endorse a vision of democracy and pluralism which does seem inherent in the idea of separate groups defining their respective needs. Thus there is agreement with Marx, along with much of contemporary philosophy and psychology, that individual identity – including the boundaries of individual choice – must be understood as arising from the social environment. Members of collectives should have the right to pursue their interests through the creative exploration of the language and rules which bind them together as members. It is only in this way that they will extend the boundaries of their own individual identities and in consequence expand the normative richness of the collective itself.

Walzer has developed these ideas in his theory of 'complex equality' about which there has been much recent discussion among political theorists. On the subject of identifying human needs, he emphasises the importance of social interaction:

> Men and women come together because they literally cannot live apart. But they can live together in many different ways...They recognize but also create one another's needs and so give a particular shape to what I will call the 'sphere of security and welfare' (Walzer, 1983, p. 65; cf. Rustin, 1985, ch. 3).

This is why at the end of the day, individual formulations of need are inevitably linked to the common aims and beliefs – the preferences – of collectives about how they should be satisfied. Their substance will vary with 'different experiences and different conceptions'. Walzer's relativism is admittedly qualified because he also accepts that there are some objective boundaries to the attribution of human needs which cannot be culturally overridden.[5]

Laclau and Mouffe have no such qualms. They argue that it is language which 'constitutes' the way in which the natural and social worlds take on their meaning for different groups – and they use language in different ways. Thus the realities which are posited via language all have equal legitimacy because there is no 'truth' or 'universality' beyond experience which can arbitrate between different interpretations of it. Laclau and Mouffe combine such epistemological indeterminacy with a defence of political pluralism which is similar to that of Walzer. The result is an unbridled relativism which renounces all 'determinisms' and 'essentialisms' – especially those of Marxism – which would argue that one form of life is better or more 'progressive' than another: 'Pluralism is *radical* only to the extent that each term of this plurality of identities finds within itself the principle of its own validity' (Laclau and Mouffe, 1985, p. 167). The idea of evaluating different social formations with respect to their success in meeting universal interests is rejected out of hand: ' "Interests" ... are a social product and do not exist independently of the consciousness of the agents who are their bearers' (Laclau and Mouffe, 1987, p. 96). Needs, therefore, are perceived as embodied in the culturally variable 'discursive position' which they believe to constitute the individual subject.

A more guarded form of relativism has been put forward by others who search for a healthier balance between the state and the individual in both capitalist and state socialist societies. In his writings on civil society, for example, Keane envisages many groups counterposing their individuality – their differently defined needs – against the centrality of the state and believes this to be essential for the well being of all. But like Laclau and Mouffe, he also explicitly embraces the cultural relativism that results from rejecting any universalisable link between such definitions:

> To defend relativism requires a social and political stance which is thoroughly modern. It implies the need for establishing or strengthening a democratic state and a civil society consisting of a plurality of public spheres, within which individuals and groups can openly express their solidarity with (or opposition to) others' ideals. Understood in this new way, the concept of democratization would abandon the futile search ... for definite truths of human existence. It would teach us to live without an assumed 'historical agent of emancipation', as it would discard, once and for all, the indefensible ideological concepts – Order, History, Progress, Humanity, Nature, Individualism, Socialism (Keane, 1988, p. 238).

And there we have it. Without debating the details, Keane is surely right that relativism is inconsistent with all traditional formulations of socialism. His only omission was not to have explicitly rejected the existence of universal human needs as well, although he may have something like this in mind by writing of 'Humanity'. Keane's sentiments are representative of a variety of post-structuralist and post-modernist writers (Lawson, 1985).[6]

Phenomenological arguments: needs are socially constructed

Finally, from a very different intellectual discipline – the currents of phenomenology and ethnomethodology within contemporary socio-logy – comes a similar questioning of abstract categories which are regarded as ignoring or distorting the complex negotiations and individual meanings which make up the reality of everyday life. Here again, the idea is rejected that there are objective and universal characteristics like objective needs which link us as humans, irrespective of culture. According to this view, social science should be primarily about the study of the complex negotiations of meaning which constitute everyday life. To the extent that it is not, ideas of social reality are a 'fictional non-existing world constructed by the scientific observer' – yet another imperialistic imposition which does little more than reflect the preconceptions and interests of the social scientists involved (Schutz, 1965, p. 58). Some ethnomethodologists go even further, arguing that 'every reality is equally real' and that 'no single reality contains more of the truth than any other' (Mehan and Wood, 1975, p. 37). The methodological and epistemological aim of such writers is clear: to call into question all explanatory and moral categories which are imposed by some groups – in this case professional academics – on to others. To this extent, they would endorse Rorty's plea that 'In the end...what matters is our loyalty to other human beings clinging together against the dark, not our hope of getting things right' (Rorty, 1980, p. 727).

Writing in this tradition, Smith argues that in the study of human need all one can do is to describe as accurately as possible the different subjective notions of need found in common discourses and the ways they are employed in specific social contexts (Smith, 1980, pp. 68–75). 'Traditional' notions of need current in discourses about social welfare are criticised as false, attributing 'objective', measurable and static attributes to the 'client'. On the contrary, he argues that need is a dynamic social construct, which in practice is closely dependent on professional practice. In a study of a Social

Service Department in Scotland, Smith shows how the needs of clients are interpreted and constructed by different professional groups. This indicates that 'needs' reflect the ideology of the particular profession, the organisational structure of the bureaucracy and certain practical constraints within which it operates (Smith, 1980, chs 5, 6; Foster, 1983, pp. 32). Implicitly, the message should by now be familiar: only *clients* can really know what they need.

Modern studies of deprivation and poverty also often loosely employ phenomenological arguments. These studies are directly related to our concerns since deprivation is often defined in terms of unmet needs and poverty with reference to the absence of material or monetary resources to satisfy needs. Since the pioneering work of Townsend (1962) and Runciman (1966), it is widely agreed that deprivation is relative in both time and space. What deprivation consists of varies over time and is dependent on the social situation (group, community, society) in which it is experienced. Indeed, needs are partly defined by virtue of the obligations, associations and customs which membership of a society entails. Thus Townsend maintains that the meanings of different commodities and conditions are necessarily variable:

> Isn't the idea of shelter relative not just to climate and temperature but to what society makes of what shelter is for? The three little pigs had different ideas of the meaning of shelter. Shelter includes notions of privacy, space to cook and work and play and highly cultured notions of warmth, humidity and segregation of particular members of the family and different functions of sleep, cooking, washing and excretion.

Even hunger is open to wide interpretation and is 'demonstrably a relative and social concept' (Townsend, 1985, pp. 667, 664). For these reasons, 'the concept of "absolute need" deserves to be abandoned' (Townsend, 1981, p. 21).

So a wide consensus in modern thought agrees that universal and objective human needs do not exist or cannot be formulated coherently. Indeed, the reader must by now be wondering what there is left to say in this book. From the political Right, Left and

Centre, from traditional disciplines and post-modernist thought, from economics, sociology, philosophy and discourse theory, from radical feminism and anti-racism, the charge is the same: the quest for universal and objective needs is a search for a will-o'-the-wisp. However, closer examination reveals that there are problems with all these schools of thought which indicate that they cannot do without the very thing that they implicitly or explicitly denounce. We explore the implications of this awkward fact in the next chapter.

2

The Inevitability of Human Needs

The coherence of the concept of social progress depends upon the belief that some modes of social organisation are better suited to satisfying human need than others. Unless increases in need-satisfaction can be shown to follow from policies which purport to promote such progress their moral purpose will be blurred. This can be seen as regards the varied attempts to defend and improve the welfare state. In light of national differences between welfare provision and differing levels of benefits within nations, some criterion is required to distinguish good and bad welfare systems, to enable the one to be defended and the other to be reformed. Again, it seems that only a coherent concept of objective need can do this work. This is why the threat posed by relativism to such a concept must be addressed and resolved in this volume. Here we begin this task by revealing internal inconsistencies and tensions within the different types of relativism outlined in the preceding chapter. As they stand, all of these positions end up implicitly presupposing what they purport to reject – some notion of universal human need.

Orthodox economics: the circularity of evaluation

On the face of it, if any discipline should be able to forego the concept of need, it is neo-classical economic theory and its normative counterpart, welfare economics. But can it? In fact, there are so many inconsistencies within the principles of want-satisfaction and consumer sovereignty, and so many problems in measuring want-satisfaction, that welfare economics cannot do without some other criterion of welfare external to the subjective preferences of individuals. Let us consider each of these issues in turn.

The idea that individuals are the sole authority in judging the correctness of their wants is severely compromised once we admit limits to people's knowledge and rationality. 'Wants based on ignorance are epistemically irrational' and there are further limits to practical rationality concerning future events and ulterior preferences (Penz, 1986, p. 63, ch. 5; Sen, 1970). 'Evaluation circularity' poses another serious problem. If wants are shaped by the institutions and processes of production and distribution which meet those wants, then they cannot provide an independent standpoint with which to evaluate the functioning of those institutions and processes. 'What is being evaluated determines, in part, the criterion by which it is being evaluated' (Penz, 1986, p. 87; cf. Steedman, 1989, ch. 11). The shaping of wants can be direct, as in much modern advertising, but more pervasive is the indirect influence of socialisation and past patterns of demand (Penz, 1986, ch. 6).

If, for the moment, we set aside these weaknesses, there are also problems in comparing the want-satisfaction of people with different want structures and in ranking levels of want-satisfaction as higher or lower. As Sen graphically illustrates, utilitarian traditions of welfare measurement which equate welfare with desire-fulfilment ignore all the ways that people lower their desires and reconcile themselves to fate:

> Our mental reactions to what we actually get and what we can sensibly expect to get may frequently involve compromises with a harsh reality. The destitute thrown into beggary, the vulnerable landless labourer precariously surviving at the edge of subsistence, the over-worked domestic servant working round the clock, the subdued and subjugated housewife reconciled to her role and her fate, all tend to come to terms with their respective predicaments. The deprivations are suppressed and muffled in the necessity of endurance in uneventful survival (Sen, 1985, pp. 21–2).

Conversely, it is inadmissable to equate the state of a person with the extent of his or her possessions, as do 'opulence' interpretations of welfare (Sen, 1985, p. 23). According to either interpretation, welfare economics lacks an objective basis for comparing people's welfare.

Finally, the principle of consumer sovereignty is undermined by the plethora of well-known critiques levelled at markets as arrangements for meeting individual wants. They include such examples of 'market failure' as the external effects of individual actions on third parties and the environment and the problems of finding market solutions to 'social' wants and unrevealed preferences. The interdependence of efficiency and distribution also interferes with attempts to separate out measures of the former from judgements about the latter. Furthermore, 'prisoners' dilemma' problems question the desirability of the free market as a choice condition. Individuals may prefer gun control to owning a gun, yet in the absence of the former express a market preference for the latter (Penz, 1986, ch. 3).

Penz, on whose analysis we have primarily relied here, draws two conclusions from this catalogue of problems and inconsistencies. First, 'want satisfaction is a principle that cannot be made measurable without additional normative judgements that are neither contained in nor entailed by the preference principle'. Second, were such external normative judgements to be drawn up:

> their insertion into the want-satisfaction principle subverts the principle's fundamentally open-ended and subjective character. Yet not to insert them leaves it open to the problems of ignorance and irrationality, of the evaluation circularity, and of noncomparability. This dilemma quintessentially reflects the shortcomings of the want-satisfaction principle and of the sovereignty conceptions that are based on it (Penz, 1986, pp. 132, 136).

Penz argues that the best candidate for these 'additional normative judgements' is some conception of human need.

The New Right: universality after all

When we consider the New Right we are confronted with the problem of implicit non-preferential standards – the belief that some preferences are objectively more important than others. For adherents are not morally neutral about capitalism. They believe that it is a *good thing* – that the productivity and freedom which they claim it engenders is worth encouraging and defending. In a more complex way, this too leads back not only to certain values which challenge individual preferences, but to values which embody notions of serious harm and need. The argument is that individuals and/or collectives will be *better off* in the long run – that their *interests* will be better served – if they prefer capitalism to some other system (Griffin, 1986, pp. 31–7).

But implicit in this argument is some objective goal which is not in itself a matter of rational preference. For *any* preference which contradicts the goal, whatever it is, will be regarded as irrational. There is no way, for example, that a conservative utilitarian can view someone who prefers to maximise the unhappiness of herself and others as anything other than irrational. And this will be the case no matter how correct – and therefore 'rational' in the more narrow sense of the term – the calculation of how to do it happens to be. Libertarians like Nozick must say much the same of a person who successfully plans to have her taxes arbitrarily increased so that her autonomy can be consistently violated as often as possible. We again end up with another form of 'circularity of evaluation' – rational preferences are seen as reducible to non-preferential standards which have themselves dictated the rationality of the preferences (Hollis, 1987, chs 5–6; cf. Penz, 1986, chs 5–6).

One way out of this circularity – a route which relativists would embrace – is to differentiate clearly between what Barry calls 'want-regarding' and 'ideal-regarding' principles (1990, ch. III.3). Want-regarding principles take as given the wants which people happen to have and pay no regard to other criteria when evaluating policies. Ideal-regarding principles embody other criteria and are essential to avoid the evaluational circularity described above (Barry, 1990, pp. xliv–lii). But do the latter have to entail anything like a notion of need? Barry, and many others espousing this distinction, think not. They reject the idea that this justifies belief in the existence of standards of evaluation which are common to all forms of life. Provided that *some* ideals are embraced and differentiated from wants then rational actions can still be differentiated from irrational mistakes.

The difficulty with this argument is that it is unable to account for why some mistakes can be seen to have the same objective consequences irrespective of the culture and value system in which they are made. For example, stock markets are only found in the cultures of advanced capitalism. Losing a very small amount of money on the market is a mistake with consequences which cannot be understood in these terms. Most cultures don't have stock markets and the opportunity to experience them. Yet there is a big difference between a small, culturally specific mistake on which nothing much depends and one which results, say, in not being able to afford to eat. In the latter case, one is harmed in an objective way that is similar to the harm which mistakes of other kinds might bring in alternative forms of society. The reasons for the harm – and ultimately for the significance of the mistake for the individual concerned – is the fact that basic needs have not been as well satisfied as they would otherwise have been. The concept of needs enables one to *compare* harm in different economic and cultural settings. Therefore, the neo-liberal emphasis on the individual right of self determination cannot be defended by arguing that needs and preferences are the same – however this right may be justified on other grounds.

Finally, the New Right's justification of both the rational efficiency and moral justifiability of capitalism depends on some conception of comparable *fitness* among economic rivals to compete. A race between a well fed and trained thoroughbred and a starving and uncoached hack can hardly be called a race at all (Brown, 1986, p. 96). Yet the possibility of such fitness, along with equity between competitors, presupposes the existence of physical, emotional and educational prerequisites which cannot be reduced to subjective preference. Just as the race horse needs oats and not sugar cubes, so the consistently successful business person and worker needs, for example, an adequate diet and appropriate education.

Nozick appears to accept this claim when he argues hypothetically for a once and for all abolition of unfair individual advantages in the market place which have been won through violations of the past rights of others (Nozick, 1974, p. 231). Why else would such violations matter? The same can also be said of Hayek when he maintains that the state should provide a minimum 'safety net' to prevent poverty – conceived in an absolute and not a relative sense. This must, therefore, correspond to some notion of objective need about which it is believed there can be a consensus (Hayek, 1960,

p. 303). As Plant (1989, pp. 14–15) argues: 'The neo-liberal takes the view that need is an open-ended, elastic concept which has no consensual hold in society, but their own view of poverty as an absolute standard of need, or of welfare as meeting this absolute standard, presumes that there is some clear consensual standard of need'.

Explicit denials that basic needs exist, in other words, are often accompanied by an implicit acceptance that they do. The denials, of course, are understandable. Since individual self-determination is at the very heart of the belief that capitalism is both the most morally just and productively efficient society, it does not serve their political purpose to underwrite any criteria by which individual preference may itself be judged as problematic.

Marxism: the cynical gaze of determinism

The desire of Marxists to reject universal human needs on the grounds of historical, cultural and economic determination is equally easy to understand. Yet, to do so leads to similar problems. To make critical judgements about capitalism requires some criterion of evaluation which distinguishes between needs and preferences – a commitment to the belief that not everything about human nature is historically relative. The upshot is a tension in Marx's own writings between two ideas of need and human nature – one uncompromisingly relativist, the other implicitly or explicitly universalist (Soper, 1981, ch. 2). Until recently, the dominant schools of Marxism have echoed and elaborated the relativist rather than the universalist strand (Geras, 1983, ch. 1). This has generated what Lee has called the 'cynical gaze' of some Marxist writers and political activists when analysing need satisfaction within capitalism (Lee and Raban, 1988, ch. 4).

To argue that what counts as need satisfaction, whether provided by the market or by the state, contains elements which are harmful, degrading, oppressive is one thing. But to condemn all or most state activity – no matter how ostensibly valuable in the relief of suffering – is plain silly and very difficult to sustain in practice. The fact is that the welfare state is contradictory, in some ways contributing to human betterment, in other ways doing the opposite (Gough, 1979, pp. 11–15). To deny this – to link the expression and satisfaction of 'true need' and its satisfaction to systemic revolutionary change while at the same time proclaiming the theoretical impossibility of specifying what the change is meant to achieve – is to live for a future empty of substantive content. It is the secular equivalent of what Hegel called the 'unhappy consciousness' of early Christian obsession with the afterlife (Hegel, 1977, pp. 126–38; cf. Norman, 1976, pp. 59–64).

For if it is denied that people have the same needs both before and after revolutionary success – if 'radical needs' in Heller's terms can only be formulated properly once such success has occurred – then how can success itself be identified? Surely the whole point of socialist politics focused on the future is to achieve dramatic improvements in the lives of individuals who will actually live in a post-capitalist society. However, the potential for revolutionary progress can only be measured against the background of beliefs about what is not being accomplished in the here and now. And the concept of basic human need is central to specifying precisely what these deficiencies are and how they might be remedied in practice (Soper, 1980, pp. 213–18; Geras, 1983, pp. 107–16). For their political programme to have any clear point, Marxists must be committed to the existence of human needs which are the same now as they will be in the future – everywhere and for everyone.

This is increasingly accepted in the late twentieth century, as universal constraints on human freedom and potentiality have been recognised and incorporated within Marxist scholarship and socialist politics. The predicaments stemming from psychology, biology and ecology are crucial here. As regards psychology, Freudian insights suggest that strategies for communal politics must take into account universal psychic conflicts within individuals which will not be dissolved into some post-communist 'pleasure principle' (Soper, 1981, ch. 8; Rustin, 1989). Timpanaro makes a similar point with respect to biological limits on human capacities (1975, p. 50; p. 45–54.): 'love, the brevity and frailness of human existence . . . the debility produced by age . . . the fear of one's own death and sorrow at the death of others', all these are constants which, though they will be experienced in different ways in different cultures and times, are features of the human condition.

To these two constraints is now added recognition of the constraints of ecology. 'If ecology's hypotheses are valid', writes Enzensberger (1976, p. 295), then capitalist societies have probably thrown away the chance of realising Marx's project for the reconciliation of man and nature. The productive forces which bourgeois society has unleashed have been caught up with and overtaken by the destructive powers released at the same time... Socialism, which was once a promise of liberation, has become a question of survival. If the ecological equilibrium is broken, then the rule of freedom will be further off than ever.

Today's green consciousness again stresses the commonality of human nature and human needs and of the predicament we face in trying to satisfy them. Together these currents have illuminated the intractability and continuity of human need. Utopian optimism has been replaced by materialist pessimism, yet one which recognises the human potential for ever-greater success in overcoming these obstacles (Timpanaro, 1975, p. 20). Thus any valid reformulation of the Marxist project needs the idea of need.

Critiques of cultural imperialism: the objectivity of oppression

Turning now to the pluralism of some radical anti-racists and feminists, they *do* believe that needs can be known in the here and now – but only by those who share the same cultural and biological background. Such fragmented relativism has proved to be both incoherent and politically destructive. The incoherence derives from the fact that even though universal needs are rejected in one breath, they are presupposed in another. It is true that different cultures sometimes articulate conflicting conceptions of need and institutionalise varying norms of what constitutes the public and the private good. Yet if groups really do possess complete moral autonomy in such formulations, then the members of one group can never justifiably criticise the activities of any other. This is precisely what is done, however, by those who would confine the truth to the boundaries of specific cultures. For example, critics of British or American imperialism rightly argue that both have resulted in a wide range of suffering: extreme poverty and poor health, little or no education and regimes involving consistent humiliation by those in power. The fact that the victims come from diverse cultural backgrounds is not viewed as a reason for assuming that their suffering is qualitatively different. Indeed, the identification of their oppression and exploitation hinges on what they have in common as the 'dispossessed' in Fanon's terms – that their basic needs and associated rights have been violated in the *same* ways.

Ironically, relativism in the name of attacks on cultural imperialism, racism or sexism only sounds plausible when agreement already exists about who and what is to be regarded as good or bad. It backfires, however, when it is realised that cultures of oppression are still cultures with their own internally consistent moralities or 'principles of validity' (in Laclau and Mouffe's terms). British imperialism constituted a coherent culture. Why then do radical pluralists believe it to have been morally wrong unless they believe that there are some things that are just not morally acceptable whatever the culture? This inconsistency turns particularly sour when such critics are unwilling to condemn violations of human need in the context of societies or communities with which they have some cultural affinity (Lees, 1986, pp. 97–8; cf. Tang Wain, 1991, pp. 1–22). The same muddled thinking has been behind some socialists being unwilling to support the right of Salman Rushdie to publish his novel, *Satanic Verses*. Once the capacity to identify barbarity is sacrificed to the false liberalism of cultural tolerance, the floodgates are opened for even more serious harm to be inflicted on those who cannot protect themselves. Rushdie's condemnation to death or 'fatwa' by Khomeini was perfectly consistent with Islamic doctrine.

Radical democrats: romanticising group morality

It is this latter point that poses severe problems for the relativism of Walzer, Laclau and Mouffe, and Keane. On the face of it, the idea that collectives should be accorded the same sorts of political rights in democracies which are ordinarily associated with individuals seems a good one. It protects minority groups from the domination of majorities and, assuming that each group will look after the basic needs of its members, thereby encourages a maximum of both cultural and individual creativity. But again, without a standard of need-satisfaction which extends beyond the cultural boundaries of the group itself, how can we be sure that definitions of need will not be adopted which are destructive to some of those concerned? There is no a priori reason why a particular group – or more accurately those who hold power within it – might not insist on a range of things from its members which are not in their interests in that they constitute a violation of their basic needs. In illustration, think of some of the ways in which most groups are in fact dominated by men and the consequences of this fact. Other examples are the practices of some religious cults which have been psychologically damaging to some of their members who have been both materially exploited and emotionally abused without their necessarily realising it.

If this is at least to be recognised, then standards external to the group must exist to evaluate what is and is not morally tolerable inside it. Similar points can be made about Keane's advocacy of the creative potential of civil society and of his argument that the state should not try to interfere with the results. Again, creativity has a double edge. The particular groups which he includes in this definition of civil society – the family, for example – can also be destructive and harmful to their members (cf. Channer and Parton, 1990, pp. 105–20) Only some form of public regulation can prevent this from occurring. But without a coherent theory of human need to inform such regulation – especially in the context of capitalism and the distorted perceptions of need which follow from it – there is little choice but to lapse into an optimistic and hazardous idealism that, when left alone, individuals and groups will always know what is best for them (Harris, 1987, pp. 13–22; cf. Osborne, 1991, pp. 201–25).[1] They won't and they don't.

Phenomenological arguments: social realities kick back

We do not have the space adequately to explore the problems of phenomenological writings in sociology and their relativistic approach to human need (Trigg, 1985, ch. 5). Commenting on the relationship between Schutz's rejection of the objectivity of social structure and the fact that he was a refugee from the Nazis, Hindess jibes:

> There can be no Schutzian politics and indeed no rational social action of any kind. The 'knowledge' of the social world upon

which such action might be based consists merely of one set of stories about the world among a multitude of others. The fascism in Europe was nothing but a pattern that some storyteller or other happened to have made up and some facts and events that he happened to be interested in. Why then did [Schutz] flee to America? (Hindess, 1977, p. 76).

We cannot account for the meaning of our actions (e.g. being a victim of Nazi persecution), for the institutional factors which help to shape these meanings (e.g. the political and economic background to the success of fascism in Germany), or for the objective character of the serious harm which can be institutionally imposed on individuals when such meanings take particular forms (e.g. the horror and consequences of the Holocaust), through suggesting that they are all reducible to individual negotiations of preference within everyday life.

Sociological theorists of deprivation sometimes qualify their ostensible relativism by a persistent belief that definitions of human need entail *some* core of objectivity. Townsend, despite his desire to abandon the idea of absolute need, also argues that objective needs *can* be distinguished from 'conventionally acknowledged' needs according to their properties of 'detachment, quantifiable measurement, reproducibility, systematic comparison and validation' (1972, p. 48). This is hardly surprising, as his writing is informed by a strong and consistent concern for the objective plight of the poor, irrespective of their own preferences or of those of others.

Thus he criticises 'consensual' approaches to assessing the poverty line in Britain, which allow a majority of a sample of the population to decide which goods and services are necessities and which not (Mack and Lansley, 1985, ch. 2). This, he argues, ignores problems of 'false consciousness'. People do not always recognise the social forces which shape their preferences and this 'obliges us to look for criteria of need other than in social perceptions'. He even goes on:

Perceptions which are filtered through, or fostered by, the value or belief systems of sectional groups, the state or whole communities can never be regarded as sufficiently representative of 'reality out there'. There have to be forms of 'objective' social observation, investigation and comparison against which they may be checked (even if these standards remain necessarily incomplete as well as necessarily creatures of socially produced modes of scientific thought) (Townsend, 1972, p. 48).

But this sits uneasily alongside the theoretical foundations of much of his other writing which persistently defines deprivation in cultural rather than universalist terms: 'Any rigorous conceptualisation of the social determination of need dissolves the idea of "absolute" need. And a thorough-going relativity applies to time as well as place' (Townsend, 1979b, p. 17). The result is at best ambiguity and at worse confusion and the appearance of vacillation (Sen, 1984, pp. ch. 14). To define deprivation – and therefore need – solely in relative terms leads to the paradox that one way of increasing the need satisfaction of the starving is to destroy enough of the food of the non-starving to bring the two groups closer together (Sen, 1984, p. 330; cf. Goodin, 1990, pp. 15–20)!

All of the examples of relativism which we have examined thus far have attempted both to denounce universal standards of evaluation with one hand only to employ them to endorse some favoured view of the world with the other. The consistent relativist must not chop and change in this way. But the consistent relativist – one who regards the whole of social life as a 'construction', each aspect of which has no more or less veracity than any other – enters a moral wasteland into which few have feared to tread. One of the few is Feyerabend (1978, pp. 8–9) who pulls no punches:

> Reason is no longer an agency that directs other traditions, it is a tradition in its own right with as much (or as little) claim to the centre of the stage as any other tradition. Being a tradition it is neither good nor bad, it simply is. The same applies to all traditions – they become good or bad (rational/irrational; pious/impious; advanced/'primitive'; humanitarian/vicious; etc.) only when looked at from the point of view of some other tradition. 'Objectively' there is not much to choose between anti-semitism and humanitarianism. Racism will appear vicious to a humanitarian while humanitarianism will appear vapid to a racist. *Relativism* . . . gives an adequate account of the situation that emerges.[2]

are chronically hungry or thirsty, he argues, the physiological motivation to secure food and water will be most powerful. However, once their bellies are full, the other and 'higher' needs emerge and these rather than hunger dominate the organism. Next in line for adults – and even more for children – will be the requirements for a safe, orderly, predictable world. When these goals have been achieved, higher needs dominate, and so on until finally an open-ended motivation for emotional and intellectual fulfilment takes over (Maslow, 1943, pp. 370–96).

In the remainder of this book we shall not use 'need' in this sense, for two reasons. First, even if we accept Maslow's typology as exhaustive – which is far from obvious – its strict temporal sequencing of the motivations in question is simply false. Some people seem far more concerned with their self-actualisation than their safety – mountain climbers, for example. Equally, in deliberating over many of the choices we make about our lives, Maslow's categories seem either to be combined or, at times, to conflict (Springborg, 1981, pp. 184–90; cf. Fitzgerald, 1977a, pp. 43–51). But second, and more to the point, there are good reasons why we should divorce the discourse of needs as universalisable goals from that of motivations or drives altogether.

As Thompson argues, one can have a drive to consume something, like lots of alcohol, which one does not need and at the same time have a need for something, like exercise or to diet, which one is in no way driven to seek. In the case of the former, the drive is not linked to preventing serious harm in some universalisable manner, even if harm can accrue in the individual if it remains unsatisfied. Addicts of certain drugs, for example, will become ill if they do not get a fix. Yet it is also the case that they would not have been harmed had they never begun to use drugs and that in the long term the satisfaction of their addiction will damage them in numerous ways – as it would anyone. In short, to have the urge to act in a particular way must not be confused with an empirical or normative justification for so doing (Thompson, 1987, pp. 13–14).

Nevertheless the emphasis on drives and motivations does alert us to the biological background to human needs: to the constraints on human needs given by our genetic structure. If needs are not identical with the drives of the human organism, neither are they disconnected from 'human nature', or the physiological and psychological make-up of *homo sapiens*. To argue for such disconnection would be to identify humanity with no more than human reason and to bifurcate human existence from that of the rest of the animal world.

In her wonderful satire on the traditional existentialist conviction – especially Sartre's – that human freedom justifies such a demarcation, Midgley makes the same point:

> Had we known no other animate life-form than our own, we should have been utterly mysterious to ourselves as a species. And that would have made it immensely harder for us to understand ourselves as individuals too. Anything that puts us into a context, that shows us as part of a continuum, is a great help ... The really monstrous thing about Existentialism ... is its proceeding as if the world contained only dead matter (things) on the one hand and fully rational, educated, adult humans on the other – as if there were no other life forms. The impression of *desertion* or *abandonment* which Existentialists have is due, I am sure, not to the removal of God, but to this contemptuous dismissal of almost the whole biosphere – plants, animals, and children. Life shrinks to a few urban rooms; no wonder it becomes absurd (Midgley, 1979, pp. 18–19; cf. chs 1–3).

We are linked to other animals in a variety of ways, through being bipedal mammals – warm blooded, suckling, naked descendants of apes, with an upright gait and flexible hands. But we also have large, developed brains and a corresponding capacity unmatched in evolution to communicate with each other, to reason and to create projects. As a direct result of our brain size, which has necessitated the relatively early birth of human babies, we have a remarkably extended period of dependence in childhood. These features roughly define human nature as distinct from that of dogs and trout, say, and set natural *boundaries* on human needs (Benton, 1988, pp. 8–15; cf. Weigel, 1986). Our mammalian constitution shapes our needs for such things as food and warmth in order to survive and maintain health. Our cognitive aptitudes and the bases of our emotionality in childhood shape many other needs – for supportive and close relationships with others, for example.

Indeed, Freud, as well as psychologists of a number of other pursuasions, argued that the impact of childhood on all aspects of conscious life cannot be overestimated. Bridging the biological, emotional and cognitive aspects of life, processes of repression and emotional self-protection in childhood are seen as erecting unconscious motivational structures which thereafter influence the everyday activities and thought processes of individuals in hidden ways. The exact character of these processes and the manner in which their influence is actually exerted on conscious activity is hotly debated. However, there can be no doubt that in understanding human action, much more requires explanation than just the conscious reasons which individuals give for what they do, and that psychoanalytic techniques can help to uncover a reality that appearance does not reveal (Frosh, 1987, Part I).

So far, so good. But, as Rose *et al.* (1984, Chapter 9) have demonstrated, the problem with much of what now passes as sociobiology is that it *confuses constraint with determination* and overestimates the extent to which innate biological, emotional and cognitive 'grammar' can be said to determine what we *should* and should not attempt. Suppose that women have a genetic predisposition, an 'open instinct' in Midgley's terms – a need, if you like – for the expression of strong maternal feelings towards their young children (Midgley, 1979, pp. 51–7). There is no problem until it conflicts with, say, their need to find employment either to explore their creative potential in other ways or just to pay the bills. In such circumstances, it is the woman and not her genes who has to make the choice about which aspect of her nature to act upon, and to this extent Sartre was right. So aside from the fact that very little has been scientifically established about the genetic background to human action and well-being – the strength of maternal feeling appears, for example, to vary enormously in women – our unique cognitive abilities as humans still leave us with the problem of deciding what we need, irrespective of what we feel that we want.

What the insights of sociobiology primarily show is that in certain situations, some decisions will be more difficult – sometimes much more – than others. What they do not demonstrate is that our evolutionary past can or should override our ability to choose and to act (Trigg, 1984, pp. 93–101). In making up our minds about what to do in particular circumstances, we should obviously take our experience of our biological 'needs' into account – to prepare ourselves for whatever difficulties we will encounter in trying to achieve the goals we have set ourselves. Fear, and the emotional anxiety that accompanies it, are good examples. Acts of bravery show that people can force themselves to do things on the basis of what they consider to be good reasons when their instincts, so to speak, are screaming the opposite. But the fact remains that the choice of both reasons and actions remains our own and is not determined by our biology. It would hardly make sense for calls to resist our biological character were this not the case – for men, for example, to refrain from whatever genetic propensity to aggression they have inherited from their ancestral hunters. Therefore, the question remains of what *we* – as opposed to our genes – should do with our lives.

Needs as goals and strategies

The word 'need' is also used explicitly or implicitly to refer to a particular category of *goals* which are believed to be *universalisable*. Examples would be: 'This person needs (and should have the goal of) more protein' or 'These families need (and should have the goal of) proper shelter this winter'. Needs in this sense are commonly contrasted with 'wants' which are also described as goals but which derive from an individual's particular preference and cultural environment. Unlike needs, wants are believed to vary from person to person. The difference between goals thought of in these distinct ways is explicitly recognised by such an uncontentious statement as: 'I want a cigarette but I need to stop smoking.'

Referring to needs as universalisable goals risks obscuring the reason why universality is imputed to some aims and not others. The imputation rests upon the belief that if needs are not satisfied by an appropriate 'satisfier' then *serious harm* of some specified and objective kind will result (Feinberg, 1973, p. 111; cf. Wiggens, 1985, pp. 153–9). Not to try to satisfy needs will thus be seen to be against the objective interests of the individuals involved and viewed as abnormal and unnatural.[1] When goals are described as 'wants' rather than needs, it is precisely because they are not believed to be linked to human interests in this sense.

All need statements conform to the relational structure: '*A* needs *X* in order to *Y*' (Barry, 1965, Section 5 A). Here whether or not *X* is a need concerns not universality but its strategic efficacy for achieving some specified goal *Y*, whatever it happens to be. Thus adequate nutrition and a new hi-fi can both be regarded as needs in this sense: the nutrition to maintain health and the hi-fi to improve one's enjoyment of recorded music (Thompson, 1987, pp. 7–8). It is evident that we need further conceptual clarification to distinguish (a) basic needs from non-basic needs, and (b) needs from wants.

When needs are viewed as universalisable goals, the Y of the piece – the avoidance of serious harm – is often implicit and the attention of those in pursuit of their needs is focused on how to go about achieving the X. Very often in the developed world, for example, the goal of acquiring food is pursued without a thought of the harm that will ensue if the pursuit is unsuccessful. The goal that is paramount is simply the fact that the shopping must be done and primary attention is on how best strategically to do it. The same point may be made about a host of other commonly perceived needs. Because the final goal toward which they are directed is not necessarily made explicit, such needs are believed to be goals in their own right rather than what they actually entail – various strategies linked by a common goal believed to be universalisable.

So what in some circumstances may be referred to as goals will in others be described as strategies. Food, shelter or clothing, for example, can be referred to in either way. Descriptions of needs are hierarchical in character. Beginning from some overall goal – like physical warmth – the means by which it is sought (e.g. specific types of clothing) again can be thought of as ends in their own right. This will be especially likely if their strategic relation to the goal remains implicit – for example, if there is no conscious formulation of the strategic link between the goal of a new coat and the more fundamental goal of physical warmth. Just as clothing may be described as either a goal or a strategy, this is also true, say, of specific types of clothes and of the money necessary to buy them. In short, the grammar of statements about human need which do not refer to drives is one of instrumentality.

Some other goal Y (either believed to be universalisable or not) must always be in the background of a specific need X being regarded as a goal in its own right. Were this not the case, it would be impossible to identify the *reason* why the goal is identified as a need and why we believe it to be worth pursuing. To understand, for example, what it means to call physical warmth or a meal a need, we must have a *prior* understanding of why these are the sorts of things which we must try to acquire if we have the goal of avoiding serious harm. If someone says, 'I need physical warmth because I just do' or 'I need a meal because I just feel like one', their use of 'need' will be unclear. We would find such statements just as incomprehensible as we would if someone said that they needed 'a saucer of mud' for the same 'reasons'. They are not 'reasons' in any ordinary sense of the term (cf. Anscombe, 1957, pp. 71–2; Plant *et al.*, 1980, pp. 26–9). Reasons for needing (or for that matter wanting) are then essentially *public*, in that they draw on a shared understanding of what sorts of strategies actually do avoid harm, or what sorts of empirical research should be done to facilitate such understanding (Doyal and Harris, 1986, ch. 4). Were this not the case, people would be unable to make mistakes about what they need through confusing needs with wants (Wall, 1975, pp. 505–6).

One cannot be be mistaken in the same sense about a want, provided that some understandable reason is given for it. If, for example, you say that you want another MacDonald's burger because you like their taste and texture, others may not agree. However, it is unclear what it would mean for them to claim that you are wrong: you have given your reasons and they are perfectly intelligible. It would, however, make sense to say to someone: 'You should have the goal of stopping smoking instead of buying another pack of cigarettes.' For here reference is made to what is agreed to be necessary to maintain the individual in an 'acceptable' state which avoids the prospect of serious harm. To use another hackneyed example, diabetics may want sugar so badly that their perception is one of need. They may well feel that they cannot 'go on' unless they achieve it as a goal. But what they need is insulin – even if they have never heard of it and do not have the capacity to conceptualise it as a preference. In fact, this is what those who died of diabetes throughout history before the discovery of insulin needed all along – both the insulin itself and the realisation that it was their lack of it that made them ill (Plant *et al.*, 1980, pp. 25–33).

A more formal way of making the same point is to note that when we both want and need things, we do so with respect to particular descriptions of them. So if it is true to say: 'I need water' then it will always be equally true to replace the word 'water' by any other word whose meaning is extentionally equivalent (e.g. 'H_2O') – which can be used to refer to the same *same thing*. On the other hand, whether or not I want something depends on my beliefs about it and not on its actual attributes. In this case, I may well want the same thing under one description (e.g. 'the perfectly poached egg in front of me') and not under another (e.g. 'the perfectly poached egg in front of me which may be contaminated with salmonella') (White, 1971, p. 114). Statements about wants, in other words, are *intentional* and referentially opaque because their truth depends on 'how a subject of experience looks out on the world' (Griffin, 1986, p. 41). You cannot want something of which you have no conception and which you are not in some way 'trying to get' (Anscombe, 1957, p. 68). Such subjectivity is to be contrasted with the objectivity of statements about needs. These are *extentional* with their truth depending on something like 'the way the world is' and not on 'the workings of my mind' (Wiggens, 1985, p. 152). Not only is it the case that you can need something that you do not want. You may need it without even knowing of its existence!

Of course it is possible that wants and needs can coincide. There are wants which are satisfiers of generally accepted needs and others which are not. So you can need what you want, and want or not want what you need. What you cannot consistently do is not need what is required in order to avoid serious harm – whatever you may want.

Needs, relativism and morality

Yet many questions still remain concerning the objectivity of needs. What needs, if any, should *all* individuals try to satisfy if they are to be said to be acting in their interests? So far, all that we have shown is that there is a commonly employed distinction between needs and wants which is rooted in the belief that there are some goals which are instrumentally and universally linked to the avoidance of serious harm, while there are others which are not. Thus, the coherence of the distinction between needs and wants – and of the belief that it can be made in any sort of objective way – is predicated on some *agreement* about what serious harm itself is. But for this agreement to exist – for us to be able to recognise the harm – there must also be a consensus about the human condition when it is normal, flourishing and unharmed (Thompson, 1987, ch. 3).

But what if there is no such agreement? There is much dispute about whether or not some needs exist 'naturally' for the individual or not. Sex, for example, is often spoken of as such a common goal. However, specific patterns of sexual activity cannot be universalised in the sense in which other 'basic' needs like a minimum quantity of food might be said to be. The fact is that what is regarded as normal sexual practice can vary between cultures and between relationships within cultures and some people seem to manage quite well in life with little or no sexual contact with others. The same point may be made of a variety of activities whose normality is more a function of cultural tradition than of any sort of biological necessity (Renshon, 1977, pp. 58–64).

Further, even if it is accepted – as presumably it must be – that there are certain needs (e.g. protein, water) which have to be met for humans to survive, it can still be argued that there are so many ways of meeting them that in practice the distinction between needs and wants tells us more about those who make it than it does about the human condition. The distinction between needs and wants, therefore, seems to be essentially normative: if agreement about values does not exist, there seems to be no further grounds for arbitration (Fitzgerald, 1977b, pp. 195–212). For example, if different groups set standards for shelter at different levels and therefore endorse different criteria of what constitutes acceptable levels of harm, to what 'higher' or 'universal' standard can an appeal be made? This is why, it has been argued, so many debates about social policy and morality tend to go round in circles.

Relativists, of course, must either explicitly or implicitly endorse the normative character of the distinction between needs and wants. What is perceived to be a need, along with the right to need-satisfaction, is not dictated by universal standards of reason or reality. For the intelligible boundaries of experience are thought to be determined by culture – the conceptual rules which individuate forms of social life. Winch sums up much post-modernist thinking on the matter in two classic sentences: 'Reality is not what gives language sense. What is real and what is unreal shows itself in the sense that language has' (1974, p. 82).

Since there is no escape from the rules and discourse of one's form of life, there is no neutral reality to which one can turn to assess which approach to need satisfaction is 'best'. Thus different ways of conceptualising purity and danger, for example, lead to conflicting beliefs about what sorts of food are clean and needed and which are unclean and harmful (Douglas, 1966, chs 1–3; cf. Douglas, 1975, pp. 47–59). The fact is that members of different cultures just do find different things morally outrageous, as sometimes do individuals within the same culture. To search therefore for a universal and and objective grounding for what amounts to no more than cultural or individual preference is, according to the relativist, to pursue an illusion.[2]

In short, what began as a relatively clear distinction – that between needs and wants – becomes extremely muddled when its basis is challenged. For if there is no rational way of resolving disputes about what is and is not generalisable about the human condition or about specific groups of humans, then what are needs for some can be said to be merely wants for others – and vice versa. Similarly, moral right in the face of perceived need becomes a matter of cultural preference or individual feeling rather than reason. Was relativism correct after all?

For now, and against the background of our criticisms in the preceding chapter, we can only respond by pointing out that there can be no doubt that such a view goes against deep moral convictions throughout the world. If need were simply a function of cultural or individual preference then we would find nothing wrong with Huxley's *Brave New World* where a diet of drugs, sex and ignorance produces a subjective contentment which is as uniform as it is awful. Further, statements of need certainly seem to be much more than just descriptions of empirical states of affairs – be they physical or social in character. They also carry with them a normative force which it is difficult to ignore and which can certainly feel as objective and universal as do true descriptive statements with no moral content (Braybrooke, 1987, p. 61). Many charities and international aid agencies bear witness to this moral force. Where groups are perceived to be extremely vulnerable to harm, the 'ought' of the obligation to satisfy need usually does seem in some fashion to follow from the 'is' of the need itself.

In Part II, we will attempt to clarify this tension through developing a theory of the human condition which is both linked to our 'nature' while not being determined by it and so recognises the importance of subjective well-being for the individual without regarding it as determining right and wrong or who has a right to what. The concept of objective and universal human needs will be shown to be central to this task. What we have seen thus far is that if such needs exist, they must be shown to constitute goals which all humans have to achieve if they are to avoid serious harm. The extent to which the choices involved in such achievement are constrained by biological drives and the unconscious will, for the purposes of this book, remain an open question.

II

A Theory of Human Need

4

Physical Health and Autonomy: the Basic Needs of Persons

Attempts to deny the objectivity of need have proved popular and superficially plausible. People do have strong feelings about what they need and these feelings can vary enormously between cultures and over time. In Britain, for example, Townsend found that as many as 44 per cent of those he defined as severely deprived felt no deprivation themselves (1979a, p. 423). Yet there also appears to be a consensus about the range of necessities which form a poverty line below which no one should be allowed to fall (Mack and Lansley, 1985, ch. 3). Conflicting evidence of this kind suggests that subjective feeling is not a reliable determination of human need, a point reinforced by the fact that we can strongly desire things which are seriously harmful and, in our ignorance, not desire things which we require to avoid such harm. But the intelligibility of this fact seems to depend on the belief that there is something objective and universal about human need: 'objective' in that its theoretical and empirical specification is independent of individual preference, and 'universal' in that its conception of serious harm is the same for everyone.

Pioneering work in philosophy by a number of recent writers has addressed this point, particularly Plant and Lesser (Plant *et al.*, 1980, chs 3–5), Braybrooke (1987), and Thompson (1987). Our own previous contribution to the debate was especially influenced by the first, as is what follows (Doyal and Gough, 1984). In ethics, similar conclusions about the objectivity of need have been arrived at especially by Gewirth (1978) in the United States, and Wiggens (1985) in the UK. At the meeting point of welfare economics, development economics and philosophy, Sen's (1984, 1985, 1987) work on the allied notion of human capabilities has also been influential. In this chapter, we shall draw on these different perspectives in developing our own theory of human need.

Needs as the preconditions for human action and interaction

We have seen that in ordinary discourse, basic needs are linked to the avoidance of serious harm – however harm might be conceptualised. In one way or another, all of the writers cited above do the same through identifying basic needs with what they argue are the conditions necessary for such avoidance. Serious harm itself is explicitly or implicitly understood as the significantly impaired pursuit of goals which are deemed of value by individuals. To be seriously harmed is thus to be fundamentally disabled in the pursuit of one's vision of the good. Thought of in these terms, the objectivity of harm is ensured through its not being reducible to contingent subjective feelings like anxiety or sadness. For one can experience both – not to mention a host of other unpleasant feelings – and still successfully achieve aims deemed important (Thompson, 1987, pp. 35–54). Basic human needs, then stipulate what persons must achieve if they are to avoid sustained and serious harm in these terms.

Another way of describing such harm concerns the impact of poor need satisfaction on the success of social *participation*. Unless individuals are capable of participating in some form of life without arbitrary and serious limitations being placed on what they attempt to accomplish, their potential for private and public success will remain unfulfilled – whatever the detail of their actual choices.[1] Whatever our private and public goals, they must always be achieved on the basis of successful interaction, past, present or future, with others. Our entire lives – even when we are alone – are dominated by what we learn from others, how they assess what we think we have learned and how they respond to changes in our actions on the basis of such assessment. In other words, we build a self-conception of who we are through discovering what we are and are not capable of doing, an achievement based on our participation in social life. In this and later chapters, the social character of human action and of the serious harm which results when it is fundamentally impaired will be further explored.

For now, it is important to recognise that harm in this sense is not just to have one's desires satisfied less than before the harm occurred. It is to be disabled to a degree which blocks new achievements which would otherwise have been real possibilities for the individual concerned. Miller puts it as follows:

> Harm, for any individual, is whatever interferes directly or indirectly with the activities essential to his plan of life; and correspondingly, his needs must be understood to comprise whatever is necessary to allow these activities to be carried out. In order, then, to decide what a person's needs are, we must first identify his plan of life, then establish what activities are essential to that plan, and finally investigate the conditions which enable those activities to be carried out (Miller, 1976, p. 134).

Because of his emphasis on the objectivity of such conditions, Miller's definition has much to commend it. Unfortunately, however, since it links the content of the needs of individuals to their plan of life, the moral significance of need-satisfaction becomes predicated on our prior acceptance of the moral value of such plans. This throws us back into relativism.

The search must be for universalisable preconditions which enable minimally impaired participation in the forms of life both in which individuals find themselves and also which they might subsequently choose if they believe their existing form of life to be wrong. Without the discovery of such conditions, we will be unable to account for the special moral significance which we wish to impute to basic need-satisfaction (Goodin, 1988, pp. 32–3). Harris sums up the consequences for the formulation of social policy as follows:

> social policies should be directed toward guaranteeing a range of life chances to the citizens of a society. The relevant life chances are those required to protect the status of individuals as full members of the community. Their purpose is to offer material opportunities to participate in the way of life of the society.

Needs, by implication, are defined as whatever is necessary to that end. An individual is 'in need' for the purposes of social policy to the extent that he lacks the resources to participate as a full member of society in its way of life (Harris, 1987, p. 101, cf. Weale, 1983, p. 35).

In what, therefore, do such 'resources' consist?

Debate about what makes humans 'human' and different from the rest of nature go back to Plato and Aristotle. Both thought that reason was crucial and the latter in particular stressed the importance of the quest for virtue, something which without reason and choice no animal could possibly pursue (MacIntyre, 1985, chs 11–12; cf. Norman, 1983, chs 2–3). Later, in the seventeenth century, Descartes restructured this idea into a rigorous dualism where the person became metaphysically divided into material body and immaterial mind. Still working within this tradition, Kant posed the problem of the components of person-hood in different terms. Against the background of the body conceived as a deterministic process, he searched for the conditions to which persons must conform if they are to be capable of initiating actions and assuming responsibility for them. Although he was not directly concerned with the character of human need, he did articulate many concepts and arguments relevant to its theorisation. Kant showed that for individuals to act and to be responsible they must have both the physical and the mental capacity to do so: at the very least a *body which is alive* and which is governed by all of the relevant causal processes and the *mental competence to deliberate and to choose*. Let us identify this latter capacity for choice with the existence of the most basic level of personal 'autonomy' (Lindley, 1986, ch. 2).

Kant's analysis of freedom anticipated the contemporary argument that the 'behaviour' of the body has to be distinguished from the 'action' that 'accompanies' it. Thus, the physiologist or biochemist will give a *causal* explanation of the movement of the body of someone running down the road. But however much evidence we gather about the motion of the runner and however successful we are in giving a mechanistic account of it, we will be no closer to identifying and explaining what the runner is *doing*. Running for a bus, escaping from a tormentor or jogging are only three of many possible interpretations compatible with the same physiological and biochemical understanding. To decide which one to opt for requires a further explanation of the agent's *reasons* for running. Among other things, this will mean discovering her aims and beliefs – her goals and the strategies which she has chosen to try to implement them. Thus in running for a bus, the agent is expressing her autonomy by doing something that she might not have done. Among other things – and this was Kant's main reason for developing the argument in the first place – this is why we may *blame* her if she acts unreasonably and admire her when she achieves her goal with originality (Doyal and Harris, 1986, ch. 3).

To be autonomous in this minimal sense is *to have the ability to make informed choices about what should be done and how to go about doing it.* This entails being able to formulate aims, and beliefs about how to achieve them, along with the ability to evaluate the success of these beliefs in the light of empirical evidence. Aims and beliefs – 'our own' reasons – are what connect us logically with 'our own' actions. The capacity to make 'our own' mistakes performs the same role as regards the successes and failures of our actions. In these minimal terms, autonomy is tantamount to 'agency. It is a clear precondition for regarding oneself – or being regarded by anyone else – as being able to do, and to be held responsible for doing, anything. Its existence is expressed in the unique repertoire of successful and unsuccessful manual and mental activities which constitutes the story of how we became who we are. It is this narrative which primarily individuates our identity as a person from that of others (Parfit, 1984, Part. III).

Thought of in this way, autonomy has little to do with stronger notions of self-ownership – of being in control of both the aims and the beliefs which inform action (Dworkin, 1988, p. 15; cf. Haworth, 1986, ch. 1). Both slaves and masters are autonomous in the terms outlined, provided that the latter give the former correct information about what they want done and allow them the scope to follow these orders in their own individual ways. Toward the end of this chapter, we show how the concept of autonomy can be strengthened to discriminate between the two groups.

A person with impaired autonomy is thus someone who temporarily and seriously lacks the capacity for action through his agency being in some way constrained. Examples would include a person who is physically forced to do something against her will or who has been duped into thinking that she has done one thing when, in fact, she has done another. Someone would fall into the first category, for example, if she was violently raped. The second category would be illustrated if someone was deceived into doing something which they did not intend, like committing a crime.[2] It makes sense, therefore, to claim that *since physical survival and personal autonomy are the preconditions for any individual action in any culture, they constitute the most basic human needs – those which must be satisfied to some degree before actors can effectively participate in their form of life to achieve any other valued goals.*

As it stands, however, such an assertion appears to be circular. On the one hand, we have argued that needs are universalisable goals which must be achieved by agents to avoid the objective harm of not doing the things which they believe that they should as well as they might. On the other hand, we have also maintained that the survival and autonomy of agents must be ensured before they can act to achieve any goal. But surely this must mean that it is misconceived to talk of the need for survival and autonomy as *goals* at all. For how can either be attained unless they have already been attained? Thompson makes a similar point as regards survival when he argues: 'in normal circumstances the questions "Do you *need* to survive?" and "Do you need to avoid serious harm?" are logically inappropriate, because they involve the category mistake involved in the questions "Is death fatal?" and "Is harm, harmful?"' (Thompson, 1987, p. 21). We seem to be reasoning in a circle.

In one sense, yes. Certainly, to the extent that survival and autonomy viewed as fixed states provide the intentional foci of other goals and strategies which are deemed to be needs, then Thompson's point about survival is well taken. But in another sense the apparent circularity of suggesting that we need to achieve the very things which our achievement of anything presupposes begins to resolve when we remember that the reality of human capacity for action is one of *degree* and *occurs over time.* Concerning survival, we appear to know perfectly well what it means to act with the goal of survival in mind. What else are we doing, for example, when we encourage sick patients to fight to get better – to increase their life expectancy? The same may be said of viewing autonomy as a basic need when we try to help those who are depressed or exploited to take more control over their lives.

The man who is struggling to stay alive – and most of us do when our lives are threatened unless we have made a conscious decision to the contrary – will not thank you for informing him that he had to be alive to do so. He may know that he can never be completely healthy but he has the goal of becoming more healthy than he is. Similarly, the woman who is trying to increase her understanding of her actions and their consequences through working during the day and going to school at night will hardly appreciate the news that she already possesses the autonomy which she is working so hard to increase. Her goal is the capacity to do more of the things which she deems significant within her culture than she is capable of at present.

In short, from now on when we talk about survival and autonomy as basic needs, we will refer to the concrete ways in which individuals or collectives can act in practice to *sustain* or *improve* the satisfaction of both. Though these needs already had to be satisfied to some degree to account for the possibility of action in general, the success of future actions will also depend on the survival chances and the degree of autonomy which has been acquired by the actor(s) at the time of their execution. To this extent, it seems reasonable to continue to refer to the goals of increasing life expectancy and autonomy as basic needs.

This said, Thompson's argument about the avoidance of harm is acceptable without qualification. If harm is the end state in relation to which basic needs take on their definition, then we must not refer to the avoidance of harm as a need. Since it becomes the *final* goal for all humans – the ultimate 'Y' in 'A needs X in order to Y' – it makes more sense to describe it as our most basic human interest.[3] For now, it suffices to note that in general terms, survival and autonomy are the basic preconditions for the avoidance of serious harm as it has been defined thus far – dramatically impaired participation in a form of life. Of course, the satisfaction of these needs does not guarantee *successful* participation. It may still fail for a thousand reasons and if this were not the case, we really would be arguing in a circle. However, it is clear that the empirical probability of any individual succeeding will be improved by greater survival chances and autonomy whoever they are and wherever they live. We must now examine what this potential for improvement entails in practice.

Survival/ physical health as a basic need

Let us begin with survival. Readers may have already become uneasy that the need for physical survival on its own cannot do justice to what it means to be a person. The victim of a motor accident who survives in deep coma on a life-support system, incapable of independent action, demonstrates why. This is not an idle philosophical point. Whether or not such victims regain the capacity to act will eventually determine their fate. Despite physical survival, if the best clinical advice continues to be that that the chances of regaining consciousness are non-existent, or even extremely remote, then the ventilator may eventually be turned off. Those who have suffered severe brain damage or who have been in long-term dementia will at some point be presumed to be almost as incapable of any ordinary human action as the person/body on the life-support system. Were it possible to decide with absolute certainty that they would not recover – as is the case for a condition like extreme Alzheimers Disease – then similar ethical questions concerning the artificiality of their survival are raised (Kennedy and Grubb, 1989, pp. 1086–116).

So it is *physical health* rather than just mere survival which is a basic human need, one which it will be in the interest of individuals to try to satisfy before they address any others. To do well in their everyday lives – whatever they do and in whatever cultural context – people have to do much more than survive. They must possess a modicum of good physical health. To complete a range of practical tasks in daily life requires manual, mental and emotional abilities with which poor physical health usually interferes. But defining health and illness is not easy and disputes rage about how this should be done. We cannot avoid confronting some of these problems here.

Those definitions of physical health which focus on physiological impairment are often referred to as 'negative' definitions because they link it conceptually with biological disease or, more accurately, with its absence. On this view, the physical health needs of individuals have been met if they do not suffer in a sustained and serious way from one or more particular diseases (Stacey, 1988, pp. 169–72; Caplan, 1981, Parts 1, 5). For our purposes, the usefulness of such a perspective should be clear. Serious diseases ordinarily disable sufferers from participating as well as they might

– and as might be expected of them – in the particular form of life in which they find themselves. Indeed, it is precisely the impairment of such participation which motivates us to describe its physical causes as abnormal in the first place (Fulford, 1989, parts 2 and 3). Avoiding these diseases will therefore be a goal which most individuals will wish to achieve. To fail to be physically healthy in this sense will be regarded as abnormal – unless there is some reason like famine or plague why most others are also failing – and complex social mechanisms have evolved in all cultures to enable their members to cope with such failure (Parsons, 1958, pp. 165–87; cf. Morgan, *et al.*, 1985, pp. 45–52).

The negative definition of physical health is both highly specific and, on the face of it, universalisable through the technical understanding made available by the *biomedical model* (Doyal and Doyal, 1984). Because of its causal character and its consequent concern with nomological regularities, this approach to diagnosis and therapy appears to provide a cross-cultural foundation on which to compare, understand and sometimes improve the physical health of people in differing social contexts. Relativists, however, might object at this point that conceptions of biological abnormality and appropriate treatment will be culturally varied: who is to say – without making ethnocentric or even racist assumptions – who is right or wrong? The problem that they like to highlight is that since what is real seems to be the by-product of the scheme of medical understanding employed to interpret experience, *rational* choice between different approaches to healing becomes impossible (Wright and Treacher, 1982; Armstrong, 1983; cf. Stark, 1982).

Let us tackle these doubts by considering a 25-year-old without employment in Chicago, a 40-year-old casual labourer from Rio de Janiero and a 12-year-old child from Nairobi, all of whom are suffering from poverty and severe tuberculosis. Whatever their cultural differences, they are alike in three ways.

First, they will all *feel ill*. Against the background of their particular symptoms and suffering, their *perceived* ability to participate as they would wish in their form of life will have been seriously violated. This perception, however, will not only be a function of how they actually feel. At the same time, their physical state must also render them functionally incapable of sustained participation in practice. After all, one can feel ill without this entailing such incapacity. It is only when impaired participation exhibits *both* factors – the subjective feeling and the physical actuality of impaired agency – that universalisability will eventually and properly be imputed to the disease regarded as responsible for the impairment (cf. Boorse, 1975, pp. 49–61). In this case, the disease is tuberculosis.[4]

Second, all three individuals may well refer to their illness by a variety of names and explain its origin and symptoms in diverse ways. However, given our technical understanding of the tubercular bacillus and its infectious consequences, it is not clear what a denial that all three had tuberculosis would mean in practice, provided that they tested positive on the basis of accurate tests. It is no more clear, for example, than it would be if someone denied that helium is a gas, that it expands when it is heated and that it does so because of the impact of heat on its molecular structure.

And third, the best available technical understanding also dictates the most effective biological and environmental approaches to prevention and cure and provides the most complete account of why they work. For all three cases of tuberculosis, the preventive measures will be those which have the effect of maximising resistance to infection through adequate housing, diet, sanitation and vaccination. The curative measures will mainly involve certain types of antibiotics.

Of course, things will not always be this straightforward. In the case of a disease like cancer, the causes are much more obscure and, although we do know a great deal about prevention, there are few cures. In radical critiques of curative medicine, it has become a truism that the nineteenth-century killer diseases – tuberculosis, cholera and typhoid, for example – diminished primarily through the evolution of a better standard of living. Epidemiological evidence makes it is equally clear that we stand a better chance of preventing than curing the twentieth century diseases of affluence such as cancer and heart disease. Yet such evidence is actually predicated on biomedical understanding. For all of the diseases in question acquire their physiological identity and their capacity for diagnosis against the background of past biomedical research.[5]

It is, of course, true that approaches to theorising physical disease and illness can and do vary. Yet unless we are dealing with relatively minor diseases and illnesses where recovery is fairly certain and nothing much turns on how they are conceptualised, or chronic diseases and illnesses where curative therapy has not proved especially effective, 'traditional' approaches find it hard to compete with medicine based on the biomedical model. This is now widely accepted throughout the world. Even where traditional medicine remains popular, biomedical understanding is employed whenever possible to treat and to prevent serious disease and illness (Len Doyal, 1987, pp. 27–40). Certainly in much of the current literature on medicine and underdevelopment, the Chinese model of 'walking on two legs' is regarded as ideal – of using traditional and biomedical approaches to therapy, whichever appears to work the best and in the most cost effective way (WHO, 1983a; cf. Kleinman, 1984). But in the case of extreme life-threatening diseases, especially those involving infection, this almost always entails the use of available biomedical technology.

In short, physical health can be thought of transculturally in a negative way. If you wish to lead an active and successful life in your own terms, it is in your objective interest to satisfy your basic need to optimise your life expectancy and to avoid serious physical disease and illness conceptualised in biomedical terms. This applies to everyone, everywhere.[6]

Autonomy as a basic need

Yet clear and potentially useful as the negative definition of physical health is, it is rightly regarded by many as problematic. For much more is involved in the preconditions for minimally disabled human action and interaction than the absence of serious biological disease (Salmon, 1984, pp. 254–60). Individual autonomy must also be sustained and improved. One can easily imagine a situation where an actor has met her primary need for physical health but is still capable of initiating very little. 'Initiate' is a crucial word here, because a person who initiates an action is presumed to do so in a fundamentally different way from a machine. The latter is understood via its mechanism and its nomological regularities, but people consist of more than the deterministic relationships between their bodily components. As we have seen, individuals express their autonomy with reference to their capacity to formulate consistent aims and strategies which they believe to be in their interests and their attempts to put them into practice in the activities in which they engage. This is why we hold them practically and morally responsible for their actions but do not, for example, do the same for machines which cannot make choices in the same sense. We may sympathise with those who get angry at machines when they are unreliable. However, we can hardly commend their rationality in doing so!

Three key variables affect levels of individual autonomy: the level of *understanding* a person has about herself, her culture and what is expected of her as an individual within it; the *psychological capacity* she has to formulate options for herself; and the objective *opportunities* enabling her to act accordingly (Faden and Beauchamp, 1986, pp. 241–56). Let us look at each in turn.

Understanding

The degree of understanding of self and culture depends on the availability and quality of *teachers*. People do not teach themselves to act – they have to learn from others. Which *cognitive skills* are learned will differ from culture to culture, but they are not totally variable. All children must learn, for example, to interact socially in minimally acceptable ways, irrespective of the specific cultural rules they follow in the process. Persistently lying to, or punching, one's fellows will never be a recipe for successful social interaction. Similarly, in all cultures, language skills are necessary as the medium through which actors learn conceptually to order their world and to deliberate about what to do in it. In this sense, individual consciousness is essentially social – the by-product of interaction with others. To the extent that consciousness is partly linguistic then it is obviously social. As Wittgenstein has shown, just as a private language cannot exist – one that is created *ab initio* by the individual – there can be no such thing as a purely private person (Doyal and Harris, 1986, pp. 80–6). The same considerations apply to learning particular *motor* skills. The problem with the Robinson Crusoe myth is that he already knew how to be so industrious (and racist!) because he had already been taught. It is not, as the song goes, that 'people who need people are the luckiest people in the world'. Everyone needs people to be anyone.

Some forms of learning and teaching will be more conducive to high levels of autonomy than others. Much will depend on what is taught. There are some activities which are common to all cultures and for which everyone must be prepared if they are to be able to participate successfully and to understand what goes on within them. Braybrooke correctly classifies these social roles as those of parent, householder, worker and citizen (1987, p. 48). To be, say, a good carpenter, cook or whatever, you must learn certain skills and learn them well. The strength of our autonomy when negotiating with experts will also be related to our understanding. In medical relationships, for example, patients who know more about medicine and health can and do demand more from their doctors and from themselves – they have more choices than they would otherwise (Gorovitz, 1982, ch. 4).

This underlines the degree to which the capacity for thinking about and doing new things must be contextualised in relation to the practical demands on particular individuals. To the degree that specific patterns of learning conform to such demands, the autonomy of the individual will be either helped or hindered. One might, after all, learn anything. However, a good and relevant education of whatever institutional form will prepare learners for participation in their culture which will both win the respect of their peers and strengthen their own self respect. This is why autonomy can be impaired in formal education, for example, by a curriculum which is irrelevant to the vocational needs of the community or the emotional needs of individual students (Entwistle, 1979, parts I–II). It can be equally damaged by the *way* in which people are taught. Without having their curiosity sparked and their intellectual confidence reinforced, the scope of their potential choices will be artificially constrained along with their ability to impact upon the world and upon others (Grundy, 1987, ch. 3). As a result, they will be objectively disabled.

Mental health

The second key determinant of autonomy is the individual's *cognitive and emotional capacity* – ultimately their *mental health*. Rationality is an important component in all the definitions of autonomy which we have considered. But what does it mean in relation to mental health? Loss of self in these terms can be explained in different ways and can take on a variety of cultural forms – anything from possession by spirits to chemical imbalance. The lack of specific aetiologies has generated a huge debate about whether all mental illnesses are correlated with physical pathology in the same sense in which physical illnesses are said to be. Some, such as the contributors in Kleinman and Good (1985) and Cox (1986), have questioned whether Western conceptions of mental illness can be applied to sufferers in other cultures (cf. Mezzicch and Berganza, 1984). This is illustrated by Obeyesekere (1985, p. 134) who writes: 'How is the Western diagnostic term "depression" expressed in a society whose predominant ideology of Buddhism states that life is suffering and sorrow?'. Hirst and Woolley (1982, Part II) have developed a powerful relativist critique of orthodox conceptions of mental illness. Indeed, some, such as Szasz (1961), have disputed its very existence and charged that psychiatry seeks to replace the proper realm of contending moral, political and religious values with a false pseudo-science.

These critiques are important because they draw attention to the care which must be taken in diagnosing mental illness in individuals from cultures different to our own. However, such arguments do not rule out the possibility of culture-free identification of emotional as distinct from physical or cognitive disablement or of some of the reasons for it. For mental illness can be primarily conceived in terms of a significant reduction to individual autonomy: 'Mental illness means only those undesirable mental/ behavioural deviations which involve primarily an extreme and prolonged inability to know and deal in a rational and autonomous way with oneself and one's social and physical environment. In other words, madness is extreme and prolonged practical irrationality and irresponsibility' (Edwards, 1982, p. 70; cf. Engelhardt, 1982). Mental health is the obverse of this – 'practical rationality and responsibility'. While there are borderline departures from rationality, and though there will be disagreement at the margins about the meaning of 'extreme' and 'prolonged', there are many deviations from rationality in these terms which will be identified as such in all cultures.[7]

Since all actions have to embody a modicum of reason to be classed as actions at all, it is difficult to give a precise definition of the minimum levels of rationality and responsibility present in the autonomous individual. Generally speaking, the existence of even minimal levels of autonomy will entail the following over sustained periods of time:

a)   that actors have the intellectual capacity to formulate aims and beliefs common to a form of life;
b)   that actors have enough confidence to want to act and thus to participate in a form of life;
c)   that actors sometimes actually do so through consistently formulating aims and beliefs and communicating with others about them;
d)   that actors perceive their actions as having been done by them and not by someone else;
e)   that actors are able to understand the empirical constraints on the success of their actions;
f)   that actors are capable of taking responsibility for what they do.

Again, like physical health, autonomy at its most basic level should be understood negatively – with reference to the serious objective disablement which will result when one or more of these characteristics is abscent.[8]

When the preceding characteristics are absent in individuals, they may be deemed either emotionally or mentally disabled. Leaving aside specific symptomatology, those who are seriously and permanently ill in this sense have either lost or never possessed a level of autonomy sufficient for more than minimally successful levels of intentional social interaction – if that. To be sure, with help, they can become less handicapped than they are. For now, our focus is on the seriously mentally ill, where at best specific aetiology is in dispute, where there is a significant impairment of social participation but where it does make sense to talk of the recovery of cognitive and emotional capacities.[9]

In serious mental illness, the absence of rationality can take a variety of forms – visual and auditory illusions, delusions or gross inconsistencies in thought patterns (Clare, chs 2–3, 1980). With psychotic depression, for example, there is an almost total loss of sense of self and an incapacity to join in everyday activities. Even in less harmful forms of clinical depression, there is still a perceived gap between actor and action. Concretely, this entails a more or less constrained sense of fatalism about what happens to sufferers in their physical and social environment. This is often accompanied by a consequent sense of anxiety about the unpredictability of life as well as a feeling of helplessness (Seligman, 1975), lack of control, (Phares, 1976), worthlessness (Beck, 1967) and defeat (Gilbert, 1984, ch. 4). In short, all of these theorists describe different ways in which depressed individuals can lose control over their lives and exhibit low levels of what we mean by autonomy. Again, the fact that the *reasons* for such loss or the ways in which individuals interpret them might be culturally variable does nothing to counter the claim that its symptoms lead to the same types of disability across cultures (Foster and Anderson, 1978, ch. 5; cf. Helman, C., 1990, ch. 10).[10]

The negation of this nightmare vision – of individuals who cannot participate in their culture, who do not understand why, who are tormented by their own imaginations, unable to do anything about it and 'kept going' by drugs – must be at the empirical heart of any *positive* conception of individual autonomy. This is reflected in the work of Jahoda (1958) who includes among her components of positive mental health: growth of self, informed self-acceptance and sense of identity, unification of life goals, tolerance for stress and frustration and 'environmental mastery'. In his recent attempt to operationalise the same concept, Warr (1987, ch. 2) distinguishes five components of mental health: affective well-being, competence, aspiration and integrated functioning and autonomy. (We differ in that we regard mental health as a component of autonomy.) Of course, none of this is to suggest that the mentally ill are completely lacking in autonomy. Everyone must have a measure of autonomy in order to do anything – irrespective of the *degree* of helplessness which they might exhibit or feel in their everyday activities. Among other things, this is illustrated artistically by the high levels of creativity shown by some severely impaired psychiatric patients and legally by the fact that many patients who are subject to compulsory psychiatric treatment are not regarded as incompetent to make informed choices about other aspects of their lives (Mason and Smith, 1987, ch. 18).

There is the possibility that in arguing the above, we will be misunderstood in two ways which we must try to rectify in advance. First, it might be argued that we are lauding asocial, individualistic values which stress independence at the expense of reciprocity and interdependence. An autonomy which pursues individual self-interest at the expense of others hardly constitutes a universalisable human need. In fact, several studies suggest that self-esteem goes hand in hand with pro-social attitudes, altruism and generosity: that those individuals who are most confident about their ability to act in the world also tend to be those who are most aware of the needs of others (Lieven, 1989). Furthermore, they often tend to be those who act to improve the conditions of others and who will not always give in when the going gets tough. For example, it was found that a strong sense of self was exhibited by young people from the northern USA who had gone and lived in the South and participated over a long period of time in the anti-segregation demonstrations there – often at the risk of their lives, comfort and immediate careers (Coles, 1967). In general terms, then, it seems likely that effective challenge to oppressive social orders is more likely the more autonomous are the challengers (Barrington Moore, 1978, ch. 3).

Second, it could be claimed that while paying lip service to Freud, our analysis of autonomy does not take on board the revolution in human understanding which he and other psycho-analytic theorists have brought about. This is because the model of choice and decision making which we advocate still basically presupposes that individuals are potentially in charge of their lives provided that the physical, educational, emotional and social variables can be got right. Many within the pyscho-analytic tradition would dispute this, arguing that even when actors are deemed autonomous through high scores on these measures – including the absence of serious mental disorder and depression – and appear to project high levels of self-determination, the reality is still one of the unconscious ruling the roost. Unfortunately, exactly how it does so remains a matter of enormous dispute among psychoanalysts, one in which it would be inappropriate for us to engage here. The fact remains that whatever the influence of the unconscious turns out to be, the more autonomous individuals are in the terms we have outlined, the more free they will be to pursue life goals. Since it is precisely the minimisation of arbitrary psychic constraints on such freedom which all psycho-analysis seeks to achieve, our theory should be regarded as complementary rather than inconsistent with its aims.

This said, we are emphatically not arguing that the enhancement of personal autonomy will necessarily increase subjective happiness. Much of the psychoanalytic tradition is convincing on this point and we have already underlined it in our own clear distinction between needs and preferences. However, Guntrip further argues: 'Freud said that at best we can only help the patient to exchange his neurotic suffering for ordinary human unhappiness. That, I believe, is too pessimistic a view, and the patient has glimpses of feeling the possibility of experiencing himself and life in a much more real and stable way' (Guntrip, 1968, p. 279; cf. Freud, 1974, pp. 292–3). In other words, what therapeutic success can achieve for individuals is an improvement in their ability to participate in or to question their form of life. The fact that such participation may be unhappy – as it no doubt often is – in no way negates its liberational potential. Indeed, if anything can minimise such unhappiness it is likely to be the sense of self-worth which successful participation can engender.[11]

Opportunities

The third variable which affects the degree to which autonomy can be increased is the range of *opportunities* for new and significant action open to the actor. By 'significant' we mean activities which are deemed of social significance in any of Braybrooke's preceding categories – parent, householder, worker or citizen – or which the actor deems of significance for the rational improvement of her participation in her form of life. This means that when we link improvements in autonomy to increased choices, we do not mean any old choices. One could choose to toss a coin all day but the process of doing so would hardly count as an improvement in the autonomy of the tosser. The choice of a brand of soap powder which is really no different from all of the others has more to do with a diminution of autonomy than its expansion (Dworkin, 1988, ch. 5). But for us to make significant choices – and to enjoy the pride and pleasure of knowing that we have successfully done so – we must have the opportunities. Those who are denied them have their freedom and their autonomy artificially constrained and are unable to explore some of their capacities as people (Haworth, 1986, ch. 6). More than anything else, it is this that makes tyranny so abhorrent.

Yet we have already seen that even the oppressed can make choices. Their lives are full of mundane choices in interpreting the rules which shape the social roles over which they have no say. Indeed, given the rigidity of these constraints and the extreme hardship which they can cause, great creativity is often shown in eking a living out of what is available, trying to maintain self-dignity and supporting the dignity of others for whom an individual feels a sense of responsibility. Were the freedom of the oppressed illusory – were there *no* opportunities – it would make little sense to encourage and to assist them to throw off the chains of their oppression. Slavery is the most dramatic example, although the same point applies to all groups in extreme and unnecessary poverty. It also underlines the political importance of the *freedom of agency* of individuals in such groups – their ability in principle to choose – even though at any given time members may do little to challenge their oppression.

What is equally clear, however, is that freedom of agency should not be confused with the higher levels of autonomy and opportunities associated with *political freedom* (Doyal and Harris, 1986, ch. 5). Our analysis of autonomy as a basic need has thus far focused on the necessary conditions for participation in any form of life, no matter how totalitarian. Individual autonomy can obviously reach greater levels than this. Where the opportunity exists to question and to participate in *agreeing or changing* the rules of a culture, it will be possible for actors significantly to increase their autonomy though a spectrum of choices unavailable to the politically oppressed. In such circumstances, actions which hitherto they could only be said to choose through interpreting the already existing rules of their particular social environment, become chosen and their own in a much more profound sense. What was autonomy becomes 'critical autonomy'

Raz makes the same point:

Significant autonomy is a matter of degree. A person may be more or less autonomous. [Significantly] autonomous persons are those who can shape their life and determine its course. They are not merely rational agents who can choose between options after evaluating relevant information, but agents who can in addition adopt personal projects, develop relationships, and accept commitments to causes, through which their personal integrity and sense of dignity and self-respect are made concrete. In a word, significantly autonomous agents are part creators of their own moral world (Raz, 1986, p. 154).

Dworkin puts it more technically:

autonomy is conceived as a second-order capacity of persons to reflect critically upon their first-order preferences, desires, wishes, and so forth and the capacity to accept or attempt to change these in light of higher-order preferences and values. By exercising such a capacity, persons define their nature, give meaning and coherence to their lives and take responsibility for the kind of person they are (Dworkin, 1988, p. 20).

The distinction between first- and second-order preferences is useful to the extent that it underlines the distinction between action which is based on a process of reflection from action executed uncritically. However, to link this difference to the conceptualisation of autonomy *per se* obscures the equally important difference between those who are and those who are not in a position to reflect critically upon and to try to change the rules of their social environment. Oppressed people must at times exercise high levels of critical deliberation of Dworkin's second-order type – within the context of *given* social institutions – simply in order to keep body and soul together. It is to do them an injustice to suggest that agonising choices which they sometimes have to make are no different from the run-of-the-mill daily actions in which we all engage with little critical reflection. At the same time, it would be foolish to argue that such people have a high level of autonomy simply because they are in a position 'to take responsibility for the kind of person they are'.

It is for this reason, that we prefer the distinction between autonomy as freedom of agency, which is compatible with relatively high levels of critical reflection, and the higher degrees of critical autonomy which are entailed by democratic participation in the political process at whatever level. For critical autonomy to be a real possibility, individuals must have the opportunity to express both *freedom of agency and political freedom* (cf. Doyal, 1990, pp. 1–13). Without both types of opportunity, they will again be objectively disabled, even though their levels of understanding and cognitive and emotional competence may be quite high. For now we will continue to focus on the former, since we are here concerned with the necessary preconditions for participation in any form of life – no matter how authoritarian. We will explore the practical, moral and political implications of the creation of critical autonomy in Chapters 7 and 11.

Problems in comparing need-satisfaction

We have now shown that certain conditions must be met before humans can assume the mantle of persons. Logically speaking, they have to be able to participate in a cultural form of life. In practice, this means that they must have the physical, intellectual and emotional capacity to interact with fellow actors over sustained periods in ways which are valued and reinforced in some way. Loss of health or autonomy entails disablement in this respect and an inability to create or to share in the good things of life, however they may be defined. Since these basic needs are the same for everyone, we appear to have found a way round the problems of ethnocentricity with which we began – a criterion for demarcating needs from wants which can be used to measure the degree of social progress which any society has achieved.

Unfortunately, however, we still face two problems. First, what is meant by 'basic'? There is little problem about identifying the most minimal levels of need satisfaction, since even the most staunch relativist would presumably not question the universality of the need for life-preserving quantities of water, oxygen and calorific intake. Neither, hopefully, would they dispute that without some learning and emotional support in childhood, all individuals will find it impossible to join in the activities of their peers. But once we ask how much more than the minimum counts as an *adequate* level of basic need-satisfaction, the consensus begins to evaporate. Second, people within different cultures attempt to satisfy their needs in profoundly different ways. Let us define the objects, activities and relationships which can satisfy our basic needs as 'satisfiers' (Lederer, 1980, p. 53; cf. Kamenetsky, 1981, p. 103). Since therefore *need satisfaction* always occurs within a given cultural context, is not the cross-cultural identification of *need* an artifact?

Let us explore the second point first. It is both true and fortunate that individuals have developed so many different approaches to need-satisfaction. Food is one of the most obvious examples. The sheer variety of culinary traditions throughout the world is truly remarkable, since the raw materials are often so similar. To be able to experiment with and choose between such traditions – as is possible in many big cities if one has the money – is a privilege almost beyond compare. The same can be said about the range of other satisfiers of basic needs – clothes, architecture, crafts – which have also evolved in such varied ways throughout human history. The fact that we all require minimal levels of, say, water and protein has, on the face of it, nothing to do with the issue of whether or not some cultural traditions are better or more progressive than others. What sense would it make, for example, to ask which type of food is better – Chinese or Indian? No doubt, someone from China or India would have their preference, as probably does the reader. Yet as we have seen, preference is something that is subjective and culturally specific. So important is culture in this respect that some people will suffer gross deprivation in order not to violate cultural taboos, especially concerning food (Braybrooke, pp. 102–4).

Second, the level of what is perceived as an acceptable level of need-satisfaction seems also to be culturally specific. The fact that people in many traditional cultures do not have the same average life-expectancy or degree of educational attainment as those in the industrialised countries does not mean that they cannot participate in their form of life in highly creative ways. We know that they often do – exhibiting much autonomy in the process, and believing that their way of life is better than that of others. Indeed, the more we learn about some 'traditional' cultures, the more attractive many of their features appear compared with our own – those which stress the importance of the obligation of the individual toward the collective, for example, along with a more serious concern for the environment. In short, the relativist might claim that to talk of individual health and autonomy outside the context of the cultures in which they find expression is to indulge in philosophical abstraction with little anthropological significance. Once one moves beyond the most minimal preconditions for participation in social life, it seems that human needs remain hopelessly relative.

Consider, for example, the problem of comparing autonomy between cultures. There is evidence to suggest that personal success defies cross-cultural analysis. The craftsman from a traditional culture who has won the respect of his peers may have much more autonomy in our terms than the college professor who considers himself and is considered by others to be a bumbling failure, and this despite the fact that the latter has a greater life-expectancy and education than the former. Further, what might appear to be an example of high autonomy in one culture – bravery, for example – may appear to be crass stupidity in another. Individual autonomy, it could be argued, is just too much a construct of particular cultural environments to be employed as a metric for helping to evaluate social progress in the way in which we are attempting (Mauss, 1985, pp. 1–25; cf. La Fontaine, 1985, pp. 123–40).

On the face of it, these are powerful arguments which do seem to suggest that the imposition of beliefs about human need by one culture on another amounts to little more than conceptual and moral imperialism. How can we plausibly maintain the universality of our theory while at the same time recognising that people and cultures do differ in their beliefs about what adequate need satisfaction entails in practice? We will address this problem with the help of a thought experiment.

Imagine an island where there is no material scarcity or environmental pollution, where there is unrestricted education in the manual and cognitive skills which the indigenous culture values, where ample opportunity for vocational choice exists, as well as a long tradition of providing emotional support for all inhabitants who conform to existing norms and laws. All things else being equal – for example, no concentration of greed and power within the general population, no prevalent genetic disease, no natural disaster – we have no reason to suspect that in the midst of such plenty there will be any major inequalities in need-satisfaction. To this extent, therefore, all of the inhabitants should have *similar* and *high* levels of health and autonomy in the terms which we have outlined, however they may conceptualise them. We would thus expect all inhabitants to be able to participate in their culture successfully if this is what they desire. So let us assume that this is exactly what we do find – a thriving and rich form of cultural life with a high degree of participation among its members.

Now suppose that on one half of our island, there is a plague, one component of which is severe dysentery which physically disables the population. It is clear that if they go to the other half which is physically healthy, they will be unable to participate in their ordinary way of life to the degree that would otherwise be the case, and that they will be perceived to be disabled for this reason – irrespective of how the disease and illness is conceptualised. Similarly, suppose that one effect of the plague is partial amnesia, making those affected forget many of the intellectual and practical skills which they have learned. Again, it is clear that they will be unable to participate as well as they could beforehand in a variety of ways, whatever explanation they may give for the memory loss. Finally, suppose that instead of physical illness or amnesia, the consequence of the plague is depression and loss of confidence in the ability to execute such skills. Again, however this may be understood, the result will be that their participation will be impaired in comparison with those who have not been so harmed. So regardless of the indigenous cosmology, by hypothesis we seem to have a situation within a single culture where we can compare high *and* low levels of health and autonomy.

Can similar comparisons be made across different cultures? Let us further assume that there are surrounding islands with similarly prosperous populations. There too we should find high levels of social participation – however this may be explained. What is regarded as normal on one island may be shunned on another without this necessarily affecting the physical health and autonomy (in our terms) of the inhabitants of either. By hypothesis then, we have a range of individuals from radically different cultures who have achieved much more than minimal levels of health and autonomy in what appears to be precisely the same sense – the sustained physical and mental capacity to participate in their culture in highly creative ways. This has been due to the availablity and characteristics of specific satisfiers, regardless of their cultural differences. (We develop this distinction further in Chapter 8.) In short, there seems to be little difficulty in comparing levels of basic need-satisfaction within *and* across cultures at above-minimum levels.

It follows that if an epidemic of dysentery, amnesia or depression strikes the other islands, there is no reason (all things being equal) to expect any difference in their disabling impact. Individuals with higher or lower levels of physical health and autonomy will be readily identified, as will their differing abilities to participate in their particular culture. Further, individuals with high levels of physical health and autonomy on one island will have more potential for high levels of participation on another, provided that they understand the rules of the alien culture. Indeed, there is no reason to believe that they will not be able to participate even more successfully than some of the indigenous population if their levels of health and autonomy are higher. The only argument to the contrary would have to contend that learning the rules of an alien culture well enough successfully to join in its activities was impossible because of the conceptual constraints imposed by one's own. Were this true, it would be impossible to illustrate in any detail what it means for cultures to differ radically since all anthropology would have to be regarded as rubbish (Doyal and Harris, 1986, chs 6–7)! But this must again mean that it is possible to compare levels of basic need-satisfaction of individuals both within and between cultures. Of course, none of this should be surprising. It is exactly these sorts of comparisons which we do in fact find in a variety of epidemiological, sociological and psychological literatures.

Finally, if such comparisons are possible, then it becomes clear in principle what it would mean to talk of optimal rather than minimal levels of basic need-satisfaction, irrespective of culture. The optimum level of physical health entails as high a life expectancy and as little disability through disease as is possible in the light of a person's genetic potential. The optimum level of autonomy can be specified in two ways corresponding to our earlier distinction between autonomy of agency and critical autonomy. The lower optimum entails the minimisation of social constraints on a person's participation in socially significant activities coupled with access to as much cognitive understanding as is necessary successfully to pursue their chosen form of life. The higher optimum will further entail access to knowledge of other cultures coupled with the critical skills and the political freedoms to evaluate their own and to struggle to change it if they choose.

We have argued in this chapter that health and autonomy are the basic needs which humans must satisfy in order to avoid the serious harm of fundamentally impaired participation in their form of life. Provided that there is nothing logically inconsistent or factually improbable about the preceding thought experiment, we have also demonstrated that it is possible in principle to compare levels of basic need-satisfaction in these terms not only within but also between cultures. In so doing, we have simply underlined the justification for the same sorts of comparisons undertaken by every national and international organisation concerned with assessing the degree of serious harm suffered by the populations which they represent.

Yet this focus on universality may have worried some readers. Certainly, we have made little mention of the distinct needs of specific groups of people. In concentrating on the needs which all members of our species have in common the discussion thus far has been genderless, raceless, classless, ageless, cultureless. We are, of course, not denying that there is a sense in which particular groups have specific needs. Obvious examples are women, groups subject to racial oppression and people with disabilities. Members of each group are commonly subject to *additional* threats to their health and autonomy over and above those which we have already outlined. As a result they require *additional and specific satisfiers* and procedures to address and correct them. The fact that this is the case, however, does not entail that the basic needs of members of such groups are any different from those of all other persons.

Indeed, most of the 'isms' which denote particular types of social and economic inequality or oppression can only be condemned to the extent that they can be shown to be inconsistent with the basic needs of individuals in the group in question. For these reasons, it is clear that there is a place in any politics of need for a politics of difference, with particular groups emphasising and struggling to improve the specific satisfiers available to meet the basic needs of their members (Lovell, 1990, part 3; cf. Rowbotham, 1979). They will know their requirements best and be most committed to the struggle for increased access to them.

Yet what should not be forgotten are the dangers of reifying these differences. Basic needs, and as we shall see the necessary conditions for satisfying them, are the same for all oppressed groups. It is precisely through such concepts that the experiences and impairments of those with specific patterns of poor need-satisfaction can be understood and appreciated by those who do not share them. Politically, this has three important functions. First, it illustrates the common bond between oppressed groups – the onslaught on their health and autonomy by those who oppress them. Second, such commonality suggests the extent to which their different experiences are in fact similar and holds open the door for a great deal of mutual understanding and sympathy. And third, this in turn makes possible joint political action with a common aim – of optimum need-satisfaction for all, whatever the specific differences between groups.[12]

5

Societal Preconditions for the Satisfaction of Basic Needs

Has our emphasis on personal autonomy smuggled in a strong form of individualism which denies the role of the social and its place in meeting needs? The answer we give in this chapter is no – we can only acquire the ability to act from the positive actions of others and they from others and so on. Any conception of agency or autonomy which ignores this fact will be an impoverished abstraction, irrelevant to understanding why humans act and choose as they do. This argument explores the societal preconditions which must be met by all collectivities if they are to survive over long periods of time thus ensuring an environment within which individuality can evolve.

The social dimension of individual autonomy

In the last chapter, we argued that for individual autonomy to be 'critical' two different kinds of freedom must be present – freedom of agency and political freedom. In further exploring the links between autonomy and freedom, many writers within the liberal tradition argue that both should be seen as the absence of constraints on actions which have not been chosen by actors themselves. As long as we are talking about physical constraints – the inhibition of autonomous choice through the exercise of brute force – then this seems straightforward.

However, 'constraint' is sometimes interpreted much more widely, as when Wolff writes: 'the autonomous man, insofar as he is autonomous, is not subject to the will of another' (Wolff, 1970, p. 14). This implies that really autonomous agents are completely *self-sufficient* in that they choose for themselves the form of life which they wish to follow, provided that this does not interfere with the choice of anyone else. On the face of it, this vision of self-determination seems plausible. Both freedom of agency and political freedom clearly do depend on agents being able to choose for themselves; and respect for such freedoms is eminently practical if all it entails toward others is doing nothing which is not in self defence.

Such an individualistic conception of autonomy cannot, however, be sustained. For even if we limit our focus to Dworkin's first- and second-order preferences – both of which are compatible with surviving creatively within an authoritarian social order – such individualism splits actors from the social environment within which their personal identity evolves. As we have seen, individuals discover who they are through learning what they can and cannot do. Individual action is social to the extent that it must be learned from and reinforced by others.

Actors are socialised into following rules – expressions of collectively held and enforced aims and beliefs. These will range from the obviously public (e.g. how to exchange one set of goods for another) to those which seem essentially private (e.g. bathing, toilet etiquette). Such rules constitute the parameters of our sense of self and of others – our individual vision of what (formally) is and is not privately and publicly possible. Thus the autonomy necessary for successful action is not compromised by the necessity to follow rules – quite the opposite. It is precisely the normative constraints of our social environment which make the specific choice to do X rather than Y a real possibility (Doyal and Harris, 1986, ch. 4; cf. Raz, 1986, chs 8, 14).

This is easily seen by differentiating between rules and individual interpretations of them. People are identified and identify themselves as players of chess with reference to the appropriate set of rules. They cannot choose to play chess unless they agree to follow these rules. But their autonomy as players is secure because there are so many different ways that they might individually select to play. Their perception of their quality as players – or even their ability to play at all – is dependent on those with whom they interact. Of course, understanding why individuals choose to act in relation to specific rules and why those rules are structured in the ways that they are is obviously more complex in the context of the wider society than is the case with chess. Personal and institutional power, for example, will always have its impact on such choices, along with a range of other goals and strategies which will be less clear – if indeed they are conscious at all – than those associated with making the next move in a game (Giddens, 1984, pp. 14–25; cf. Lukes, 1974, pp. 11–25). The fact remains, however, that the intelligibility of individual action stems from rules and thereby the existence of those social collectivities which sustain them both.

Writing about the rules of language, Doyal and Harris stress the same links:

> The repertoire of actions you perform is therefore like the vocabulary of the language you speak. It is the collective possession of the social group within which those actions are performed and that language is spoken . . . Thus it is fundamentally mistaken to view yourself as acting with total self-sufficiency – by yourself and for yourself – without reference to anyone else. Social life is an essential characteristic of individual humans, unlike the situation of an individual tree which just happens to be in a forest. Grown from a seed in isolation, a tree is still a tree; but humanity is the gift of society to the individual (Doyal and Harris, 1986, p. 80).

But this must mean that the opportunity to express individual autonomy requires much more than simply being left alone – more than *negative* freedom. If we really were ignored by others, we would never learn the rules of our way of life and thereby acquire the capacity to make choices within it. For Robinson Crusoe to have been such an individual success in isolation required many years of previous social contact with those who taught him the skills he later used!

In other words, to be autonomous and to be physically healthy, we also require *positive freedom* – material, educational and emotional need-satisfaction of the kind already described (Berlin, 1969). Against the background of the general socialisation on which their cognitive and emotional capacity for action depends, autonomous individuals (who are not slaves) must understand *why* they should not physically constrain the actions of others and must possess the emotional competence to act accordingly. But again, they can only learn to follow the rules embodied in such constraint with positive assistance. Further, to wish to act in an unconstrained fashion still entails participating in a form of life to which the positive actions of others give substance. For example, for an individual to deliver a successful lecture involves much more than her listeners not intervening to stop it! They must also have the physical, intellectual and emotional competence to give serious consideration to her arguments. Otherwise, why should the lecturer bother?

These arguments expand the reasons outlined in the previous chapter for linking the concept of serious harm with that of impaired social participation. Without the necessary need-satisfaction to avoid such fundamental impairment, individuals will not be able to explore the boundaries which their form of life provides for the expression of their physical, intellectual and emotional potential. Such arguments are incorporated within more recent formulations of citizenship theory by Marshall, Tawney, Titmuss and Townsend (Harris, 1987, chs 3–5).

Since the protection of the health of individuals, their learning and the growth of their emotional maturity are themselves social processes, they necessarily entail individuals interacting in social groups. These groups will often be quite small – families, classes in schools, friends and workmates, for example – and their membership will overlap the membership of other groups. To the degree that all members follow more or less the same rules concerning what they perceive to be the most significant aspects of their everyday life then they can be said to share the same *culture*. To the degree that some members have a particular set of rules pertaining to some but not all significant aspects of social life which only they and close associates follow – and which may or may not conflict to some extent with the dominant culture – then they can be viewed as belonging to a *sub*-culture.[1]

From now on we will focus only on the former, with two important qualifications. On the one hand, we agree with Archer (1988, p. 19) that too much emphasis on cultural integration can lead to 'inattention to the presence or absence of alternatives at the systemic level' and an 'unwillingness to concede any modicum of differentiation in the population'. On the other hand, despite the existence of such normative variety, it also seems clear that specific networks of rules can be identified which conceptually organise the practical means by which large groups of individuals seek to satisfy their basic needs and which stipulate which sorts of satisfiers will be regarded as normal and acceptable by the majority of their members. Provided that it is not regarded as an independent variable which determines the detail of individual activity, 'culture' remains the most useful expression to denote the presence of such normative consensus and, to the degree that it exists, to individuate one consensus from another.

Four societal preconditions

As is the case with individuals, there are necessary societal preconditions which have to be satisfied by such collectives if they are to survive and flourish over long periods. These concern the normative structure of the group – the rules within which individuals order their everyday lives and which embody the goals which they must collectively achieve if they are to continue to provide each other with mutual support. There are four such goals which are the same for all cultures (cf. Williams, 1965, chs. 2–3; 1979, ch. II.3). First, any society must produce sufficient need-satisfiers to ensure minimal levels of survival and health, alongside other artifacts and services of cultural importance. Second, the society must ensure an adequate level of biological reproduction and child socialisation. Third, it must ensure that the skills and values which are necessary for production and such reproduction to occur are communicated throughout a sufficient proportion of the population. And fourth, some system of authority must be instituted to guarantee adherence to the rules by which these skills are successfully practised.

Individual action which is directed toward the achievement of societal preconditions – even without actors necessarily thinking of their aims in these terms – illustrates what Giddens calls the 'duality' of the structure of human action (Giddens, 1984, pp. 24–8, ch. 6; cf. Cohen, 1989, ch. 1). Without individual capacity for action there can be no social structure and without social structure there can be no individual capacity for action. Giddens states: 'By the "duality of structure" I refer to the essentially recursive character of social life: the structural properties of social systems are both medium and outcome of the practices that constitute those systems' (Giddens, 1982, pp. 36–7; cf. Archer, 1988, pp. 87–94). It is for this reason that individual health and autonomy must always be achieved in an institutional context and that the long-term survival of social institutions will depend on whether or not it is. For similar reasons, Braybrooke also emphasises four categories of social role which are practically identical to our four societal preconditions (Braybrooke, 1987, pp. 48–50; Doyal and Gough, 1984, pp. 18–21). Let us now examine each in turn.

Production

In all cultures, it is necessary somehow to create the food, shelter and other satisfiers required for (what are defined as) 'normal' levels of health to be achieved collectively. This need for *material production* constitutes the economic base of each society and poses a vast range of practical problems which it must solve if its members are to sustain themselves. Of course, these arrangements will vary in detail between cultures, especially when they exist in radically different physical environments. Nomadic, hunter-gatherer, agricultural and industrial societies all approach their material tasks in different ways. Yet they all share similar problems in trying to get nature to do their bidding and all face obstacles about which they can agree despite cultural differences.

Doyal and Harris have argued that these core activities are 'constitutive' of social life generally and are at the heart of our ability to understand the similarities between alien cultures and our own (Doyal and Harris, 1986, ch. 7; cf. Archer, 1988, ch. 5). Unless, for example, an anthropologist can at least identify some activities in another culture which he is convinced are the same as those in his own then he will be unable to *translate* the aliens' language and thereby to enter the collective consciousness of their rules and norms. He does this through being able recognisably to *join in* such activities *before* he has learned the alien language. This will be necessary both to convince the aliens that he is human and friendly and to establish the translation bridgehead he needs securely to link their language with his.

Neither aim is achievable unless constitutive activities possess a basic intelligibility which does not depend on their meaning within a mode of discourse linked to a particular culture. This illustrates the *practical* constancy of various aspects of productive activity, irrespective of culture. Not only does such constancy put paid to forms of relativism which claim that reality is little more than a reflection of cultural norms. The reasons behind the success and failure of constitutive activities also reveal a constant pattern of practical *reason* which is equally immune to cultural variation. For example, if you try to build a roof with an inappropriate pattern of supports, it will fall down – and for the same reason, whatever your culture. Further, an anthropologist would look silly trying to grow food or to understand how it was grown without grasping the practical significance of water – whatever the aliens call it.

Constitutive activities will include, therefore, aspects of material production which are *common* to all cultures, as well as how such aspects are socially organised. Since Marx and Durkheim, it has become accepted that all production is essentially social. Humans are not genetically endowed with the physiology or mentality to enable them to survive on their own – let alone in any sense to prosper. Barrington Moore argues, for example, that successful production requires group interaction in the form of a division of labour:

> Every known human society displays a division of labour ... Even in a non-literate society with a very simple economy and abundant resources, not all tasks are equally attractive all of the time. Under more complex economies the differences, of course, become very striking. Thus, in the division of labour, as in systems of authority, we are again concerned with an implicit social contract subject to perpetual testing and renegotiation ... [and which] ... serves to regulate an inherent and unavoidable conflict, though one whose intensity varies greatly in time and space. This is a conflict among (1) the demands and requirements of the individual worker or household for food, clothing, shelter and a share in the amenities and pleasures of life; (2) the needs of the society as a whole; (3) the demands and requirements of the dominant individuals or groups (Barrington Moore, 1979, pp. 31–2).

In short, for the satisfaction of basic needs to be sustained satisfactorily, social relations of production are required which are suited to this collective end.

The sphere of material production is broader, however, than the process of people interacting with nature to produce goods. It encompasses, as Marx argued, the related processes of exchange, distribution and consumption – the whole set of activities from planting the seed to eating the meal (Marx, 1973, pp. 88–100). Once it is realised that all forms of production are social and thereby require some sort of division of labour, then the need for an appropriate system of exchange becomes obvious. If people cannot produce what they need for themselves and those for whom they accept responsibility, then they must have some other means of acquiring it.

This entails a set of rules by which they can trade the goods and services which they have produced with those they need. Whatever this system of exchange might amount to – barter, reciprocity or markets of various kinds – it will in part constitute a system of distribution which allocates goods and services in specified ways to particular groups or persons. However, distributive systems must also stipulate rules by which individual entitlements are negotiated – decisions about who should get what. These will be linked to factual beliefs about the importance of particular individuals or families for material production and to moral beliefs about the justice of whatever degrees of inequality are tolerated. So the mechanisms of exchange and distribution vary widely between cultures (Sahlins, 1974, ch. 5). The point, however, is that they all have mechanisms which, whatever their normative details, must guarantee levels of production which are sufficient at least for group survival. In fact, of course, most cultures do much better than this.

Reproduction

For forms of life to exist over time, their modes of production must also provide the material foundation for successful biological reproduction and socialisation – the process which 'begins with ovulation and ends when the child is no longer dependent on others for necessities and survival' (O'Brien, 1981, p. 16). This includes two separate elements: procreation, and infant care and socialisation. Whenever we use the term 'reproduction', from now on we shall mean these activities and no other.

It may seem strange to regard the former as intrinsically social. However, mating and childbirth, as Eisenstein argues, always occur against the background of specific rules:

> None of the processes in which a woman engages can be understood separate from the relations of the society which she embodies and which are reflected in the ideology of society. For instance, the act of giving birth to a child is only termed an act of motherhood if it reflects the relations of marriage and the family. Otherwise the very same act can be termed adultery and the child is 'illegitimate' or a 'bastard'. The term 'mother' may have a significantly different meaning when different relations are involved – as in 'unwed mother'. It depends on what relations are embodied in the act (Eisenstein, 1979, p. 47).

This said, whatever the cultural specificity of procreational rules, say of confinement and kinship, they must enable the safe execution of the constitutive activity of childbirth and aftercare – both for the mother and infant (Moore, 1988, ch. 3). The cultural form again has a universal core.

Equally, the survival of cultures will depend on the the minimal satisfaction of basic pre- and post-natal health needs. For cultures to do better than just survive, higher levels of satisfaction will also be necessary. Many now argue that the early recognition of the close relationship between procreative and societal success contributed to the evolution of both patriarchy and private property. Men were physically capable of subduing and raping women against their will, particularly when their dependence and vulnerability were increased by child bearing. Both facts, along with the male bonding which accompanied them, enabled men to take control of the reproductive cycle through the domination of womens' bodies. As this became common, so did the perception of women as commodities to be traded for social benefit, thus – as opposed to Engels, who saw it the other way around – laying the psychological and normative grounding for the evolution of the institution of private property (Lerner, 1986, ch. 2; cf. Meillassoux, 1972, pp. 93–105).

Some contemporary feminists have criticised such speculative anthropology as exaggerating the degree to which the social importance of women should be identified with their role in biological reproduction. It is clear that despite these reproductive demands, they have always continued to play an active – often the predominant – role in most aspects of production as well. The separation of the processes of production and reproduction and the identification of women with reproduction undervalues or denies the importance of their labour in the productive sphere. This in turn reinforces sexist stereotypes of the naturalness of men controlling the cycle of material production, and hides the fact that without women both productive and reproductive cycles would grind to a halt (Jaggar, 1983, ch. 6). The validity of this critique does not, however, obviate the fact that activities associated with procreation can be differentiated from those concerning production in our first sense. Any critique of conventional anthropological wisdom which argues that women face a double burden because of their procreational as well as *other* productive roles, still implicitly recognises the appropriateness of distinguishing between them.

The other dimension of reproduction in any society will be the care of infants, and their socialisation into correctly understanding and following basic rules fundamental to their present and future well-being. These rules concern activities which are again either constitutive or culturally specific. The former will be the same for all cultures and be directed toward the satisfaction of basic needs (e.g. learning that certain activities are physically dangerous and potentially painful). The latter will vary with culture and might or might not be so directed (learning the language of the culture as opposed to learning some of its more exotic customs). As with the biological dimension of procreation, the achievement of both types of aims will be shaped by the social environment in which it occurs:

> What young people are taught and how they are taught depend on the type of adults desired. What should young people accept as food or as appropriate toilet habits? What should they accept as legitimate authority? What skills and interests should they acquire? These are all determined by prevailing social values including, in contemporary society, values about the proper place of the children of working-class parents, of ethnic minority parents, and of course, about the proper place of women (Jaggar, 1983, p. 152).

Historically, the social context within which the early socialisation of infants has occurred has always been some form of family structure, though with a wide variation of kinship patterns.

Documenting and explaining the social character and complexity of such patterns has long been a central theme of anthropology (Naroll, 1983, ch. 10). At the same time, many feminist writers have linked the social organisation of the family to forms of patriarchal oppression. However for our purposes here, we must focus primarily on the lack of symmetry between the biological and social dimensions of reproduction outlined above. Many studies have indicated that biological parentage does not necessarily make someone effective in the early socialisation of infants, a point which further undermines any attempt to reify the biological maternal role (Moore, 1988, pp. 21–30). Yet however varied the structure of the family may be and however oppressive many of its forms are to women, the survival of cultures will still depend on the success with which such early socialisation takes place.

Cultural transmission

The societal preconditions of production and reproduction involve the manipulation of the physical environment so that goods and services of particular kinds can be either created or consumed. None of this would be possible without sufficient cultural understanding on the part of the members of the social groups involved – without knowledge of the beliefs which have proved successful in achieving these practical goals in the past. We have seen that actors are not born with such understanding, nor will they necessarily be pre-disposed to accept the particular approach to production and distribution of the social group of which they are a part. After early childhood and with increasing conceptual complexity, both must continue to be learned from others in the context of formal and informal education. This will in turn be based on an already existing body of norms, laws, traditions and rituals which define the predominant cultural values of the form of life involved – the rules by which one form of life is individuated from another.

Social structure and culture are reproduced through the instantiation of these rules by groups of individuals who interpret them in ways which they deem 'the same'. The process of such instantiation is another universal characteristic of all sustained cultures, one which we shall call 'cultural transmission'. For this to recur through time, patterns of communication must be established which conform to and reinforce dominant normative patterns. As Williams argues: 'The emphasis on communications asserts, as a matter of experience, that men are not confined to relationships of power, property and production. Their relationships, in describing, learning, persuading and exchanging experiences are seen as equally fundamental' (Williams, 1973, p. 18). The social organisation of such communication will require its own normative structures – educational institutions are the most obvious example. Yet whatever the institutional detail, the socialisation which occurs as a consequence must prepare individuals for specific productive and procreative roles within the division of labour in which they are expected and expect themselves to participate. Two specific types of understanding must be transmitted for this to be achieved.

The first concerns *technique*. Each culture will possess a collective memory of how its previous members learned to tackle their most important productive and reproductive tasks. At the least, this will involve what, following Habermas, we may term 'technical' and 'practical' understanding, the former concerned with the successful manipulation and prediction of natural processes and the latter with successful communication with others (Habermas, 1971, pp. 301–17; cf. ch. 7). Unless enough of both types of understanding are transmitted to a sufficient number of people and are adapted to new demands, the material base of the culture and of the basic need-satisfaction of its individuals will deteriorate.

Second, each society will require rules to *legitimate* acquisition, exchange and distribution in ways which link different types and amounts of labour with what people receive for their work (Giddens, 1984, pp. 28–34). For individuals to be able to plan to meet their material needs, they must know and accept that they will be allocated goods and services in return for their labour, provided that it conforms to certain rules. The absence of sustained conflict in a society suggests that aspects of its distributional system have been internalised irrespective of its particular hierarchical character and the specific level of need-satisfaction of its members. Consider the stability of some traditional cultures with poor levels of need satisfaction, or the web of beliefs which convinces many individuals within capitalist societies that the market is a natural and fair mechanism for the organisation of production, consumption, exchange and distribution. You do not have to be a Marxist to see that without the acceptance of such principles – especially in times of high poverty and unemployment – the survival of capitalism would be threatened (Williams, 1979, pp. 31–49).

Authority

Finally, it is clear that the mere existence of sets of rules which combine to form a culture in our sense will not guarantee their perpetuation or implementation. Individuals can break the rules – as opposed to just interpreting them in ways which involve no threat to social cohesion. This poses both opportunities and problems for the individuals involved. On the one hand, it creates the possibility for social change – provided that enough individuals decide to break the rules in the same way or, which amounts to the same thing, to follow a new set of rules capable of sustaining a different culture. Without this possibility, social change would be both inexplicable and pointless to advocate, even in the face of forms of life which are unhealthy, exploitative and tyrannical for the majority of their members (Gouldner, 1971, pp. 218–25; cf. Giddens, 1979, ch. 1). On the other hand, the prospect of social change creates potential difficulties. For we have also seen that the individual potential for sustained and improved health and autonomy is entirely social in character. It depends on the collective acceptance of a range of rules which institutionally define the social roles required for a division of labour to be a productive success. If too many individuals decide to break the rules at one time then everyone's short-term need-satisfaction will be threatened, whatever longer-term advantages revolutionary change might engender.

So despite the prospect that it may be abused and ultimately provoke collective rejection, there must be some system of *political authority* – backed up by sanctions – which will ensure that cultural rules linked to need satisfaction will be taught, learned and correctly followed. The exact character of such authority will vary enormously, depending on the size, complexity and level of differentiation of the societies concerned. Yet however centralised or dispersed the authority may be, it must be effective in its own terms if the society in question is to persist (Giddens, 1979, p. 108; cf. Barrington Moore, 1979, pp. 15–31). Indeed, the further one moves from Durkheim's vision of traditional society towards the 'organic solidarity' of industrial nations, the more important this becomes. Hegel was one of the first to recognise that a successful 'civil society' or capitalist market economy necessitates some form of central authority (Avineri, 1972, chs 7–9; cf. Taylor, 1975, chs 14–16).

In short, a 'state' is required which through its normative structure and the power it commands, ensures that the rules which underpin the survival and success of the collective as a whole are both taught and enforced. The material manifestation of political authority in this sense will always be some form of government, a system of justice and mechanisms for law enforcement. Again, one does not have to approve of the legal system of any particular society to recognise that if its most fundamental rules are consistently and widely broken, then it and its members will either perish or be incorporated into another system where basic individual needs stand a better chance of being met.

In general, then, these four societal preconditions – production, reproduction, cultural transmission and political authority – refer to the structural activities which any minimally successful mode of social life must be able to carry out. They also refer to concrete goals whose achievement must be planned for and sustained over time. The degree to which individual needs are capable of being satisfied in principle will depend in practice on the degree of such success. Similarly, the success of a form of social life will in turn be predicated on the health and autonomy of its members, assuming, of course, that they share roughly the same central values concerning what is expected of them, how to do it and what will happen if they do not. For now, it is an open question what these central values should be to ensure more rather than less need-satisfaction. On the face of it, there are many conflicting value systems which have been and are still capable of mediating more than just minimal levels of such satisfaction. We shall explore what sorts of rules might facilitate optimal levels in the next chapter.

Emphasising the interdependence between individual need-satisfaction and societal preconditions in this way should make it clear that we are not adopting the sort of abstract individualism which is so often exhibited by utilitarian writers and politicians. There is much more to human welfare than the individual calculation of which actions will lead to the most happiness. Yet, it should be equally clear that we do not accept forms of sociological functionalism which presuppose that individual actors simply mirror the structural properties of their social environment. Again, were this the case it would be impossible to explain social change since the individuals involved would never see the point of trying.

The only criterion for evaluating forms of life which will be advocated here is the extent to which they enable basic individual needs to be satisfied. But this must mean that individual needs are conceptualised in ways which are *independent* of any particular social environment no matter how much their satisfaction may depend on it. Otherwise, any evaluation of normative structures with respect to associated levels of need-satisfaction would be circular. It is the moral feasibility of such an evaluation to which we must now turn.

6

Human Liberation and the Right to Need-Satisfaction

So far we have argued that health and autonomy are basic needs common to all humans irrespective of culture. We have further shown that there are specific societal conditions for the satisfaction of both needs. But we have not been concerned with the moral issue of whether people's needs *should* be met. Not everyone accepts that they have an obligation to aid those in serious need. Without such a moral theory we can only preach to the converted. This is by no means a pointless task. Given the assaults of relativism, and the withering attacks from upholders of rather crass forms of individualism – the 'me-now' ethic – in recent years, those who uphold the morality of meeting basic needs require as much rational support for their beliefs as possible. But their arguments need situating within a broader moral context if others are to be convinced. Otherwise why should they be expected to move from the 'is' of need to the 'ought' of the responsibility to do something about it?

Plant and Lesser have outlined a general answer to this question which calls attention to the fact that

> those who have developed moral outlooks, however different, that command certain ends or require certain duties to be performed are logically committed to a conception of basic needs. Ends (however different) and duties (however varied) can be pursued and performed only by human beings acting autonomously; and therefore any moral view to be coherent must recognize the maintenance of human life and the development of autonomy as basic obligations (Plant *et al.*, 1980, p. 93).

This important insight requires further exploration.

In particular, does their argument apply only to obligations to meet basic needs *minimally*, or can it be extended to higher and even optimum levels of need satisfaction? Plant *et al.* (1980, p. 94) maintain that 'the level of satisfaction in question is going to be a matter of normative dispute, but this does not render the whole conception ineffectual'. However, unless it can be shown that individuals have a right to more than the bare minimum of need-satisfaction, an ineffectual outcome seems likely. But if we are obligated to meet needs at a higher than minimal level, is everyone entitled to an *equal* level of satisfaction – even strangers or enemies? If so, how should this be accomplished against the background of scarce resources and the limited ability of economic systems to redistribute them? If there is a moral obligation to provide charity, should it not begin at home? The morality of meeting need, and to what degree, are the subjects of this chapter.

Duties, rights and moral reciprocity

To be a person rather than just a living body or animal entails more than consciousness and an ability to communicate and to formulate aims and beliefs. The individual must also be the bearer of responsibilities. As writers like Rousseau and Durkheim so vividly argued, the very existence of social life depends upon the recognition of duties toward others – that in one's interaction with others there are some things that one should and should not do. Whatever their specific content, the normative structures of particular cultures would be unintelligible were it not for the assumption that their members could accept responsibilities toward, as well as recognising them in, others.

Not only does social life require moral responsibility; the same can be said for the success of our own individual participation within it. Unless we happen fortuitously to have the power to inflict our will on others, social success will depend on our capacity to understand what our moral responsibilities are and on our willingness to act accordingly. Indeed, it is the existence of such moral conscience in ourselves that underpins the central dilemma of individual existence: what is the right thing to do in the circumstances in which we find ourselves. The duties which moral responsibilities entail are just as *real* for us in our social lives as is our physical environment. For example, a statement to the effect that someone is acting in accordance with a specific duty has empirical conditions under which it will be true in the same sense as do descriptive statements about the natural world (Platts, 1979, p. 243; cf. Arrington, 1989, ch. 4).

The reality of duties apparently entails the reality of *rights* – the entitlement of one group of individuals to what is required for them to carry out obligations which they and others believe they possess. However, the logical relationship between rights and duties is highly complex.[1] For this reason, we shall argue that duties only entail rights against the background of an already existing network of moral beliefs which clearly specify the conditions of entailment. As White argues: 'The various rights and duties of husband and wife, child and parent, employer and employee, different ranks in an institution, etc. arise not mutually from each other, but jointly from the common system in which all participate' (White, 1984, p. 70). So, for example, if the 'common system' dictates that you have a duty to tell the truth, others in turn can be said to have the right to be told it. And the same applies to you. It is in this sense that rights and duties are reciprocal and that rights which really do constitute entitlements have corresponding duties to which some individual or group is capable of conforming. It is also why individuals who refuse to act in accordance with this reciprocity (e.g. criminals) may lose entitlements which others do not.[2] Again, the capacity of individuals to recognise and exercise such reciprocity is what makes social life a possibility at all.

With this in mind, we shall address the issue of the morality of meeting needs in two stages: first, the right to minimal need-satisfaction, and second, the right to 'optimal' levels of need-satisfaction. Within each stage, we shall distinguish between the rights and duties of those who share the same culture and the rights and duties of all, irrespective of culture.

The right to minimal need-satisfaction of those sharing the same culture

Let us begin with an individual *A* who believes that she has a duty of some kind toward others in group *B* who expect her to act accordingly. Also assume that she is aware of and accepts the legitimacy of their expectation. The group in question could be a small face-to-face community or a large anonymous collectivity. But whatever its size and however well its members know each other, for her and them to believe that she should do her duty presupposes that they also believe that she is in fact able so to do. In other words, 'ought' implies 'can'. Gewirth argues as follows:

> X's initial 'ought' statement also logically commits him to accepting the positive responsibility of helping other persons. For suppose X's doing z is impossible without other men's providing various kinds of essential conditions or services, which I shall call p. Hence when X says 'I ought to do z' he must also accept the statement 'Other men ought to do p.' For since 'ought' implies 'can', if it is right that other men not do p, without which X cannot do z, then it is false that X ought to do z. To put it otherwise, if one endorses some end, then one must also endorse the necessary means to that end, at least prima facie or in the absence of superior counter-considerations (Gewirth, 1982, p. 94; cf. Weale, 1983, pp. 37–47).

Therefore, the ascription of a duty – for it to be intelligible as a duty to those who accept it and to those who ascribe it – must carry with it the belief that the bearer of the duty is entitled to the level of need-satisfaction necessary for her to act accordingly.

Thus A must believe that she has the right to such satisfaction if, say, she suddenly becomes impoverished but is still expected by the members of B to execute the duties she did before this occurred. For *without at least minimal levels of need satisfaction, A will be able to do nothing at all, including those acts that are specifically expected of her.* And the same applies to those who believe that they have a right to A's actions. They also must accept that unless her basic needs are minimally satisfied, she will be unable to do what they think she should. Therefore, she has a right to such satisfaction in proportion to the seriousness with which they take her duty and expect her to comply with it. And the converse also holds (cf. P. Jones, 1990, pp. 44–6).[3]

Of course, the acceptance of such a right does not specify exactly how it should be respected in particular circumstances. The members of B, for example, may accept that A has a right to a minimal level of need satisfaction without accepting that they have a corresponding duty *directly* to provide it. This will be likely if, say, welfare agencies exist which have the institutional responsibility for meeting needs. But remember: someone or some group must accept the duty to act for *A* if her right is to have substance. Therefore, the members of *B* cannot escape from the responsibility at least to *contribute toward A*'s minimal need-satisfaction – provided that an *agency* exists for this purpose, that it can be shown that otherwise *A*'s minimal need-satisfaction will not occur and that *A* is regarded by the members of *B* as continuing to have duties toward them. The form that such assistance may take can either be direct support through actually providing *A* with the goods and services which she requires (or the money to acquire them) or indirect support through funding for whichever welfare agency is doing the job instead (Goodin, 1985, pp. 151–3).

Apart from such positive support, the other thing that *A* can morally expect of the members of *B* is 'forbearance' – that her negative freedom will also be respected and that they will not act in ways which directly prevent *A* from doing her duty. This would make as little sense as it would for *A* to try to impede the members of *B* from doing their duty toward her (Gewirth, 1978, pp. 249–50). Note the difference, however, between this emphasis on the right to forbearance and that of a libertarian like Nozick. As we have seen, he conceptualises rights in a fundamentally asocial way which imputes entitlements to individuals with respect to their 'inviolability'. According to this view, we have the right to do what we *want*, provided that it does not keep anyone else from doing the same. Our view is rather that we must have the right to do what others think that we *should*, provided that they take their expectations seriously. Their duty to forbear is essentially social and follows from their adherence to a given set of moral beliefs.

In general, therefore, to the degree that *A* and the members of *B* share a reciprocal moral relationship of the kind outlined, then they must be seen as *equals*. This equality has nothing to do with the relative quantities of their material possessions. Rather it reflects the premiss that equal levels of need-satisfaction lead to equal potential for assuming shared moral duties – for achieving equal dignity in the social pursuit of individual goals. When this does not occur, the disadvantaged suffer not because they *have* less than others but because they can *participate* less in their respective form of life. It is their impaired agency rather than their inequality as such that should be the focus of our moral concern (Raz, 1986, pp. 227–40; cf. Gewirth, 1978, pp. 206–9).

So far, we have focused our argument for the existence of a right to minimal need-satisfaction on individuals who accept that they are bound by reciprocal moral duties. Remembering the dangers of imputing too much conceptual·uniformity in the process, let us now generalise this to all members sharing a culture – a common normative vision of the good. We have seen how moral codes – systems of rules dictating which actions are to be regarded as right and wrong – provide much of the social cement which bonds individuals into a consensus about who is entitled to and responsible for what. The key characteristic of such moral imperatives is our willingness to ascribe goodness and badness to individuals on the basis of whether or not they at least try to act in accordance with their prescribed rules. Wiggens (1985, pp. 170–1) sums it up nicely:

> A social morality . . . is not just any old set of abstract principles. It is something that exists only as realized or embodied (or as capable of being realized or embodied) in a shared sensibility, and in the historically given *mores* and institutions that are themselves perpetuated by it. It is only by virtue of participating in it, that ordinary men as actually constituted are able to embrace common concerns and common goals that can take on a life of their own and be perceived as enshrining values that enjoy what Hume sometimes called 'moral beauty'.

In other words, virtue itself in part entails conformity to those rights and duties which stipulate what it means to be a *member* of such a 'social morality' or culture, whatever one's role within it.[4]

But for the same reasons we have just outlined, to condemn or punish an individual for not being virtuous, or to praise and reward someone for the opposite, presupposes that they have a choice one way or the other – that they could have acted otherwise. It must follow that a precondition for blaming *anyone* within a culture for acting immorally and expecting them to do better in the future is respecting their right to the minimum level of need-satisfaction necessary for them to do so. It is therefore contradictory to regard someone we believe to share our vision of the good as capable of doing better in ways that we think that they should and then not to help them attain at least the *minimal* wherewithal to do just that.

The right to minimal need-satisfaction of 'strangers' in other cultures

But does our sense of moral imperative only apply to members of our own culture? Obviously not. While it would be absurd to overestimate the capacity of organisations like Oxfam and War on Want to solve the problem of dire poverty in the Third World or to eradicate the political and economic conditions which cause it, they do represent a very strong sense of the right to aid of those who suffer and the duty to give of those who do not. These feelings reflect an implicit application of the arguments described above to all persons everywhere. And justifiably so. For moral imperatives know no national boundaries – provided that those who proclaim their belief in the good really do mean it.

To take a topical example, if we think that individuals should not be killed for their beliefs or for what they write and publish about them, then we identify this position as one aspect of what we accept to be the moral good. It is the *categorical status* of this principle which leads us to condemn *anyone* who violates it, whether they are a member of our own culture or of another which embodies opposing moral views. But to say of those in another culture – 'In my opinion, you should act otherwise' – again presupposes that they *can* and that they have the right to minimal need satisfaction to the degree that we are capable of providing it. Thus, to see a starving mother in another society trying unsuccessfully to feed her infant carries with it the conclusion that she should be better able to fulfil whatever obligations toward her child we impute to her. Given such imputations, we take on the obligation to try *in some way* to help. The general response that 'something should be done' to satisfy the minimal needs of those even in radically different cultures is due in part to the fact that they hold up a nightmarish mirror in which those in more comfortable nations can see themselves reflected – knowing that they should act in some way but finding themselves too incapacitated to do so. To use Shakespeare's image, they see 'the heath' and themselves as the 'poor, bare, forked animal' unprotected on it (Ignatieff, 1984, pp. 38–44).[5]

Many of us feel that we would be entitled to expect help in such circumstances and would reciprocally grant others the same right. Even those who would not do so usually find it necessary to attempt some justification for rejecting universal rights to minimal need-satisfaction. Apart from racist doctrines which proclaim that some members of *homo sapiens* are not fully human, the most common justification for not giving strangers minimal aid is that in one way or another it will undermine their ability to care for themselves. Hardin, for example, argues:

> If poor countries receive no food aid from outside, the rate of their growth would be periodically checked by crop failures and famines. But if they can always draw on a world food bank in time of need, their population can continue to grow unchecked, and so will their 'need' for food. In the short run a world food bank may diminish that need, but in the long run it actually increases that need without limit (Hardin, 1977, p. 17).

But, as long as the focus remains on minimal basic needs, such arguments remain inconsistent. They presumably presuppose that actors in dire need should do something about it, yet deny them access to the minimal health and autonomy necessary for them to do so (O'Neill, 1986, ch. 4).

We are not, therefore, suggesting that anyone *must* accept that all humans have the right to minimal need-satisfaction. Neither must they recognise it as their duty to do what they can to ensure others achieve it. The infliction of suffering is, and always has been, a feature of individual and collective human irrationality. And by 'irrationality' we do not, of course, mean of no 'instrumental advantage'. Holding morality aside, it will always be in someone's short-term interest to exploit others to the point of desperation and death. However, the fact remains that there is widespread opposition to such an extreme version of egoism. There is an almost universal belief that it is morally wrong to do nothing when confronted by someone in dire need whom one can do something to help. Otherwise the general revulsion that is felt at genocide would be inexplicable. Equally difficult to understand would be the disquiet many philosophers and social theorists have about forms of utilitarianism which give succour to a majority wishing to inflict severe hardship on a minority. Indeed, it is precisely to account for these problems that Hume incorporates an appeal to universal moral 'sympathy' into his more sophisticated version of egoism. Similar appeals to universalism also characterise the recent revival of naturalism in moral theory (Norman, 1983, chs 5, 11).

In other words, a moral consensus of a sort has existed for some time about minimal need-satisfaction which emphasises the unfairness of some people being unable to participate in their culture or to develop their individuality. Among other things, this accounts for the lasting popularity of the rhetoric of justice and equality, even among oppressive political regimes . The link between severe need and entitlement is a powerful one supported by both reason and feeling.

The right to optimal need-satisfaction among members of the same culture

The argument so far has justified the rights of all peoples to the *minimal* satisfaction of their basic needs. It has not, however, provided a justification for anything more than the avoidance of gross suffering, or enabling people just to 'get by'. Let us now extend the argument to higher levels of need-satisfaction, up to and including 'optimal' levels.

Fulfilling one's perceived obligations in public and private life usually involves much more than the minimal amount of action made possible by a minimal level of need-satisfaction. There will always be some goals which individuals take very seriously and which they believe that they have a duty to achieve *to the best of their ability*. These will usually be aims which they perceive as central to the conduct of their lives, the successful achievement of which will determine whether or not they will regard themselves and be regarded by others as of high moral character. Personal goals of this kind are informed by cultural values – the types and levels of performance expected by those toward whom one experiences moral obligations. Thus attempts at excellence are symbolic of the commitment to a specific way of life and thereby to a particular vision of the good. The degree of this commitment will ultimately be judged by others who share the same values. In these situations, for us to expect *less* of ourselves than our best, or to believe that less would be acceptable to those to whom we are obligated, calls into question our and their commitment to the shared good which informs our action. It would mean that the good was not really believed to be *that* good after all.[6]

If, however, we agree that those who are committed to the same morality have the duty to do their best – to be good in its terms –

then this commits us to a further belief: the *right* of those concerned to the goods and services necessary for their best effort to be a realistic possibility. It is inconsistent for us to expect that someone else should do their best and also to think that they should not have the wherewithal to do so – the *optimal* as opposed to the minimal satisfaction of their basic needs. And, of course, the same applies to ourselves. The only way in which this conclusion does not follow is for us to believe that, all things being equal, less than the best effort is compatible with the pursuit of the good.

But again, what would 'the good' mean in this context? If we really take our moral beliefs seriously, then we have no option but to take equally seriously the entitlement of other members of our community to those things which will optimise their capacity for moral action. As was the case with minimal need satisfaction, this entails two things: negatively, not inhibiting persons from trying to do their best, and positively, doing what we can to provide access to the same levels of need-satisfaction that we claim in our own pursuit of moral virtue. All other members of our own culture who take their morality seriously incur the same duties toward us and for the same reasons (Gewirth, 1978, pp. 240–8).

Of course, what is regarded as 'best' and 'optimal' in the above terms will vary between cultures, depending on their particular moral codes and the resources which are available for need-satisfaction. Therefore, when we use the the term 'optimal' we are obviously not maintaining that those who share moral values have a right to *everything* that might conceivably reinforce their pursuit of moral excellence. Since the scope of such satisfiers is potentially infinite, no individual or group within the culture could assume the corresponding duty of providing them and without such a duty there can be no identifiable right. Our point is rather that the members of specific cultures will already have reasonably clear ideas of what doing one's best amounts to *in practice*. These will be linked to exemplars of what ordinary individuals can hope to achieve if they apply themselves to the best of their ability, along with theories about the levels of health, learning and emotional confidence which are usually associated with such application. To be consistent, therefore, a commitment to a vision of the good must be linked to that culture's best available understanding of what is required for optimal individual effort. Consistency also dictates that everyone who is expected to do their best – and is encouraged to try to do so – is given a fair share of the resources available for this to be a real possibility.

But 'fair' in what sense? So far we have shown that all individuals within the same moral order have an equal right to optimal need satisfaction and an equal claim on the resources necessary to achieve this end. If we return to the island of plenty to which we referred in our defence of the universality of needs, there is no problem. Since there is no scarcity, as Hume says, the 'jealous virtue of justice would never once have been dreamed of' (Hume, 1963, p. 184). But if many of the goods and services there suddenly become unavailable – because, say, of a natural disaster – then satisfaction of need will have to be reduced accordingly. All things else being equal, this will have the same basic effects on everyone whose needs should have been optimally met when there was no scarcity. For example, mortality and morbidity rates will rise and access to education and emotional support will decline in proportion to the degree and type of scarcity involved. Even in these circumstances, however, the individual's right to equal and optimal need-satisfaction remains just as strong, and overrides rights to the satisfaction of *preferences*. After this practicable degree of equality of need-satisfaction has been achieved, nothing in our argument so far dictates how any remaining surplus should be distributed.

It is this sort of argument – one based on both moral entitlement and pragmatic efficacy – which is behind social policies which advocate equal access to *high* levels of health care and other welfare services. Especially within a competitive economy and culture, it is irrational to exhort the disadvantaged to do their best to help themselves, without making provision for the need satisfaction which they require to do so.

Unfortunately, such qualified egalitarianism is no more identifiable today than throughout human history. In all societies conflicts of interest are present and those with power and privilege usually fight tenaciously to defend the high levels at which they satisfy both their needs and wants, irrespective of the damaging consequences on others with whom they may claim to share the same values. We have already considered some of the ways the powerful try to legitimate their advantages. Yet as Hegel made clear in his analysis of the relationship between master and slave, if we dominate others so much that their own contribution to *our* personal growth is devalued in the process then the price for the resulting contradiction will ultimately have to be paid (Hegel, 1977, pp. 104–11). Broadly speaking, this price can take two forms. First, the pursuit of short-term gain can threaten system 'accumulation': for example, lack of investment in the education of the British workforce is partly to blame for the current economic vulnerability of the nation (Finegold and Soskice, 1988). Second, unfair domination threatens system 'legitimation' – some sort of believable affirmation by those who are being dominated that they accept the legitimacy of their domination and of those who dominate. Whatever affirmation they do give will be unconvincing if their health and autonomy are impaired when they make it. Both of these potential costs are part of the explanation for the development of Western welfare states (Gough, 1979, chs 3–4).

Commitment to a conception of the good shared with others – even including the putative good of capitalism itself – entails, therefore, commitment to their right to pursue it with the same seriousness which we reserve for ourselves. To deny them as much may lead to subjective happiness in the here and now but is inconsistent with both moral virtue or any coherent theory of social justice. No doubt many in power will ignore such advice and continue to line their pockets in the hope that they will never have to pay the long-term price. As individuals, they may be lucky but that does not make them right. You can lead a horse to the waters of reason but it is true that you can't make it drink (Gewirth, 1978, pp. 190–8)!

The right of aliens to optimal need-satisfaction

So far we have seen how a collective commitment to optimum need-satisfaction should follow from a collective commitment to a vision of the good and to a system of rights and duties associated therewith. But what of social justice among those who do *not* share the same system of moral values and, therefore, the same moral vision?

The measure of our moral commitment is our willingness to take seriously its categorical character – its applicability to everyone and not just to those with whom we already profess agreement. If our good is *the* good then we must believe that *all* individuals should do their best to act accordingly – irrespective of their own moral values. If one believes, for example, that female circumcision is an affront to all women, or that the isolation of old people is an outrage, then the practice must be morally condemned – whatever the justification used by participants. However, if we believe that others should do their best to be good in our terms then we must also accept that they have the *right* to try do so. Yet for this prescription to be any more than a hollow moral abstraction, it also follows that they should have the right of access to those conditions which make such a choice a real physical, emotional and intellectual possibility: the right to *optimal* need-satisfaction. Indeed, given the enormous intellectual and emotional difficulties associated with moving from one morality to another, we should want our moral opponents to be in as good a shape as possible.

So consistency dictates that we must support the right to optimal need-satisfaction of strangers about whose moral beliefs we know nothing *in proportion* to our own commitment to the truth and superiority of our vision of the good. To be victorious in bullying the weak and feeble is morally defeating. Like the slave, even if they say they agree, you can never be sure that they really do. Whatever personal gratification their agreement may bring in the short term, it will not be long-lasting. If a concern for virtue in the face of what is believed to be barbarity leads to the repression of the very preconditions for the optimal pursuit of virtue – the optimal need-satisfaction of all of the potentially virtuous whatever their current beliefs – then the resulting bland conformity of action is a form of conceptual and emotional slavery. It is not the responsible moral choice which any morality should demand of its followers.

Thus far we have argued that to the degree that individuals take any vision of the good seriously, they have a duty to respect the right of all others who are deemed human to do their best to adopt the same vision. The idea of common human needs entails the right even of strangers to optimal need-satisfaction. In an appendix to this chapter we discuss the rights of *enemies* and the justice of war, qualifying this right in the case of those regimes and their agents who are seriously assaulting the need-satisfactions of others, either within or without their national boundaries. However the criterion justifying this qualification remains that of generalising optimal need-satisfaction to all peoples.

Special obligations and the optimisation of need-satisfaction

So much for rights; what of duties or obligations? In practice, the right to optimum need-satisfaction will entail not only acts of forbearance but also positive acts to make available the goods and services necessary for such decisions to be a material and psychological possibility. In short, we all have a responsibility, a duty, an obligation to help all humans to optimise their need-satisfaction.

If this argument is accepted, it places an onerous responsibility on us all. The extent of dire needs throughout the world is staggering. How are individuals supposed to fulfil the duties specified, when they will naturally be preoccupied with satisfying the needs and wants of those whom they already know and for whom they feel a strong and explicit sense of responsibility (e.g. family and friends)? And how can everyone throughout the world have a right to optimum need-satisfaction when it is not clear whether agencies exist which can act to ensure the right to even minimal need-satisfaction? As O'Neill argues, 'rights discourse often carries only a vague message to those whose action is needed to secure respect for rights. Widespread acceptance of the abstract rhetoric of rights coexists with widespread failure to respect rights' (O'Neill, 1986, p. 117). Can this be avoided?

To explore this question further, let us begin by hypothesising a day at the beach. Suppose that the peaceful situation dramatically changes and a child is seen swimming for his life, caught by strong currents and being swept out to sea. Who is responsible for saving him – for respecting the need for survival which he himself is struggling to satisfy? If there is a lifeguard, the first response will no doubt be that it is he who has a 'special responsibility' to do exactly this. He has voluntarily assumed this duty because it is stipulated in his contract of employment which also guarantees certain rights for himself (e.g. to regular payment). But suppose he does nothing. Who else should act on the child's behalf? Would it make sense, for example, for everyone to shout: 'We're not going to do anything until it is clear that his father and mother – who also have a special responsibility for his welfare – will do nothing.' Hardly. The child has a right to help not because of his contractual relationship with anyone else but because of his 'dire need' (Goodin, 1985, p. 111). Everyone else who is in a position to intervene to satisfy his need for survival has a moral responsibility to do so – everyone, that is, who takes their vision of the good seriously.[7]

But how is this responsibility to be apportioned? It should clearly not be on the basis of some fractionalisation, where, for example, if there were 200 swimmers present each would share 1/200 of the responsibility. To the degree that each individual is in a position to satisfy the needs in question – in this case through stopping the drowning – then they each share full responsibility for its occurrence. The only thing that can mitigate this responsibility is the fact that they cannot act without endangering their own basic need-satisfaction (e.g. through being unable to swim) or they honestly think that they will interfere with the success of others who are acting appropriately. This aside, any decision on whether or not the delay of onlookers is justifiable will depend on whether or not they wait too long for the needs of the child to be met. The fact that this may be difficult to determine is more a counsel for not taking any chances than it is for the avoidance of an undeniable duty to help. Goodin – on whom this analysis greatly depends – aptly makes the point: 'The limit of this responsibility is quite simply, the limit of the vulnerable agent's needs and of the responsible agent's capacity to act efficaciously – no more, but certainly no less' (Goodin, 1985, p. 135).

So responsibility for the drowning boy rests with all those on the beach. Yet if our theory is to be plausible, it must also be applicable to people in need whose distress *we do not directly witness and can do nothing directly to satisfy*. What are our practical obligations to strangers when weighed alongside our special duties toward those who for whatever reason are 'close' to us, or our duties toward strangers whom we are in a position to help directly? If need satisfaction begins at home, so to speak, then how far are we responsible for those who don't live there and with whom we have no direct contact? Let us consider in turn the case of strangers within and without our national boundaries.

The problem begins to resolve when it is accepted that it is not only agents but *agencies* – social institutions of one sort or another – which can act to ensure need-satisfaction, provided that they have adequate powers and material support. Individuals by themselves are clearly unable to stop the decline or encourage the improvement of the need-satisfaction of persons with whom they have no contact. The same cannot be said of a collective which contains individuals who do have the contact, along with the expertise and the resources, to intervene appropriately. It is through their support for such agencies – or through the policies which they support or oppose if they are members of such collectives – that individuals must discharge their moral responsibilities for the need-satisfaction of strangers (Gewirth, 1978, pp. 312–19). So returning again to our example, many local citizens who do not themselves use the beach may and should recognise their responsibility to contribute toward the protection of those who do. Thus they may collectively support the costs of a lifeguard – someone with special responsibilities for need-satisfaction founded on his training and unique skills.

But why stop there, and confine one's concern only to the beach round the corner, so to speak? All swimmers on all public beaches have the same need and therefore right to protection. It is this that morally justifies the strict duty to submit to *taxation* for such purposes. Otherwise, the moral irrationality or confusion of individual personalities will generate the 'free rider' dilemma – it will be in the interest of all to enjoy the security a lifeguard provides, but in the interests of none to resource his provision. The same argument applies to resourcing, say, the local ambulance service, the nearby hospital and all other agencies who might have to look after those who have been injured as the result of accidents. It is also the rationale behind preventive measures like the public provision of, say, swimming lessons and swimming pools. In other words, there is a strict duty on individuals to ensure that they participate in the collective need-satisfaction of strangers through their support for relevant institutional agencies (Plant *et al.*, 1980, pp. 93–6; cf. Gewirth, 1982, pp. 59–66).

Such duties go to the heart of all rights-based justifications for the *welfare state*. Since, in a variety of national contexts, many of the institutions of the welfare state have shown themselves capable of considerable success in the alleviation of need (as we suggest in Chapter 13), we have gone some way toward justifying the practicality of our emphasis on rights and duties. For the fact is that much higher than minimum levels of need-satisfaction have been, and therefore can be, obtained. Equally, whatever their recorded abuses, there is no indication that state institutions of welfare must necessarily lead to a diminution in such satisfaction, especially as regards the basic need for autonomy. In practice, as well as in theory, we must always desire the optimum satisfaction that can be obtained for those whom we wish to do their best to pursue our vision of the good. That we might debate what this level practically entails and how it should be given effect does nothing to detract from the moral imperative of collectively helping others to reach the high levels of need-satisfaction which we already know can be achieved. Equally, in the process of doing so we must be careful not to create institutions of welfare which in practice frustrate autonomy through artificial and bureaucratic constraints on individual choice.

Yet the problem of our responsibility for the needs of strangers in other nation states still remains. If there is no justification for confining our responsibilities to our local neighbourhood, any further limitation of duty would be arbitrary. This must mean that we have a responsibility to help all those who are in need *everywhere* – even when the particular state agency which has formal jurisdiction over them does nothing (Singer, 1979, p. 23). This brings us finally to the Third World. Given the scale of the deprivation of those in need and the consequent enormity of their right to need-satisfaction, how can moral responsibility be interpreted so that it makes practical sense for individuals who live thousands of miles away in a developed country? First World individuals *qua* individuals can do little directly and effectively to satisfy Third World need (Fishkin, 1982, p. 75). Indeed, if their only effort is through specific acts of charity, it may even be potentially damaging by detracting from the importance of institutional intervention.[8]

Therefore, just as everyone has a strict duty to support the collective provision of welfare within their own national boundaries, so we have the same obligation internationally. We have the duty to help create and sustain agencies which can act effectively to relieve suffering throughout the world (Goodin, 1985, pp. 163–7). Like national welfare states, these agencies could be financed through a system of taxation – an 'international need tax'. The details of such a system of taxation along with how its revenues should be allocated between relief and investment remain a matter for further discussion. For now, the important point is that the call for such a system is based on our theoretical analysis of the relationship between need and rights *and* has a practical purchase on current international realities. There are many aid agencies already in existence which cry out for the extra funds that such a system of taxation could provide. To be specific, the World Health

Organisation has recently estimated that 14 million children die every year in the Third World of illnesses which could either be easily prevented through cheap vaccination or cured through cheap treatments (UNICEF, 1987, p. 5). The distribution infrastructure for helping these children already exists. To the extent that First World citizens do nothing to help them, these childrens' blood is literally on their hands.

Yet, to conclude, it might still be objected that our emphasis on the international rights of those in need has only focused on the issue of minimal need-satisfaction. Even if we are correct about this, aren't we still deluded in our stress on the moral importance of *optimal* satisfaction for such people? We think not. Once national boundaries are no longer seen as demarcating self-contained spheres of moral responsibility, and it is accepted that that we respect the right of citizens of our own nation state to optimum need-satisfaction through collective welfare agencies, it follows that we have just as much responsibility toward those in need in other states as well. The fact that the initial focus of agencies of need-satisfaction must be on minimal requirements says more about the practical and political constraints under which the agencies are operating than it does about our responsibility to remove those constraints as soon as possible. It is precisely this progression from a concern with minimal need-satisfaction to much more than this that is reflected in what is morally best about existing welfare agencies. Our argument is that everyone who can has a strict duty to strive for the same process of progression among those in need in the poorest countries. If it is accepted that we have a duty to support the creation or sustenance of agencies of need-satisfaction throughout the world and that this is in principle a feasible moral and political goal, then why settle for less?

Relativism and the prospect for human liberation

So it is healthy and autonomous humans doing their best who fuel creativity and can lead to an explosion of cultural richness which can potentially be tapped by everyone. It is this potential which has been so eloquently stressed by writers like Walzer, Keane, and Laclau and Mouffe. Unfortunately, one cannot say the same about the relativistic conclusions which they reach about human need and, by implication, the right to its optimal satisfaction. Taking this right seriously entails accepting the *existence* of basic needs as well as the fact that there are some approaches to their optimal satisfaction which are objectively better than others. As we have seen, the relativism which characterises much of the post-modernist tradition in recent European thought denies the possibility of doing either and thus renders itself incapable of doing anything other than defending one or another cultural status quo (Callinicos, 1990). As Vincent argues: 'despite its progressive association with the campaign against imperialism, what the doctrine of cultural relativity allows in practice is a surrender to what John Stuart Mill called the "despotism of custom"' (Vincent, 1986, p. 55; cf. Anderson, 1983, pp. 45–55).

What could it mean, for instance, to claim that people in the Third World, suffering from a disease characteristic of underdevelopment that could be cured or prevented by the application of Western medical technology do not need to take advantage of such knowledge? Similarly, what would be the point of suggesting that women who are kept in ignorance of their potential as persons do not need and have no right to free themselves from patriarchal control which narrowly restricts their education and the scope of their social interaction? In what sense could they not need to? The only justification we can see is the one which the relativist would opt for – people cannot 'need' what they do not want. Yet we have already seen that people quite often confuse their wants and needs, sometimes with disastrous results.[9]

All of us require as much help as we can get in learning how to optimise the satisfaction of the needs of ourselves and of others – how individually and collectively to pursue the goal of *human liberation*. The best understanding we can acquire in this respect is the one which is the most *practically* efficacious, irrespective of its cultural origins. Some understanding is indisputably better than others in this respect (Doyal and Harris, 1986, pp. 148–55). Relativism spuriously closes off the consciousness and practice of some groups from others and denies as impossible the many conceptual and practical bridges which have already been erected between cultures throughout human history. During this time, humans have time and again refused to be constrained in their choices by the conceptual boundaries of their culture – with progressive results for us all.

The theoretical link between the optimisation of choice and the human liberation which basic need-satisfaction makes possible has a long history. It was an essential part of the Hegelian background both to Marxism and to classical liberalism (Taylor, 1975, pp. 546–64). The key difference between these approaches has been their conception of the social and economic context within which such freedoms could best express themselves: individually through the market, or collectively within a more centrally planned and/or communitarian society. Arguably applicable in either case, Hegel's view seems to us to be still the most fruitful: that the more we learn about what we are capable of doing, the more we learn about ourselves. In this process – one which always involves the rejection or negation of what is accepted as true and beyond question – we discover what is contingent about the social and natural world (e.g. slavery or supernaturalistic accounts of killer diseases) and what is necessary (e.g. the need for literacy to have access to different cultural traditions, or the necessity to drink unpolluted water to stay healthy). Hegel also accepted that such learning is essentially social and argued that it has its own characteristic patterns of historical development, which expand the bounds of human creativity at the same time that they destroy those cultural structures which artificially inhibit it (Plant, 1971, chs 6–7; cf. Norman, 1976, chs 5, 6).

In some of his writings, Marx develops similar ideas – again focusing on the unnatural constraints which prevent humanity achieving all that it is capable of. The key difference between the two is that Marx argues that a programme of political action exists to remove such constraints. He claims that people are potentially in charge of their own destinies rather than, as Hegel suggests, swept along by a river of history which they might understand but can do little about. For Marx and for all those who believe that the condition of humanity can be improved through the careful application of the best available knowledge, the owl of Minerva flies at dawn *and* at dusk, albeit perhaps more safely as the day wears on! And accompanying this belief is an enormous responsibility. For if humans do possess the power to alter history, the task is to keep trying to bring about those alterations which are necessary conditions for human liberation – the satisfaction of the health and autonomy needs of as many humans as possible to the highest sustainable levels. The tragedy of relativism is that through proclaiming the incoherence of debates about how this goal should be achieved, its supporters – whatever their intentions might be – lend support to those who wish to prevent such change.

Entertaining the idea that humans as a species have indeed made progress in their capacity to satisfy their needs – that objectively there are some ways and some choices that are better than others in achieving this – is not to succumb to cultural imperialism or to claim that in everything the Rest should mimic the West. It is simply to insist that those who are denied such choices are disadvantaged compared to those who are not, and that this will be the case whatever the culture and for contingent, alterable reasons. It is also to maintain that to the extent that Western scientific, intellectual and political traditions facilitate such choice, and in the process lead to higher individual levels of health and autonomy than would otherwise be the case, then they can and should be seen as more humane and progressive (Nickel, 1987, pp. 71–9).

Of course, the same can be said for other traditions of satisfying basic needs. For example, it is clear that Indian and Chinese approaches to health and healing have much to offer Western medicine in understanding how individual states of consciousness affect a wide range of physiological processes. What is not the case, however, is that what constitutes the best medical care for specific illnesses or the best education for the accomplishment of particular goals is simply a matter of cultural preference (Doyal, 1987, pp. 35–8). The same applies to all modes of understanding about those constitutive activities which must be executed successfully in all cultures if they are to survive and flourish.

We have argued that a belief in the existence of human needs in conjunction with a consistent belief in a moral vision of the good lends strong support for a moral code that the needs of *all* people should be satisfied to the *optimum* extent. This entails corresponding duties on individuals – to act where appropriate to relieve the suffering of others and to support national and international agencies which can effectively do so. The ultimate goal of the acceptance of such responsibilities is the liberation of humankind through the optimisation of significant choice within and between cultural forms of life.

Appendix: The rights of enemies to need-satisfaction

Is not the argument in Chapter 6 taking the doctrine of love thine enemy too far? Surely it would be wrongheaded to support the right to optimal need-satisfaction of enemies with whom we are, for example, at war. If we really believe that everyone has this right, then does it follow that there can be no such thing as a just war, or rebellion where there is the deliberate taking of human life? Let us try to answer this question through envisaging two groups, *A* and *B*, whose countries are adjacent. Suppose that *A* is a democracy committed both in theory and in practice to the optimisation of need-satisfaction among its members and all other groups, irrespective of their cultural differences. *B*, on the other hand, is ruled by a minority concerned only to optimise its need- and want-satisfactions but not those of the majority who are ruthlessly exploited. In light of the moral right of strangers to optimal need-satisfaction, consider three scenarios: where *B* attacks *A*; where the majority of the population of *B* revolt against their oppressors; and where *A* attacks *B*.

Assume that *B*'s rulers support warfare against *A* because it is seen as the only way to gain territory or new labour or to silence the alternative which *A* offers to B's population. Further, assume that *A* opposes *B* through encouraging its majority to revolt because it regards B's rulers as violating their rights. Yet *A* is opposed to warfare on the grounds that this would be imposition of their values through force rather than rational persuasion. *B* then attacks *A* and in the process kills and injures members of its population. In these circumstances, it would indeed be justifiable for the army of *A* – which there can be no doubt it needs in case of just such an eventuality – to attack the army of *B* and to incapacitate as many of its members as is necessary to stop the attack. If this means killing them, then so be it. For it is *B* which has violated the rights of *A*, in precisely the same sense as an individual who tries to murder or otherwise harm another violates their rights. In both cases, *self-defence* is appropriate since it is only in this way that the individual or group can protect their potential for *future* need-satisfaction and their capacity for virtue in relation to the pursuit of their vision of the good. Since self-defence cannot be effective while the defender at the same time respects the right of the attacker to optimal need-satisfaction, the attacker forfeits these rights and in proportion to the severity of the threat posed (Walzer, 1977, ch. 4). The same argument can also be employed to justify some forms of imprisonment and again underlines the reciprocal character of rights and duties.

Can we justify on similar grounds the right of *B*'s population to pursue armed revolution against their rulers? The theory of just war can be applied to civil rebellion against tyranny or political oppression, as Locke and others have argued (Geras, 1989, pp. 185–211). Our theory focuses this right on a specific conception of grave social injustice. Given their unambiguous and extreme attack on the basic need-satisfaction of their own people, members of the government and their agents have lost their right to such satisfaction for the same reason that members of their army did when *A* was itself attacked. This right may be qualified on consequentialist grounds, if a calculation of the 'balance of suffering' suggests that the suffering from rebellion outweighs that of the status quo; but that is all. Otherwise, rebellion will be justified if all other channels of defending the right to basic need-satisfaction have been denied by those who are also actively engaged in the process of attacking this right. The justice of the rebellion, however, will not just concern the inequity of *B*'s rulers. Also of relevance will be the rebels' commitment to the goal of universal and optimal need-satisfaction and to constitutional policies designed to ensure the feasibility of its achievement – if they are victorious. Both will ensure, among other things, that in victory the rights of the vanquished will be protected.

Finally, is *A* justified in attacking *B* with the aim of replacing its current regime with one which does respect the right to universal and optimum need-satisfaction? Here, perhaps counter-intuitively, the answer must usually be no. For the operative word is 'attack'. To try to force agreement with a form of life through causing harm – rather than harming to defend the right to choose a form of life – will almost always be counter-productive if the aim really is to win moral consensus rather than material gain. No matter how morally justified such an attack may feel, it cannot usually be based on reason, and any consensus that it generates will remain suspect. Against the background of such a plurality of conflicting visions of good throughout the world, it is crucial that under ordinary circumstances national/cultural boundaries be respected by those who share different moral visions (Walzer, 1977, ch. 6; cf. Rawls,

1972, pp. 378–9). Without a strict acceptance and enforcement of related rights and duties, it will always be too tempting for the *B*'s of the world to attempt to export their own particular brand of misery or for the *A*'s to intervene in a situation where, despite their good intentions, they are still denying local people the chance to choose their destiny for themselves. Since it is these people who know the details of their situation best, outside interference which attempts to impose solutions to perceived injustices can still go badly wrong.

For this reason, the above argument is qualified if liberational forces within *B* which are trying to overthrow the government through the use of force call on *A*'s help. If the armed rebellion is justified on the grounds outlined above, then in principle it is deserving of outside resources. Whether it should be resourced in practice will depend, among other things, on the extent to which it is believed that those receiving help will commit themselves to the goals and strategies of universal basic need-satisfaction. Outside resources, however, are not the same as armed intervention. Despite the preceding arguments in support of national sovereignty, the one case where armed intervention is justified – the Vietnamese invasion of Cambodia is a possible example – is where an attack by the rulers of a country on its people is so extreme that their physical and mental capacity to retaliate is completely undermined, whatever outside aid they are given (Arkes, 1986, pp. 232–42; cf. Pogge, 1989, pp. 242–5). Not to intervene in the face of such helplessness because of national boundaries would be as wrong in this case as it would be in the case of a helpless individual in similar need confronted with an attacker. Far from being a cry for violence, therefore, such an argument is both a reiteration of the right of those under direct attack to self-defence and a plea for real tolerance.

So much for *jus ad bellum* – the justice *of* war. What about *jus in bello* – justice *in* war? Suffice it to say that none of the above arguments entail that those fighting just wars or rebellions have unlimited discretion concerning the methods of warfare. The rules which govern such discretion can be divided into two categories: those concerning the category of persons against whom violence may be directed and those concerning the manner of attack. The first draws a distinction between combatants and non-combatants and decrees that only the former should be the subjects of deliberate violence, notwithstanding the difficulty in drawing a line between the two. Thus in our previous example, once the individual attackers of *B* have been incapacitated, then they regain all of the rights to optimal need-satisfaction which they lost by virtue of their attack on *A* – to the degree that this does not hamper *A*'s forces from continuing effective defence. Given their desire to persuade them of the moral merit of their culture and to join their cause against *B*, members of *A* should sustain the health and autonomy of their captives as well as they can under the circumstances. Applying these rules to the scenario of a domestic revolution, Geras concludes that only direct agents of oppression should be attacked, the regime's: 'leaders, soldiers, police, security agents, jailers, torturers; in general those warring on its behalf, those involved in imposing and enforcing oppressive laws' (Geras, 1989, p. 198). Violence against the remainder of the population can never be condoned.

Concerning appropriate methods of warfare, the doctrine of 'minimum force' is appropriate. The forms of fighting should be capable of stopping enemy combatants, but they should not in any way cause gratuitous suffering (Gewirth, 1978, p. 215). So *A* should not use arms or methods which will permanently harm *B*'s members *after* they have been incapacitated or have divulged under interrogation whatever knowledge is required for the purposes of defence. Again, this would lessen their ability to do their best to follow the path of virtue in *A*'s terms and, indeed, would help to convince them that *A* was morally no better than *B*. Such selectivity in the treatment of prisoners and the choice of weapons is morally required irrespective of *B*'s behaviour, provided that morality in this respect does not hamper effective self-defence. The horror of chemical and nuclear weapons, along with methods of torture, is not just that they kill and permanently maim. It is that they deprive those who have been affected – assuming that they survive – of even the chance to choose to follow the form of life of those who caused their injuries. Because the aim is to destroy or completely manipulate the victim, their autonomy and humanity are discarded as an irrelevance (Nagel, 1971–2, pp. 140–1). To do this to a fellow human – whatever the circumstances – is a moral wrong of the highest order.[10]

7
Optimising Need-Satisfaction in Theory

Even if we assume that there is general agreement within a society that priority should be given to the optimisation of need satisfaction, we are not yet out of the relativist wood. There may be little consensus over which strategies best achieve this goal and/or, whether or not it can be reconciled with other aims and beliefs. Human history has created so many different patterns of production, reproduction, communication and government that views on appropriate social arrangements will often be disputed, even when final goals are agreed. On the one hand, we must judge what optimisation entails in terms of those real choices which the broad span of contemporary theoretical and practical understanding makes possible. Hegel is at least right to the extent that the Owl of Minerva must consistently look back as she tries also to fly forward! On the other hand, however, there may be fundamental disagreements about what such choices entail in practice – about what specifically should be done to achieve the aims which they embody. This may be the case, for three reasons.

First, the effectiveness of particular technologies may be disputed. Given the need for nutrition in order for individuals to maintain optimum health, what kinds of foods best fit the bill? Or since the need for specialised education must be satisfied in order to create optimum levels of competence in particular skills, what is the most successful approach to teaching them? What is scientifically and technologically correct and incorrect can itelf be a matter of dispute. Some scientifically-based technologies do indisputably work, are useful in the pursuit of basic need-satisfaction and are more effective than others. However, other technologies are more uncertain in this respect – some associated with genetic engineering, for example – and require further debate for their liberational potential (or lack of it) to be understood (Yoxen, 1983, ch. 5). The question of appraisal is therefore shifted, from questions about the practical efficacy of a technology to how it should be designed, how extensively it should be employed, who should control it ... and so on. Without this sort of understanding – which is not so much about technical effect as about its human and social impact – the use value of the technology will be either unrealised or misappropriated.[1]

Second, disputes rage over the appropriate social policies to optimise need-satisfaction. Examples include the respective roles of preventive versus curative health policies, the content and processes of education, universality or selectivity in social security, techniques for redistributing income and wealth, land reform and a million and one other issues. Again, we can make a rough division between those social policies which indisputably do work and those over which there is considerable disagreement. An example of the former would be the policy to teach all capable children in Britain to read and write. The amount of legal compulsion which should be employed to regulate the environment illustrates the latter. Of course, even when strategies for optimising need-satisfaction are hotly contested, those involved must believe that the debate is worth having and that it makes sense to talk of correct and incorrect solutions which transcend preferential barriers. Yet commitment to this fact alone does little to resolve such debates or to demonstrate that a rational resolution is a possibility.

And third, even if a consensus were to emerge about ways of resolving these issues, other dilemmas will remain about what it means to optimise need-satisfaction against the background of resource constraints (Nevitt, 1977). When there is simply not enough of what is indisputably needed to go around, the age-old question of politics recurs – *cui bono*, or who gets what? Thus while it may be accepted that some technologies and cultural practices will benefit everyone, others will only be relevant to specific groups (e.g. educational techniques for infants or special housing facilities for elderly people). How do we resolve disputes about which group gets what? The same debate shifts to individuals when we examine the allocation of resources on a micro level and recognise the inevitable conflicts of interests which ensue. Some of the most dramatic examples obviously occur in medicine, when decisions have to made about the allocation of life- saving treatments (Bell and Mendus, 1988, chs 2–5; cf. Daniels, 1985, chs 1–2). Equally, at the macro level, there may be disagreements about which types of need-satisfaction should be prioritised in legislative programmes – environmental improvement, a better health service or improved educational services. Conflicts of interests will be represented by formal or informal lobbies consisting of individuals with their own moral, political and professional priorities.

The goal of optimising need-satisfaction faces severe problems of moral and practical indeterminacy when confronted by disputes of this kind. In many instances, it will not be clear what the right answer is or even what it means to talk of one right answer (Doyal, 1990, pp. 1–16). A further dimension of such indeterminacy is the relationship between what *should* be done to optimise need-satisfaction in relation to the arguments which we have put forward and what *can* be done in terms of specific political and economic realities. As usual, ought implies can. However, the 'can' of this particular piece is and always will be debatable. For example, one open question is the extent to which people who are already privileged will be willing democratically to put the satisfaction of needs before preferences, and the extent to which it will be morally acceptable to reduce their autonomy through forcing them to do so in the name of the rights of the poor. In some situations (e.g. legislation against racial harassment) there might be general agreement. In others (e.g. a quota system of positive discrimination in employment) there may not. Nothing that we have said thus far has in any way indicated how such specific debates and issues should be resolved. In this chapter, we will work toward a resolution through addressing two issues.

The first concerns communication. What can be done to ensure that the policy which is adopted has emerged from a debate that is most likely to yield the most rational and efficient solution to the problem of need-satisfaction under consideration? Often the most that we can hope for is not certainty, but the knowledge that the answers have evolved from communication which has been as open and critical as possible. This is especially important, since the decision reached is likely to be a compromise which purports to serve the interests of as many of the contestants as possible. Unless we can discover procedures which can optimise the rationality of debate about need-satisfaction – one which demonstrates the objective acceptability of some forms of consensus against the background of disagreement – we will again be confronted with relativist doubts.

Second, accepting that our emphasis on individual autonomy and equality commit us to some form of political democracy within which debates about policy should be pursued, what form should it take? If we veer in the direction of a strong central democratic state, we risk undermining individual autonomy. Combine the moral indeterminacy of many of the policy decisions which have to be made with the threat to liberty if they are executed in a mechanistic way by an authoritarian state bureaucracy and it is clear why Braybrooke argues that 'strict final priority of need-satisfaction' must give way in practice to what he calls 'role relative precautionary priority'. Here different social and cultural group-ings should have a say about which satisfiers are most appropriate for their needs and which will be prioritised when there are disagreements and/or resource constraints (Braybrooke, 1987, ch. 6). Again, democratic majorities may not otherwise play ball. Conversely, if we move in the opposite direction to a completely decentralised democracy, we appear to pose the same risk for the efficiency and long-term planning that optimised need-satisfaction also demands.

Clearly, we require some combination of these two principles. If the principle of precedence becomes too role-relative and precau-tionary, then needs risk collapsing into preferences with all of the difficulties we have seen that this entails. In short, unless we can find generalisable answers to the preceding questions, the objective foundation of any programme to improve, let alone optimise, need-satisfaction is called into doubt. Human liberation will remain an appealing but utopian fantasy.

In our view, Habermas and Rawls are the two writers whose work offers the most hope in resolving these difficulties. Their work has been both influential and controversial and they incorporate into their theoretical perspectives a conception of objective and universal human need which has influenced our own. Both ground notions of individual rights in what Habermas calls 'generalisable interests' and Rawls refers to as 'primary goods'. Furthermore, they are also concerned that their vision of the good has a purchase on political practicality, with Habermas focusing on the rationality of political debate and Rawls on the constitutionality of political formations. In this chapter, we shall briefly outline and criticise some of their ideas with the aim of demonstrating their contemporary importance for the moral and political pursuit of need-satisfaction.

Habermas and rational communication

Working within the tradition of the Frankfurt School, Habermas is acutely aware of the tensions within Marxism between reason and morality, where the aim is to found a completely new social order uncontaminated by the tarnished bourgeois goals of the Enlightenment (Roderick, 1986, pp. 41–50). Yet such ambitions cannot, alas, be justified without reference to those very goals. Consequently, Habermas accepts the inevitability of an agenda of reform rather than systemic change, an agenda guided by the goal of optimising 'generalisable interests'. In principle, such interests are determined by the answer to the question:

> how would the members of a social system, at a given stage in the development of productive forces, have collectively and bindingly interpreted their needs... if they could and would have decided on the organization of social intercourse through discursive will-formation, with adequate knowledge of the limiting conditions and functional imperatives of their society? (Habermas, 1976, p. 113).

Hence the problem of reason becomes that of establishing the principles by which the most effective policies for meeting such interests can be determined.

Habermas argues that there are two intellectual traditions within which this issue has been tackled, both of which are essentially flawed. The first derives from Weber and is identified with the organisational and managerial structure of capitalism. Here reason is transformed into little more than the ability to manipulate humans in ways which maximise their collective efficiency but which also arbitrarily restrict their freedom and distort their creative potential. According to Habermas, such a transformation degenerates into the dogmatic imposition of the values of those in power. For since human values are inevitably involved in the creation of public policy, and since the equation of reason with instrumentality entails that 'values are in principle beyond discussion', it follows that 'a collective value system can never be achieved by means of enlightened discussion carried on in public places' (Habermas, 1974, p. 271). Yet it is precisely such discussion which enables humans to transcend arbitrary constraints on their freedom placed by social environments into which they are born but to which they have not given their informed consent.

Alternatively, traditional Marxism dogmatically equates reason with the interests of the working class, assumed to be the embodiment of the progressive forces of history. Yet as a collective, working people have shown little potential for fulfilling the millennarian aims of many Marxists and have at best a mixed record in offering effective opposition to the worst excesses of capitalism. Certainly, what has been done in their name has often shown itself to be a political and economic failure because it has ignored the fact that 'unless they are connected with protest potential from other sectors of society no conflicts arising from such underprivilege can really overturn the system – they can only provoke it to sharp reactions incompatible with formal democracy' (Habermas, 1970b, pp. 109–10).

In his search for an effective model of democratic reason which is capable of serving the interests of everyone, Habermas therefore rejects these two traditions and instead looks to the normative structure of language and communication themselves. He envisages an 'ideal speech situation' where communication is undistorted by the particularity of ideology and where generalisable interests can be collectively conceptualised and pursued in an efficient and rational fashion. His argument is not that the conditions for such pristine dialogue and debate can actually be found in existing social structures, but rather that if we do not assume that such conditions could exist, the very rationale for inquiry and debate itself grinds to a halt:

No matter how the intersubjectivity of mutual understanding may be deformed, the *design* of an ideal speech situation is necessarily implied in the structure of potential speech, since all speech, even intentional deception, is oriented toward the idea of truth... In so far as we master the means for the construction of the ideal speech situation, we can conceive the ideas of truth, freedom, and justice (Habermas, 1970a, p. 372).

The normative structure of this construction is seen as implicit in sincere efforts to communicate. When made explicit, it consists of pragmatic rules which stipulate conditions under which argument can occur at its most fruitful, rational and democratic.

For our purposes, three such rules are of particular importance in determining how debates about the optimisation of need-satisfaction should be conducted. First, all participants should possess the best available understanding concerning the *technical* issues raised by whatever problem it is they are trying to solve. Habermas argues that all humans have an indisputable 'cognitive interest' in being able to intervene in the world or society, with predictable consequences which are deemed of value. Such instrumental control 'is governed by technical rules based on empirical knowledge. In every case they imply conditional predictions about observable events, physical or social. These predictions can prove correct or incorrect' (Habermas, 1970b, pp. 91–2). There is now a vast fund of knowledge of this sort in natural science and technology, and to a lesser extent, in the social and behavioural sciences. If solutions to problems about the optimisation of need-satisfaction require such 'technical' understanding, problem-solvers must have access to the best available nomological and factual knowledge relevant to the tasks at hand.

Second, if disputes about such knowledge threaten the optimisation of need-satisfaction, their rational resolution will require specific *methodological and communicational skills*. On the one hand, accepted principles of empirical assessment will be crucial – the methodology, for example, of controlled trials. On the other hand, communicational skill, or what Habermas calls 'hermeneutic understanding' will be necessary to apply such methods effectively and to discuss their outcome. As much as possible, it guarantees 'within cultural traditions, the possible action-orienting self-understanding of individuals and groups as well as reciprocal understanding between different individuals and groups' (Habermas, 1971, p. 176). To the degree that we participate in any social activity, we must also possess such 'practical' understanding and Habermas outlines a range of further pragmatic rules – a hermeneutic method – which must be adhered to in successful communication. These include the importance of telling the truth in a comprehensive and understandable fashion and doing so in a way which engenders trust and at least the potential for agreement (Roderick, 1986, pp. 73–105).

Third, communication which is intended to lead to improved technical and practical understanding – and thus the possibility of optimising need-satisfaction – must be as *democratic* as possible. Given the scope and complexity of the natural and social sciences, those with relevant knowledge must be able to contribute to discussions about how such optimisation should be achieved. Successful democratic debate will be impossible if it is dominated by vested interests, including those of 'experts', which place unwarranted constraints on its direction, content and length. McCarthy summarises Habermas as follows: 'the consensual basis of communication is disrupted if one party's right to perform the speech acts...is called called into question, on the grounds, for example, that his role or status does not entitle him to do so, or that his acts contravene accepted norms or conventions' (1978, p. 289). Thus the normative structure of debates within social policy about the optimisation of need-satisfaction is just as important as the availability of correct technical information and methodological expertise.

Insofar as participants in such debates conform to the above standards, Habermas contends that the most rational solutions to problems about optimisation will be those which achieve the widest consensus.[2] Indeed, he equates truth itself with such a consensus: 'We attribute truth only to statements to which...every responsible subject would agree if only he could examine his opinions at sufficient length in unrestricted and unconstrained communication' (quoted in McCarthy, 1978, pp. 419–20). However, some critics have argued that such a view of rational debate is hopelessly idealistic, since all known speech situations are dominated by the contingencies of power and resource constraint (Lukes, 1982, pp. 134–48; cf. Keat, 1981, pp. 180–90).

Habermas's response – which we endorse – is that his vision is admittedly counterfactual and constitutes a political goal rather than an actually existing state of affairs. Nonetheless, the normative structures which are thus idealised are implicit in the methods and content of the ordinary arguments which currently do take place in what he refers to as the 'life world' of everyday private and public communication. The 'more or less diffuse...unproblematic background convictions' implicit in such ordinary discourse become 'rationalised' to the degree to which they are made more explicit through critical communication which conforms to his ideal. It is only in this way that one can properly contemplate the relevance of particular beliefs embedded within cultural traditions to the solution to technical and practical problems concerning need-satisfaction (Habermas, 1981, p. 70; cf. White, 1988, pp. 92–103).

At their best, institutionalised debates among professionals derive their rigour from the commitment to expose ideas and arguments to collective evaluation which is designed to root out factual mistakes and logical inconsistencies. Properly-run case conferences and clinical audits in medicine are good examples. The success of other attempts to expand the scope of human understanding will depend on inquirers developing 'communicative competence' – assimilating rules of discourse and social interaction orientated toward 'truth, freedom and justice' (Habermas, 1970a, p. 372). This includes the belief that some arguments are more rational than others, along with the conceptual and methodological capacity to discover which are which. Thus the potential for rationality to dominate the political process is linked to a moral vision which Habermas shares with Rousseau. It is a belief in the basic goodness of ordinary people and their potential to live, work, create and communicate together in harmony and to use practical reason peacefully to resolve their disputes and to optimise their need-satisfaction.

Yet despite his optimism, Habermas is acutely aware of the difficulties of reconciling his vision of human liberation with existing social realities. He argues that the life world where the everyday dramas of action and interaction occur has been 'colonised' – dehumanised and compartmentalised – by the organisational and instrumental rationality of capitalist enterprise and the state (Roderick, 1986, pp. 134–5). The task of liberational struggle is to peel away the false ideological beliefs about what it is impossible for individuals and collectives to try to achieve, beliefs which lead people to define the fragmentation of everyday life within capitalism as natural and to equate capitalism itself with social progress. In the case of the individual, Habermas links such struggle with the therapeutic methods of Freud and psychoanalysis.

For the collective, the economic and political analysis of Marx and Marxism serve a similar role. The critical character of both perspectives is crucial: 'In self-reflection, knowledge for the sake of knowledge comes to coincide with the interest in autonomy and responsibility. For the pursuit of reflection knows itself as a movement of emancipation' (Habermas, 1971, p. 197–8). Recent events in Russia and Eastern Europe reveal the fruits of such reflection and the degree to which its critical focus extends beyond the institutions of capitalism.

More specifically, the codified knowledge of professionals must be made to confront the rationalised life-world – the 'experientially-grounded knowledge' – which ordinary citizens develop through such self-reflection. Otherwise, the power of vested interests will go unchecked – their experience of the life-world will be reified in ways which simply reinforce their prejudices. This is especially the case in welfare states, the rules and legality of which are often divorced from the experiences of recipients. According to White (1988, p. 113), Habermas argues that this 'juridification' is the:

> objective redefining of the client's lifeworld which... requires an incessant process of 'compulsory abstraction' of everyday life situations. This is not just a cognitive necessity in order for everyday situations to be subsumable under legal categories, but a practical necessity in order that administrative control can be exercised. Juridification thus exerts a *reifying* influence on the lifeworld, which, when combined with the enhanced claims to *expertise* of social workers and other administrators in the newly redefined categories of life, produces an insidiously expanding domain of dependency. This domain comes to include the way we *define*... family relations, education, old age, as well as physical health and mental health and well-being (White, 1988, p. 113).

But it is at this point that Habermas confronts a problem which he never adequately solves. Given the degree to which the consciousness of so many people has already been distorted by the misguided trust which they have placed in experts – medicine is again another good example – it is not obvious how they are supposed to acquire the confidence, understanding and power to act differently. Habermas looks for the instruments of progressive change in those groups which he believes have resisted the corruption of instrumental reason. By far the most significant of these is the women's movement which, among other things, is well known for its attacks on the patriarchal colonisation of public discourse (Habermas, 1981). But given the lack of political power of such progressive groups and the continued influence of those vested interests which dominate existing institutional channels of communication, what would a feasible political programme to optimise need-satisfaction look like?

However vague his explicit recommendations to overcome this, Habermas's message is clear enough, at least as it affects our own arguments. For the optimisation of basic need-satisfaction to be meaningfully and democratically negotiated – for liberation to begin to be a practical proposition – individuals must have the right and the health and autonomy sufficient to work together to achieve it.[3] That is to say, they require social institutions which stipulate how these rights and need satisfactions will be guaranteed, to the extent that they actually can be. That the most powerful economic forces in the world today – capitalism and state socialism – have both shown themselves to be problematic from this perspective only underlines the importance of reconsidering the constitutional relationship between the state and the individual with these aims in mind. Within competitive capitalism, inequalities in basic need-satisfaction mean that some citizens have an unearned advantage over others, however much emphasis is placed on civil liberties. Conversely, under state socialism, or what is left of it, individuals have a formal right to basic need-satisfaction but the absence of civil liberties has compounded the difficulties centrally planned economies face in delivering the goods. Surely, some synthesis of what is best in both political traditions must be possible. But what might it look like?

Rawls, justice and optimal need-satisfaction

What is required is a theory of justice which integrates both positive and negative rights. This must provide a vision of the good which seems practically feasible and consistent enough with the pursuit of individual interests to be convincing to those who may have to make material sacrifices in order to bring it about. Rawls attempts to construct such a vision in *A Theory of Justice* (1972), one which has been refined by several sympathetic commentators in the wake of an enormous volume of critical response.

He begins with an attack on relativistic conceptions of justice, particularly utilitarianism and intuitionism. The former ultimately equates justice with aggregate happiness and as a result cannot take human rights seriously, for reasons we have already examined. The latter maintains that morality is objective but that its only correct source is human intuition which is unclouded by vested interests. This might seem reasonable if the individual is Gandhi but worrying if it is Pol Pot. Rawls argues instead that judgements about justice must be based on reason and universality and he attempts to demonstrate the truth of a range of constitutional principles which incorporate positive and negative rights in the manner required (Rawls, 1972, pp. 22–40). In so doing, he adopts a theory of rationality with similarities to that of Habermas.

Reviving the seventeenth and eighteenth century tradition of social contract theory, Rawls begins by envisaging a hypothetical negotiation between a range of individuals about the provision of 'primary goods' which comprise 'rights and liberties, opportunities and powers, income and wealth' (Rawls, 1972, pp. 92–3). These are freedoms, goods and services which are necessary to formulate life plans and successfully to act on them. Rawls assumes, on the one hand, that all of the participants in this 'original position' share a basic understanding about the natural and social world. For example, they would have accurate technical and practical skills in Habermas' sense, including an appreciation of economic institutions and psychological motivations. Yet on the other hand, the participants are all under a 'veil of ignorance' in that they have no knowledge of their own particular circumstances – who they are, how they make their living, how much wealth they possess, their family background, and so on (Rawls, 1972, p. 19; cf. Lessnoff, 1986, ch. 7).

What they do know is that they have to specify the constitutional principles that will determine their positive and negative rights in the society in which they will have to live after they have agreed them. No one who is a party to the decision knows how they will fare after the collective decision has been made – which social role they will occupy with how much status and privilege. Thus, like Habermas, Rawls is keen to remove the threat which vested interests pose to rational deliberation – to exclude from the negotiating process 'knowledge of those contingencies which sets men at odds and allows them to be guided by their prejudices' (Rawls, 1972, p. 19). This will be especially true if what is being decided is as important as the rules which will hereafter constrain individual action within the body politic.

Under these circumstances, Rawls argues that rational as opposed to subjective self-interest dictates a system which will maximise the individual capacity to define and pursue life-plans irrespective of where the participants find themselves on the day of reckoning. The situation is analogous to that of a child told to slice a cake fairly by ensuring that she will not know in advance which piece she herself will receive. Rawls claims that in such circumstances, rational participants will be concerned to protect themselves if they wind up belonging to the group of the least well off. Therefore, the constitutional principles negotiated in the original position will embody a 'maximin' criterion through ensuring that the benefits of this least privileged group will always be optimised. Two such principles are then seen to follow. The first concerns 'fundamental rights and liberties', and the second 'economic and social benefits' (Rawls, 1972, p. 63).

The first thing that those in the original position will agree is that their rights and liberties should be guarded to ensure a democratic mode of political organisation. These rights are:

> roughly speaking, political liberty (the right to vote and to be eligible for public office) together with freedom of speech and assembly; liberty of conscience and freedom of thought; freedom of the person along with the right to hold (personal) property; and freedom from arbitrary arrest and seizure as defined by the concept of the rule of law. These liberties are all required to be equal by the first principle, since citizens of a just society are to have the same basic rights (Rawls, 1972, p. 61).

It will only be through the protection of such liberties that those negotiating within the original position can ensure that, if afterwards they find themselves without power and resources, their own freedom and dignity will not be abused by others who for whatever reason have both in abundance. Put another way, putative violations of individual rights will be subject to public debate while at the same time Habermas's other communicational advantages of democracy will be maintained.

The second principle is divided into two subsidiary principles, the first concerning social inequality and the second equal opportunity. As regards the former, Rawls argues that the maximin model of decision making leads to his 'difference principle' – that social inequality will only be rationally tolerated to the extent that it benefits the least well off. Suppose, for example, that 10 men produce 10 units of goods which are distributed equally amongst them. Now suppose that 5 of the men, in response to higher income, agree to more demanding work and produce an extra 5 units, making 15 in all. So long as they receive no more than 4 extra units in recompense, there will be something left over for the other 5 men. Despite the increase in inequality of income of the new arrangement, the increased production made possible by the activities of the first 5 results in a higher level of potential consumption for the other 5. Rawls's argument assumes that the least well off actually do receive as much as possible of the increased surplus which is produced. Provided that there is not some other arrangement which will benefit them even more and that we remove envy from the list of primitive attributes assigned to those in the original position, he claims that the latter state of affairs is more just than the one which preceded it (Rawls, 1972, pp. 538–9).

In so reasoning, Rawls does not reject the egalitarianism of a writer like, say, Tawney, who maintains that excessive inequality leads to unacceptable reductions in individual dignity, confidence and autonomy. Indeed, he argues, for example, that without self-respect, 'nothing may seem worth doing, or if some things have value for us, we lack the will to strive for them. All desire and activity becomes empty and vain, and we sink into apathy and cynicism. Therefore the parties in the original position would wish to avoid at almost any cost the social conditions that undermine self-respect' (Rawls, 1972, p. 440) The crucial moral issue, in other words, is not just about the serious harm which inequality can cause. It also concerns how to minimise this harm while at the same time optimising the goods and services which are available for avoiding other types of serious harm. So inequalities can only be morally defended to the degree to which they can be shown to serve the interest of the least well off – through the increased production believed to follow from the presence of economic incentives.

Rational constitutional negotiators will also select a further constraint on the legitimation of social inequality. Rawls maintains that when inequalities are defended on economic grounds, there must be *equal opportunity* for everyone to compete for the most desirable positions whatever their existing location in the social hierarchy. This is important for reasons both of efficiency and morality. Without equal opportunity those who are best qualified for positions will not necessarily get them – something which would not be in the interests of the least well off since they would potentially suffer as a consequence (Rawls, 1972, p. 303). And, as regards morality, it will be unfair for those who have least not to have the choice to try for more, even if they actually decide to stay as they are. Without such choice, they will not only be 'excluded from certain rewards of office such as wealth and privilege'; they will also 'be debarred from experiencing the realization of self which comes from a skilful and devoted exercise of social duties... one of the main forms of human good' (Rawls, 1972, p. 84).

The degree to which access to primary goods is optimised will depend on the extent to which the preceding constitutional principles are adhered to. As we suggested earlier, the result combines elements of both classical liberal and socialist thinking. The first principle ensures that since the basic liberal freedoms are guaranteed, democratic debate will lead to improved understanding of the natural and social world with a consequent expansion of collective and individual choice. In practice, this means recognising the value of the accumulated civil and political rights achieved, for example, in the Western democracies. For example, to deny individuals the right to free speech, to freedom of assembly, to not being imprisoned without a proper trial, to being secure from cruel and unusual punishment from civil authority – all, among other things, central planks of the American Bill of Rights – is to deny them the capacity to flourish as humans whatever the ostensible identity of the political system in which they find themselves.

The first component of the difference principle recognises the productive potential of the market but also argues that there comes a point where levels of inequality simply cannot be justified for such economic reasons. The socialist moral bite of the difference principle is the constraint which it places on such rationalisations through insisting that they be linked to optimising access to primary goods for the least well off. Were it the case that income differentials actually had to be costed in these terms, the degree of inequality found in even the most egalitarian industrial society would prove excessive. Further, the surplus that would accrue as a result of correcting it would increase the overall amount available for further redistribution.

The principle of equal opportunity also combines similar constitutional and redistributive concerns. On the one hand, it entails procedures of 'pure procedural justice' which forbid arbitrary and prejudicial constraints on opportunity (e.g. because of class or race). On the other, it also follows that every child will have access to enough primary goods to ensure that those who are 'similarly endowed and motivated' will be able to make roughly equivalent choices of life plans (Rawls, 1972, pp. 83–90, 301). In other words, the equal opportunity principle provides a guide for estimating whether or not the amount of surplus generated by the difference principle has been properly redistributed. In practice such distribution will entail a wide range of radical measures which will be expensive as well as contested by those already in positions of power and privilege – everything from increases in the provision of health, educational and other welfare resources, to severe restrictions on the right to inherit property.

Rawls's attempt to combine aspects of liberalism and socialism would make little sense without his theory of primary goods. Negotiators in the original position are presumed to be reasoning consequentially to optimise their own individual self-interest. Yet they will be unable to do so without some knowledge of those goods and services which are preconditions for all individuals to formulate and act on specific life-plans. Equally, without an understanding of these same preconditions, we would be unable to know what the achievement of equal opportunity means in practice, once we have rejected its equation with either strict equality of outcome or formal equality of opportunity (Dworkin, 1981, part 2). Yet despite the importance of primary goods, Rawls says very little about the exact ways in which they serve the explanatory role he gives them. He opts for a 'thin' theory of the good because he wants it to be as neutral as possible between different visions of the good which should be allowed to compete in the sort of constitutional democracy he favours (Rawls, 1972, pp. 395–9). However, the ignorance that this imposes on his participants in the original position becomes so great that, as many critics, have argued, they may well decide that it makes more sense to gamble their future in the hope that they will be among the better off (Plant *et al.*, 1980, pp. 126–31).

Revising Rawls

To avoid this problem, Rawls must show why the least well off will on his calculation still be able to *flourish* as individuals. To do this, he requires the theory of needs which we have already elaborated with very much the same ends in mind. For it to be clear that their best interests will be served no matter where they find themselves when the social dice finally fall, those in the original position must define 'best interest' in relation to the optimal health and autonomy which they will require to compete fairly or cooperate with those who have been more fortunate. Even those who do not aspire to more than they are allotted will still presumably wish to live their life to the full within the material parameters which they choose.[4] In short, Rawls's difference principle should be expanded to state that *inequalities will only be tolerated to the extent that they benefit the least well off through leading to the provision of those goods and services necessary for the optimisation of basic need-satisfaction.*[5]

The optimisation of need-satisfaction will also be a necessary condition for the practical achievement of those fundamental rights and liberties held sacrosanct by the first principle. Rawls is ambiguous on this point. On the one hand, he makes it clear that he realises that the value of rights and liberties conceived of as negative freedoms will be minimised for those who are unable to take advantage of them for social and economic reasons. For example, he argues that 'the worth of liberty is not the same for everyone. Some have greater authority and wealth, and therefore greater means to achieve their aims' (Rawls, 1972, pp. 204–5). On the other hand, he also maintains that the first principle should have lexical priority over the second principle. Indeed, in a later essay, he claims that questions about social and economic provision should not be the subject matter of constitutional negotiation at all (Rawls, 1982, p. 52).

Unfortunately, this will not do. For as Pogge aptly puts it, in a situation where there is formal freedom but extreme poverty, the poor are in many obvious ways unfree on account of their poverty. The existing ground rules provide no legal path on which they can obtain more than a part of what they need...If the account of social primary goods is to reflect a plausible notion of human needs then it cannot deny the fundamental role basic social and economic needs actually play in a human life. But the insistence on the preeminence of the basic (civil and political) rights and liberties constitutes just such a denial (Pogge, 1989, p. 133).

He later argues that the

> first principle would then require that an institutional scheme should, if feasible, guarantee to every participant sufficient socio-economic goods for meeting the basic social and economic needs of a normal human person participating in the relevant social system. When normal persons differ, this minimum – the same for all – is defined so that it suffices for the greater needs (within the normal range). I refer to basic social and economic needs, so defined, as the *standard basic socio-economic needs* within some social system (Pogge, 1989, p. 143)

In the formulation of his 'general theory', Rawls avoids this criticism through placing both of his main principles on the same level of priority in circumstances of severe scarcity. Here, 'All social primary goods...are to be distributed equally unless an unequal distribution of any or all of these goods is to the advantage of the least favoured.' (Rawls, 1972, p. 303). Our analysis thus far has demonstrated the difficulty faced by the principles of lexicality in his 'special theory' when applied to more affluent economic environments. When general indicators of economic success are disaggregated, the effects of the pockets of poverty which remain will always obviate attempts to prioritise negative over positive freedoms.

Thought of in these terms, therefore, the result is really not two principles of justice but one with three components. The first concerns the right to basic need-satisfaction of the sort for which we have argued in Chapter 6, including the protection of civil liberties in relation to their impact on the optimisation of autonomy. The second morally justifies whatever inequalities are required for such satisfaction to be optimised. And, remembering that the material reasons for unequal opportunity will have been already removed by the effects of the revised first principle, the third principle becomes purely procedural and stipulates the legal constraints on bringing about social inequalities. It is this reading of Rawls which we positively endorse and which will inform subsequent chapters.

In summary, then, Rawls's formulation of his social contract should not be taken as representing an actual negotiation which might occur between the framers of a new and just constitution. Rather it is similar to Habermas's ideal speech situation in that its arguments and its vision are *implicit* in much contemporary political debate (e.g. about the welfare state). The only way of integrating positive and negative freedom – of ensuring that effective participation in the economic and political process can be guaranteed in principle – will be through the optimal satisfaction of basic needs. This will necessitate a state with appropriate juridical and redistributive capacities. This is why the *moral* right to optimal need-satisfaction derived in Chapter 6 must be translated into *constitutional* rights guaranteed by public authority. In short, the individual liberties enshrined in classic liberalism are shown to be both compatible with and, if taken seriously, dependent upon the creation and/or success of certain socialist-inspired institutions of the welfare state.

Of course, as is already the case, the detail of welfare provision and the practical levels at which it can be feasibly pegged in specific national and local environments will be open to negotiation and debate. Without trying to fix such levels on *a priori* grounds, Habermas and Rawls reinforce each other in their insistence on certain ground rules if outcomes are to be rational and just. This underlines the feasibility of the moral visions of both and leaves a wide scope for individual variation and preference. In some circumstances, for example, economic development may be given priority over improved health care or there may be a local desire for more attention to the environment than for greater access to higher education. Similarly, there may be diversity in the organisation of government and in other aspects of the political process (Pogge, 1989, pp. 156–8).

The empirical conditions for the optimisation of the need-satisfaction of the least well off will often be an open question and each of these options is possible in principle within a Rawlsian constitution. What cannot be negotiated away, however, are the inalienable rights of the least advantaged to have their need-satisfaction prioritised in this way and the relevance of basic needs in our terms for this purpose (Meyers, 1985, ch. 2). In the previous chapter, we attempted to show how this followed logically from the conception of the pursuit of good. Although it is partly derived consequentially from a similar but implicit theory of need, Rawls's general theory can be read as having much the same aim (Pogge, 1989, pp. 39–43; cf. Kukathas and Pettitt, 1990, pp. 69–73).

Critiques of Rawls

In placing so much emphasis on Rawls's theory of justice, we are not denying that there are problems with his view. Indeed, the critical literature here is vast, and important criticisms have come from both sides of the political spectrum.

On the Left, commentators like Miller and MacPherson have argued that many of Rawls's specific arguments, as well as the type of society that is implicit in the conclusions he draws from them, are too closely wedded to existing capitalist forms and thereby beg a range of questions concerning scarcity, production and redistribution. Socially, he simply presupposes the existence of a class society in which inequalities are inevitable. Economically, he at best propounds some variant of market socialism – proclaiming the virtues of competition and incentives. This ignores their human costs and the concentrations of corporate and managerial power which have much more to do with the institutions of capitalist economies than with the laws of supply and demand. Such is the scope of this power, it is argued that it is futile to expect capitalist vested interests to permit any real encroachments on its wealth and privilege (MacPherson, 1973, pp. 89–90; cf. Miller, 1975, pp. 215–30).

The problem with such arguments is that they too beg the question. At best, they minimise the importance of the social progress that has been made in welfare states within the developed capitalist nations. At worst, they amount to little more than the unsubstantiated claim that under socialism there would be far fewer problems of scarcity and far fewer violations of individual liberties

(Gutmann, 1980, pp. 145–56; cf. Buchanan, 1982, pp. 128–32, 145–49). These criticisms now have a hollow ring. The contribution of planning to solving problems of production and distribution is now questioned by many in the Second World. There are similar disputes over the degree to which the liberational potential of democracy is compatible with state ownership and control of the economy and political system. In relation to these arguments, the events of 1989 and 1990 constitute the most exciting developments in international socialist politics since the Second World War. If even Russian communists are willing – after a fashion – to explore the compatibility of their own beliefs with ideas similar to those of Rawls, then surely we can expect the same of Rawls's First World critics!

Some Marxist critics of Rawls also reject his general idea that a right can be said to exist to those primary goods necessary for the achievement of equal opportunity. The discourse of rights is charged with being legalistic, coercive and individualistic. The enforcement requires bureaucratic/legal procedures which can ride roughshod over the multifaceted nature of individual need and necessitate sanctions which only the state can impose – an institution which is said to be coercive under capitalism and redundant under communism. Since rights form the ground-rules for present-day individualistic, selfish and class-ridden societies, they are said to have no raison d'etre under communism. In other words, constitutional rights are seen as either ineffective or redundant (Campbell, 1983, ch. 2). These critiques are also flawed. The enforcement of rights and duties does not always imply sanctions. Alternatives include education, counselling and other policies geared to the prevention of abuse. Further, political authority and codified rules are universal features of all societies. Different conceptions of the good life will always abound and will need reconciling or arbitrating. For this to happen without unjustly infringing the autonomy of individuals will always necessitate in some sense the codified recognition of the existence of individual rights.

Yet aside from those already mentioned, there are further problems in Rawls's work. Like Habermas, he gives little insight into the question of political strategy: of how in different economic, cultural and political environments groups can strive to implement his principles with any hope of success. However, it is clear that even without such answers, Rawls's ideas can help to clarify the goals of a need-oriented society. They are the goals of any feasible socialism which takes individual rights seriously – the vision of healthy, educated individuals struggling together to look after themselves and each other in ways which fairly optimise their creative potential as persons.

Those who criticise Rawls from the Right take up a different attack which has two main components, both of which were briefly introduced in Chapter 1. First, it is argued – most recently and coherently by Nozick – that the classic liberal emphasis on respect for individual autonomy is threatened by the compulsion which must be associated with theories of positive rights. This is the case since the goods and services to which individuals would be entitled are not necessarily earned by them and have to be paid for by someone. Since charity is ruled out because the entitlement is strict, the only other possibility is some form of taxation. But as those who are taxed cannot refuse to pay if they so choose, Nozick argues that their negative rights are being unjustifiably violated (Nozick, 1974, p. 174). And since similar violations would inevitably accompany the implementation by the state of anything approximating Rawls's difference principle and the principle of equality of opportunity, what might be pronounced a theory of justice turns out to be the opposite.

The second criticism is related to the first in that it draws attention to the *expense* of respecting positive rather than negative rights. After all, the argument goes, it costs nothing to honour the individual's right to free speech, privacy, security of property and so on. Individuals simply need to be left alone to get on with their lives. However, positive rights – particularly of the sort that Rawls envisages – cannot be associated with strict duties in the same way. For here the task is to provide rather than to forbear, and resource constraints may make this impossible. If in the context of scarcity duties are impossible to act upon or there is no clear way of deciding between competing claims, then it follows that the rights were only apparent in the first place (Cranston, 1973, pp. 66–7). Thus it makes no sense to talk of someone having a right to, say, forms of health care or education which are beyond a nation's expense. Again, the only coherent foundation for the kind of redistributive policies which Rawls advocates is charity and not constitutional reform.

Both of these criticisms are flawed. Nozick's argument is based on a Lockean view of ownership which is essentially individual – you and only you are entitled to decide what to do with the fruits of your labour. Once it is realised, however, that production is a social process in which many mix their labour, any rights associated with ownership can no longer be focused exclusively on the individual (MacPherson, 1962, ch. 5; cf. O'Neill, 1981, pp. 319–21). Therefore, provided that the political representatives of those who are directly or indirectly responsible for production agree to taxation for redistributive purposes, Nozick can hardly complain. Further, both positive and negative rights incur the expenditure of resources and therefore cannot be differentiated in this respect. If the protection of security of property is to be taken seriously, it will require more than just the hope that others will exercise their duty to forbear. Some form of police and judicial system, for example, will be required (Plant, 1986, pp. 36–8). More important still, it will require a strong sense of moral reciprocity among the citizenry. However, if such reciprocity amounts to little more than libertarian platitudes about liberty rather than the material wherewithal for its concrete enjoyment, a reticence on the part of the dispossessed to forbear will hardly be surprising.

Even if the preceding arguments against Rawls are in our view unfounded, there do remain several inadequacies and lacunae in his work which need rectifying. The first of these concerns the relative lack of attention paid to theories of democracy and to citizen participation. It would appear that a Rawlsian constitution is possible which yields a society of benign bureaucrats with little popular political participation. The Webbs, no doubt, would have interpreted him in this way and found little in his work to be contrary. Given our emphasis on the necessity for maximum participation in defining and implementing need-based policies, this significant silence on his part is of obvious importance.

Developing this criticism, Gutmann rehearses the four classic arguments for optimising and equalising participatory opportunities in the political process: to protect oneself and one's group against tyranny by others (the traditional justification of democracy), to produce better policies through involving in the decision-making process those who are directly affected by the decisions (Habermas's primary defence), to encourage self-development and a capacity for political judgement (J.S. Mill's emphasis along with a range of later Fabian writers) and to guarantee the equal dignity of all citizens (Tawney and T. H. Marshall's chief concern). The strength of all of these views when taken together motivate her to add a fourth constitutional principle to Rawls's three with which we agree: *to diffuse political power to the maximum extent consistent with his principle of distributive justice* (Gutmann, 1980, pp. 178–81, 197–203).

Such a participatory principle would have to remain subordinate to his redistributive goals, since achieving the latter is a necessary condition for the success of the former. Thus Gutmann argues that attempts to extend participatory opportunities in the context of an unjust and inegalitarian society – the development of community control over schools in the USA in the late 1960s, for example – illustrate how this may actually widen inequality in a number of ways. Hence the image of freedom and democracy will be no more than that, unless the constitutional principle of equality of opportunity is given substance through being matched with the principle of equality of need-satisfaction (Gutmann, 1980, pp. 191–7; cf. Gutmann, 1982). Yet this in turn will be impossible unless something like Habermas's goals of communicative competence are embodied in the ways in which production, reproduction, education and the exercise of authority are publicly planned and regulated. Otherwise, the understanding necessary to optimise such satisfaction and, therefore, to optimise democracy itself will be lacking. This is why Gutmann's analysis also supports measures such as industrial democracy, the decentralisation of much policy-making to the local level and public accountability over bureaucracies and professional groups.

A second notable absence in Rawls's writing concerns those specific groups for whom justice in his terms will be especially hard to achieve. On the one hand, this neglect might be seen to be reasonable, given the universality of his theory and the way in which it sets standards by which the treatment of everyone can be judged. On the other hand, the difficulty of implementing something like the principle of equal opportunity for some groups does have a structural dimension in all cultures which needs to be addressed. This is particularly true, for example, in relation to the explicit and implicit impact of patriarchy on inequalities between men and women. As for general inequality, Pateman (1988, p. 43) has argued that Rawls:

merely takes it for granted that he can, at one and the same time, postulate disembodied parties devoid of all substantive characteristics, and assume that sexual difference exists, sexual intercourse takes place, children are born and families formed. Rawls' participants in the original contract are, simultaneously, mere reasoning entities, and 'heads of families', or men who represent their wives... Rawls's original position is a logical abstraction of such rigour that nothing actually happens there.

To the degree that Rawls smuggles patriarchal assumptions into his formulation of the original position, then Pateman's argument is well taken. If men alone are present in the original position – and by hypothesis men who define themselves as 'heads of families' at that – then the social contract which they then agree will hardly recognise the *specific* primary goods which women require for equal opportunity to be an individual and social reality rather than an ideal abstraction. Yet it does not follow from this deficiency that Rawls's general method and conclusions ought to be rejected, provided that the characteristics of the negotiators is altered to embrace Pateman's critique.

Suppose that negotiators will also not know which *sex* they will be once the constitution is agreed. Given the idealised character of Rawls's thought experiment, there seems no more reason to exclude this possibility than many of the other counterfactual assumptions which his model embraces. If this is specifically done in relation to reproduction, a range of rights follows from our reading of Rawls general theory concerning the specific needs of women. These include access to free and safe contraception and abortion. Without both, women cannot be said to exercise freedom to formulate and act upon their life chances to the same degree as men. It is precisely for these Rawlsian reasons that they should be included in the list of need satisfiers to which all women should have access as a matter of constitutional right.

When we move to the sphere of social reproduction, however, more difficult questions of principle are raised. On the one hand, the physical, mental and moral immaturity of small children (leaving aside the thorny question of the age at which they cease to be children) justifies their right to protection against artificial impediments to their development as healthy and autonomous adults. On the other hand, the specific needs of the mother – or any other primary carer of a child – imply that the maximum freedom to experiment in alternative child-care arrangements should be encouraged which is consistent with the provision of such protection. The necessity here, as elsewhere, is to stimulate choice by altering legal and normative constraints which institutionalise restricted forms of child care ... but not through exposing the child to unnecessary harm. As regards both efficacy and morality, the correct course of action in specific situations just may not be that clear. And this will be the case even assuming that there has been agreement about the general rights of both carers and children.

As Habermas suggests, any rational and effective attempt to resolve the potential tension between ostensibly conflicting goals such as these must bring to bear both the codified knowledge of experts *and* the experiential knowledge of those whose basic needs and daily life world are under consideration. In the case in point, the voices of the children, the carers and the experts must all be heard before a final decision is negotiated. It is in this sense that, along with the communicational and constitutional conditions for the optimisation for need-satisfaction outlined above, justice requires both centralised authority with organisational and academic expertise and a thoroughgoing democratisation of as much of the planning and governmental process as is consistent with our basic moral obligations. It requires a *dual strategy of social policy formation* which values compromise, provided that it does not extend to the general character of basic human needs and rights. Any successful communicational and political strategy for the optimisation of need-satisfaction will of necessity, therefore, contain elements of both generality and particularity. To paraphrase Kant, justice without participation is empty and participation without justice is blind.[6]

Internationalism, ecology and future generations

At the end of Chapter 6, it was argued that a radical internationalism follows from an acceptance of the universal human right to optimum need-satisfaction. While it may be psychologically understandable that individuals are hesitant to allocate resources to strangers in other lands, morally they have no option but to accept that they should – provided that they are committed to a vision of the good and wish to remain consistent with it. Certainly, once we accept the case for a rights-based 'welfare state', we are, in Myrdal's terms, morally constrained to go 'beyond the welfare state' to respect the same rights to optimum need-satisfaction on a global scale (Myrdal, 1960).

While paying lip service to it, Rawls's own theory neglects the problem of global justice, presumably because the idea of a hypothetical contract governing a constitution for the entire world is so far-fetched and daunting (Rawls, 1971, pp. 171–82). Yet the application of something like Rawls's veil of ignorance to its solution leads to Myrdal's conclusion. If we assume that those in our version of the original position will not know which country they will inhabit, it seems clear that they will be equally concerned with the international right of *all* individuals to the optimal need-satisfaction which this will require (Pogge, 1989, ch. 6). In actual discussions about how such optimisation should be attempted, the focus is usually on transfers and capital flows from the North to benefit those in most serious need in the South.

Debates about how to achieve this aim are as complex as they are contested. To further the goal of international optimal need-satisfaction, we have argued, for example, for the creation of an international need tax within the developed nations. But which agencies should administer it, given that most governments in the developed and underdeveloped world have shown themselves not to be committed to significant redistribution? The ideal agency for world redistribution would be a democratic *world* government which would implement the same Rawlsian constitutional principles that we have outlined for nation states. This in turn would require the creation of international agencies of welfare focused either on direct provision or on the coordination of existing national welfare agencies. To be sure, when one considers the power of the national and international vested interests throughout the world, along with the impotence of potentially pre-figurative organisations like the United Nations to counteract it, such institutions remain a distant dream. Yet the daunting character of the aim of creating them does not obviate their moral justifiablity (Pogge, 1989, pp. 259–61; cf. Goodin, 1985, pp. 154–69). It simply underlines the urgency of the task and the many different levels of political activity which it entails.

In the meantime, liberational political struggle continues throughout the Third World with some successes, including constitutional reform of the kind endorsed above. For a variety of reasons – the most current being massive debt to First World banks – different regions of the Third World are increasingly realising that they must cooperate economically and politically to counter the power of the developed world. As such alliances emerge, a more equitable redistribution of wealth from the North to the South will rightly remain a dominant aim (Cammack *et al.*, 1988, ch. 7). Its accomplishment should not be divorced from the task of creating or improving international agencies of the preceding kind.

Redistribution, however, is only one part of the moral agenda of optimal need-satisfaction. If strategies for more social equality and for the acceleration of economic development within the Third World neglect the *environment*, then ultimately they will be self-defeating. If, for example, the environment is seriously polluted, increases in real income will not necessarily lead to an improvement in individual health and autonomy. Indeed, one of the lessons of the developed world is that the opposite is the case if greater wealth has the effect of increasing access to such hazards – contaminated food products, for example.

Further, environmental pollution can lead in the long term to economic development itself being threatened. This can occur through damage to natural resources required for production or through the effects of hazards on both producers and consumers. Counteracting both again requires legal regulation by an appropriate system of international political authority (World Commission on Environment and Development, 1987, ch. 12). The Rawlsian negotiator will concur if, again, she is unaware of the country in which she will be placed after agreement on a constitution has been reached and if her veil of ignorance does not shield her from the ecological facts necessary for her to protect her best interests.

Of course, such an authority would stand no chance of success unless its regulatory activity were combined with an international reallocation of goods and services which would make it economically feasible for underdeveloped countries to act accordingly. The universality of the principle of the optimisation of need-satisfaction, along with consequentialist reasoning along Rawlsian lines, both dictate that nations which have already economically benefited from exploiting the environment have a moral duty to ensure that poor nations who are now similarly tempted share in this benefit. Provided that the right of individuals everywhere to optimal need-satisfaction is respected, it will then be possible for underdeveloped countries better to resist economic policies which might pose short-term increases in such satisfaction but which are also environmentally irresponsible. Also, given the organic character of the earth's eco-system, it is self-evident that the long-term consequences of environmental irresponsibility are unsatisfactory for everyone, irrespective of where they happen to live in the world (Taylor, 1986, ch. 6). There is literally no escape.

Finally, even if the optimisation of human need-satisfaction through ecological *space* has been attended to, we still have to confront the question of our moral responsibility for optimised need-satisfaction through *time*. Do we have duties toward future generations in this respect and if so what are they? This is a particularly important question since levels of present need-satisfaction can always be raised at the expense of the environmental resources available to future humans who will be in need. One thing is clear. On purely utilitarian grounds, our obligations are obscure. To know that our family line or cultural traditions will continue into the future is unlikely to outweigh our desire for higher levels of need-satisfaction in the here and now (Parfit, 1984, pp. 480–6). Similarly, rights-based arguments seem to offer little support to intergenerational redistribution: it is unclear how we could ascribe rights to beings who have not even been conceived and cannot assume corresponding duties even in principle (Partridge, 1981, pp. 243–64).

This said, there is something morally uneasy about denying that present generations have any responsibility to protect and conserve the environment for more than purely short-term considerations. This is the case for three reasons which, when combined, affirm the existence of the rights of future individuals to at least the same levels of need-satisfaction which we have shown to be possible in the present.

First, if we have special duties toward those who we know our direct intervention can protect from harm, it follows that we must at least have environmental responsibility for those generations which overlap our own. We should do nothing that will interfere with their pursuit of optimal need-satisfaction. Yet if this is accepted, then it seems impossible empirically to isolate the environmental needs of this generation from those of the people who follow it. The integrity of the environment cannot be temporally sliced in this way.

Second, Rawlsian arguments also suggest the profound unfairness of environmental irresponsibility (Rawls, 1972, Section 44). While perhaps it would be too far-fetched to expect representatives from the future to return to the present to sit in on constitutional negotiations about environmental protection, this does not work the other way round (Goodin, 1985, pp. 172–3). We can imagine a veil of ignorance where those in the present do not know if they will be reawakened in some future generation but do understand what the relationship will continue to be between their needs and the environment. In these circumstances, it would be surprising if the outcome of their negotiations was ecologically irresponsible. Once again, the success of this argument is predicated on the existence of human needs – or primary goods thought of in these terms – which are universalisable over time and about which negotiators have knowledge. Were this not the case, they would have no way of linking their present and future interests (Feinberg, 1980, p. 181).

But third, and perhaps most important of all, a commitment to a contemporary moral vision of the good makes little sense applied only to present generations. To so damage the environment as to jeopardise the long-term survival of a form of life which we believe embodies the good is to renounce our commitment to that good – no more and no less. Such forms of life, like persons, have an inherently narrative structure or *telos*. Yet unlike persons, the narrative associated with beliefs about the good stretch indefinitely into the future. If we believe a form of life to be good, then its story *should* continue. What would it then mean for someone to argue that while they support the moral values and achievements of their favoured form of life in the present, they really don't give a damn what happens to it in the future? Such a response can only suggest a lack of commitment to the moral worth of the form of life in the first place. For it must mean that the person involved does not want future generations to be in a position to do what they now themselves believe to be morally right. We can no more consistently undermine the ecological possibility of future virtue –

whatever we believe to constitute virtue – than we can that of the present.

At the beginning of this section of the book, we distinguished needs from wants by reference to the preconditions for the avoidance of serious harm. These conditions can be regarded as goals which all humans should have in common, if they are to be able to act in their objective interests. We end the chapter by outlining the environmental constraints on the right to optimised need-satisfaction for which we have also argued. Human needs, therefore, are those levels of health and autonomy which should be – to the extent that they can be – achieved for all peoples now, without compromising the foreseeable levels at which they they will be achieved by future generations. In the long term – if there is to be one – an awareness of the delicacy of the biosphere must go hand in hand with any feasible commitment to the optimisation of need-satisfaction. Taking rights seriously means doing the same for the environment.

We have argued that there are two necessary conditions for successful struggle for the achievement of optimised need-satisfaction. First, participants must have accurate understanding of the social and physical environment which they are attepting to improve. Second, the objective opportunities for change must really be present within these environments. But there is also a third condition which we can only mention here. In the face of frustration and possible danger, participants will require the classic Greek virtues which MacIntyre has recently done so much to rehabilitate – reason, courage, truthfulness and a willingness to sacrifice. Ironically, some may think, successful political struggle will also entail the classic Christian virtues – particularly charity with respect to those with whom one disagrees and faith and hope that participation will contribute toward a more just distribution of material, intellectual and emotional resources – even when it fails in the short term.[7]

Without the pursuit of individual virtue in all of these terms, the dream of optimising need-satisfaction for everyone will remain exactly that. There is no 'river' of history or process of social determination which will – in and of themselves – bring about the required changes. No matter how much their social environment may be ripe for transformation, individuals will need to work virtuously in their personal, vocational and political lives to bring it about. Moreover, the more we succeed, the more we will have reinforced the collective potential for further action towards the same goal. Indeed, as we have seen, it is usually those who already have relatively high levels of health and autonomy who most often challenge established authority with success. Therefore, if we take virtue seriously it cannot be divorced from our vision of a more liberated future – one where we protect existing levels of need-satisfaction and work for their improvement in whatever ways we can.

III

Human Needs in Practice

8

Measuring Need-Satisfaction

In Part II we have argued that basic needs exist which are objective and universal but our understanding of which changes, and typically expands, through time. We also recognised that these needs are met by innumerable specific satisfiers, which do vary across cultures. Here, we must again address the many problems which flow from this duality of universality and particularity. Can we articulate what physical health and autonomy mean in terms which are universal yet measurable? What does optimising need-satisfaction entail in practice? Can we devise measures which directly assess levels of satisfaction? These are the sorts of questions asked in this chapter. None of them is novel. Indeed, they have all been tackled in the rapidly-growing literature on 'social indicators', the 'basic needs approach' and the 'human development' concept. It is therefore with this body of literature that we begin our analysis of human needs in practice.

Social indicators and other direct measures of human welfare

A diverse collection of empirical indicators designed to assess 'need-satisfaction' is now commonly used throughout the world. Though these have older roots, the 1960s saw a new interest in direct non-monetary measures of well-being in the 'First' and the 'Third' Worlds for both theoretical and practical reasons.

Theoretically this stemmed from dissatisfaction with national income as a measure of total product, let alone human welfare. Gross Domestic Product (GDP) sums the net values added of those

151

goods and services produced within the monetised sectors of an economy. In its unadjusted form it excludes peasant and other production for direct consumption (which can amount to 40 per cent of total product in less developed economies) together with the vast range of unpaid activities and services performed chiefly by women within the domestic sphere (which can amount to 40 per cent in the more developed economies). Yet as a measure of welfare GDP per head is still more deficient. It takes no account of the composition of output between need-satisfiers and luxuries, nor of the distribution of welfare between groups and within families, nor of the impact of production and consumption on human well-being (unless well-being is defined in terms of those things which GDP measures), nor of the side-effects of production on the environment and the biosphere and hence of the sustainability of future production and welfare (Miles, 1985, ch. 2).

These deficiencies are well known – indeed they are in one sense misplaced as critiques in that GDP was not initially devised to measure either aggregate production or welfare. But during the last half-century such inadequacies have led to the search for alternative measures of welfare (Miles, 1985, ch. 2). To begin with, Drewnowski and others associated with the UN Research Institute of Social Development developed the concept of 'level of living' – direct measures of need-satisfaction in various areas of life. This was subsequently theorised by other social scientists, mainly in the Nordic countries. Von Wright (1963) developed the distinction between objective welfare and subjective happiness in this context. Allardt (1973) then broadened the approach from material level of living to embrace those aspects of life usually the subject of the personal and political realms. In this way he distinguished three fundamental dimensions of objective well-being – 'having', 'loving' and 'being' – while retaining the contrast with subjective well-being (see also Galtung, 1982).

These theoretical developments reflected, and contributed to, practical developments. In the First World, governments began to move on from Keynesian economic management to broader responsibilities for social planning, and this in turn required the construction of new statistics for modelling and control purposes. Social reporting was developed in the USA and spread via such publications as the British government's *Social Trends*. In 1973 the OECD identified a 'list of social concerns common to most member countries' and subsequently specified and constructed social indicators to monitor progress with respect to these concerns (OECD, 1976).

In the Third World in the 1960s and 1970s, respectable rates of growth in some regions failed to prevent worsening levels of relative and even absolute poverty, an experience which generated an explicit 'basic needs approach'. 'Economic growth', measured by rates of change in GDP, was criticised as an index of both 'development' and 'welfare'. Attempts to chart the latter led eventually, via a focus on employment and income distribution, to an explicit concern with 'basic needs' (Wisner, 1988, ch. 1). In 1976 the International Labour Organisation adopted a Declaration of Principles and Programme of Action for a Basic Needs Strategy of Development, and in 1978 the World Bank initiated work on basic needs. These and other initiatives set in motion programmes to collect and collate indicators of basic need-satisfaction, typically prioritising a small set of basic needs such as nutrition, primary education, health, water supply, sanitation and housing.[1] Many advantages were claimed for the basic needs approach as both a goal and a set of policy priorities for Third World countries (Streeten, 1981, chs 18–19; Stewart, 1985, ch. 1). The goal was applicable to the concerns of all people and it was widely acceptable and hence appealing to international aid agencies. Above all it was morally sound: 'putting basic needs first', some argued, was closer to what should be the fundamental objectives of development. Trivial sums of money could be shown to relieve vast areas of suffering. As a means of prioritising policies in a context of limited resources it integrated separate issues into a coherent package, yet could justify concrete programmes for specific vulnerable groups.

Yet despite theoretical advances and political advantages the movement for social indicators and human development appears to have run into the sand. Politically, the social indicators movement was weakened in the 1980s, especially in the English-speaking world, by the rise of neo-liberalism. The resulting IMF-led policies of 'structural adjustment' in the Third World paid scant regard to basic needs, human development or quality of life (Cornia *et al.*, 1987). By the 1980s many countries were experiencing falling growth rates and spreading absolute poverty. At the same time the basic needs strategy was also criticised by Third World critics as being an imperialist riposte to their demand for a New International Economic Order. Instead they stressed the prior need for the underdeveloped nations to reduce their economic dependency on the West (Wisner, 1988, ch. 1; Miles, 1985, p. 169).

Undoubtedly, the crises facing the international economy contributed to what some identified as a crisis facing the social indicators or 'human development' movement in both the South and the North. So too did the impracticality of some basic need strategies, the 'breathtaking innocence of socio-political reality' exhibited by some (Leeson and Nixson, 1988, p. 34, cf. ch. 2). But well before this time the relativist wave, documented in Chapter 1, was eroding the conceptual foundations of such strategies. The basic needs approach, it was argued, incorporated arbitrary postulates about human nature, in particular Western cultural values, and about social change, in particular a uniform, linear model of development. Instead an anthropological approach to evaluating quality of life was advocated (Rist, 1980). At the macro-level this entailed a greater emphasis on community and participation as ways of understanding the needs of particular social groups. In many ways, and in some hands (e.g. Johansson, 1976), this represents a positive contribution to developing the sort of cross-cultural understanding of human need advocated in this book. However, elsewhere it has helped to discredit any notion of universal human need.

The decline and fall of the social indicator/human development movements was due first and foremost to the lack of a unifying conceptual framework (cf. Sen, 1987, p. 25). The earlier theoretical innovations noted above all suffer from one overriding defect. None of them demonstrates the universality of their theory, nor, the other side of the same coin, tackles the deeper philosophical questions raised by relativism. Either the very idea of a universal approach is rejected: 'Needs are constructed by the social structure and have no objective content' (Rist, 1980, p. 241). Or, more commonly, the theoretical possibility of universal needs is granted, but their concrete assessment is perceived as beyond reach due to the cultural and political bias of concepts and evidence.[2]

Thus Galtung (1980, p. 72) grants that basic human needs exist, but are 'perverted' or 'contaminated' by Western conceptions, categories and lists. We can approach the universal core only by generating alternative non-Western lists of needs. A universal list is a dangerous illusion, even though he holds out the prospect of getting closer to it via dialogue between contending lists. In the same vein, Carr-Hill begins from the recognition that 'measurent work and statistical work in general are not politically, socially or theoretically autonomous activities', and proceeds to a real fear that technical solutions can replace fundamentally political problems. 'There are then two possible consequences: either one does not construct indicators at all ("because they are ideological"), or one constructs those indicators most suited to one's political predilections' (Carr-Hill, 1984, pp. 180, 176). He adopts the second approach, but cannot then gainsay any alternative system of indicators put forward by proponents of different value systems. Back to relativism. Yet it is not enough to attack relativism in the abstract and to argue for the existence of basic needs in theory. We must show what they entail in practice, especially the practice of applied social research.

Satisfiers and 'intermediate needs'

While the basic individual needs for physical health and autonomy are universal, many goods and services required to satisfy these needs are culturally variable. For example, the needs for food and shelter apply to all peoples, but we have seen that there is a potentially infinite variety of cuisines and forms of dwelling which can meet any given specification of nutrition and protection from the elements. We have called all objects, activities and relationships which satisfy our basic needs 'satisfiers'. Basic needs, then, are always universal but their satisfiers are often relative. Sen has made a similar point in his analysis of poverty: 'Poverty is an absolute notion in the space of capabilities but very often it will take a relative form in the space of commodities or characteristics' (1984, p. 335). The same point has been made by some contributors to the literature on basic needs and social indicators (e.g. Lederer, 1980). The existence of basic needs or capabilities which are universal to all people is quite consistent in theory with a rich variety of ways in which they can be met and a wide variation in the quantity of satisfiers required to meet them. But to measure need-satisfaction in practice further stages of analysis are necessary.

In a series of papers Sen (1984, 1985, 1987) has developed a concept and measure of well-being which contributes to this task.

First, he draws a distinction between a commodity and its set of characteristics or desirable properties (Lancaster, 1966). A meal, for example, may have the properties of satisfying hunger, establishing social contacts or providing a centre for family life. Conversely, a number of distinct commodities will often share one or more characteristics, as when all (or most) foodstuffs have the characteristic of satisfying hunger. Second, he argues that these characteristics must be distinguished from the 'functionings' of persons – what a particular person can achieve or succeed in doing with the set of commodity characteristics at her or his command. The set of functionings which persons can choose – their 'freedom of choice' of functionings – he calls their 'capabilities'. Functionings and capabilities are in turn distinguished from the final state of mind of that person, such as happiness or desire-fulfilment. Hence Sen constructs an analysis of consumption and welfare, richer than that of orthodox economics, as follows:

Commodities → Characteristics → Capabilities/Functionings → Mental states

We propose to integrate Sen's framework with our own. His model suggests that there are *two* alternatives to either wealth (commodities) or utility (subjective end-states) as measures of well-being: 'capabilities/functionings' and 'characteristics'. Let us look at each in turn.

First, it is apparent that our basic needs for physical health and autonomy are closely related to functionings. But Sen can be criticised for not developing a systematic list of functionings and capabilities, despite his own helpful applications of his framework. It is just this which, we claim, our theory offers. The first task of operationalisation is thus directly to measure the degree of satisfaction of our basic individual needs using cross-cultural measures. In Chapter 9 we show that considerable progress has been made in doing just that. Nevertheless, certain conceptual and empirical problems remain, which often leave us confronting a hard choice between universalisability and operationality. How can basic need-satisfaction or 'objective welfare' be charted without either embracing relativism or working at such a level of generality that the relevance of our theory for specific problems concerning social policy is lost?

Second, as Sen suggests, to avoid this we must complement the first approach with one based on satisfiers and their characteristics. 'Satisfier characteristics' are a subset of all characteristics, having the property of contributing to the satisfaction of our basic needs in one or more cultural settings. Let us now subdivide this set further to identify *universal satisfier characteristics*: those characteristics of satisfiers which apply to all cultures. Universal satisfier characteristics are thus *those properties of goods, services, activities and relationships which enhance physical health and human autonomy in all cultures*. For example, calories a day for a specified group of people constitutes a characteristic of (most) foodstuffs which has transcultural relevance. Similarly 'shelter from the elements' and 'protection from disease-carrying vectors' are characteristics which all dwellings have in common (though to greatly varying degrees). The category of universal satisfier characteristics thus provides the crucial bridge between universal basic needs and socially relative satisfiers.

Given the instrumental character of statements about human needs outlined in Chapter 3, universal satisfier characteristics can be regarded as goals for which specific satisfiers can act as the means. For this reason, and because the phrase is less clumsy, let us refer to universal satisfier characteristics as *intermediate needs*. If this reasoning is correct, such needs can provide a secure foundation on which to erect a list of derived or second-order goals which must be achieved if the first-order goals of health and autonomy are to be attained. As Braybrooke (1987, ch. 2.2) points out, the construction of such lists is a common practice and there is a 'family of lists of needs' which have emerged from very different studies. However international organisations like the OECD, national governments and private individuals have all propounded different lists.[3] Some items like food and water appear on all of them; others like 'recreation' or 'command over goods and services' do not. The problem with such lists is their *ad hoc* character. By contrast, our theory dictates which intermediate needs are most important for basic need-satisfaction, why this is so and why they are the same for all cultures. These intermediate needs can be grouped as follows:

Nutritional food and clean water
Protective housing
A non-hazardous work environment

A non-hazardous physical environment
Appropriate health care
Security in childhood
Significant primary relationships
Physical security
Economic security
Appropriate education
Safe birth control and child-bearing

The only criterion for inclusion in this list is whether or not any set of satisfier characteristics universally and positively contributes to physical health and autonomy. If it does then it is classified as an intermediate need. If something is not universally necessary for enhanced basic need-satisfaction, then it is not so classified, however widespread the commodity/activity/relationship may be. For example, 'sexual relationships' is not included in this list, because some people manage to live healthy and autonomous lives without sex with others. Similarly, an item which is found to be harmful to health and autonomy in one social context (e.g. high-rise housing in Britain) will not be included if in other societies it is not found to have this effect (see e.g. Douglas, 1983, pp. 171–2).

There is one partial exception to our definition of universal satisfier characteristics. Significant biological differences *within* the human species may occasion specific requirements for distinct satisfier characteristics. The most significant of such differences by far is the sex difference between men and women. We shall argue in Chapter 10 that this entails one further universal satisfier characteristic, the satisfaction of which is essential to the health and autonomy of one half of the human race. Women require access to safe birth control and child-bearing if they are to enjoy the same opportunities to participate in their respective societies as men.

The evidence about what is universally necessary is derived from two principle scientific sources. First, there is the best available technical knowledge articulating causal relationships between physical health or autonomy and other factors. Second, there is comparative anthopological knowledge about practices in the numerous cultures and sub-cultures, states and political systems in the contemporary world (Braybrooke, 1987, chs 2.3, 2.4; cf. Mallmann and Marcus, 1980). Thus both the natural and social sciences play their part in rationally determining the composition of intermediate needs. As we shall see, however, this is not to devalue the contribution of Habermas's 'practical' understanding discussed in Chapter 7.

Like all taxonomies, this list of intermediate needs is, in one sense, arbitrary. Its groups are 'verbal wrappings' or 'labels' designed to demarcate one collection of characteristics from another. Moreover, the word-labels used will be ambiguous – they will 'not contain or exhaust the meaning of the need identified' (Judge, 1980, p. 280). Ambiguity can be reduced by increasing the numbers of characteristics or 'need categories'. Yet the larger the set, the greater the problems in comprehending the totality of human needs. At the end of the day, however, the actual categories do not matter. Whatever the taxonomy, our theory requires that the sole condition for selection is the universality of the satisfier characteristics.

Thus we propose to measure need-satisfaction defined in terms of (i) basic needs and (ii) intermediate needs. There is a third interpretation of need-satisfaction, but it will feature infrequently in this volume. This entails measuring the consumption of specific satisfiers in a particular social context. To determine which satisfiers constitute necessities at a particular place and time requires distinct research methodologies pioneered by, for example, recent poverty research and 'social audits'.[4] In particular, codified knowledge needs to be complemented by a rich input of experiential knowledge from the people living the particular lives under investigation. Some of these issues will be broached in our concluding chapter, and the poverty research is partially utilised in Chapters 9 and 10. Otherwise, our analysis will stick resolutely to those intermediate needs which must be satisfied if the basic needs for physical health and autonomy are themselves to be satisfied.

Standards of basic need-satisfaction

The next problem concerns the *standards* with which measures of need-satisfaction are compared and shortfalls in need-satisfaction calculated. As regards *basic* needs, we have already made clear in Part II that we endorse neither an absolute minimum standard nor a culturally relative one. The former cannot be drawn simply with reference to biological data, since our understanding of what it is possible to alter shifts – and typically expands – through time. The second would mean sliding back into culturally distinct and incomparable metrics which would negate our whole project. Instead, we propose a third standard – the *optimum*.

In Chapter 4 the optimum degree of basic need-satisfaction was defined at two levels. At the first, health and autonomy is such that individuals can choose the activities in which they will take part within their culture, possess the cognitive, emotional and social capacities to do so and have access to the means by which these capacities can be acquired. Let us call this the 'participation optimum'. At the second level, optimum health and autonomy is such that individuals can formulate the aims and beliefs necessary to question their form of life, to participate in a political process directed toward this end and/or to join another culture altogether. This we refer to as the critical optimum. In neither case does optimum imply 'maximum'.

In practice, the physical and mental health requirements for participating in a culture and for questioning and improving that culture will be the same. It is in the domains of cognitive understanding and social opportunities for participation that the two levels of optimisation diverge. The critical optimum will extend to embrace opportunities to acquire advanced knowledge of other cultures and to exercise political freedom as well as freedom of agency. Following the argument in Chapter 6, it is to need-satisfaction at the critical optimum level that all people have an entitlement.

What is required, then, is a standard of critical optimum levels of health and autonomy. In practice this can mean either the best level of need-satisfaction achieved anywhere in the world at the present time, or a better standard than this which is materially feasible at the present time. Both standards raise complex issues concerning generalisability, the global politics of need and economic sustainability. For the time being we shall skirt around these problems. Using the term in the first sense, let us define the critical optimum according to the most recent standards achieved by the social grouping with the highest overall standards of basic need-satisfaction. A variety of social categories could be used to delimit the best-off groups – social classes, income categories, racial groups, men as opposed to women – within or across countries. Thus how the optimum is operationalised will in part depend on the task at hand. In much of this book we shall use the social grouping which is most meaningful on a global scale – the nation state.

Our operationalisation of optimal need-satisfaction, therefore, will be linked empirically to the actual performance of those nations with the highest levels of physical health and critical autonomy. There is a choice here between using different 'best practices' drawn from different states – Japan for life expectancy, Sweden for economic security, and so on – or using a single nation which on average is the best performer. The latter has the advantage that this level of need-satisfaction is demonstrably feasible and that any possible trade-offs between different needs and between the needs of different groups of people will have been discounted (Naroll, 1983, p. 64). Not only does 'ought' imply 'can'; 'is' implies 'can' too (Williams in Sen, 1987, p. 96). As the data in Chapter 12 show, the best performing nation today is Sweden.

Of course, for much of the Third World an optimum standard like this is unrealistic at the present time. Though such an optimum remains the only logical and moral criterion that can be applied to judge need-satisfaction in the long term, this does not rule out lower standards being used as strategic goals in the medium term. For less developed nations, lower positions can be derived by identifying those countries which achieve the best results at any level of (orthodoxly defined) economic development. In Chapters 12 and 13 we agree with those who argue that Costa Rica can serve as an exemplar nation for the middle-income countries of the Third World, and that, before 1977 and its present civil strife, Sri Lanka was a star performer among the poorest nations of the world.

Standards of intermediate need-satisfaction

Given the preceding arguments, the next stage is to determine the levels of intermediate need-satisfaction – for each universal satisfier characteristic – which yield optimum levels of basic need-satisfaction. This raises the question of how intermediate need 'inputs' are related to the 'outputs' of physical health and autonomy. We shall discuss this question in Chapter 10, but a more general observation can be ventured here. In a study of the impact of the environment on mental health, Warr develops a 'vitamin model' which we believe is applicable to this task. He notes that the availability of vitamins is important for physical health up to, but not beyond, a certain level: 'At low levels of intake, vitamin deficiency gives rise to physiological impairment and ill-health, but after attainment of specified levels there is no benefit derived from additional quantities. It is suggested that principal environmental features are important to mental health in a similar manner' (Warr, 1987, pp. 9–10; also Goldstein, 1985).

This holds for physical health and other components of autonomy as well. In other words, a particular level of satisfaction for each intermediate need is required if human health and autonomy are to be optimised, but beyond that point no further additional inputs will improve basic need-satisfaction. For example, the ratio of doctors to patients is positively associated with certain measures of survival in low-income countries, but not in high-income countries. This suggests that the effect of quantity of medical provision on physical survival reaches its asymptote at some intermediate level. To take another example, once a dwelling is safe, warm, not overcrowded and supplied with clean water and adequate sanitation, no further improvements – in space, amenities, luxury fittings and so forth – will enhance the *need* satisfaction of its inhabitants as they pertain to housing. These improvements may well meet subjective desires and enhance the satisfaction of wants, but they are irrelevant to the evaluation of need-based welfare.

Warr goes on, however, to note that some vitamins have a contrary impact: in very large quantities they become positively harmful. These he calls AD components after the vitamins A and D (and conveniently acting as a mnemonic for 'additional decrements'). The same will be the case with some intermediate needs. For example, certain health-generating foods if eaten in excess can cause ill-health and become life-threatening. For these categories of satisfiers, there is a plateau of food consumption on either side of which too little or too much is harmful. The same is probably true of too much security in childhood and adulthood and some other satisfiers of intermediate needs. The two sorts of relationship are shown in Figure 8.1. Thus the crucial task in constructing indicators of need-satisfaction is to ascertain *the minimum quantity of intermediate need-satisfaction required to produce the optimum level of basic need-satisfaction* measured in terms of the physical health and autonomy of individuals. In the spirit of Rawls, we could call this level the *minimum optimorum*. It is apparent that this target combines the search for minima in satisfiers with the search for optima in outcomes, but that unlike other approaches which emphasise the importance of basic needs, it subordinates the former to the latter. For instance, *if*, on the basis of the best available knowledge, further improvements in education provision can enhance a population's physical health or critical autonomy, then it follows that their needs for education are not at present being optimally satisfied and that they should be regarded as in a state of objective deprivation.

Figure 8.1   *The relation between intermediate and basic need-satisfaction*

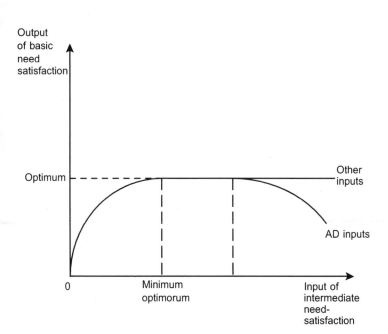

Source: Derived from Warr (1987) Figure 1.1, p.10.

A qualification must be made to this procedure in the case where universal satisfiers or intermediate needs are substitutes for one another, or complement one another, within specified ranges of values. As an example of substitutability, a warmer environment or reduced heavy labour will reduce the food requirements of humans (Cutler, 1984, p. 1121 *et seq.*). The evidence of complements between basic needs is strong: for example, female literacy contributes to health, nutrition, and lower fertility (Burki and Ul Haq, 1981, p. 171 *et seq.*; Stewart, 1985, ch. 5). More research is needed on all these relations and their linkages. Where either complements or substitutes exist, the minimum level of consumption of input A cannot be specified without knowing the level of consumption of inputs B, C, etc. (Mallmann and Marcus, 1980). This apart, however, all intermediate needs should be satisfied up to the *minimum optimorum* level. Where they are of the AD type, this should be below the point where additional decrements appear.

Another qualification concerns the ecological constraint to generalisability discussed in Chapter 7. It is conceivable that for some intermediate needs (particularly health and education services) the point at which provision ceases to enhance basic need-satisfaction lies so far to the right on Figure 8.1 that the minimum optimorum position cannot be universally achieved with available resources. In this case a *constrained* optimum is called for, specifying the highest level of basic need-satisfaction which is generalisable over the relevant population. A strong moral case was advanced in Chapter 6 for regarding the population of the whole world as the only relevant group when defining generalisability. This entails an operational notion of 'sustainable' economic development, an issue which is tackled in Chapter 11. Again, however, in making actual strategic choices in the here and now, a less universal conception of the relevant population may well be the only feasible one. For all practical purposes, this will mean the populations of those nation states which are representative of specific types of socio-economic constraints and which do well in relation to all the levels of individual need-satisfaction.

Problems in devising social indicators of need-satisfaction

But what exactly does 'do well' mean in this context? We still require valid and reliable 'social indicators' to assess the degree of success in meeting both the basic needs for physical health and autonomy, and the intermediate needs identified above. Yet, since all such indicators are surrogate measures – proxies for the strictly unmeasurable concepts which underlie them (Carley, 1982, p. 2; Miles, 1985, p. 16–18) – there will always be scope for proper debate about the suitability of any measure as an index of the satisfaction of any need. Let us consider the remaining problems identified in the literature under four headings.

Validity

How valid is 'calorie consumption per head as a proportion of FAO requirements' as a measure of 'adequate and appropriate nutrition'? Is 'overcrowding' captured by a measure of 'proportion of people living at a density of more than two persons per room'? There is always the danger of focusing on whatever happens to be easily measurable. Associated with this is the risk of substituting an 'input' for an 'output' or an 'outcome'. An example of both dangers would be measuring 'learning' by 'years of attendance at school'. Of course, such a counsel of excellence risks paralysing all attempts to chart the human condition. In practice, when direct measurement is impossible, some 'translation' must be supplied which links the desired standard to the feasible measuring instrument (Carr-Hill, 1984, p. 183; Streeten, 1981, ch. 21). While we must learn from current best practice, our theory does offer some help. It defines a clear set of final outcomes – individual health and autonomy – from which intermediate 'inputs' can be derived. In this way it provides a theoretical rationale for accepting some commonly used social indicators (such as life expectancy), rejecting others (such as 'leisure') and identifying important lacunae (such as indicators of 'children at risk' or 'social isolation').

Disaggregation and distribution

All compilers of social indicators must face the question of how far and how to disaggregate their data. Three broad alternatives can be distinguished, of which we shall use two.[5] The first is to chart differences between *individuals*, for example by using the proportions falling below some benchmark (e.g. below 2000 calories a day). Our theory focuses attention on absolute not relative differences, and in particular on the absolute standard of the worst off. Consequently, it endorses this sort of indicator rather than indicators of the average conditions of a group, such as life expectancy. Using this first method, different sets of individuals may fall below the benchmarks in different domains of need. The second method is to disaggregate measures of need-satisfaction between groups which score consistently high or low marks, such as men and women or members of social classes. Chapter 12 presents indicators of need-satisfaction distingushing between women and men.

Composite indicators of well-being

Unlike national income per head, the social indicators approach results in a messy profusion of domains of need, each often measured by more than one indicator. This has led to a search for a composite indicator which will capture well-being in a single figure. There are two approaches here.

The first entails weighting several indicators to form a single one. The Physical Quality of Life Index (PQLI) is one such which has been much used in the development literature (Morris, 1979). The PQLI is a simple unweighted average of indices representing infant mortality, life expectancy at age one and basic literacy. Need-satisfaction in these domains can be measured from the most minimal to an optimum defined in much the same way as we have done. So, infant mortality is ranked on a scale from, at one extreme, the worst national level recorded since 1950 to, at the other extreme, a 'best conceivable' level taking into account the present achievement of Sweden, the world leader. Similarly, life expectancy is scaled from the lowest recorded national level since 1950 to the likely average maximum assuming that unforeseeable developments do not extend the normal human lifespan (77 years, two years longer than the then Swedish level). Weighted equally alongside the percentage literacy rate these constitute the PQLI.

Unfortunately, this measure can be criticised on conceptual as well as methodological grounds (Streeten, 1981, pp. 387–90). We have implied above that one domain of intermediate need-satisfaction cannot be traded off against another (except where there is clear evidence of complementarity or substitutability). No amount of childhood security can compensate for lack of shelter today; nor can better nutrition offset a dangerously polluted environment. Rather each domain should be assesed separately and evaluated according to the minimum or minimum optimorum standard. Furthermore, the PQLI endorses a minimalist notion of health and autonomy – acceptable for charting how badly we are doing but not capable of extending onwards to measure broader human progress. It also sidesteps the communicational and constitutional procedures without which progress towards optimal levels of need satisfaction is impossible.

The recently published UNDP Report (1990) has constructed a Human Development Index (HDI) along similar lines which has attracted a lot of attention. It combines life expectancy; literacy; and income for a decent living standard (using as its measure of a 'desirable or adequate' level of the last, the average official 'poverty line' in nine Western nations). It marks an advance on other indices by developing a clearer theoretical formulation of human development as the formation of human capabilities and the use people make of their acquired capabilities for participating in various activities. This also clearly owes much to Sen's work and is similar to our own. However the HDI is still susceptible to the criticisms of all existing composite indexes outlined here.[6] Such criticisms apply *a fortiori* to more complex, multi-faceted indices such as Estes' (1984) Index of Social Progress which combines together 11 subindices covering 6 dimensions of social progress using 44 social indicators. Here, in the absence of a solid theoretical foundation, the huge weight of measurement threatens to topple the entire edifice.

An alternative approach to the problem of aggregation (Streeten, 1981, pp. 390–4) is to use average life expectancy or some other measure as *the* indicator of human development. Recent research suggests that it is highly correlated with doctors per head, calorie supply and, even more significantly, with literacy (Stewart, 1985, ch. 4). Our theory explains why life expectancy is so crucial for any consideration of human need. However, it does so by extending this focus on survival to a far broader concern with optimal physical health and personal autonomy. Unless a valid indicator of this entire syndrome is discovered, the problems of compositing more than one indicator will remain. Until then, social indicators are necessarily disaggregated. Though we should not foreclose the search for summary measures of human well-being, the idea of a single indicator (like GNP per head) will probably remain a search for the Holy Grail.

Who decides? Quantitative vs qualitative research into human needs

Lastly, there is the perpetual dilemma facing research into needs. If it is agreed that both subjective preference and professional/ bureaucratic dictates are suspect in determining what needs are and how they are measured, who is to decide on the appropriate social indicators and how? (Bradshaw, 1972). The consensual answer to emerge in the last two decades is 'participation' (Streeten, 1984, pp. 974–5). Effective and informed participation on the part of the population whose needs are being assessed is vital, and has yielded impressive results at village level. By itself, however, an emphasis on participation is no panacea. Among other things, it can advantage the already-privileged through their ability to manipulate the information process and can sacrifice the common good to sectional interpretations of it.

Our approach offers some clues to overcoming this dilemma. We have already seen that our theory is essentially 'iterative': universal and objective needs can be shown to exist but the ongoing growth of knowledge continually modifies and improves our understanding of intermediate needs and how they can best be satisfied. This new knowledge in turn feeds back into and alters the indicators for the evaluation of social policies. The appropriate indicators of inter- mediate needs are continually open to question and improvement as a result of the growth of codified and experientially-grounded knowledge. This applies *a fortiori* to the process of determining culturally specific *satisfiers* (e.g. specific types of food with partic- ular nutritional content).

For the moment, let us note that our theory endorses the use of both quantatitive and qualititative research methods (see Bryman, 1988, especially ch. 6). Except for the very smallest groups, the evaluation of need-satisfaction must necessarily involve quantitative social indicators: numerical statistics which summarise conditions pertaining to groups of people. There are other advantages of such data, notably that they enable one to compute the degree of difference in need-satisfaction between groups, or their rate of change over time. Nevertheless, this does not rule out a role for qualitative research in providing an understanding of the meaning of actions, and thus in devising and refining indicators of basic need-satisfaction. Both quantitative and qualitative research have a role to play in deepening our understanding of what it means in practice to meet human needs. But at any point in time it will be quantitative statistics to which one initially turns when charting progress in this respect.

Starting with basic needs for physical health and human autonomy we have demarcated 'universal satisfier characteristics' – those characteristics of need satisfiers which are common to all cultures – and used these to determine categories of 'intermediate needs'. The target standard of satisfaction of each characteristic is the minimum necessary to secure optimum individual health and autonomy, in turn defined as the highest standard presently achieved in any nation state. Constrained versions of the optimum and the minimum optimorum standard are also advocated for use in specific circumstances. To chart both basic and intermediate needs we ideally require social indicators which are valid, distributive, quantitative and aggregated, but which are open to revision. These indicators should be amenable to disaggregation between groups. In this way profiles of the need-satisfactions of nations, cultural groups and other collectivities can be compiled.

Though all the above has been argued with respect to individual needs, the same methods are applicable to our societal preconditions. That is, we need to identify – and measure – those societal preconditions which enable people everywhere rationally and democratically to identify and optimally satisfy their basic needs. This is tackled in Chapter 11.

In the meantime the basic structure of our theory is summarised in Figure 8.2., on the following page. Though such a diagram cannot do justice to the complexity of the issues, it does illustrate the two crucial dimensions. First, it demarcates the levels of the theory, distinguishing between universal goals, basic needs, intermediate needs, specific satisfiers and societal preconditions. Second, it illustrates the theory's distinction between participation within a social form of life and human liberation. The figure summarises the analysis so far and can act as a guide to the operationalisation of the theory in Part 3.

Figure 8.2   *The theory in outline*

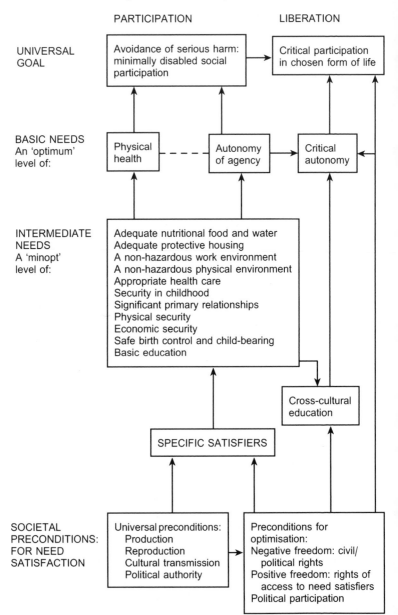

9

Physical Health and Autonomy

How can the satisfaction of *basic* needs be empirically evaluated? The reader will recall the distinction drawn in Chapter 4 between the ultimate goal presumed by our theory – the avoidance of serious harm regarded as the fundamental and sustained impairment of social participation – and the basic needs for physical health and autonomy. These needs were seen to be the universal conditions for achieving this goal. Our intention here is to operationalise physical health and autonomy and to suggest cross-cultural indicators of both.[1]

Figure 9.1 elaborates the top part of Figure 8.2 and illustrates the major steps in our approach. First, we consider direct measures of

Figure 9.1 *The relation between participation, health and autonomy*

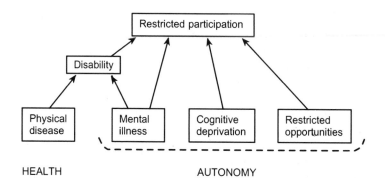

survival and of disability, conceptulised as the restricted ability to peform an activity regarded as normal for a human being, where this restriction is the result of physiological or emotional impairment. Second, we turn to cross-cultural measures of physical disease utilising the biomedical model. The remaining three sections operationalise the three components of personal autonomy distinguished in Chapter 4: mental illness, cognitive deprivation and restricted opportunity to participate in socially significant activities. By the conclusion we hope to have shown how the basic need for physical health and autonomy can be charted empirically.

It will be apparent from Figure 9.1 that we conceptualise and operationalise health and autonomy in the negative way argued earlier. The WHO in a famous definition puts forward a positive definition of health as 'a state of complete physical, mental and social well-being'. However, though frequently quoted it is just as often ignored, and for good reason: it is unclear how such a positive conception of health can be measured (Caplan, 1981, parts 1, 5). Our approach is to define and measure physical health negatively as the minimisation of death, disability and disease. And similarly to define and measure autonomy negatively as the minimisation of mental disorder, cognitive deprivation and restricted opportunities. However, we consider that these two negatives make a positive: together they constitute a rounded, yet operational, conception of that state of objective well-being which the WHO has sought to identify.

Survival and disability

We have seen that survival is, so to speak, the bottom line of the need for physical health. Unless individuals are alive, they do not even have the chance of becoming ill, much less of doing anything else. Provided we leave aside some interesting questions about long-term coma, there is not much dispute about what survival means empirically. You are surviving as a person if you are capable of any intentional activity. We have argued that individuals have a right of access to the means to survival to the degree that they are physically capable of it. Of course, if they do not survive it would be strange to say that they are then in any way deprived. The dead cannot be deprived of anything since they cannot do or participate in anything. It is this fact that makes death such a personal tragedy

(Nagel, 1979, ch. 1). Yet persons are also deprived if their *survival chances* are artificially limited by social and economic circumstances which are alterable.

The most relevant indicators for such deprivation will be mortality rates and life expectancy – a measure indicating the number of years someone of a particular age in a particular population would live if patterns of mortality prevailing at that time were to stay the same throughout her/his life. In Britain, for example, the average life expectancy at birth is 75 years; in Guinea it is 42 years (World Bank, 1988, Table 1). The infant mortality rate (deaths before the age of 1 per 1000 live births) and the under-5 mortality rate (deaths before the age of 5 per 1000 live births) are invaluable indicators of a wide range of health and social conditions. UNICEF (1987) uses the latter, rather than GDP per head, as its key indicator of social progress when comparing nations. Hicks and Streeten (1979), as we have seen, regard life expectancy as probably the best overall measure of basic need-satisfaction.

The major limitation of aggregate mortality-based statistics is that they do not reveal the distribution of life chances between individuals and groups. One solution is to calculate rates for people from different class and other groupings within nations. In Britain today, for example, this reveals that children of unskilled workers are twice as likely to die before their first birthday as those of professionals (Whitehead, 1988, p. 229). Another approach is to measure individual variations in life chances using various measures of the dispersion of age-at-death (LeGrand, 1987; Silber, 1983). All of these calculations however encounter conceptual and statistical problems (Carr-Hill, 1987, p. 516). The search goes on for a valid yet sensitive index of differential survival chances, but this certainly does not invalidate the use of such well-known and widely available indicators as life expectancy.

Yet as Streeten (1981, p. 363) has put it: 'life can be nasty, brutish and long'. Physical survival and health do not coincide and there are many problems in using mortality statistics to measure ill-health. The cause of death may be a different condition or pathogen to that which has caused disease and illness during life. As a consequence, data on cause of death are often not strictly comparable. Most important of all, mortality only provides information about lethal diseases and omits morbidity caused by others. In Britain today, for example, cancer figures large in mortality data and arthritis not at all, despite the greater prevalence of arthritis as a cause of disability. So alternative, direct measures of poor physical health are required.

Given our stress on the importance for individuals of the competence to participate fully in their form of life, the most direct method of measuring poor physical health is to measure functional or structural *disability* without appeal to medical disease categories. The WHO *International Classification of Impairments, Disabilities and Handicaps* (1980) makes a distinction between these three terms consistent with the outline of similar concerns in Chapter 4. *Impairment* refers to 'any loss or abnormality of psychological, physiological or anatomical structure or function' which represents deviation from some norm in the individual's biomedical status (WHO, 1980, p. 29). These represent disturbances at the organ level, and can be classified according to the bodily system which is affected – intellectual, visceral, skeletal and so on. Second, *disability* refers to the consequent 'restriction or lack of ability to perform an activity in the manner or within the range considered normal for a human being'. Here the focus is on compound or integrated activities applicable to the whole person, such as tasks, skills and behaviours. It indicates the way that 'functional limitation [impairment] expresses itself as a reality in everyday life' (WHO, 1980, p. 28; cf. Fulford, 1989, Part III). And third, *handicap* refers to any social consequence of disability 'that limits or prevents the fulfillment of a role that is normal (depending on age, sex, and social and cultural factors) for that individual' (WHO, 1980, p. 29). Handicap can only be operationalised in a specific social context.

The relationship between the concepts can be represented as follows:

Disease $\rightarrow$ Impairment $\rightarrow$ Disability $\rightarrow$ Handicap

Disability occupies an intermediate position between the biological notion of impairment and the socially contextual notion of handicap. If it can be operationalised in a cross-cultural way, it will provide a useful contribution to measuring basic need-satisfaction.

A recent study within Britain marks an advance in assessing disability, in ways which could in principle be applied anywhere.

Modifying the WHO classification, it distinguishes 10 main areas where disability can be experienced: locomotion, reaching and stretching, dexterity, seeing, hearing, personal care, continence, communication (being understood and understanding others), behaviour, and intellectual functioning (memory, clarity of thought processes) (OPCS, 1988a, p. 10). Information was collected from survey respondents or their carers about the nature of their disabilities in each category, and on the complaints which gave rise to them. Using a methodology congruent with our theory, it evaluated severity of disability within and between these 10 areas and on this basis constructed an overall index of disability. A set of judges drawn from professionals, researchers, people with disabilities, carers and voluntary organisations was asked to arbitrate on severity. It is evident that this approach attempts to draw on and to reconcile both codified and experiential knowledge.

For example, a man with arthritis in his spine and legs, and suffering from a stroke which affects one side of his body and from a heart condition, was adjudged to fall in severity category 6 (out of 10 ranging from slight (1) to very severe (10)). His locomotion was impaired – he always needed to hold on to something to keep his balance and he could not bend down and pick up something from the floor. The same held for his dexterity. For example, he had difficulty picking up and pouring a kettle of water. While this may not *handicap* a person in all cultures – males are not normally expected to undertake certain domestic duties in many cultures – there can be no doubt that as a scale of *disability* the measure is applicable to all humans everywhere. For such disabilities will reduce, all other things being equal, the effectiveness with which any individual can participate in social activities requiring those capacities reduced by the disablement. On this basis the survey concluded that 14.2 per cent of adults suffer some form of disability in Britain: 6.2 per cent suffer severely (categories 5–7) and 2.2 per cent very severely (categories 8–10) (OPCS, 1988a, Table 3.2). There is nothing save lack of resources and/or political will to prevent such studies being undertaken in all nations to enable the comparative prevalence of disability to be calculated.[2]

Special attention has been devoted to designing indicators of impairment and disability among children. This requires a theory of the 'normal' range of development of children in physiological, cognitive and anatomical terms. Another study by the OPCS in the

UK (1988b) found that 3.2 per cent of Brtish children suffer from some form of disability, computed in an analogous way to that in adults, O.8 per cent of whom are very seriously disabled. Again this sort of research could be applied to any and all cultures, but in its absence there are some proxy indicators of child impairment and disability which permit crude comparisons to be drawn of child health throughout the world. They include the prevalence of low-birth-weight babies, slow gain in height and weight, excessive weight/height ratio, small head circumference, poor motor co-ordination and various sensory deficiencies. For many of these conditions some scattered comparative information is available (see UNICEF, 1987, Part 3).

Pain was excluded from the OPCS study on the grounds that it is an impairment rather than a disability. Yet acute or chronic pain is for many people a crucial part of their illness and relief of that pain enhances, in however small a way, their ability to act and interact with others. Again, there are awkward conceptual and practical problems here because the perception of pain is known to vary between cultures, and across individuals within cultures. Neverthe-less, beyond a certain threshold, pain is pain in any culture and its persistence, if it is preventable with available techniques, constitutes serious harm to all persons in the same way as preventable death or disability.[3]

Physical disease

Measures of disability using this sort of methodology are invaluable in charting the prevalence of poor physical health. But to explain and understand these findings requires theories of physical disease and mental illness. In the case of physical disease we have already argued in Chapter 4 that the biomedical model provides an unrivalled framework for classification and explanation. Embodying a nega-tive definition of physical health, this generates an 'extensive' specification of many diseases, rather than an 'intensive' definition of illness *per se* (Busfield, 1986, p. 35). Precisely because of its technical efficacy, the biomedical model now dictates the conceptual scheme which is internationally employed to identify patterns of ill health within populations: the International Classification of Dis-eases (ICD). Hence all of the statistical data which provide information about national and international patterns of mortality and morbidity incorporate the disease classification of the biomedical model (e.g. OPCS, 1986; WHO, 1988). Indeed, it is precisely such data which are used by many to attempt to illustrate the failures of the model in relation to debates about prevention and cure.

Thus the medical *causes* of disability can – in principle – be charted, as shown in Table 9.1. In contemporary Britain, musculo-skeletal, eye and ear diseases cause most severe disability, along with diseases of the nervous sytem, notably strokes. The chief causes of disability would differ in poorer countries, but this methodology is appropriate to all.

Table 9.1   *Frequency of complaints causing disability. UK*

	%
Infection	1
Neoplasms	2
Endocrine and metabolic	2
Blood	1
Mental	13
Nervous system	13
Eye	22
Ear	38
Circulatory	20
Respiratory	13
Digestive	6
Genito-urinary	3
Skin	1
Musculo-skeletal	45
Congenital	0
Other/vague	6

Notes

1   Survey of 10 000 adults living in private households (i.e. excluding those living in communal establishments such as nursing homes and hospitals).
2   Percentages add up to more than 100 as some people have more than one complaint.
3   Diagnostic terms based on ICD categories attributed to complaints as described by interview respondants.

Source: OPCS (1988a) Table 4.3

The ideal way to ascertain the prevalence of physical disease would be a medical consultation/examination of a random sample of the relevant population to detect the presence of illness independently of people's subjective definitions yet utilising their unique experiential knowledge. Such medical surveys are rare, though they are becoming more common in some Western nations (Blaxter, 1986; Cartwright, 1983). In the absence of that ideal, recourse must be had to two other data sources. The first is administrative records of the utilisation of formal medical services. This can embrace hospital admission and discharge records, and records of patient contacts with primary-health providers in the community. The second source of morbidity data comprises less rigorous field surveys, small-scale epidemiological research and questionnaires on self-reported health in general household surveys.

Each of these has its drawbacks. The former is influenced by levels of provision, monetary and non-monetary factors affecting access, and many other factors. The latter will be subject to cultural influences and the other problems bedevilling subjective appraisal of health. While we have ruled out subjective assessment as a decisive measure of ill-health, it does not follow that self-perception is irrelevant when combined with other indicators. When checked against doctors' records or other clinical measurements, laypersons' self-reports in the UK have been found to agree remarkably well (Whitehead, 1988, p. 224).

Though we have argued that the biomedical model provides a cross-cultural metric with which to compare disease prevalence, it is still a daunting task to estimate the number of cases of different types of disease on an international basis. One heroic attempt to do so for Africa, Asia and Latin America, based on the WHO *Special Programme for Research and Training in Tropical Diseases*, is reproduced in Figure 9.2 alongside estimates of mortality from specific causes. Though the two parts of the figure are not strictly comparable, it reveals the importance of diarrhoeal diseases for both survival and ill-health in the Third World, while also illustrating the differences in patterns of disease provided by mortality and morbidity statistics. The general types of physical disability which accompany serious manifestations of these diseases are undisputed.

Figure 9.2 *Proportions of mortality and disease prevalence of the major infectious diseases and malnutrition, in Africa, Asia and Latin America, 1977–8*

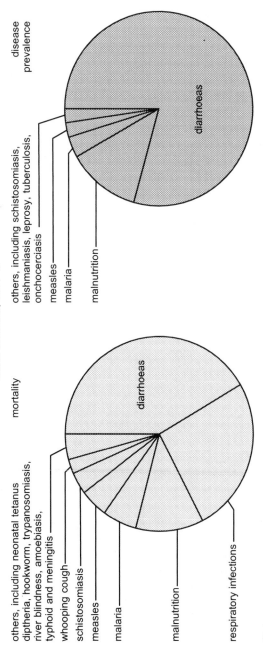

Notes:
* Disease prevalence excludes respiratory diseases for which no reliable estimates exist.
** Based on estimates from the World Health Organisation and its Special Programme for Research and Training in Tropical Diseases, confirmed or modified by extrapolations from published epidemiological studies performed in well-defined populations (Walsh and Warren (1979) Table 1).

Source: Open University (1985) Figure 3.3, p. 19.

Autonomy and mental illness

We have seen that there is more to the necessary conditions for successful social participation than the absence of physical disease. To begin with, it is clear from Table 9.1 that mental illness (including senile dementia, depression and phobias) is a major contributor to disability in contemporary Britain. We have contended in Chapter 4 that a culture-free concept of mental illness can be constructed in terms of impairments to rationality. Yet its further operationalisation requires us to return to some of the problems raised there (Busfield, 1986, ch. 2).

The fact that the aetiology of most mental illnesses is unknown or disputed means that they are commonly diagnosed using a syndrome of symptoms together with details about the personal and social background of patients, rather than physical measurement. Hence the consistency of the diagnosis is more often open to dispute than with physical disease. Also, despite our earlier optimism on the subject, there is evidence that the experiences and symptoms of mental illness differ across cultures, even where the medical profession is using the *same* model of mental illness in all of them. For example, the symptoms associated with depression have been found by many studies to vary between cultures. Non-Western 'sociocentric' cultures exhibit lower frequencies, or the complete absence of, certain components of depression common in Western 'egocentric' cultures, such as guilt and thoughts of suicide. However, at the same time, they exhibit higher frequencies of certain somatic symptoms (Marsalla, 1985, p. 303; Beiser, 1985).

Despite these problems, careful comparative research has shown that in all cultures serious mental illness impairs social participation. This is revealed by the *common core* of disabling symptoms found by all the studies to underly these variations in experience. For example, a study of depression among Senegalese, New Yorkers, and South-East Asian refugees in Canada, using a careful lexicon of culture-specific ways of expressing distress together with other means of ensuring translatability, found significant differences in symptoms. Yet underlying these differences were many experiences in common, including hopelessness, indecisiveness, a sense of futility and anergia. Among the somatic symptoms were palpitations, dizziness, lack of breath and persistent poor health (Beiser, 1985). The WHO Collaborative Study on Depression

(1983b) found that patients from five countries experienced high frequencies of sadness, joylessness, anxiety, tension, lack of energy, loss of interest, difficulty in concentrating and feelings of inadequacy. Again, reviewing a variety of cross-cultural studies of schizophrenia, Murphy (1982, ch. 4) concluded that, though cultural variations in symptoms and the development of the condition are substantial, schizophrenia sufferers exhibit common features in all societies for which we have information. Valid comparisons *can* be drawn about the incidence of disablement accompanying diagnosed schizophrenia in different societies.

Indeed, there has been considerable progress in the development and acceptance of uniform international taxonomies of mental disorder during the last four deacdes (Busfield, 1986, pp. 42). The two major schemas are the mental disorder sections of the International Classification of Diseases and the American Psychiatric Association's Diagnostic and Statistical Manual of Mental Disorders (DSM-III). Though there are some interesting differences between them which have yet to be resolved, they constitute a real achievement in operationalising the cross cultural diagnosis of mental disorder (Beiser, 1985, pp. 289–90). Using these diagnostic categories, comparisons can be made of the impairments to autonomy across countries and groups.

This said, in practice there are even greater defects in using administrative and survey data to chart the transcultural prevalence of mental disorder than is the case with physical disease.[4] Future indicators will require a variety of sources to fill the gaps (Warr, 1987, ch. 3). But this is to suggest that they can in principle be filled, building on the foundation of already existing universalisable measures.

Learning and cognitive skills

Now let us turn to the second component of personal autonomy – learning and cognitive skills. We have argued in Chapter 4 that the degree of comprehension individuals have of themselves and their culture depends on the *understanding* which they have of the knowledge and rules of that particular culture, along with their ability to reason consistently about them. Many basic skills will be common to all cultures, including language and basic motor social skills – those necessary to join in 'constitutive activities' of the sort introduced in Chapter 5. Despite criticisms of his work, Piaget does provide evidence that there are some general stages of cognitive development through which the human infant normally passes, at least up to the age of 2, while always stressing the interplay of biology and social environment in this development (Piaget, 1952; Dasen, 1977). The acquisition of language, about which more in a moment, is widely recognised as the most crucial cognitive skill enabling individuals to impose order and understanding on their world.

Beyond these common components, however, the competences required by different cultures will vary so much that again we are faced with difficulties in operationalisation. Clearly the capacity for thinking about and doing new things must be contextualised in relation to the practical demands on particular individuals. The ability to operate a computer will contribute little to a person's basic autonomy in a subsistence economy, and the same applies to agricultural skills in post-industrial societies. To the degree that an individual's patterns of learning conform to such specific demands, his autonomy will be either helped or hindered; he will either be disabled or not.

To begin with, then, measures of learning must be *culturally specific yet 'objective'*. In other words, the competences designated as central in any culture will be those necessary to enable members to understand and interpret the rules of that culture – to possess the potential to participate successfully in that culture in a way which will both win the respect of their peers and strengthen their own self-respect. For example, the percentage of young people in Britain who lack the linguistic, numerical and scientific skills to prepare them for the employment tasks available can in principle be computed and compared with with other Western countries (Prais and Wagner, 1985; Finegold and Soskice, 1988). In the industrialised world, the level of formal education achieved – as charted by the International Standard Classification of Educational Development (ISCED) – may provide a valid comparable indicator of such learning (UNESCO, 1974; OECD, 1986, ch. 2). Yet this will not be applicable to other social settings where different indicators will be required.

Underlying these contrasts, however, will be certain skills common to all or most societies. Let us return to *language*. It is generally accepted by educationalists that self conception and the potential for intellectual growth go hand in hand with fluency of language use. The world does not present itself through experience which is already, as it were, conceptually prepackaged. Order and understanding must be imposed via the medium of language. For this reason, the richness of someone's language is influenced by, and in turn influences, the extent and variety of their world, along with what they can and cannot successfully do within it (Doyal and Harris, 1986, chs 4–6; Freire, 1985, ch. 2). The cognitive dimension of autonomy expands in relation to linguistic proficiency.[5]

Essential to this process in societies using a written and not just a spoken language is *literacy* – the ability to read, say, an official form and write a letter of complaint about it (Coombs, 1985, pp. 52–7, 279–81; Carr-Hill, 1986, p. 300). To keep individuals from becoming literate in literate societies, therefore, not only artificially limits their autonomy through constraining their volition and imagination. It also cuts them off from their inscribed cultural heritage – its history, literature, skills – and its current political and social life. It would, of course, be foolish to underestimate the autonomy of people who are illiterate. They may be superbly creative from a variety of cultural and technical perspectives and highly regarded by their families and peers. Even so, it is not ethnocentric to claim that their autonomy would in principle be increased by the expanded consciousness and intellectual ability that literacy provides. This is why so many illiterate people struggle to study – often under difficult circumstances – to acquire this skill. Indicators of literacy are critical elements in a cross-cultural index of autonomy, for all but a few of today's cultures. The latest estimates suggest that nearly 900 million adults, the majority of them women, are denied this most basic competence (UNDP, 1990, p. 27).

Other common skills, such as basic mathematics and knowledge of the physical and biological sciences, are being demanded by the forces of internationalisation in the world economy. While these cannot be conceived as culture-free characteristics of human knowledge, their empirical necessity in the modern world lends support to the use of those educational indicators which measure competences in these fields. Notwithstanding the methodological problems (see Spearitt, 1990) cross-cultural measures of these skills are being developed by educational researchers. For example, the proportion of 13 year olds able to solve identical intermediate-level mathematical problems was found to vary from 40 per cent in South Korea to 18 per cent in the UK and 9 per cent in the USA, according to one recent study (IAEP, 1988, p. 17; cf. IAEEA, 1988). In other words, the expansion of the global economy is homogenising the demand for certain intellectual competences in a way that makes this component of autonomy increasingly comparable across the world. Yet this is superimposed upon a wide diversity of specific skills which also contribute to personal autonomy in particular cultural settings. An ideal set of measures should capture both the common and the variable elements.

In all of these ways the cognitive component of autonomy embraces the intellectual and physical skills required to participate in those activities deemed of cultural importance. As Naroll (1983, p. 136) puts it, this entails a positive vision of self-respect and of respect by others:

> To gain and hold esteem, a man or woman must perform skilfully and conscientiously the social roles assigned to him or her by the culture. A person who knows these roles and performs them well – who understands and assumes the full social responsibilities called for in the moral code of his or her people – is said by the Chinese to have 'ren'. In Yiddish, such a person is called a 'mensch', a *real* person. A mensch, a person with ren, gains respect in the eyes of family, friends, and neighbours. And so gains his or her own self-respect.

To be denied the cognitive capacity for such self-respect is to be fundamentally disabled and seriously harmed, irrespective of who you are or where you live.

Social roles and opportunities to participate

Thus who an individual is – how they are regarded by themselves and others – is partly a reflection of the sorts of things they regularly and recurringly do. We have argued that human autonomy also entails the *opportunity* to participate in some form of socially meaningful activity. To be denied the capacity for potentially successful social participation is to be denied one's humanity. Someone may be perfectly healthy in body and mind, and well equipped with culturally relevant knowledge, yet unable to realise these capacities through lack of opportunity. Prisoners by definition have their autonomy curtailed, however creative and healthy they may be in all other respects. Having social roles is a universal attribute of human autonomy, notwithstanding the diversity of cultural expectations about how they are defined and allocated. The roles associated with the four societal preconditions identified in Chapter 5 are common to all social groupings above a certain size, and consequently hold great significance in all cultures. Thus it is the opportunity to participate successfully in roles relating to all four of these societal processes to which we should turn to operationalise this aspect of autonomy in a cross-cultural way.

Threats to autonomy can stem from two quarters: role deprivation and role stress (Marsalla *et al.*, 1985, p. 312; Warr, 1987, ch. 12). The former refers to exclusion from any socially significant activity, in particular from all four of our universal social roles. The latter refers to an unmanageable conflict between different social roles such that the opportunity to do well in any of one of them is threatened. Let us illustrate both threats to social participation via two case-studies: unemployment and women's 'dual burden'.

Across all societies, probably the most important type of activity is *labour* – where people translate a part of themselves into something which they produce or maintain or, more often, help others to produce and maintain. Labour in this sense can be either manual or mental, and takes two forms: paid or unpaid. *Paid labour* is particularly important for individual autonomy in most societies because the income that it creates provides direct access to other intermediate needs. According to Freud (1961, p. 80), paid employment is our most important tie to reality. Further, as Barrington Moore (1978, ch. 1) has powerfully argued, deliberate participation in the overall division of labour in one's society is a crucial component in the evaluation of self-worth.

The importance of opportunities to participate in activities associated with societal production is illustrated by evidence on the way mental health suffers with unemployment – evidence which has accumulated at an alarming rate in the 1980s as unemployment itself has mushroomed in many parts of the First and Third Worlds. A recent survey of cross-sectional studies, conducted mainly in advanced Western countries since 1960, reveals a persistent association between unemployment and poor psychological ill-health on 13 different measures, including affect, experience of strain, negative self-esteem, anxiety, depressed mood, psychological distress, neurotic disorder and suicide (Warr, 1987, ch. 11; cf. Smith, 1987).

Research evidence is also clear on why enforced unemployment has this effect. Jahoda (1982, p. 59) sums up most of the benefits of paid employment, other than the receipt of income, as follows: 'The imposition of a time structure, the enlargement of the scope of social experience into areas less emotionally charged than family life, participation in a collective purpose or effort, the assign-ment... of status and identity, and regular activity'. Notwithstand-ing the negative impact of some forms of work on emotional and cognitive competence (discussed in the next chapter), such findings show how harmful to conceptions of the self is *exclusion* from this type of social participation.

Cross-cultural indicators of opportunities to participate in employment, or of barriers to this, are difficult to construct. Comparative data on unemployment, or economic participation rates, are strewn with problems, especially in nations where formal labour markets are poorly developed (Godfrey, 1986, ch. 1). Though the ILO regularly publishes such statistics, they ignore the extensive participation in the informal labour market, along with subsistence agriculture. Similarly, we lack reliable indicators of the status attached to reproductive activities, and of the freedom of different groups to choose or not to choose this social role. Yet our understanding of these weaknesses, against the background of the information which we do possess, suggests the sorts of indicators which might be developed.

The second threat to successful participation is role stress – an unmanageable conflict between the demands of two or more social roles which inhibits successful participation in any of them. Far and away the most important practical example of this is the dual burden of productive and reproductive labour mainly faced by women. In Chapter 5 it was argued that reproductive labour is a universal societal precondition for successful basic need-satisfaction and in most societies the care and socialisation of children is an apparently valued social role. Yet so often in practice its functional necessity and moral worth conflict with its unpaid status, and with the more valued role of paid labour. Throughout the First, Second and Third Worlds the evidence is overwhelming that women increasingly labour under a dual burden of responsibility for unpaid domestic work as well as paid employment. The growing research on domestic work shows that the resulting tension between reproductive and productive labour is one factor which can induce high levels of anxiety, overload and depression in women in Western societies, and thus impair still further their ability to participate successfully in their form of life (Warr, 1987, pp. 230–1).

For many people it is participation in our other two societal preconditions – cultural transmission, and the framing and enforcement of social rules – which constitutes a socially significant activity, and this too requires charting in a cross-culturally valid way. Perhaps the best single indicator of the opportunity for such participation is the amount of 'free time' they have available, after satisfying personal and family needs (sleep, meals, personal hygiene, domestic work) and contracted activites (work or study). Time budgets reveal large variations in this potential for participation, according to gender, family size and occupation, in particular (OECD, 1986, ch. 4; Seager and Olson, 1986, #13). Many disadvantaged groups throughout the world face an unenviable choice between no work and excessive hours of work, both of which inhibit these broader forms of participation. In particular, time budget studies graphically illustrate the obstacles to broader social participation which women encounter as a result of their dual burden.

Critical autonomy

In raising the issue of the direct or indirect control which individuals have over the cultural and political rules of their form of life, we confront much broader issues about freedom and autonomy and the positive and negative freedom which different groups require to pursue their life goals. So far, we have focused on the universal conditions for effective participation in any social group. We still need to consider how to operationalise those second-order processes which enable people to situate and challenge the particular rules into which they are born, or, for whatever reason, find themselves. Critical autonomy entails the capacity to compare cultural rules, to reflect upon the rules of one's own culture, to work with others to change them and, *in extremis*, to move to another culture if all else fails. For now, let us focus just on the educational conditions for critical autonomy. The others will be addressed in Chapter 11.

Just as there is more to physical health than survival, so there is more to the cognitive aspects of individual autonomy than culturally specific skills or even literacy and the other skills associated with constitutive activities. It must also entail the teaching of *different* cultural traditions and the provision of a forum where these can be openly discussed and debated. But how can something as open-ended as the educational component of critical autonomy be operationalised and measured? We suggest two building blocks to begin with. The first is access to the rules and knowledges of other cultures. A good indicator would be knowledge of a standard international language. There are probably about 4000 distinct living languages in the world today but a majority of the world's population speak one of just five: English, Chinese, Hindi, Spanish and Russian (Crystal, 1987, pp. 286–9). Second, there is the motivation and understanding to take advantage of this – an appropriate curriculum to enable people to explore other cultures and make sense of what they find there. To argue that people from any culture do not need access to the classics of literature of other cultures, or to the contemporary vocabulary of science and technology, is to lapse into particularly destructive forms of both dogmatism and relativism. Again, it can make no sense of the intense personal sacrifices made, for example, by many uneducated families in traditional cultures to provide access for their children to such cognitive liberational potential. We discuss what the realisation of such potential might mean for educational practice in the next chapter.

In short, learning plays a dual role in enhancing autonomy. First, it provides (or rather could provide) the linguistic and practical skills and the appropriate knowledge to enable individuals to participate successfully within their own culture. Second, it can begin to release individuals from the confines of that culture and provide them with the conceptual wherewithal to evaluate it in the light of knowledge about the other cultural practices which have emerged on our planet. It is only in this sense that they can at least be regarded as having *chosen* their normative environment, even though they may still not have the opportunity physically to leave it. Thus higher learning leads on and out from autonomy which is blinkered by one cultural tradition, towards critical, liberational autonomy and the satisfaction of Maslow's 'highest' need for self-actualisation.

This vision of autonomous liberation constrasts dramatically with the repressiveness of many cultural practices and illustrates the potential conflict between what we may call internal and critical autonomy. Successful participation may entail accepting the unacceptable: performing roles which undermine critical autonomy even as they facilitate participation in a particular culture. An example from certain groups in Africa and the Middle East is female circumcision and other practices harmful to the physical and mental health of women. Another example is the claim on time and the sheer mindlessness of much contemporary television which can be argued to constitute a formidable barrier to self-emancipation and the enhancement of critical autonomy. According to Baudrillard television culture no longer reflects signifieds but signs. Media and masses simulate each other in a cycle of 'hyperreality' divorced from any end purposes in meaning (Baudrillard, 1983, pp. 98–9). Leiss argues that in these circumstances: 'Previous categories of need dissolve, and the resulting fragments are subjected to regular reshuffling into new patterns ... the sense of satisfaction and well-being becomes steadily more ambiguous and confused' (Leiss, 1976, pp. 88–9).

Of course, against this it can be argued that, by dissolving older particular forms of cultural identity, mass communication has facilitated the emergence of more universalist identities of communicative rationality as conceived by Habermas and discussed in Chapter 7. Yet such arguments must be weighed against the danger to individuals of the consequent devaluations of meaning and language (Lash and Urry, 1987, pp. 288–92, 296–300). To avoid ethnocentric dogmatism, sensitive measures of critical human autonomy must take such factors into account through identifying the potential modes of cognitive and emotional participation within all cultures and the artifical constraints which inhibit individuals from joining in.

We have argued that individuals have a basic need for physical health and autonomy which can be operationalised in the ways outlined above. Table 9.2 brings together our suggested cross-cultural indicators of both. Except for life expectancy, all of these are negative. That is to say, they measure a lack of empirical components of health and autonomy. Of course, several indicators are not available, even for wealthy countries, let alone the Third World. This is especially true of measures of autonomy. If our theory is correct, however, it provides an outline of the direction which research into such indicators should take.

Table 9.2   *Suggested indicators of basic need-satisfaction*

Basic need components	*Suggested indicators*
Physical health	
Survival chances	α Life expectancy at various ages (including disaggregated and distributional measures)
	α Age-specific mortality rates, especially infant and under-5 mortality rates
Physical ill-health	β Prevalence of disabilities, according to severity
	β Prevalence of children suffering from developmental deficiencies, according to severity
	β Prevalence of people suffering from serious pain
	β Morbidity rates for various disease categories
Autonomy	
Mental disorder	β Prevalence of severe psychotic, depressive and other mental illness
Cognitive deprivation	χ Lack of culturally relevant knowledges
	α Illiteracy
	β Lack of attainment in mathematics, science and other near-universal basic skills
	β Absence of skill in world language
Opportunities for economic activity	β Unemployment, and other measures of exclusion from significant social roles
	β Lack of 'free time', after accounting for productive and reproductive activities.

Notes

α   Reasonably reliable universal or near-universal data.
β   Data for few countries only, but where there is a clear idea of operationalisation.
χ   More speculative suggestions for indicators.

10

Intermediate Needs

In Chapter 8 we introduced the notion of 'universal satisfier characteristics': those 'inputs' which, according to the best available knowledge, contribute positively to the 'output' of individual health and autonomy in all cultures. We identified eleven such characteristics, which we called 'intermediate needs'. In this chapter, we shall elaborate on each of these, trying to do two things. First, its inclusion will be justified by referring to the scientific evidence linking particular universal satisfier characteristics to either physical health or autonomy as they have been operationalised in the preceeding chapter. Often there is no sharp dividing line between the two: a 'physical health satisfier' like nutrition will also affect cognitive and emotional development if seriously deficient, while an 'autonomy satisfier' like childhood security will also affect physical health if seriously deficient. Second, we shall specify cross-cultural indicators for each intermediate need or, where these are unsatisfactory or unavailable, propose alternatives.

To avoid becoming physically ill, people must live in a healthy environment and have access to a range of goods and services of sufficient quantity and quality. In other words, a necessary condition for the physical health of each individual is a number of inputs which mediate between them and their environment. Each related intermediate need will have a material base which will be identifiable within the terms of biomedical understanding. We shall group these into the following five categories:

1 adequate nutritional food and clean water
2 adequate protective housing
3 a non-hazardous work environment
4 a non-hazardous physical environment
5 appropriate health care.

Figure 10.1   *Social components of depression*

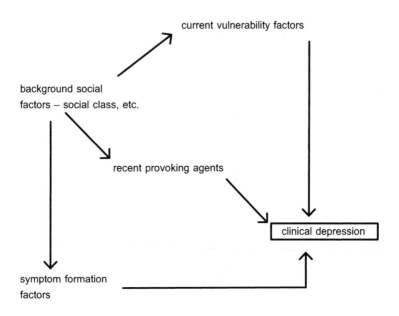

Source: Brown and Harris (1978a) p. 48 *et seq.*

Can we demarcate intermediate autonomy needs in a similar way? In the case of the *emotional* component of autonomy we shall begin with Brown and Harris's (1978a) important study of the social origins of depression among women. Employing a highly sophisticated methodology, they argue that depression and the loss of autonomy that it entails are 'an understandable response to adversity'. In classifying the various social components of this adversity, they employ the model shown in Figure 10.1. Recent provoking agents, such as divorce, a child leaving home or some other specific personal difficulty perceived to be long-term, act as sufficient conditions for the onset of depression. Current vulnerability factors, such as unemployment, the absence of a close and confiding relationship and the loss of a mother at an early age, play a role as necessary conditions for developing serious depression. Still other 'background social factors' predispose some *groups* to depression and thereby suggest their increased susceptibility to provoking agents and vulnerability factors. There are much higher rates of depression, for example, among working-class than among middle-class women. Finally, symptom formation factors influence the severity of depression. They include the loss of significant others, the age at which the loss occurred and the number and degree of past experiences of depression. While it may well be true that the precise value of the variables in their model will vary with culture – for example, the emotional significance of specific members of the family – there seems little reason to doubt its overall applicability across cultures.[1]

Of course, we realise that Brown and Harris's research concerned women only. However, in our search for universal needs which both sexes share, it still seems to us to be highly suggestive. From their model we can extract four social factors which inhibit mental health: an emotionally deprived childhood, the loss or absence of significant others, insecurity and economic deprivation. In turn this suggests that we can identify four further intermediate needs which contribute to an enhancement of emotional autonomy:

6 security in childhood
7 significant primary relationships
8 physical security
9 economic security.

To this list we must add a tenth – appropriate education – as a condition for the enhancement of the cognitive component of autonomy. The social determinants of access to valued social roles – our third aspect of autonomy – are held over for discussion in the following chapter.

Lastly, there are certain biological differences within the human species which require specific intermediate needs for all who share those characteristics. The most important is the sex difference between women and men, though of course over the millennia an enormous weight of social differentiation has accrued to this biological difference. The most notable implication of this fact for our theory is that the capacity of women to bear children entails a further category of intermediate need for them and them alone: the need for safe birth control and safe child-bearing.

Now let us consider each intermediate need in turn.

Food and water

In order to maintain bodily functions a minimum intake of energy
is required, known as the Basal Metabolic Rate. The FAO
calculates the 'critical' energy· needs of humans as 120 per cent
of this rate, a level which will vary according to age, sex, average
body weight, environmental temperature, level of physical activity
and other factors, such as pregnancy or breast-feeding. For an
average 65kg man aged 20–39, the critical energy need is estimated
to be 1800 calories a day; for a 55kg woman, 1500 calories a day.
However this is the absolute minimum required to sustain bodily
functioning. The energy 'needs' of a 'moderately active' person are
much higher according to the FAO – 3000 calories a day for the
man and 2200 for the woman. These are the best estimates of the
calorific needs to maintain health and to avoid the illness
associated with under-nutrition (FAO/WHO, 1973; Cutler, 1984,
p. 1121 *et seq.*). Of course specific amounts of other nutrients, such
as protein, vitamins and iodine, are also required to ensure growth
and health.

If someone consistently falls below this level, then chronic undernutrition ravages the body, lowers resistance to other illnesses and
produces weakness and debility which generate a downward spiral
of need-deprivation and an increasing incapacity to do anything
about it. There is a close association between calorific inadequacy
and malnutrition, the prevalence of babies with low birth-weight
and the prevalence of wasting in the second year of life.
Furthermore the lack of specific nutrients is associated with
specific diseases: for example vitamin A deficiency with xerophthal-
mia, causing blindness; other vitamin deficiency with beri-beri,
pellagra and scurvy; and iodine deficiency with mental retarda-
tion, hearing and speech defects, spasticity and many other
difficulties (UNICEF, 1987, p. 121). Malnutrition is also a problem
in the developed world, where most people have enough to eat but
consume a range of things which violate their health needs in quite
different ways (Clutterbuck and Lang, 1982).

The most widespread indicator of nutritional adequacy is the
FAO calculation of daily per capita calorie supply as a percentage
of requirements. It reveals widespread unmet need in parts of the
Third World. For example, the FAO Fourth World Food Survey
(1977) found that 17 per cent of people in India fell below the

absolute minimum 'critical' energy intake as defined above (Cutler, 1984, p. 1129). Taking the numbers falling below the average calorific needs shows even more extensive nutritional deprivation. In sub-Saharan Africa in the early 1980s, for instance, the *average* daily calorie supply was only 91 per cent of requirements (World Bank, 1985, Table 24). These figures are however very crude: they calculate food supply and make an estimate for animal feed and food lost in processing and distribution. However, they do not take account of waste in cooking, nor of maldistribution between classes and other groups within a country or members of households. Furthermore, the FAO/WHO estimates of calorific requirements themselves have been criticised on various grounds. In a useful survey, Sen (1984, p. 351), for example, argues that there is a danger of circular reasoning in linking these with physical characteristics such as body weight. This can result in underestimates of the relative malnutrition of women.

For these reasons it would be wise to buttress indicators of food intake with more direct measures of the actual consequences of food disparity. One such is the WHO estimates of the proportion of children suffering from wasting and acute malnutrition, defined as abnormally low weight-to-height ratios. These show that in many of the poorest countries more than one in ten children under 5 suffer from severe malnutrition (UNICEF, 1987, Table 2).[2] More sensitive indicators are needed if deficiency in consumption of other nutrients and if malnutrition in more affluent countries is to be charted.

Adequate and replenishable supplies of safe water are a complementary need. The drought which often accompanies modern famines also brings with it acute thirst and dehydration which can kill and damage more quickly than lack of food. Yet even where water is plentiful in the Third World, it is not necessarily either accessible or safe. Many infectious diseases are specifically water-borne and spread through lack of clean water. It is estimated, for example, that in 1975 diarrhoeal diseases caused between 5 and 18 million deaths in Asia, Africa and Latin America, and by 1980 the WHO claimed that 80 per cent of all illness in the world was due to exposure to contaminated water. These diseases affect children in particular and contribute most to their high rates of mortality. This represents a monumental amount of illness for those affected but also underlines the plight of millions of women who must provide water everyday for their families. They spend large amounts of time in this way, often in a weakened state from illness generated by the very water they carry (Agarwal, 1981, pp. 29–32).

In charting unmet water needs it is now generally accepted that, while purity is important, quantity of water is the first priority. One ILO study proposes 21 litres per person per day as a desirable target, or 112 litres per person per day on average if unequal distribution is taken into account (Stewart, 1985, p. 124). In a related way, the WHO estimates the numbers who have access to adequate, safe drinking water (see UNICEF, 1987, Table 3). Once again, however, more sensitive indicators are required, which would chart the presence of lead, mercury, nitrates and other contaminants in water supplies throughout the world.

Housing

Adequate housing is the next important intermediate need which must be satisfied if illness is to be avoided. On the face of it, what constitutes adequacy here is more open to cultural relativity than food. It might be argued that given the wide social variation in what is regarded as a 'dwelling' – not to mention climatic variations – any attempt to find a common yardstick of adequacy must be doomed from the start. Some have argued that the concept of the slum is impregnated with 'Northern' values (Drakakis-Smith, 1979); others that Western standards have dictated quite inappropriate policies in meeting the housing needs of the Third World (Turner, 1972). The UN (1977, p. 3) has declared that housing standards should be guided by nations' own climatic, economic, technical and social circumstances. All of these views reflect valid concerns. Do they then rule out the recognition of some universal housing characteristics common to all people? We believe there are three satisfier characteristics related to housing which, if not met, are everywhere inimical to physical or mental health.

First, a dwelling must offer reasonable protection from climatic extremes, from exposure and from pests and disease-carrying vectors. It should be able to withstand the normal demands of weather, provide adequate sanitation and, in colder climates, appropriate heating and insulation. The most obvious index of a shortfall in accommodation is homelessness itself. Millions of people throughout the world sleep on pavements, under bridges or elsewhere in the open and are deprived of all these benefits at great cost to their health and autonomy.

Second, there is plentiful evidence that poor or non-existent sanitation contributes to the bacterial contamination of water supplies discussed above. One of the most debilitating parasitic diseases of underdevelopment – schistosomiasis – is caused by the urine of infected people contaminating a water supply that is then used by the uninfected for washing or swimming. Well over 200 million people suffer from this problem throughout the world. Disease can also be transmitted directly from human faeces without water contamination. Untreated infected waste creates a breeding ground for flies which can transport and deposit the deadly microbes it contains directly on food, or into the eye producing trachoma, for example – a disease affecting millions and often leading to partial or total blindness (Open University, 1985, chs 3, 4).

Third, dwellings which are overcrowded can also undermine the health of their occupants. Overcrowding involves the experience of excessive social demands and lack of privacy and has been linked to physical and psychological withdrawal and a general feeling of debilitation. Of course, overcrowding is associated throughout the world with poverty, racial discrimination and other factors which independently affect health. However, the effect of cramped housing itself remains strong even when these other influences are taken into account. The weight of evidence from different societies now suggests that overcrowding contributes, among other things, to respiratory illness, slow physical and cognitive development in children, and stress and depression in adults – all factors contributing to physical illness and impaired autonomy (Murie, 1983, ch. 1; Douglas, 1983, pp. 171–3).[3]

According to the Brundtland Report (1987, p. 250) much housing in the Third World is deficient on all these grounds:

Low income accomodation generally shares three characteristics. First, it has inadequate or no infrastructure and services – including piped water, sewers, or other means of hygienically disposing of human wastes. Second, people live in crowded and cramped conditions under which communicable diseases can flourish, particularly when malnutrition lowers resistance. Third, poor people usually build on land ill-suited for human habitation: floodplains, dusty deserts, hills subject to landslide, or next to polluting industries (cf. Hardiman and Midgley, 1982, ch. 8; Jones, 1990, ch. 4).

For example, outside Quito, Ecuador, large communities occupy flimsy shacks built on stilts above sewer marshes, connected by slippery planks where one step can spell death for a child (*The Economist*, 30 April 1983). Such conditions blatantly fail to meet our universal satisfier characteristics, yet social indicators to quantify housing needs are sparse. The WHO estimates suggest that a large majority of inhabitants in the Third World (85 per cent in rural areas in 1985) lack basic sanitation (UNICEF, 1987, p. 114). The only comparable global information on overcrowding comes from unreliable and out-of-date statistics on the number of persons per room, collected by the UN (UN, 1987, Table 4.5; UNDP, 1990, Table 17). There is little by way of other suitable cross-cultural indicators of housing need.

The situation is different in the richer countries. Though some housing in industrialised countries remains inferior, the general trend is one of marked improvement in both space and amenities since the Second World War. A recent Swedish study even proclaimed that 'when there is almost universal access to basic conveniences (running water, sewage drainage, toilets and central heating) it is no longer possible to measure the distribution and change in the housing standard with these indicators' (Erikson and Åberg, 1987, p. 5). Yet in Britain, due to inadequate heating and insulation, winter death rates among infants and elderly people are much higher than in summer – unlike the pattern in many other advanced nations with harsher climates (Douglas, 1983, p. 170). Once again, none of this implies that we view conventional Western housing *forms* as necessarily superior to others. Neither does it deny that official state definitions of housing need can sometimes be horribly wrong, evicting people from accommodation which they regard as satisfactory and housing them elsewhere in conditions which may actually harm their levels of physical health and autonomy. The main point is that such mistakes can be identified by reference to precisely the same criteria whatever the specific context in which they occur.

A non-hazardous work environment

Aside from the home, the other aspect of their environment which most immediately affects an individual's physical health and autonomy is their workplace. Work conditions can pose serious harm in three ways. First, excessive hours of work can physically and mentally enervate people. Especially since the Industrial Revolution this has been a threat to those in the weakest positions in the labour market, whether nineteenth-century English factory children or twentieth-century child labourers in Third World sweatshops, whether Southern slaves or Sri Lankan estate labourers, whether paid men or unpaid women. In principle, time budget studies can be used to chart those working excessive hours, as discussed in the previous chapter.

Second, a hazardous work environment can threaten physical health via occupational injury and disease. Occupational illnesses fall into two categories. On the one hand are those specifically associated with certain types of production process and/or materials. For example, the incidence of bladder cancer in the dye industry has risen with the use of betanaphthalamine (Doyal and Epstein, 1983, p. 32). In the agricultural sector, especially in the Third World where there is little effective government regulation, the use of toxic pesticides poses a special threat (Bull, 1982; Eckholm, 1982, ch. 6). On the other hand, some of the more common diseases such as bronchitis are less strongly correlated with particular occupations, making it more difficult causally to link the one with the other. However, when we focus on the distribution of deaths from specific causes by occupational class, the degree to which work constitutes a contributing factor seems clear (Open University, 1985, ch. 10). A second method of charting harmful work conditions is directly to assess the presence in the work environment of hazards, such as dust, noise, exposure and air pollution. Unfortunately most of this information is available only for certain Western nations (OECD, 1985, Table 16.1). Data for the UK shows that these hazards threaten most those who are the least well-off – a pattern likely to be universal.

Thirdly, certain forms of work can impair the autonomy of workers. De-skilled, excessively repetitive and machine-like work almost by definition cannot stimulate a person's powers or provide a positive sense of self. Warr's extensive summary of research findings shows that opportunities for control, skill use and variety together and singly affect well-being. In particular, lack of control over job content induces depression, anxiety and low self-esteem. Work demands which are both too high and too low can also undermine well-being as defined in Chapter 9 above (Warr, 1987, chs 5, 7). Undoubtedly many people in the world today have their autonomy impaired rather than stimulated by the work they are forced to do, but at present we have no idea how many. Despite much theorising on deskilling, the evidence is ambiguous that jobs in modern industrial societies are on balance leading to a reduction of autonomy at work. Indeed, some evidence from Sweden suggests that overall job autonomy has risen over the last two decades, though mental strain has also increased (Åberg, 1987; cf. Cooley, 1980, ch. 2).

A non-hazardous physical environment

More generally, the wider physical environment itself contributes to our health – or undermines it. Even in situations of satisfactory provision of water, nutrition, sanitation, housing and occupation, a hazardous environment can still maim and kill. We have already seen how carcinogenic pollutants at work can cause cancer among an otherwise affluent and healthy population. They can also damage the environment more generally as disasters in modern industries, such as those at Bhopal and Chernobyl, have recently demonstrated.

When we focus on water and air pollution, the situation is similar. Here one culprit is industrial effluent. Even toxic wastes which are not dumped directly into streams and rivers but onto land sites can pose severe problems, because they can leach into the surrounding water table, the sudden appearance of illness being the only indicator of their presence. Similarly, air pollution takes its toll, especially in areas of dense population where there are high concentrations of industry and/or motor cars. Despite a vast improvement in air pollution levels in Britain and other Western countries in the past three decades, the correlation between certain respiratory diseases and remaining concentrations of sulphur emissions still gives cause for concern (Stern *et al.*, 1984, pp. 110–12).

Such environmental problems are even more acute in parts of the underdeveloped world. In 1980, 15 000 inhabitants of part of Cubatao, Brazil – referred to by environmental groups as 'the valley of death' – were relocated because of the mutagenic effects of the high levels of atmospheric contamination. A similar illustration of extreme water pollution is the Bogota River in Colombia, one of the most contaminated in the world. Here huge levels of organic and inorganic effluent – with particularly large amounts of arsenic, copper and mercury – enter the river upstream to be drunk downstream by people in the nearby villages. Much evidence testifies to the fact that these are by no means isolated incidences and are inseparable from the social and economic exploitation accompanying the development process (Eckholm, 1982, ch. 6). What is clear is that the criteria by which environmental problems can be evaluated are the same for everyone. DDT, for example, is just as bad for an Islamic Mullah as it is for the Pope and for precisely the same biological reasons.

The quality of the natural environment is now charted in a much more satisfactory manner than a decade ago by such international organisations as the UN (1987) and OECD (1987). Indicators of air pollution, including emissions of carbon monoxide, nitrogen oxides and sulphur oxides, are crucial in charting general environmental degradation (see Chapter 11). Better for our purposes here are the actual concentrations of dangerous pollutants, such as smoke particles and nitrogen oxides in populated areas.[4] Water quality is increasingly monitored in many nations, and data is also available on the coverage of waste treatment plants. There are many other sources of environmental degradation which impact on physical health or autonomy: for example, traffic noise is a growing threat in many parts of the world. Finally, health surveys can directly monitor levels of exposure to dangerous substances such as lead. Employing such knowledge, the UN and other international agencies lay down minimum safe levels for exposure to many pollutants, which enables the numbers exposed to higher levels to be charted.

Health care

Acting on the recognition of the intermediate needs described above would help reduce many of the hazards which violate the basic need of individuals throughout the world for physical health. Yet the availability of medical care – preventive, curative and palliative – will always be a necessary additional input to good health. It has become a truism that a major part of the decline in mortality in the First World over the last century has been due more to environmental improvement than to the provision of curative medicine (McKeown, 1976). But we have already argued the moral case for therapeutic treatment whenever it can improve people's long-term health. There is no question, therefore, but that access to effective medical services employing the best available techniques constitutes an intermediate need. Yet we cannot devise indicators of access to 'effective' health care unless we say a little more about the nature of different healing systems and of 'Western' medicine in particular.

Western curative medicine is not, of course, unproblematic and there can be no doubt that it has been widely abused in violation of individual health needs. Despite the expenditure of vast resources, biomedical research has led to little effective treatment for the killer diseases of developed societies – cancer, heart disease and hypertension. Furthermore the dangers of modern medicine are legion. There are the iatrogenic problems directly induced by doctors – through the overprescription of a wide range of potentially harmful and/or addictive drugs. There are also indirect hazards, including what has sometimes been called the medicalisation of health problems – the use of the biomedical model to obscure the economic and political causes of ill health. The more conservative medical research is, the more it will restrict itself to the conceptualisation and treatment of illness *only* in specific aetiological terms – identifying the cause of tuberculosis only as a specific infection, for example, and ignoring avoidable environmental circumstances. This can lead to health resources being spent on expensive diagnostic and curative technologies rather than on preventive measures which are more cost effective. Finally, the degree to which medicine is dominated by technology has led to serious problems with the doctor–patient relationship. Patients are often mystified by and alienated from the vast array of apparatus at the doctor's disposal. And since doctors gain much of their diagnostic information from machines rather than from communication with patients, they do not necessarily develop the very communicational skills which are required for effective therapy and for health education and promotion. The end result is even further dependence on doctors for the individual management of health problems, a reinforcement of their economic and social status and an inducement to oppose needed changes in their professional practice (Doyal and Doyal, 1984).

Yet dramatic as they are, none of these problems entails the wholesale condemnation of medicine premised upon the biomedical model of disease. For one thing, curative medicine often does cure! The fact that an overemphasis on the specific aetiology of disease can detract from its environmental, political and economic causes does not obviate therapeutic efficacy where it exists. Such success covers the obvious examples of diagnostic methodology and related technology, surgery, antisepsis, anaesthetics, antibiotics, vaccination and a range of strategies focused on the management of diagnosed illness – hormonal and chemical replacement therapies and the relief of pain in terminal care, to name but two. Thus even if much more emphasis were to be placed on the prevention of disease, cure and effective management would remain of the utmost importance in any system of medical care. Paradoxically, against the background of some claims that Western medicine is ethnocentric, those areas of the world where its therapeutic success has been most dramatic in recent times are Third World countries rent by infectious disease (Len Doyal, 1988, pp. 35–8). For example, potentially lethal bacterial infections are curable with antibiotics, and many effective preventive programmes have involved immunisation or other therapies which have resulted from biomedical understanding.

To claim that the biomedical model detracts from prevention, that it has been employed to nourish those very social relationships which help to create unhealthy environments, that it is not always cost effective or that it has an urban bias, suggests a programme of action to correct these distortions rather than one which would seek a new model of medicine altogether. It is clear that the present global priority should be *primary care*, designed to identify and treat illness at an early stage and to educate workers and users into the politics and practice of prevention (WHO, 1978, 1987; Open University, 1985, ch. 9). Given the expense of high technology medicine and the meagre health budgets of underdeveloped countries, there is no alternative in the short run.

Thus, the ideal social indicators for this intermediate need will chart people's access to appropriate health care. In practice, the most widely available and reliable indicators are for the *provision* of medical inputs. Though these are not ideal, research on international variation in life expectancy and infant mortality rates provides strong support for the view that primary health care provision can diminish mortality and associated disease (Stewart, 1985, ch. 7; Cumper, 1984, ch. 3). The provision of medical inputs, including doctors, nurses and paramedics *does* make a difference through the potential availability of cheap curative and preventive therapies. A crude but generally available indicator of equality of provision here is population per physician or per nurse. This has improved since 1965 in all regions of the world, but differences between countries have remained astonishingly wide – in Britain in 1980 there were 650 people per doctor compared with 69 390 in Ethiopia (World Bank, 1988).

For many poor people, however, the presence of health services means little if they are not accessible, owing either to geography or to cost. Direct indicators of health care *utilisation* are therefore important – the numbers immunised against diseases like tetanus, measles, polio and TB being especially relevant. Also useful, though less reliable, are the WHO's estimates of numbers of people with 'access to health services'. Paradoxically, access appears to vary inversely with need: in the early 1980s about two-thirds of people in countries with very high under-5 mortality rates had no such access (UNICEF, 1987, Parts 3, 4). The accessibility of health care also varies according to its method of organisation. In all countries, most people can only afford medical care above the most basic level if they are members of collective cost-sharing schemes, for which measures of effectiveness are also required (OECD, 1985, Table 1; Jones, 1990, ch. 6).

Security in childhood

A belief in the centrality of a secure childhood for the development of an autonomous adult personality is a core feature of all schools of psychology. Moreover, we know of no traditional belief system which does not also uphold this view, despite wide cultural variations in how children should be loved, taught and enabled – indeed in the very idea of childhood (Korbin, 1981, ch. 1; MacPherson, 1987, chs 3, 8). Accepting that a person's identity is continuous through time, such 'childhood needs' are in one sense constituent of a person's autonomy rather than an input into it. However, the length and centrality of childhood development justifies the separate identification of childhood security as an intermediate need, the satisfaction of which will influence levels of adult autonomy.

The awesome power which significant others have over us when we are young is summarised by Seligman (1975, p. 137):

> Human infants begin life more helpless than infants of any other species. In the course of the next decade or two, some acquire a sense of mastery over their surroundings; others a profound sense of helplessness... If a child has been helpless repeatedly, and has experienced little mastery, he will believe himself to be helpless in a new situation, with only minimal clues. A different child with the opposite experience, using the same clues, might believe himself to be in control. How early, how many, and how intense the experience of helplessness and mastery are will determine the strength of this motivational trait.

This is written by a leading exponent of behaviour as learned control or helplessness. However, few would dispute that it is those with whom the child most strongly identifies – as opposed to children themselves – who through their support and encouragement are most responsible for increases in autonomy. The Freudian tradition affirms this point, but offers a different and more far-reaching account of the psycho-dynamics involved.

What factors shape the growth of autonomy in children? A recent WHO study proposes a four-fold classification of the psycho-social needs of children, believed to be applicable across cultures and stages of development (WHO, 1982; Kellmer-Pringle, 1980). The first is the need for love and security. This is met initially by the child experiencing from birth onwards a stable, continuous, dependable and strongly affective relationship with parents or parent-substitutes. It does not preclude negative emotions so long as they do not involve excessive and/or arbitrary physical punishment or degradation. Young children have a need for consistent and dependable attitudes and behaviour if their sense of personal identity and worth is to flourish. It seems likely that the security of a known place and familiar routines are also important contributory factors here.

Second, there is a need for new experiences to foster cognitive, emotional and social development. Play is a crucial means by which children undertake this sort of early exploration and learning, and all children require the time and opportunities for it. Third, children need praise and recognition and positive feedback within a framework of clear rules which are perceived to be just. Fourth, there is the need gradually to extend responsibility to children, beginning with simple personal routines and moving on to more complex responsibilities towards others. Much is known, then, about the universal needs of children and how best to foster their satisfaction. Research on aggressiveness, for example, has found that authoritarian families tend to have the most aggressive children, but that permissive families do not have the least aggressive. Rather the latter appear to come from families where there are clear rules of behaviour combined with a warm loving relationship (Lieven, 1989).

Ideas of what constitutes good parenting will of course vary across cultures, and so, in consequence, will definitions of child abuse and neglect. This makes comparisons of societies as regards their treatment of children peculiarly hazardous (Channer and Parton, 1990). But we need to start with the fact that all cultures do have ideas and rules about what constitutes acceptable behaviour towards children. On this basis Korbin (1981) analyses 'idiosyncratic' child abuse and neglect which falls outside the self-defined bounds of any society. She argues that it is more prevalent where the following factors are present – a low cultural value attached to children; discrimination between groups of children, and against some groups such as illegitimate, orphaned or female children; inappropriate beliefs about the capacities of children at different developmental stages; and the absence of a wider network of kin and community beyond the immediate family concerned with child care. Other cross-cultural studies suggest that, while the use of some physical punishment in child-rearing is widespread, frequent punishment is more common in more complex societies (Levinson, 1989, chs 2, 4, 6).

In all parts of the world many children suffer a serious shortfall in the basic prerequisites for autonomous and healthy development, yet social indicators of this lack are woefully inadequate. In line with the 'vitamin model' adopted in Chapter 8, we are not using as a yardstick some notion of an 'optimal' childhood, even if such a thing could be defined. We know that children can often endure substantial neglect, insecurity and misfortune with their autonomy intact, even if the reasons for this are by no means understood. All we are looking for is the *minimal* quantum of security, stimulation, recognition and responsibility necessary to ensure the opportunity for optimal flowering of each individual's autonomy. In practice there is little information of any kind available, and we must rely on the crudest of proxy indicators.

A growing phenomenon about which there is some crude information concerns the 'street children' who live completely without family ties. It has been estimated that in the Third World some 100–200 million children live on the streets, with 40–50 million in Latin America and the Caribbean alone. Perhaps one third live independently, trying to support themselves materially, but returning home occasionally; while an estimated 7 per cent are abandoned and have no parent-figures to provide them with any psycho-social resources. The only state intervention in most cases is harsh and punitive – when the child eventually falls foul of the law (MacPherson, 1987, p. 204; cf. Allsebrook and Swift, 1989). In Rio de Janiero, they even have to contend with killer squads of hired gunmen who 'cull' these street children like so many vermin (*Guardian*, 21 April 1990). Limited but growing evidence is also available of the numerous ways in which children are abused and neglected in developed countries. A recent estimate of the prevalence of sexual abuse of children in Britain, for example, suggests that up to 10 per cent may have been affected (Bentovim and Vizard, 1988; Laurence, 1988). The continuing absence of data on such a crucial component of objective welfare is itself revealing – reflecting the veil of secrecy with which many aspects of family life are still surrounded.

Significant primary relationships

Another intermediate need is a set of *significant primary relationships* – a network of individual reinforcers who provide an educative and emotionally secure environment. The work of Brown and Harris, referred to above, indicates that the loss of a spouse or close friend, or significant isolation, can lead to a person becoming more vulnerable to depression and mental breakdown and can enhance its severity. It is useful here to distinguish (a) primary support groups and (b) close and confiding relationships. Naroll (1983) gathers together findings from an impressively wide range of societies and cultures to support a more general theory of 'moralnets' – those primary groups that serve as a normative reference group. Weakened moralnets, he argues, are correlated with mental illness, suicide, crime, child abuse, wife battering and many other indicators of arrested individual autonomy (Naroll, 1983, Part II).

It is likely that more people in developed, industrial societies are harmed by the absence of strong primary support groups than in Third World societies. Several British surveys, for example, have shown that about one fifth of elderly people experience a significant degree of isolation (Tinker, 1981, p. 163). On the other hand, a comprehensive Swedish survey using different measures could find no evidence that loneliness had increased between 1968 and 1981 and put the proportion affected at about 2 per cent (Axelsson,1987). Though there is little correlation between *number* of social contacts and a subjective feeling of loneliness (which is harmful to a positive sense of self), the latter is heavily influenced by the *quality* of social contacts, whether the absence of close friends or the loss of a lifetime companion. Moreover, the problem of loneliness is particularly acute for those who feel that nobody relies on them or, alternatively, who feel that they are in a situation of extreme dependence on others (Tinker, 1981, ch. 11). People living in residential homes can experience a bizarre combination of lack of privacy and utter isolation. A Manchester study of elderly people in homes, for example, found that many did little more than watch television and verbal interaction was extremely limited (Evans *et al.*, 1981, ch. 6). It cannot be doubted that such isolation harms the individual's sense of self and leads to a spiral of disablement and diminishing autonomy. The degrees to which different cultures tolerate or even promote isolation of this kind varies widely even within Western societies. It is much rarer, for example, in Italy than in Britain or the United States (Finch, 1989).

A close and confiding relationship may be a universal satisfier of similar importance. Even if individuals are in generally supportive social environments, their daily lives will inevitably be beset by a variety of problems. These need not always be very dramatic but at times they will be. Usually such problems present themselves as 'puzzles' in Kuhn's terms to be solved against the background of the conceptual and practical skills of one's paradigmatic culture and subculture(s) (Kuhn, 1962, ch. 4; cf. Doyal and Harris, 1986, ch. 1). As he argues, they only become a threat if they remain unsolved despite repeated attempts. Hence people require more than just a generally supportive social background for their autonomy to be maintained. This is the case for two reasons.

First, there are persistent failures which must be adjusted to and discussed at length both to ensure that their ego is not unrealistically impaired and to prepare them for future corrective action. This often requires a great deal of time and the highly textured emotional and intellectual support which can only come from someone who knows the individual extremely well. Second, because in their public lives actors are necessarily oriented toward their relationships with *others*, any detailed exploration of self – desires, beliefs, ambition, commitment, weakness, strength – is usually limited. This is where the private context of personal development becomes crucial. The depth, complexity and range of human potential is pretty much unlimited and its unravelling and cultivation is an essentially social activity. Consequently, the time and energy to facilitate both can only come from someone who is highly committed to the task and expects to be helped themselves in a reciprocal way. It is supportive relationships of this kind which define the private space of individual self-development. Their importance explains the dramatic and sometimes dangerous sense of loss that may be experienced when they disappear – however difficult and even unhappy such relationships may have been (Brown and Harris, 1978a, pp. 173–9; Freden, 1982, ch. 6). This may also explain the near-universal desire for a 'proper' funeral when loved ones die, a demand of workers and peasants the world over, despite the cost frequently involved (Streeten, 1984, pp. 973–4).

Social indicators of the presence of primary support groups are currently being developed, though the most readily available – data on people living alone – is the least valid. Information on the quantity of interaction with partners, relations and friends is more valuable; but again, too much social integration can be harmful to autonomy, particularly critical autonomy. The best indicators therefore are those that measure the *quality* of primary networks –

in particular, how much a person can rely on others when in need – and the *choice* people have in selecting their networks. At present such indicators are available only for a few high-income countries (Axelsson, 1987; Finch, 1989).

Economic security

Security is the next intermediate need which must be satisfied if individual autonomy is to be sustained and expanded. Without security of the person and of those primary possessions geared to the satisfaction of other basic needs, serious harm can occur. Research on helplessness, for example, suggests a close link between high levels of autonomy and a sense of control over the quality, constancy and consistency of one's environment (Seligman, 1975). That is to say, uncertainty about the consequences of intentional activity is destructive to both self-expression and creativity. Everything that we have said about the maintenance and development of individual autonomy has presupposed that actors can do two things. First, they can plan for and attempt to bring about a particular future – at least for themselves. And second, they can do so through a network of rules, rewards and human relationships which they assume will continue in more or less the same form in the immediate future. The result of insecurity in either context is trauma – a loss of external control and sense of self of dramatic proportions which can culminate in mental illness or even death. By far the quickest way to destroy someone's autonomy is arbitrarily to punish and humiliate them for no apparent reason, denying them any right of appeal. It is hardly surprisingly that such random acts of oppression constitute one of the few things which will generate a sense of outrage and injustice in all known cultures (Barrington Moore, 1978, ch. 2; cf. Bettelheim, 1986). Let us distinguish economic and physical security and look at each in turn.

Economic insecurity has been endemic throughout human history: the sudden loss of harvests, the unpredictable vagaries of the weather, the unforeseen death of cattle have always spelled disaster for the majority of humankind and continue to do so. Since the eighteenth century the capitalist industrial system has added to these threats a new source of economic insecurity: the loss by the proletariat of access to the means of production, the utter dependence on securing waged labour and hence the overwhelming threat of unemployment. In much of the developed world in the post-war years full employment policies, income maintenance programmes and state provision of social services have all – to varying degrees and with differing rates of success – mitigated some of the sources of insecurity in modern industrial societies (Esping-Andersen, 1990, ch. 2). But new forms of economic insecurity have also arisen – especially the potential of a permanent surplus population in both First and Third World countries with at best only a tenuous entitlement to economic subsistence.

Let us define economic insecurity as the objective risk of an unacceptable decline in someone's standard of living, where 'unacceptable' refers to a threat to their capacity to participate in their form of life. One relevant measure constructed by Esping-Andersen (1990, ch. 2) is an index of 'decommodification' to measure how far incomes are protected by collective income maintenance schemes – whether public or private – against contingencies such as old age, sickness, disability and unemployment. Another indicator is a participation-based measure of 'poverty' of the sort developed by Townsend. 'People may be said to be deprived if they do not have, at all, or sufficiently, the conditions of life – that is, the diets, amenities, standards and services – which allow them to play the roles, participate in the relationships and follow the customary behaviour which is expected of them by virtue of their membership of society'. Poverty can then be defined as the lack of resources (usually money resources) to obtain these conditions of life (Townsend, 1987, pp. 130, 140; cf. 1979, chs 1, 6). It is clear that freedom from poverty (if defined in this way) constitutes a universal satisfier characteristic – a necessary condition for people to be able to participate in their society and, if they so choose, to challenge its values.[5]

Comparable cross-national indicators of such poverty are rather underdeveloped. One crude measure is to use an agreed proportion of average income in a society as a poverty line, although it must be stressed that this is not ideal and does not entail acceptance of a crude 'relative' definition of poverty (Hedstrom and Ringen, 1987). Once an operational standard has been found, a 'headcount' measure of the numbers falling below it can be compiled.[6] Some such indicators are now available for several Western countries.

They show remarkable variations in the extent of economic insecurity between such countries. For much of the Third World, an even more minimal index of economic insecurity is often used. This computes the numbers of people falling below an 'absolute' poverty level, usually defined as that income below which a minimally adequate diet plus essential non-food items are not affordable. According to rough World Bank calculations for 1977–84, almost one half of the population of those low income countries for which information is available fall below this line, and high proportions are also found in some middle-income countries such as Ecuador and Malaysia (UNICEF, 1987, Table 6). Of course, such measures are woefully inadequate as indicators of economic security associated with optimum levels of physical health and autonomy. We return to this issue in Chapter 11.

Physical security

Physical insecurity – exposure to violence against individuals – can arise from the criminal activity perpetrated by one person against another or from the organised violence of the state. Yet in both cases there are serious obstacles to be faced in establishing a common metric of physical insecurity. Unless these are confronted, agreement about what constitutes physical security will not be possible between people upholding different moral values.

Concerning individual crime, there are well-known problems in defining it in culturally comparable ways and in evaluating the morality of criminal activity. Furthermore, if individuals are acting to protest against a moral order which they reject and/or in order to satisfy basic needs for which they have no other obvious source of fulfilment, then 'criminal' actions can be an expression of the strongest form of autonomy. The courageous protests of the Chinese students in 1989 is testimony to this point. Certainly, if the bystander rejects the same moral order then it will be tempting to regard such actions as progressive and laudable (Stankiewicz, 1980, ch. 2; cf. Smith, 1983, ch. 5).

Yet to yield to this temptation without taking into account the arbitrary threats which certain types of crime may pose to the personal security of others – perhaps including the bystander – cannot be successfully defended. For it is often the case that behind justifications which equate crime with rebellion is a conception of individual needs very like the one outlined in this book. If everyone has a right to the same level of basic need-satisfaction then this must apply as much to the victims of crimes as it does to those whose violated needs are employed to try to legitimate criminality. This is why terrorism and criminal activity against civilians are so inconsistent with the humanist rhetoric that sometimes fuels them (Johnson, 1982, ch. 8; cf. Geras, 1989).

Even if this and similar arguments for the commensurability of crime are accepted, there are still many well-known methodological and empirical problems in deriving indicators of physical insecurity from official statistics – problems which are compounded at the international comparative level (Bottomley and Pease, 1986, chs 1, 2). In the face of these difficulties there appear to be two ways forward. First, we can use official statistics on homicide as a proxy measure of threats to physical security stemming from other citizens. Homicide has a broadly comparable meaning across nations, is less influenced by differences in law and practice than other categories of crime and is reasonably accurately reported in all societies (Wallace, 1986). Second, these data need to be complemented by the victim studies developed in Britain and elsewhere in the last decade. Though not trouble-free, these provide more objective and comparable information than official statistics on several aspects of physical insecurity – whether caused by individual citizens or by agencies of the state (Bottomley and Pease, 1986, pp. 22–32).

In fact, violence at the behest of the state dwarfs that inflicted by individuals. Yet, to talk of the state being involved in crime opens the way to a host of philosophical problems, if the acts in question do not violate any laws. The advantage of equating justice with what happens to be on the statute books is the consequent ability to explain why the law has so dramatically altered over time and why it continues to vary between cultures. The disadvantage of such legal 'positivism' is its relativism and the consequent inability to make intelligible any conception of natural justice linked to the satisfaction of basic needs (Campbell, 1983, chs 2, 4). Without such a conception, the very idea of an unjust state would become contradictory, leading to absurd ethical consequences (e.g. the morality of the murder of Chinese students demonstrating peacefully and of other arbitrary acts of oppression, provided that they are allowed in law). For this reason and others which cannot be explored here, we shall assume that it does make sense to refer to unjust state violence.

Indicators of unjust state violence are, then, intellectually conceivable though they are frequently unavailable. Many peoples have experienced sporadic or sustained violence sponsored by the state either in the form of localised armed conflict or of execution, torture and imprisonment. Each year Amnesty International documents thousands of cases of people deliberately killed by government agencies acting beyond the limits of their national law – of executions that evaded the judicial process. How many others have had their physical and mental health destroyed by torture and imprisonment it is impossible to say, but the sort of indicators which would chart this can be readily envisaged (Amnesty International, 1983, 1984). Another source of data – on war deaths, available from the UN – does not and cannot incorporate views about the justice of the struggles which have shattered the lives and health of so many people, yet measurement of these forms of state violence must have their place among valid indicators of physical insecurity.

Education

Turning from the emotional to the cognitive component of personal autonomy we must now discuss the role of *education* in human well-being. The crucial role of learning, language and literacy in expanding autonomy has already been discussed in Chapter 9. UNESCO (1974) defines learning as 'any change in behaviour, information, knowledge, understanding, attitudes, skill or capacity which can be retained and cannot be ascribed to physical growth or to the development of inherited (instinctive) behaviour patterns'. We now need to address the contribution to this process which can be made by education – the system of teaching mainly young children and adolescents in formal institutions. Once again, however, we face both conceptual and methodological problems in evaluating education in a transcultural context.

In the Third and First Worlds, the 1960s and 1970s witnessed a growing distrust of orthodox-style state education in favour of what is called 'human-centred learning' and, in Brazil and elsewhere, 'education for liberation'. Following Freire (1985) and others, this encouraged a 'spontaneous' form of popular education which accorded total respect to popular culture and common sense. Yet this strategy has increasingly encountered philosophical contradictions and practical problems. More relevant and in tune with our theory is Gramsci's analysis which stresses both the unique knowledge of the 'educator-agent' and the valid elements in the everyday knowledge of the people.[7] This favours an education practice of direction coupled with the ability to listen and to utilise the experientially-grounded knowledge of the community. Education will contribute more to personal autonomy, we would argue, where it approaches the communicational forms outlined in Chapter 7.

If this is accepted, it implies that access to appropriate formal education is a universal pre-requisite for the enhancement of individual autonomy. 'Appropriate' here refers to the content of what is taught and to the way it is taught. The former entails a core curriculum of subjects, more or less the same for all cultures, including basic numeracy, general social skills, physical and biological processes, general and local history and vocational abilities which are relevant to future employment. Ideally, learning of this kind readies students for active participation in the entire spectrum of practices/choices on which the continuation and, hopefully, the improvement of their well-being depend. Despite cultural differences in educational policy among the world's nations, foundation studies of the type described have been at the heart of the global expansion in education since the early 1960s. Ideally, then, we require culturally unbiased and internationally comparable indices of educational attainment in all the key subjects noted above. In practice we have comparable data only for the key competence of literacy, and the reliability of even this has been questioned. Mention has also been made in Chapter 9 of the need for further comparative studies on educational achievement in the subjects of such a core curriculum.

If indicators of learning are to chart the outcome, indicators of education should measure the *access to inputs* of teaching which contribute to this outcome. However, in the absence of direct measures of proficiency, recourse must be had to data on the formal educational experience of populations (Coombs, 1985, chs 2–3; Jones, 1990, ch. 7). This can be measured in a variety of ways such as number of years of completed study, the school/higher education/occupational qualification obtained, the educational level reached (as indicated by the International Standard Classification of Education), the number of years spent at different levels of the education system, age on completion of study, and participation in adult education. Such information is relatively abundant for Northern countries and is expanding for the South. Studies of the effectiveness of teaching are a different matter, and indicators of how well children are taught are almost non-existent. Yet without this, quantitative data on inputs alone cannot capture the contribution which formal education makes towards enhancing autonomy. This must qualify any inferences drawn from measures of access to education and the quality of life of the students concerned.

When we move from autonomy of agency to critical autonomy, even this degree of educational access is insufficient. To criticise and to make choices *between* the current rules of one's own culture and the rules of others requires a broader, transcultural knowledge. However proficient someone is in knowledge of her own culture she will be unable to subject it to searching scrutiny without a knowledge of other social systems and an understanding of the rules of comparative method. Tyranny is not only achieved with force. The passivity and constraints on consciousness and imagination on which it depends are engendered by the type of secondary and higher education – or lack of it – which citizens receive. Therefore, a curriculum oriented toward the avoidance of tyranny – whatever the culture or country involved – must include the teaching of *different* cultural traditions and provide a forum for these to be discussed and debated openly.

It is just such an enlightened capacity which the best of higher education strives to achieve. Further and higher education, despite their many defects, provide a major path towards expanded consciousness in the contemporary world, as witnessed by the sacrifices so many are prepared to make to obtain them. Measures of access to higher education collected by UNESCO are not ideal, but they have some value as proxy indicators of critical autonomy. Ideally, however, we need educational indicators which directly tap people's access to the knowledge of other cultural traditions and of scientific method – access to the critical learning discussed in Chapter 9.

Safe birth control and child-bearing

Women's capacity to bear children carries with it a specific threat to their physical health and autonomy. A significant proportion of women's illness stems from the female reproductive system, the hazards associated with childbirth and the degree to which women are given primary responsibility for childcare. Especially in the Third World, where disease is generally much greater, poverty can combine with the preceding factors to produce what has been called the 'maternal depletion syndrome' where the mother and child become much more vulnerable to infectious diseases. With respect to autonomy, the impact of childbirth can be as rewarding as it can be devastating. Which it is will depend greatly on the degree to which pregnancy is chosen by or forced upon the woman involved. One of the most important dimensions of autonomy is the sense of control that individuals have over themselves and their environment. Even in the best of circumstances, pregnancy can threaten this in obvious ways, but the threat is multiplied if the choice about whether or not to become a mother is removed as well (Petchesky, 1984, chs 9–10; cf. O'Brien, 1981).

According to the 1966 UN Declaration on Population, 'the opportunity to decide on the number and spacing of children is a basic human right' (UN, 1975, p. 8). To implement that, the report goes on, requires programmes of education, direct provision of contraception, abortion and sterilisation and treatment for sterility and subfecundity. However, the object of family planning should also be the enrichment of women's lives and their personal autonomy. A woman's right to control over her fertility should not be abridged by the state, any social group or her partner. Where birth control is not available, the prospect of an unwanted pregnancy is ever-present for heterosexual women. For many this will end in the need for an unlawful abortion, entailing further anxiety and loss of control as well as a serious threat to health and even life (Lesley Doyal, 1985, pp. 4–7). In other countries, notably the Soviet Union, contraception is limited but lawful abortions are common, with resulting threats to objective well-being.

Even where contraception is legal and available, the danger to women's health and autonomy from reproduction has not ended. Family planning programmes can push poor and illiterate women into forms of contraception, such as depo-provera injections, which they cannot control but which family planners can. Men may be uncooperative, or may relinquish responsibility for the problem if women choose methods to which they object. This can strongly motivate women towards the forms of contraception which are more dangerous to their health, notably the pill and the IUD. The pill, for example, certainly involves a greater risk of circulatory disease and probably both breast and cervical cancer too. The IUD does the same for pelvic infection. In short, in the name of sexual liberation, women have been used as guinea pigs in the search for a contraceptive technology which men find acceptable (Pollack, 1985). Probably no finer example exists of the extent to which sexism and patriarchy can remain hidden by the ideology of technological advance.

Societies pursuing family planning policies in accordance with UN guidelines provides an index of *de jure* rights. To assess the extent to which different women actually control their reproductive lives, data are also required on the use of contraception. For example, according to the World Bank (1988, Table 28) the percentage of married women of childbearing age who practise, or whose husbands practise, any form of contraception apparently varies between almost zero in several African countries to 83 per cent in Britain.

We conclude by drawing together in Table 10.1 the universal satisfier characteristics and the social indicators to chart each of these suggested in the course of this chapter. To make the indicators comparable we have defined them all negatively, i.e. they measure *lack* of satisfaction or *unmet* intermediate needs. Most of these indicators provide direct measures of the lack of a certain satisfier characteristic but in some cases they measure deficiencies in health or autonomy related to that lack. For example, babies suffering from deficiency diseases provide an indirect, proxy measure of inadequate nutrition. Here we are drawing on those sorts of indicators outlined in Chapter 9 to chart basic need-satisfaction, but using them in specific contexts to enrich our assessment of intermediate need-satisfaction.

Table 10.1 illustrates the rich pattern of need-satisfactions which should be charted in any comprehensive 'audit' of the liberational opportunities offered to individuals in particular nations, groups or

Table 10.1 *Suggested indicators of intermediate need-satisfaction*

Universal satisfier characteristics	Social indicators
1 Food and water Appropriate nutritional intake	α Calorie consumption below FAO/WHO requirements β Other nutrients consumption below requirements α % lacking access to adequate safe water α % suffering malnutrition/deficiency diseases* α % low birthweight babies* β % overweight/obese*
2 Housing Adequate shelter Adequate basic services Adequate space per person	β % homeless β % in structures that do not protect against normal weather α % lacking safe sanitation facilities β % living above specified ratio of persons per room
3 Work Non-hazardous work environment	β Incidence of specified hazards χ Incidence of job tasks undermining emotional/cognitive autonomy α Deaths/injuries from work accidents* α Deaths/illness from work-related diseases*
4 Physical environment Non-hazardous environment	β % experiencing concentrations of pollutants > specified levels: air, water, land, radiation, noise
5 Health care Provision of appropriate care Access to appropriate care	α Doctors/nurses/hospital beds per population < specified levels α % without access to community health services α % not fully immunised against specified diseases

cont. p. 220

6 Childhood needs

Security in childhood χ % of children abandoned, abused, neglected

Child development χ % lacking stimulation, positive feedback, responsibility

7 Support groups

Presence of significant others χ % without close, confiding relationship

Primary support group β % with no/very low social contacts
χ % with nobody to call on when in need

8 Economic security

Economic security α % in absolute poverty
χ % in relative poverty (participation standard)
β % with poor protection against specified contingencies

9 Physical security

A safe citizenry α Homicide rates
β Crime victim rates

A safe state β Victims of state violence
α War victims

10 Education

Access to cultural skills α Lack of primary/secondary education
α Years of formal study < specified level
β Lack of specified qualifications

Access to cross-cultural knowledge α Lack of higher education

11 Birth control and child-bearing

Safe birth control α Lack of access to safe contraception and abortion

Safe child-bearing α Maternal mortality rate*

Notes

α Reasonably reliable universal or near-universal data

β Data for few countries only, but where a clear idea of operationalisation

χ More speculative suggestions for indicators

* Indicator of health or autonomy related to a particular universal satisfier characteristic

cultures. Of course, many of the indicators suggested are not novel. However others are innovative and are absent as yet from the international literature on social indicators. Measures of children's needs, for example, are few and far between. Still others commonly featured in lists of social indicators are noticeable by their absence. We believe that this illustrates the way a theory of universalisable human need can select from existing measures, and suggest new measures, of need-satisfaction. One thing, we hope, is clear. Our theory of human need has a purchase, albeit at times a tenuous one, on existing evidence of need-satisfaction throughout the world.

11

Societal Preconditions for Optimising Need-Satisfaction

In Chapters 6 and 7, we argued that everyone has a moral right to optimal need-satisfaction. We now need to consider how this moral right translates into specific positive rights – how rights to need-satisfaction can be specified and delivered, and how our procedural preconditions for rational deliberation can be approximated in real-world political processes and institutions. Only then can we evaluate how closely different societies approximate to the ideal of a just society. Moreover, all this must be discussed within the global and ecological constraints to need-satisfaction outlined earlier. Clearly, this is a daunting task, raising profound issues about economic, political and ecological feasibility, which cannot be addressed in the depth they deserve. What we shall attempt to do here is to devise indicators of positive and negative rights in relation to yardsticks of what might feasibly be achieved for countries at different levels of economic development. These standards can then be used to compare countries in terms of their procedural and material preconditions for optimising need-satisfaction and to indicate the direction of improvement and human progress.

More on the universality of human rights

Socialist writers have often been critical of liberal thinkers for being concerned with individual liberties while at the same time remaining silent on the importance of the material necessities of life. Indeed at times socialists have accorded priority to need-satisfaction over and above liberal rights: 'first food, then morality', wrote Brecht. Since the Second World War both Eastern bloc countries and Third World nations have contended that civil–political rights without socio-economic rights are a sham and have sought to extend the concerns of the United Nations and other international agencies into the latter area (Vincent, 1986, chs 4, 5). Others have contended that the Western conception of rights is blind to the reciprocal sharing arrangements which throughout the greater part of human history have been the main means of ensuring that weaker members of a community share in need-satisfaction. For instance, many cultures without legal codification provide better care for elderly people than those using the formal discourse of rights.[1]

It should be clear that these criticisms directly echo our own. In one sense the whole of Chapters 9 and 10 have been concerned to operationalise precisely those 'claim-rights' so often ignored in earlier liberal thought and by the contemporary New Right. This was done by charting *outcomes* in terms of need-satisfaction, irrespective of the legal forms existing in different societies.

Some Third World nations (in particular the 'Group of 77' of UNCTAD) also advance a second critique of Western concepts of rights, arguing that they are blind to the limitations on the autonomy of nation states (Vincent, 1986, ch. 5). In assuming the state to be the key actor safeguarding human rights, the West's approach ignores the very real inequalities between states stemming from the political/military domination of the big powers and the economic dominance of the central capitalist states, financial institutions and corporations within the world economic order. In other words, one can envisage a democratic country wishing to improve the welfare of its citizens which is powerless to do so because the nation state itself is so constrained – whether by powerful enemies or allies, or by its economic dependency. This 'Southern doctrine' on human rights emphasises the duty of colonial powers to grant political independence and, above all, the right of Third World nations to economic development via a New International Economic Order or some other set of global relations (Vincent, 1986, ch. 5; Galtung, 1980, p. 89 *et seq.*). The 'dependency' literature also sometimes claims freedom from national dependency as a basic need (Seers, 1982; Wisner, 1988, ch. 1).

This critique raises important questions about the political economy of a world order in which the rights of all people are taken seriously, but they are postponed to the final part of the book. Our intention here is to show how rights to need-satisfaction can be conceived and charted in practice. The global and politico-economic obstacles to improved human well-being, and the appropriate strategies for moving us forward, are vast issues which require separate treatment. Yet properly interpreted, the international discourse of rights provides a powerful yardstick with which to evaluate the performance of different societies in providing the material and procedural conditions for improving need-satisfaction. This still leaves open the reasons *why* different nation states do better or worse than others – one reason being precisely the actions of *other* nation states.

But in accepting Second and Third World criticisms of the *content* of the Western notion of human rights, we are not endorsing a rejection of the *concept* of human rights. Those critiques which see human rights as merely an ideological sham, obfuscating the real inequalities and injustices which still pervade the social and economic fabric, are in our view counterproductive and dangerous. Procedural rights are themselves a vital means by which substantive human needs are better protected. There is, again, a mutual relationship between the two which is at the heart of all liberational struggle and which has an even greater poignance in Third World environments of both impaired need-satisfaction *and* curtailed procedural rights. As Bowles and Gintis put it (1986, pp. 169–70):

> The discourse of rights, then, is no more bourgeois than it is aristocratic, or Protestant, or proletarian. It has been the object of a variety of intense and cross-cutting social struggles, its progressive tendencies deriving in significant part from the contributions of dominated and oppressed groups. Moreover, the discourse of rights has served as a source of bonding and a framework for the expression of group demands, rather than reflecting a social philosophy or a political ideology.

In short, insofar as political doctrine and practice militate against the optimal satisfaction of basic needs because of their violation of one or more of the liberal rights, then they are an obstacle to human liberation and must be condemned. This is true as much for the rights of women within the Iranian state as it is for the rights of blacks in South Africa or on the south side of Chicago. It is true of everyone.

Procedural preconditions for negative freedom

Civil and political rights

Our theory justifies the assessment of civil and political rights on several grounds. First, they are necessary preconditions for critical autonomy. Second, they empirically ground the duty which we owe to others in our belief that they should be able to understand and to act upon the merit of our vision of the good. They will hardly be able to do this – or to expect the same of us – if we and they are subject to arbitrary constraints on individual autonomy as a result of abuses of these rights. Finally, civil and political rights enable people to engage in open and rational debate and thus to improve decision-making about how to optimise need-satisfaction.

These arguments entail the set of basic rights and liberties addressed in Rawls' first principle of justice. They can be grouped as follows (Pogge, 1989, p. 147):

'Basic political rights and liberties, together with the guarantee of their fair value.
Basic rights and liberties protecting freedom of conscience.
Basic rights and liberties protecting the freedom and integrity of the person.
Basic rights and liberties covered by the rule of law'.

To assess the extent to which these are respected means looking in each society at the scope of their codification and their effective protection in practice.

A vast network of institutional arrangements has accrued in those nations where these rights are best respected. Corresponding to the distinction between spread and effectiveness, two factors are usually identified in explaining comparative variations. First, the rights must have some lawful basis if governments are consistently to uphold them. This usually entails codification in a state constitution, though recent research suggests that this is not in itself a guarantee against gross infringements (Pritchard, 1988, p. 143 *et seq.*). The second factor concerns the mechanisms of redress made available by governments to individuals whose rights have been infringed. The emphasis here is on judicial independence and due process, which requires that the state does not deny an individual's freedom without showing cause and following proper legal procedures. One study has found judicial independence to be positively associated with respect for civil rights across nations (Pritchard, 1988, p. 151). However, the consistency with which due process rules and legal principles are followed also independently affects the quality of justice in a state and requires separate assessment (Cingranelli and Wright, 1988). A nation's respect for civil rights entails *de jure* institutions and *de facto* processes which operate to this end – and are seen to do so.

The correct place to begin in operationalising these basic rights is surely the United Nations Declaration of Human Rights. Adopted by the General Assembly in 1948, this historic document constitutes the first attempt by a more or less representative global body to agree on a set of universal civil and political rights. It has been followed by a stream of other declarations and conventions, including the 1963 European Convention on Human Rights, the 1959 Declaration of the Rights of the Child, the 1975 Declaration on the Rights of Disabled Persons, and the 1979 Convention on the Elimination of all Forms of Discrimination Against Women – to mention just a few. Many of these have been codified in the International Covenants on Civil and Political Rights (ICCPR) and Economic, Social and Cultural Rights (ICESCR), both of which came into force in 1976.

The rights enshrined in these documents broadly encompass those entailed by Rawls's (unamended) first principle plus several rights to social and economic resources and treatments to enable people to enjoy a 'fair value' of these liberties. The narrower civil and political rights include the following:

Guarantees of equal freedoms, such as freedom of thought and the right to associate.
Protection against the state, such as freedom from torture, indefinite detention without trial and compulsory religion.
As means to these rights, legal rights, such as the right to due process and to be considered innocent until proved guilty.

Personal rights, such as rights to inter-racial and homosexual relationships between consenting adults.

The right to political participation, including rights to form trades unions, to peaceful political opposition and to multi-party elections by secret and universal ballot.

Equal rights for women and ethnic and other minorities in each of the above categories.

Though the UN itself does not publish regularly updated surveys of how far its declared rights are enforced or trampled on throughout the world, there are some independent studies which attempt to do just that (Gastil, 1984; Cingranelli, 1988). The most comprehensive is provided by Humana (1986). He has drawn up 40 separate rights, the majority of which are civil, including equal rights for women and minorities. Using a variety of sources, he has measured the extent to which these are upheld in practice in 120 countries. For each he has weighted the degree of their observation, varying from unqualified respect at one extreme to 'a constant pattern of violations' at the other. On this basis, he has constructed an overall index weighting certain rights more heavily on the grounds that their infringement represents *direct* intimidation and violence against the individual – a sure sign that personal security as an intermediate need in our terms is being dramatically violated. These infringements are: serfdom, slavery, forced or child labour; extrajudicial killings or 'disappearances'; torture or coercion by the state; compulsory work permits or conscription of labour; capital punishment by the state; court sentences of corporal punishment; and indefinite detention without charge (Humana, 1986, pp. 2–4). Humana's index captures one important aspect of our procedural preconditions for optimum need-satisfaction in the contemporary world, and we shall use it to chart comparative procedural need-satisfaction in Chapter 12.

Political participation

Civil rights alone cannot indicate the extent of political participation and citizen influence on the general policy-making process and on the resolution of debates about the content of specific policies. Also important here is the capacity of individuals to think about, to advocate and to join in attempts to change the normative and authority structure of the form of life within which they live. If a social environment is to facilitate the growth of individual autonomy, it must itself be open to alteration and improvement. As we have seen, for the most progressive changes to occur – for policy decision-making to be at its best – open debate is crucial, with the maximum possible number of relevant expertises brought to bear on the problems at hand. Again, *democracy* is an irreplaceable prerequisite for optimising human need-satisfaction.

But if it is to be an indicator of political participation, what does democracy entail in practice? The term must be unpacked if it is to provide a useful tool for operationalising political participation. Democracy is not an all-or-nothing state of affairs, but a continuum along which political systems can be ranked as more or less democratic. There is a variety of dimensions of political systems which can be charted by specific indicators (Pogge, 1989, §13; Lane and Errson, 1987, chs 6, 7). Three are crucial for our purposes: the 'democraticness' of basic political structures, the opportunities for citizen participation and the responsiveness of the state to such participation. Let us consider each in turn.

Citizens may influence the decisions of the political system either directly or indirectly. Without denying the role of small-scale, participatory forums, the referendum is the most prevalent form of direct participation. However in practice it is used infrequently and suffers from other defects as a mechanism to secure procedural justice (Lane and Errson, 1987, p. 211). Hence we shall focus here on representative democracy as it has developed over the last two centuries. Within representative systems, the most general preliminary indicator of political participation is the degree to which political parties are allowed to exist and to compete for power in a free and fair electoral system. In practice this will entail the following features. First, the relevant citizenry should be as universal as possible, the only major disenfranchised group being children below the age of majority. The spread of universal suffrage for women as well as men is thus a key indicator of procedural progress. Second, competing parties must be tolerated both in the constitution and in practice. In some countries, several parties are tolerated but not allowed to become the focus of political opposition that would pose any real threat to government.

Indicators charting these basic features of political systems are reasonably well developed. The formal right of adults to vote is near universal today; restrictions on it mainly pertain to women in certain Middle Eastern countries and non-whites in South Africa (Seager and Olson, 1986, Table 29). Indicators of genuine party choice are also available from various sources using different definitions (Kurian, 1984, Table 43; Wesson, 1987). According to Humana (1986, p. *xv*), in 1984, 1.9 billion people, 40 per cent of the world's population, were governed by some system of multi-party democracy; 2.4 billion (51 per cent of the total) by one-party, one-person or similar forms; and 440 millions (9 per cent of the total) by direct or effective military rule. Things have obviously improved in Eastern Europe since these data were collected. However, they still reveal how far short many nations fall of the minimal preconditions for political participation.

But formal indicators such as this tell us little about how much practical influence individuals and groups have in shaping and implementing the social rules which bind all human collectivities – those which concern our societal prerequisites. For this, we must analyse the degree of actual citizen participation in a polity. Voting levels in elections provide one reliable direct measure of participation in the formal political process. Apart from those countries where voting is compulsory, there are good theoretical reasons for expecting variations in electoral turnout to reflect the degree citizens feel that their welfare is affected by their political actions (Korpi, 1983, pp. 53–5).

Beyond this, other forms of citizen participation can be distinguished which can be grouped into 'autonomous' and 'mobilised' forms. Indicators of autonomous participation would include speaking, writing and participating in demonstrations. Such evidence is available for certain countries, such as Sweden (Szulkin, 1987). Possibly more important is the need for evidence on the extent of the self-organisation of citizens into pressure groups and social movements, along with their spread and effectiveness. Indeed, without autonomous activity of this sort any democratic constitution remains an empty shell.

Finally, we must consider the responsiveness of state agencies to citizen pressure. Within modern representative democracy, different forms exist which modify the degree to which they approximate procedural justice (Pogge, 1989, pp. 153–6). Variations are found in a) the electoral system, from 'first past the post' systems as in the UK to true proportional representation systems as in many

European countries; b) the pattern of government formation – typically minimum-winning party coalitions, though other types are found; and c) the type of regime, whether presidential, cabinet government or committee parliamentarianism (Lane and Ersson, 1987, ch. 7). Citizen influence will also very much depend upon the degree to which the political system is centralised or decentralised. The division between federal and unitary states is crucial here, especially in more populous nations. So too is the existence of democratically-accountable lower tiers of government with real powers. There is no simple way in which the resulting variety of forms of representative government can be evaluated as better or worse, but Lane and Ersson (1987, Table 7.9) have devised a method to compare European polities according to the degree of mass influence they afford. They conclude that even within these parliamentary democracies the degree of citizen influence varies markedly.

In all these ways, different polities permit their citizens widely different opportunities to influence policies. The greater the enfranchised citizenry and its level of electoral participation, the greater the state's tolerance of diverse political parties, the more responsive the system of government to public opinion, the more extensive the domain of economic and social life subject to effective democratic influence by citizens, the more citizens are mobilised within a wide variety of autonomous movements – the more rational will be the ongoing process of resolving disputes. Though such procedures cannot in isolation guarantee the pursuit of strategies to optimise need-satisfaction, in combination with the other societal preconditions discussed in this chapter they do offer the surest chance of success. This will be so whatever other specific characteristics of the people or their polity.

Material preconditions for positive freedom

Yet as we have argued throughout, the right to optimal need-satisfaction entails much more than civil rights and opportunities for political participation. It also requires the right to the optimal satisfaction of those basic and intermediate needs already identified. These have proved more difficult to monitor because the potential gap between *de jure* and *de facto* rights is greater. The fact that such rights entail substantial claims on resources means that the government of a poverty-stricken country cannot, with the best constitution and will in the world, ensure that these rights are respected in practice. Conversely, another nation may do well in meeting needs without recognising their status as rights at all. In Chapter 10 direct measures of need-satisfaction have been endorsed. Here we complement this by elaborating the material preconditions which underly *de facto* social rights.

Meeting human needs in practice requires a system of production and reproduction that delivers and distributes the necessary need satisfiers. To operationalise this right entails entering the domain of economic and social processes. Referring back to the societal preconditions introduced in Chapter 5, we must turn our attention from cultural transmission and political authority to those aspects of material production and social reproduction which all societies have in common and which have the potential of meeting needs.

A model of material production

We have seen that if a social system is to reproduce itself through time, its members must apply their labour to the natural resources of their environment and to the stock of means of production to create the range of goods and services which they require to survive as individuals. A portion of these will provide inputs for the processes of biological and social reproduction. In almost all societies this Promethean task occupies the bulk of people's waking hours from the end of childhood, or earlier, until death. Yet it is our open-ended capacity for expanding production which distinguishes humankind from all other species. Hence labour is for most people both a condition of servitude and an expression of their creativity (Marx, 1961, ch. 7). We shall concentrate here on the elements of material production common to all societies, saving consideration of specific modes or systems of production for Chapters 12 and 13. To do this we require a model of what all human economic activity has in common, and the way this affects levels of need-satisfaction. The most significant attempts to construct models which are culture-free, yet which are operational, have emerged from the 'basic needs' school of economic development. Our model draws on that work, in particular that of Stewart.[2]

Figure 11.1   *A model of material production*

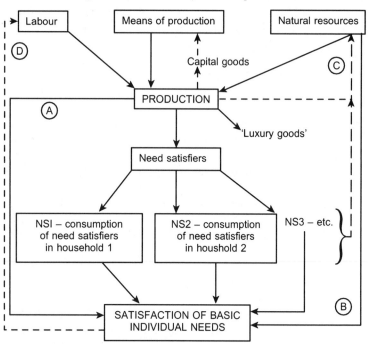

A. Direct effect of production process on basic need satisfaction
B. Direct effort of natural environment on basic need satisfaction
C. Effect of production and consumption processes on natural resource base
D. Effect of basic need satisfaction on labour capacities.

Figure 11.1 presents an abstract model of production, whereby resources at the top are transformed into need satisfactions at the bottom. In bringing about this transformation, all economies must ensure that three processes occur at some level of effectiveness: production, distribution and need-transformation.

All *production* begins with resources: manual and mental labour; natural resources including all attributes of the global environment; and humanly-constructed means of production. These resources are then allocated to productive units within which human labour, knowledge and organisation transform the raw material into outputs of goods and services. At this point the model diverges from orthodox economic theory by distinguishing three categories of output: need-satisfiers, 'luxuries' and capital goods. Capital goods are products which are not made available for current consumption, serving instead as means of production with which to produce future output. When these are set aside the remainder can be divided into two. Need-satisfiers are those goods and services which satisfy substantive individual needs within any particular economic structure. Luxury goods are all other goods and services, including consumption goods other than basic need-satisfiers and goods such as weapon systems which do not enter into the production of other products. This distinction between satisfiers and luxuries is critical in devising a more sensitive measure of need-satisfaction than Gross Domestic Product (which broadly includes all three kinds of output).

At the second stage, the quantum of consumption goods and services must be distributed between consumption units. For the vast majority of the world's population, consumption takes place within multi-member households, though the constitution of households of course varies between cultures. Hence from the perspective of our theory, it is the distribution of need-satisfiers between and within households that has a critical bearing on need-satisfaction. Of course, not all need-satisfiers are discrete items consumed by individual households. Some, such as malaria eradication teams, are pure public goods which are non-excludable and indivisible: people in the vicinity cannot be prevented from enjoying their benefits, and the enjoyment of them by one person does not prevent their enjoyment by others. Others are divisible goods with substantial externalities, such as a vaccination team which will tend to have spillover benefits (Stewart, 1985, p. 21). In these cases the relevant consumption unit is not the household, but a geographical group, such as a village, or a social category, such as members of a firm's welfare scheme. The agency of distribution is different, but the centrality of distribution as a stage in transforming resources into need-satisfactions remains.

At the third stage, the need-satisfiers are consumed, processed and transformed into individual need-satisfactions. This processing of inputs into need-satisfactions we shall label the need-transformation process. One part of this processing takes place, for most people, within 'households' and involves (a) the allotment of need-satisfiers between individual members of the household, and (b) the conversion of these inputs into the 'output' of basic need-satisfaction – into individual health and autonomy. The first step alerts us to the importance of distribution and consumption inequalities *within* the household and to the factors which affect this, in particular gender differences. The second focuses attention on the efficiency with which these inputs are transformed into need-satisfactions, and the factors which bear on this such as the social structure of the household, the stock of durable consumption goods available to it, the knowledge of practices relevant to meeting needs and the provision of collective goods and services in the community. In the same way it is desirable to evaluate the effectivness of need transformation within schools, health centres and all other collective sites of need satisfaction.

Two other factors also have a bearing on the need transformation process. On the one hand, work or the labour process can have a positive and negative bearing on health and autonomy, illustrated by path A in Figure 11.1. Since the monitoring of the work environment was discussed in Chapter 10, we shall not discuss it further here. On the other hand, the need-satisfaction of people is also affected by the natural and humanly-constructed environment (although the difference between the two has been blurred by industrialisation). One of the economic functions of the natural environment is the performance of services which directly satisfy human needs (Jacobs, 1989). Examples include the provision of amenities, such as wholesome air and water and an aesthetically pleasing landscape. It is increasingly recognised that modern forms of production can degrade or pollute the quality of this environment and diminish the quantity of previously 'free' products. This direct impact of the environment on need-satisfaction is indicated by path B in Figure 11.1. Again, since indicators of environmental quality were discussed in Chapter 10, and are addressed again below, we shall say no more about them here.

Having traced the transformation of resources into need-satisfactions, there is a fourth stage to consider. All successful economies must ensure that productive resources are replenished to enable at least a similar level of output to be produced in future rounds of production, a process we may call *material reproduction*. Sustainable production requires that labour, means of production and the natural resource base are all capable of at least equivalent levels of output in the future. The replenishment of capital goods requires that a certain proportion of output is devoted to investment. The positive and negative impact of production and consumption processes on the biosphere and natural resource base must also be taken into account. The Brundtland Report defines 'sustainable development' as 'meet(ing) the needs of the present without compromising the ability of future generations to meet their own needs' (1987, p. 43). This feedback effect is illustrated by the 'C' arrows. Lastly, the renewal of the human capacity for labour illustrates the crucial productive impact of basic need-satisfaction: the recognition that meeting needs is not only morally correct but can be economically rewarding via the enhanced capacities of the labour force – arrow D (Streeten, 1981, pp. 348–53; Streeten *et al.*, 1981, ch. 4). A new economics that is truly needs-based must point out the human and ecological waste if capital is perceived as the only renewable resource.

Hence the material factors which will determine the level of need-satisfaction of individuals, whatever the nature of the economic system they inhabit, are:

The total quantity, composition and quality of need satisfiers produced.

The pattern of distribution of these satisfiers among consumption units (households).

The effectiveness with which these satisfiers are transformed into individual need-satisfactions (partly reflecting the intra-household distribution of satisfiers), together with the direct impact of labour and the environment on need-satisfactions.

The rate of depletion/accumulation of capital goods, the natural resource base and human resources.

At this point, the reader may feel that we have taken a roundabout route to state the obvious. Hopefully, any such scepticism will be dispelled when this approach is compared with traditional national income accounting. For this is not even as refined as Stage 1 of the analysis above – making no distinction between need-satisfiers and other products – and pays no attention to the other three stages. Furthermore, this model is applicable to all types of economy – to pre-capitalist, capitalist and state socialist systems.

The model provides in principle a method to evaluate economic performance *across* different economic systems, without the dangers of circular reasoning which vitiate the reliance of neo-classical economics on internal preferences as a measuring rod (Steedman, 1989, ch. 11). It is obvious that economic growth – as traditionally measured – may not enhance need-satisfactions. A rise in the total output of an economy may take the form of 'luxuries' which do not satisfy needs, or satisfiers may not be distributed to those who need them. Ignorance or other constraints may prevent extra satisfiers being translated into enhanced need-satisfactions, excessive labour or despoliation of the environment may offset rising levels of satisfaction in consumption, or the growth may all be at the expense of future resources and future need-satisfactions. Hence conventional measures of GNP cannot serve as proxy indicators for levels of need-satisfaction.

Indicators of system performance

Yet something must take its place if we are to be able to compare, and to begin to explain, the ability of different economic and social systems to meet needs along a spectrum of 'better' and 'worse'. Here we outline the sorts of indicators needed to assess the capacity and potential of a nation or some other unit to respect 'socio-economic rights' in practice. Again, we can do no more than summarise some of the novel thinking in this area on which a theory of need can draw.

1.   *Production* At the first stage of production, we require aggregate measures of the output of need satisfiers over a period of time. To do this, some satisfactory yet workable way of distinguishing satisfiers from 'luxuries' is required. In some cases it is easy to identify need satisfiers, such as rice in a subsistence economy. However it is usually more complicated. In most modern economies where there is a choice of foodstuffs, any particular foodstuff (such as rice) is not *ipso facto* a basic need-satisfier because there are many substitute sources of, say, carbohydrate and protein available. Rice is a basic need-satisfier in a rice-based subsistence economy, but not in modern Britain or Singapore. Furthermore, a packet of rice on the supermarket shelves usually consists of a bundle of characteristics (e.g. rice, packaging, and

perhaps an advertised free gift) which the consumer might not disentangle, not all of which could remotely stand as need-satisfiers.

Ideally some method is required to estimate the aggregate value of the specific satisfiers produced in an economy. For example, using a similar distinction between basics and luxuries Cole and Miles (1984, pp. 135–9) have outlined a technique for ranking goods and services as more or less basic.[3] Employing related techniques, more sensitive measures of the rationality of production systems could be developed. However difficult this is in practice, the prescriptive conclusion is clear. All other things being equal, it is the aggregate production of need-satisfiers, rather than of all goods and services, which will influence aggregate levels of health and autonomy, and hence opportunities for social participation. This alone will not provide a measure of better or worse in the production sphere because, as Sen argues (1984, ch. 12, p. 294), the rate of conversion of primary goods or basics into 'primary powers' or need-satisfaction levels can vary for many reasons.[4] But it would be a great improvement on purely utilitarian calculation. Without at this stage introducing distributional issues, we may conclude that an economy which prioritises the production of need-satisfiers will, all things being equal, enhance overall opportunities for successful participation to a greater extent than another economy with the same aggregate output but with a higher share of 'luxury' production.

2. *Distribution* At the second stage of the model, considerations concerning distribution must be introduced. In Chapter 7, Rawls's principles were modified to engender one basic principle relevant to socio-economic arrangements. Everyone should have access to that minimum level of intermediate need-satisfaction required to optimise basic need-satisfaction – to the 'minopt' introduced in Chapter 8. In each domain everyone should have access, for example, to the nutrition, shelter, support groups or education which will enable them to participate in their form of life as effectively as they are able. Up to this point the appropriate distributional principle is one of strict equality, though in the real world this will obviously remain an ideal.[5] Given the ideal, poverty would still be possible but only with respect to wants as opposed to needs. Which patterns of distribution actually provide optimum access to such satisfiers must for now remain an open question.

Our purpose here is a different one: to combine measures of production and distribution to generate a 'Rawlsian' measure of *the real income of the worst off*. Comparison of this level across nations and other groups would indicate, all things being equal, how close or distant are their material preconditions to some feasible ideal. Let us consider how such a measure could be constructed.

To begin, which groups are most in need – are the least well off in Rawls's terminology? A plethora of direct measures of need-satisfaction have already been advanced in Chapter 10, and in each case the 'worst off' or the 'least advantaged' can be identified in substantive terms: the worst fed, the worst housed, the most insecure, and their equivalents for all our other intermediate needs. However, as critics of Rawls have pointed out, this (and analogous procedures) will normally entail that different sets of people are worst off on different counts. In the absence of a single measure of well-being we are unable to combine these different domains to identify the 'worst off' overall. The best and most practicable way forward, Pogge argues, is to identify percentile groups at the bottom of the income distribution. The percentile chosen is of course arbitrary. There is a strong moral case for comparing the very poorest household in different groups, but this measure would lack reliability and any broader validity. The bottom 20 per cent would comprise a significant group and provides a benchmark with which to compare the distributive justice of societies (Pogge, 1989, §17. 5).

Next, how is real income to be interpreted? Ideally we require measures of the value of the need-satisfiers consumed by different groups. In practice we must make do with data on the overall distribution of total incomes, on the plausible assumption that the bulk of the expenditures of the poorest groups will be on satisfiers (as culturally identified in their specific economy).[6] In comparing economies, the relative prices of the satisfiers will vary and many subsistence goods in less-developed countries will have no market price at all. These problems complicate international comparisons of real *per capita* incomes using official exchange rates. To overcome this, 'purchasing power parity' estimates of exchange rates are increasingly being calculated. These reprice a standard bundle of commodities in country X at the prices prevailing in a standard country, usually the USA, making suitable estimates for the prices of untraded subsistence goods in the Third World. National incomes per head can be compared at these new exchange rates, to give a more realistic (if still inaccurate) picture of real income per head (World Bank, 1987, pp. 268–71). Given data on income distribution, the real *per capita* income of the worst-off 20 per cent, or any other quantile group, can then be calculated. In 1980 the real income of the worst-off, defined in this way, varied from less than $US100 in several African nations to $US4400 in Sweden.

Finally, having established rough measures of the real income of the worst off, what is the optimum standard by which they should be judged? The standard is not a minimal criterion of poverty, as was discussed in Chapter 10. Rather the issue is to determine what levels of real income of the worst off are compatible with our best available knowledge about what is required for optimal need-satisfaction. Only then can we argue that any specific national performance should be improved, particularly in the context of such wide disparities in national incomes. To do so we must begin with the world's best performance, which, according to the data sources for Tables 12.2 and 13.1, is Sweden. The experience of Sweden and other leading European welfare states suggests that income redistribution towards the less well off can be combined with economic dynamism to provide high levels of need-satisfaction. High income countries who provide for their poorest citizens a real income significantly lower than the Swedish level are thus arbitrarily depriving them of feasible levels of need-satisfaction.

For the bulk of the Third World, however, such high levels of need-satisfaction pose impractical standards for the purposes of moral evaluation. For countries at lower levels of development, a constrained Rawlsian measure could be constructed by using those nations, at a given stage of development, that exhibit the highest real income for low income quantiles. The data used in Table 12.2 in the next chapter suggests that these countries included Sri Lanka (in the low income category) and Yugoslavia (in the medium income category, if we exclude those newly industrialised nations such as Hong Kong which have higher *per capita* incomes than some OECD member states). Of course, to countenance such a constrained measure is not to renege on the goal of optimisation nor to endorse present global arrangements which engender such contrasts of wealth and poverty. Indeed, until it is demonstrated that it cannot be universalised, the real income of the worst off in Sweden will continue to serve as a measure of international injustice. It is quite possible to accept that this is the case, while at the same time recognising that for different types of underdeveloped countries, the optimum must be given a feasible interpretation. Indeed, it was precisely this recognition that led the WHO to allocate different goals of physical health for under-developed countries with low, middle and high levels of aggregate income.

3. *Need transformation* Research into the third stage – the mechanisms affecting the transformation of consumption into need satisfactions – is slight. In principle it entails comparing, for any household or group of households, consumption levels of satisfiers with indicators of basic and intermediate need-satisfaction. The higher the ratio of need-satisfaction over consumption, the more 'efficient' is the need-transformation process. Though this ratio offers a promising avenue for research, we cannot attempt to operationalise it here.

This still leaves open the important issue of the distribution of satisfiers and need-satisfaction *within* the household. There is now plentiful evidence from around the world that systematic inequalities exist within families. In many Third World countries, women are more deprived than men as regards nutrition, health and literacy. Daughters are more deprived than sons in many components of need-satisfaction (Sen, 1984, chs 15, 16). In First World countries, similar patterns are found among adults for such components as income, education and employment (Norris, 1987, ch. 4). Women perform the bulk of unpaid labour within the household and are frequently responsible for meeting the basic needs of all family members including the children, yet they have access to a smaller share of household resources than men (Elson, 1991; Pahl, 1980, 1989).

As well as being morally wrong, such inequalities undermine the overall process of need-transformation. The education and health of women is perhaps the single most important factor determining the effectiveness with which satisfiers are transmuted into healthy and autonomous household members. For example, cultures and households differ in their knowledge of water and food contamina-tion, and this differential knowledge has a considerable impact on the health of populations (Stewart, 1985, pp. 78, 121–4; Jones, 1990, p. 119). Investment channelled to women has a higher rate of return, and improves child welfare more than investment channelled to men. Thus we require indicators of sex bias and intra-family distribution to chart the optimising potential of the material framework of need-satisfaction. (They are also of course important measures of 'fair equality of opportunity' and positive liberty). Unfortunately, we know of no valid, reliable and available indicator for this task, though the sex ratio of populations may provide a proxy indicator (Sen, 1990).

4.   *Material reproduction* Lastly, we need to chart the material reproduction process – the sustainability of economic activity over time. To operationalise the general idea of economic sustainability requires specifying the 'economic functions' of the natural environment and proposing indicators for each. These can be divided into three, of which we will discuss two here. Together they provide a measure of total 'environmental consumption' (Jacobs, 1989, p. 3). First, there is the provision of resources – energy, raw materials and directly consumed goods. These will be either non-renewable (e.g. minerals), renewable (e.g. water) or continuing (e.g. solar energy). Without at this stage proposing desirable rates of resource consumption, we can suggest indicators to simply chart the utilisation rates of each for different societies and groups. One critical and reasonably reliable measure of non-renewable resource use is energy consumption *per capita*, though ideally it should exclude that derived from continuing or renewable sources of energy such as solar power and hydro-electricity.

The second economic function of the natural environment is assimilation of wastes, through degradation, absorption, dispersal and storage. Pollution develops when the first three methods of assimilation are insufficient to cope with the total quantity of wastes produced. At certain levels of specific wastes, this may trigger problems in the third economic function of the environment – the continuation of life-support systems (e.g. climate). Direct indicators of waste production are becoming more commonplace as the seriousness of these threats becomes more apparent. They include measures of solid waste generated, and emissions of various gases and particulates in the air. The World Resources Institute has made an heroic attempt to construct an index of greenhouse gas emissions, which is utilised in Chapter 12. Beyond this point, it is impossible to assess threats to material reproduction within the confines of the nation state since they raise issues at a global level, discussed in the next section.

Economic sustainability and the rights of future generations

All that we have said so far must, of course, be qualified by the necessity of taking the needs of future generations into account. The societal precondition for material reproduction, in particular, alerts us to the global and inter-temporal constraints on optimising the need satisfactions of the present generation. We cannot leave this chapter without briefly addressing how these moral concerns can be monitored in practice. This entails looking more closely at the meaning of 'economic sustainability' though we cannot confront many of the contentious issues which this raises. There are logical problems in constructing measures to evaluate paths of development which cannot be foreseen. However, we can assess the empirical and structural obstacles to sustainable development and hence to the optimisation of need-satisfaction for people in the future.

In practice, a range of possible interpretations of sustainability can be identified (Jacobs, 1989, 1990). We may say that an economy is sustainable when current environmental consumption (as defined above) does not reduce the opportunity of future generations to enjoy the same level of environmental consumption. This interpretation involves no less than perfect intergenerational equality. If the resource in question is not expanding, this amounts to a time discount rate of zero – the same value is placed on all future times as on the present. By contrast, a minimal interpretation of economic sustainability might be simply that level of economic consumption which, according to current predictions, is likely to avoid some kind of ecological catastrophe. In practice however, for many environmental functions, these two thresholds may already coincide. 'Sustaining present levels of environmental consumption of, for example, tropical rainforests, would not actually prevent catastrophe: these levels are leading to it. That is, the minimal threshold might demand a lower rate of consumption than the maximal, in which case the two effectively collapse into one' (Jacobs, 1989, p. 5).

In such cases it may not be too difficult to specify reasonable yardsticks of desirable environmental consumption. For example, the rate of use of a renewable resource (e.g. fishing) should not exceed its regeneration rate, subject to the proviso that the total 'stock' exceeds a critical level where the ecosystem is sustainable. In the case of non-renewable resources, such as fossil fuels, the total output should not exceed total 'inputs' to the stock, whether from known reserves becoming economic, from new reserves being discovered, from recycling or from substitution. Waste disposal should be maintained at a level below that where total pollution increases, subject again to the proviso that the existing absolute level of pollution does not threaten life support systems. When, in time, such standards are internationally agreed (as they are currently being agreed for the emission of 'greenhouse gases') then the performance of individual economies can be evaluated against these yardsticks.

But we can already say certain things. Per capita energy consumption in the West is some 80 times greater than that in sub-Saharan Africa. About one quarter of the world's population consumes three quarters of the world's primary energy. If energy consumption per head became uniform worldwide at current industrial country levels, then by 2025 a global population of 8.2 billion would require about 55 billion kW of energy per year – compared with 10 billion kW at present, or with 14 billion kW by 2025 if per capita use remained unchanged (Brundtland Report, 1987, pp. 169–70). This illustrates the fact that present energy patterns in the First and Second Worlds are probably unsustainable, and certainly ungeneralisable. There can be little doubt that much of the excess energy and resource use in the First World goes to support the satisfaction of wants, not of basic needs.

One other issue is posed as soon as need-satisfaction is conceived of over generations. The size of the future human population is not a parameter but a variable which the present generation has the power to control within certain limits. The question of economic sustainability cannot be isolated from the question of what is a desirable future level of population. As the Brundtland Report (1987, p. 55) says, 'the sustainability of development is intimately linked to the dynamics of population growth'. Given global limits on aggregate production-through-time, there will be a trade-off between future population size and future levels of need-satisfaction. UN projections predict a phenomenal rise in global population from 4.8 billion in 1985 to 6.1 billion by 2000 and to 8.2 billion by 2025. More than 90 per cent of this increase will take place in the Third World. Furthermore, the level at which future world population might stabilise is very sensitive to the date by which fertility rates fall to replacement level. If this point is reached in 2010 (just twenty years away), then global population will stabilise at 7.7 billion by 2060. If, however, this point is not reached until 2065, then global population would almost double again, exceeding 14 billion by 2100.

Such population projections must be related to estimates of the population-supporting capacity of agriculture and other food sources. These are sensitive to the progress which is made towards a more rational diet in the North. Cattle and poultry raised on cereals consume between 3 and 9 kg for each kilogramme of edible meat produced (Brandt Report, 1980, p. 101). However, this says nothing about all our other intermediate needs, some of which, such as housing, health and education, are costly to meet even at modest levels. Nor does it take on board the case for meeting needs to the optimum extent.

To optimise need-satisfactions for the present and unavoidable future population of the planet it would seem that population growth should be lowered as much as is compatible with avoiding harm to contemporary levels of health and autonomy. This may occur as a spin-off of improved need-satisfaction (Commoner, 1980): improving female education, in particular, is likely to reduce birth rates in the longer run (Cochrane, 1977; H. Jones, 1990, p. 164). However, this cannot be a counsel for complacency, owing to the fact that a high potential growth rate is already 'stored up' in the present, very young populations throughout much of the world. Speed is therefore of the essence, and this entails a specific birth control policy centred on the widest availability of safe forms of contraception. It has been argued in Chapter 10 that such a policy – if implemented properly – would also contribute to enhancing women's autonomy. Provided that authoritarian forms of population control are avoided, the aggregate interests of the present and future generations would appear to be congruent here. Indicators to monitor this would include the existence of pro-active, pro-choice family planning policies, and, to assess outcomes, measures of fertility. Of course, none of this is to argue that population growth in the Third World is the main threat to a sustainable global economy. On the contrary, a more salient threat is the excess consumption of the First World coupled with forms of production which damage the biosphere.

Table 11.1   *Suggested indicators of societal preconditions for optimisation*

Societal preconditions	Examples of social indicators
Respect for civil/political rights	α Index of respect for UN rights
Political participation	α Index of representative democracy β Voting rates χ Indices of citizen influence within polity
Material bases for rights to need-satisfaction: Production of satisfiers	χ Value of production of 'basics' per head
Distribution of satisfiers	β Real income of lowest percentile groups (as proportion of best-achieving country at each stage of development)
Need transformation	χ Ratio of need satisfaction to consumption of basics α Sex ratio of population
Material reproduction	α Non-renewable energy consumption per head β Greenhouse gas emissions per head α Total fertility rate

Notes

α   Reasonably reliable universal or near-universal data.
β   Data for few countries only, but where a clear idea of operationalisation.
χ   More speculative suggestions for indicators.

We have identified certain procedural and material preconditions for optimising need-satisfaction and suggested system indicators to chart each. These are listed in Table 11.1. Whatever the culture, these indicators either provide or suggest evidence about the ability of a social system to meet the needs of its members. In Chapter 12 we shall use such indicators to chart how effectively different groups of countries guarantee the societal pre-requisites for rational policies to improve human need-satisfaction. Of course, such an international audit of need-satisfaction cannot begin to *explain* the findings which result. This requires a global theory of the political economy of need-satisfaction, something which is briefly sketched in Chapter 13. The above discussion has also taken for granted the nation state as the basic unit for measuring and comparing need-satisfactions. Again, this implies no such privilege when we turn to explanation. The capacities of states, and the constraints within which they operate, vary enormously – between great and small powers, between the economically advanced and the underdeveloped, and so on. The *responsibility* for the poor performance of a certain society may not lie within the boundaries of that society. But all such questions are left to one side at this stage. The first task is to monitor the present situation, and that requires nationally-based indicators which are applicable to all societies, irrespective of their beliefs.

12

Charting Human Welfare: Need-Satisfaction in the Three Worlds

Beliefs about the benign or malign effects of modernisation on human welfare seem to go in swings. The nineteenth-century trust in social progress was severely undermined by First World War, the interwar crisis of capitalism, the emergence of fascism and Stalinism and the horror of Auschwitz. Yet for a period after the Second World War the belief in a rational path of progress revived, as both welfare capitalism and state socialism held out the promise of directing society to improve human well-being. In the 1970s and 1980s pessimism came to the fore again with internationalists pointing to the immiseration of the Third World, still dominated and exploited by neo-imperialist relationships, and the environmental and green movements giving dire warnings of unsustainability and eco-crisis. These sources of 'rational pessimism' are themselves challenged and undermined by the post-modernist contention that no single path of progress can be conceived of, let alone charted.

Charting objective welfare[1]

We believe that a coherent theory of universalizable human need can help to resolve this ongoing debate. Our rejection of the post-modernist critique of the possibility of any notion of progress does not substitute in its place a cosy view of inevitable betterment. Rather, it entails a rational audit of objective human welfare: a sober assessment of the state of need-satisfaction in the modern

247

world, of past trends and of future possibilities. Are levels of human welfare rising or falling? Is inequality in need-satisfaction narrowing or widening between nations and groups of people? Our theory argues that empirical answers can be given to these questions, subject to the availability of data, and we begin to sketch them out in this chapter. But the answers will not be unitary: the very structure of basic and intermediate needs entails a disaggregated assessment of need-satisfaction. It is logically possible that modernisation has enhanced levels of satisfaction in some domains of need while degrading them in others. Similarly, of course, the objective welfare of some peoples and groups may flourish while that of others may deteriorate.

Thus far, we have suggested indicators to measure the satisfaction of basic and intermediate needs and of their material and procedural preconditions. Here these will be combined to construct social profiles of the objective welfare of groups of nations in the First, Second and Third Worlds. While some are group averages, many of the indicators will focus on shortfalls in need-satisfaction among the most deprived. To illustrate their applicability to the needs of particular groups, we also present some comparative data on the well-being of women and men.

This project is scarcely original. Chapter 8 briefly reviewed the social indicators movement, and we shall draw extensively on this body of knowledge here. Since we are dependent on available data there is little empirically new in what follows. However, we believe that our theory can make a contribution in three ways. First, it helps to order currently available social indicators, by providing a clear concept of universal basic need from which to derive a more rigorous taxonomy of intermediate needs and societal prerequisites for their optimal satisfaction. Second, from the mass of available social statistics, the theory outlines criteria for separating those which provide valid measures of objective human welfare from those which do not. And third, it helps to identify gaps in existing data, where important components of need-satisfaction are presently uncharted and proposes new indicators to fill them.

The last century and a half has witnessed a prodigious expansion in the planet's productive capacity, such that the value of global monetised output in the mid-1980s was reckoned at $13 trillion. This averaged out to about $2500 per head of the world's population; equivalent to the income per head of present day

Yugoslavia or Portugal. But given the grossly unequal distribution of resources in the contemporary world any global average of need-satisfaction is misleading. The low-income countries consume only 5 per cent of this output, though they contain 49 per cent of world population, whereas the advanced Western countries, accounting for only 16 per cent of world population, claim 65 per cent.

In comparing different national levels of need-satisfaction therefore, we shall follow conventional practice by distinguishing between the economically advanced, developed or industrialised world of the 'North' and the less advanced economies of the 'South'. Within the industrialised world we distinguish between the capitalist 'West' and the state socialist 'East'. Since the data reaches only as far as the mid-1980s, we can conveniently ignore the political and economic transformation of the Soviet bloc countries over the last two years and treat them as an entirely separate category. We shall also use the common labels of First World (capitalist), Second World (state socialist) and Third World to describe these three groups of countries. Within the Third World, 'low' and 'middle' income countries are distinguished, while China and India – in population terms the Jupiter and Saturn of the world system – are treated as separate categories. Our concern here is with the very real differences between nations and political systems which existed up to the mid-1980s and what we can learn from them about the most appropriate social and economic policies for optimising need-satisfaction.

Basic and intermediate needs

Table 12.1 presents some summary indicators of individual need-satisfaction for these groups of nations, using whatever is available from the indicators discussed in Chapters 9–11. The following account however also draws on other material and supplements the 'snapshot' picture given in Table 12.1 with some description of trends over the recent past.

We begin with human survival. Life expectancy at birth (row 4 of Table 12.1) has improved greatly in all regions of the world in the three and a half decades since 1950. In South-East Asia it has increased by as much as 18 years, from 41 years in 1950 to 59 years in 1985. Levels in the First World have also continued to improve,

Table 12.1   *Substantive need-satisfaction in the Three Worlds*

	Third world				Second world	First world	World
	China	India	Other low income	Medium income			
1 Pop., 1986 (m)	1054	781	663	1230	396	742	4885
2 GNP/head, 1986	300	290	242	1330	(2059)	12964	2780
3 GDP/head ppp, 1980	–	573	(760)	(2594)	–	9699	(3879)
Survival/Health							
4 Life expectancy, 1986	69	57	50	61	72	75	64
5 Infant MR, 1985	36	105	119	66	23	9	61
6 Under-5 MR, 1985	50	158	193	108	27	12	94
7 Low birth weight (%)	6	30	24	12	6	6	14
Autonomy							
8 Literacy, 1985 (%)	69	43	46	73	(c.100)	(c.100)	70
Intermediate needs *Water/nutrition*							
9 Safe water, 1983 (%)	–	54	33	59	(c.100)	(c.100)	–
10 Calories, 1982	111	96	92	110	132	130	111
Housing							
11 Overcrowding, 1970s (%)	–	–	–	(61)	13	2	–
Health services							
12 Pop/phys., 1981	1.7	3.7	11.6	5.1	0.34	0.55	3.8
13 Access, 1980–3 (%)	–	–	49	(57)	(c.100)	(c.100)	–
Security							
14 War dead, 1945–85 (%)	0.2	0.1	1.0	0.4	0.0	0.0	0.3
15 Homicide, 1987	–	–	–	(8.3)	1.9	3.8	(4.6)
16 Poverty, 1977–84 (%)	–	48	(55)	(33)	–	–	–
Education							
17 Adults: sec.ed. (%)	16	14	(9)	10	42	30	16
18 Adults: post-sec. ed. (%)	1.0	2.5	(1.4)	4.8	(8.9)	11.7	3.7
19 Students: sec.ed (%)	39	35	23	47	92	93	51
20 Students: post-sec. ed. (%)	–	–	3	14	20	39	19
Reproduction							
21 Contraception, 1985 (%)	77	35	21	50	——66——		50
22 Maternal MR, 1980–7	44	340	510	130	——10——		250

Notes

The definition of 'low' income, 'middle' income and 'industrial market' economies follows the World Bank (1988, p. 217). However data for the state socialist countries have been recomputed to include eight countries: Albania, Bulgaria, Czechoslovakia, German Democratic Republic, Hungary, Poland, Romania and the USSR. Four high-income oil-exporting nations in the Middle East are exluded from these country groups, though they are represented in the global averages. There are many problems in equating 'development' with income per head (Thirlwall, 1983, ch. 1), but the organisation of world statistics makes it difficult to present the data organised according to some other variable. Countries in groups are weighted by population except where noted. Numbers are in brackets when data is available for fewer than half the countries in that group.

Since there are well-known problems in comparing per capita incomes across nations, two separate measures are provided. Row 2 shows average GNP per head in $US at current exchange rates, whereas row 3 shows average GDP per head (unfortunately only for 1980) in $US at 'purchasing power parities' which reveal differences in national real incomes more accurately (World Bank, 1987, pp. 268–71). Unfortunately this information is not yet available for all nations.

– = not available.

Definitions and sources
(by row numbers)
1   Total population, 1986, millions (World Bank, 1988) Table 1.
2   Gross national product per head in 1986 in $US using average exchange rates for 1984–6 (World Bank, 1988) Table 1.
3   Gross domestic product per head in 1980 in $US at 'purchasing power parities' (World Bank, 1987) Box A.2.
4   Life expectancy at birth in years, 1986 (World Bank, 1988) Table 1.
5   Infant mortality before one year of age, per 1000 live births, 1985 (UNICEF, 1987) Table 1.
6   Mortality of children under 5 years of age per 1000 live births (UNICEF, 1987) Table 1.
7   Proportion of babies weighing under 2,500 gm (UNICEF, 1987) Table 2.
8   Percentage of persons aged 15 and over who can read and write, 1985 (UNICEF, 1987) Table 1.
9   Access to drinking water, as defined by WHO, 1983 (UNICEF, 1987) Table 3.
10   Daily calorie supply per head as percentage of requirements, 1983 (UNICEF, 1987) Table 2.
11   Percentage of housing units with more than 2 persons per room, various years 1970s (UN, 1987) Table 4.5.
12   Population (thousands) per physician, 1981 (World Bank, 1988) Table 29.

cont. p. 252

13   Percentage of population with access to health services as defined by WHO, 1980–3 (UNICEF, 1987) Table 3.
14   War deaths between 1945 and 1985, as percentage of population in 1986 (UN, 1987) Table 9.11.
15   Homicides per 100000 population (WHO, 1989) Table 10.
16   Percentage of population with incomes below that where a minimum nutritionally adequate diet plus essential non-food requirements is affordable, as estimated by World Bank (UNICEF, 1987) Table 6.
17   Proportion of adults who have ever entered secondary education; various years between 1970 and 1982 (UNESCO, 1989) Table 1.4.
18   Proportion of all adults who have entered post-secondary education; years between 1970 and 1982 (UNESCO, 1989) Table 1.4.
19   Number of secondary school pupils of all ages as percentage of children of secondary school age (generally 12–17 years), around 1985 (World Bank, 1988) Table 30.
20   Number of students enrolled in all post-secondary education, schools and universities, divided by population aged 20–4, around 1985 (World Bank, 1988) Table 30. Details of coverage are given on p. 303.
21   Percentage of married women of childbearing age who are using, or whose husbands are using, any form of contraception, whether traditional or modern methods (UNDP, 1990) Table 20.
22   Annual number of deaths of women from pregnancy-related causes per 100000 live births (UNDP, 1990) Table 11.

---

but since the rate of improvement has been slower, the relative inequality in survival chances has diminished. Yet as the table shows, great differences persist even within the Third World. While China's life expectancy approaches that of the North, low-income African countries in particular fall well short of achievements elsewhere. In nine sub-Saharan African countries life expectancy actually declined between 1979 and 1983.

The infant mortality and the under-5 mortality rate are other sensitive measures of survival chances. Infant mortality has registered an even steeper improvement, more than halving since 1950 in many nations. Yet here the relative gap remains almost as wide, because the First World countries too have maintained their improvement. Moreover, the 1980s have witnessed some regression, as in North-East Brazil, for example, where infant mortality rates are actually rising (UNICEF, 1987, p. 16). The under-5 mortality rate in India and other low-income countries is many orders of magnitude higher than in the West. On both measures China does much better than its income level would predict. Within the industrialised world, the state socialist nations do almost as well as the advanced Western nations in terms of life expectancy. They continue to lag on the other indices, while the USSR experienced an absolute regression in survival chances in the 1970s (Davis, 1988).

Direct and comparable indicators of disability and disease prevalence are much harder to come by. Aside from mortality rates for specific diseases there are few data on the prevalence of those suffering from them. One estimate of the incidence of malaria and cholera in the early 1980s based on laboratory or clinical reports collated by the WHO shows how persistent a cause of disablement these diseases remain (World Resources Institute, 1987, Table 16.4). A direct measure of (child) health for which we have broadly comparable data – low birthweight babies, shown in line 7 of Table 12.1 – exhibits a narrower range of cross-country variation than do mortality statistics. The pattern is broadly the same, except that China's achievements shine more, and India's less, brightly. However comparable data for most other serious diseases – in both the South and the North – are not available, nor is there an operational measure with which to compare their impact on disability. The continuing absence into the 1990s of valid and reliable international statistics on morbidity is a remakable indictment.

In their absence recourse must be had to cause-specific mortality rates. For well known reasons rehearsed in Chapter 9, mortality statistics cannot be used as straight-forward indicators of morbidity. However such statistics do provide some information, albeit indirect, about patterns and severity of diseases for those who are still alive. It is highly probable that if a given sample of a population has suffered and died from a disease that others in the population who have survived will have suffered too. This is why mortality statistics are employed in epidemiological research into the causes of mortality *and* morbidity, research which is crucial for the design of effective programmes of prevention. Table 12.2 summarises recent global data, illustrating the familiar predominance of infectious and chronic disease in the South and the North respectively.

When we turn to direct measures of personal autonomy comparable evidence is also scant. A WHO study (1973) of psychiatric patients in nine countries (Denmark, India, England, the USSR, Czechoslovakia, the USA, Taiwan, Nigeria and Columbia) found substantial agreement in the specific diagnosis

Table 12.2   *Number of deaths in major categories of cause by WHO region (thousands)*

	Developing Countries	%	Developed Countries	%
Infectious and parasitic diseases*	16 020	40	810	8
Neoplasms	2 200	5	2 050	19
Circulatory and certain degenerative diseases†	7 620	19	5 710	54
Perinatal conditions	3 080	8	170	2
Injury and poisoning	1 980	5	690	6
Others and unknown	9 240	23	1 240	12

* Including diarrhoeal diseases, influenza, pneumonia, emphysema and asthma.
† Including diabetes mellitus, stomach and duodenal ulcer, chronic liver disease and cirrhosis, nephritis, nephrotic syndrome and nephrosis.

Source: H. Jones (1990) Table 5.3, p. 110.

of schizophrenia and estimated that some 50 million people – about one per cent of the world's population – suffer from this particular form of mental illness. Many are institutionalised and endure appalling conditions of overcrowding, squalor, brutality and neglect (Cohen, 1988, ch. 1). Sartorius estimates that more than 100 million people – some 2 per cent of the world's population – suffer from depressive disorders (1974, cited in Marsella *et al.*, 1985, p. 299). It is possible that for some groups in the Third World, levels of mental health have deteriorated in recent decades with the acceleration of economic and social change, notably the extension of market relations and the erosion of communal ties. Though these and similar studies are not foolproof against the dangers of importing diagnostic stereotypes, the overwhelming evidence is that mental disorder is widespread and severely intereferes with the successful social participation of sufferers (Marsella *et al.*, 1985; Beiser, 1985).

Evidence on the cognitive component of autonomy is only widespread and reliable as regards literacy (row 8). This has recorded a steady but slow improvement since 1950. Then 55 per cent of the world's population over 15 years of age was literate; now 70 per cent of a population twice as great is. However the rate of increase slowed down measurably in the later 1970s and 1980s, and vast numbers remain deprived of this most basic requirement for enhanced autonomy. This is especially the case in most low-income countries (with China a notable exception) and in several Islamic nations where many women still cannot read and write. On the other hand, some Latin American countries have joined the First and Second Worlds in achieving near-universal literacy. Of course, illiteracy alone is quite inadequate as an indicator of cognitive deprivation. Unfortunately, however, we have no systematic knowledge about shortfalls in other socially appropriate skills nor of access to other cultural traditions.

Comparable cross-cultural indicators of the other components of autonomy are scant. The most widespread data on social opportunities for participation are statistics on employment in the formal sector, but even those are unreliable. The obstacles to effective participation posed by caste, race, gender and other attributes can only be revealed by disaggregated data, a procedure which is only attempted for gender in Table 12.3 below.

Turning now to some of the intermediate needs identified in Chapter 10, we begin with access to *clean water* (row 9). Though the safety of water supplies in the First World is not absolutely guaranteed – with threats from lead, nitrates and other contaminants – the extent of unmet needs is far greater in the Third World. Excluding China, 86 per cent of Third World urban dwellers and only 44 per cent of rural dwellers have access to safe water supplies, though these figures mark an improvement since 1970 when the respective proportions were 65 per cent and 13 per cent (UNICEF, 1987, p. 114). Once again the situation is worst among the poorest, predominantly African, countries.

The record of *malnutrition* is one of global improvement coupled with life-threatening regional shortfalls. The global improvement is significant and not to be underestimated: in all regions, with the notable exception of sub-Saharan Africa, the average daily availability of calories, protein and fats per person improved between 1961 and 1984, in Asia by substantial amounts. The tremendous expansion of global population over this period especially in the Third World was accompanied by a rising availability of food. However, these very broad averages conceal real deficiencies and some critical qualifications must be registered.

First, in most low income countries the situation is very bad and getting worse. Excluding China and India, average calories and protein per person have fallen, such that by 1982 the former amounted to on average only 92 per cent of requirements. In 21 of the low-income nations daily calorie supply per head was lower in 1985 than 20 years earlier in 1965. Second, the distribution of food within countries bears no necessary relation to needs. For example in Brazil, a medium-high income country and a major food exporter, over 50 per cent of children are undernourished (Coimbra, 1984, pp. 321–8). In countries with high rates of infant mortality almost two fifths of children under five suffer from mild-moderate or severe malnutrition; in Bangladesh as many as 21 per cent from severe malnutrition (defined as less than 60 per cent of the desirable weight-for-age). More than one fifth of babies aged 12–23 months also exhibit signs of wasting in countries of the Third World (with some exceptions, notably China) (UNICEF, 1987). Even in the First World undernutrition is reappearing alongside malnutrition in some of the richest nations, like the USA. In conclusion, undernutrition and malnutrition remain a devastating reality in a world where sufficient food for all is available, and even in many nations where there is more than enough to go round.

Housing conditions are deteriorating in some cities in the Third World while they are improving in most in the First World. Row 11 of Table 12.1 presents a minimal (and none-too-reliable) standard of housing occupation, showing the percentage of *households* living at densities of more than 2 people per room (the proportion of *people* living at these densities would be higher). It reveals acute overcrowding in the middle-income countries, and still greater overcrowding for the few low-income countries for which we have data. Significant numbers are still grossly overcrowded in the Eastern bloc, but few in the West live at these densities. There has been some improvement in access to adequate sanitation among Third World urban dwellers, with an increase from 34 per cent in 1970 to 62 per cent in 1985, but virtually no change in the deprivation of rural dwellers, 85 per cent of whom still lack adequate facilities. When these data are coupled with the lack of clean water and the unsuitable geography of much low-income housing discussed in Chapter 10, we can assert conclusively that housing needs are satisfied to a far lower extent in the Third World than in the First, with the Eastern bloc countries falling somewhere in between. Of course, in the West, many people are homeless, overcrowded or live in unsanitary conditions while some in the

Third World are well-housed. Nevertheless these data suggest that shortfalls in meeting housing needs exhibit extremely wide variations between First and Third Worlds.

Access to *health services* is approximated in row 12 by a rather crude, but generally available, indicator: population per physician. This ratio has improved since 1965 in all regions of the world, but country differences have remained astonishingly wide. There is a strong link with GDP per head, but again China and, in this case, India have greater provision than would be predicted from their economic resources, as do the Second World nations. The WHO's estimation of the proportion of populations with 'access to health services' in the early 1980s (row 13) shows that, excluding the two giants, about one half of people in low-income countries have none at all. More surprisingly perhaps, the situation is almost as bad in a wide range of middle-income countries. These figures may exaggerate access which is often limited by geography. While there has been a remarkable improvement in the coverage of specific health programmes, such as immunisation and oral rehydration therapy to combat diarrhoeal diseases, hundreds of millions continue to be denied access to basic health care of the sort called for by the WHO. Nor is this problem entirely overcome in the First and Second Worlds. For example between 35 and 40 million people in the USA have no certain entitlement to medical treatment (Renner and Navarro, 1989).

Physical insecurity is assessed in rows 14 and 15 of Table 12.1 using data on war-related deaths and homicide. Wars have continued to claim lives, killing almost 22 million people since the end of the Second World War. Such threats to personal security are gross but extremely localised: the main countries to suffer in the last two decades have been Nigeria, Bangladesh, Vietnam, Cambodia, Iran and Iraq. This concentration on some of the poorest Third World nations has exacerbated the suffering endured by people already living at low levels of need-satisfaction (cf. Sivard, 1989, p. 22). Statistics on homicide also reveal a very uneven incidence with a few countries – Guatemala, El Salvador, Columbia, Thailand and the USA – experiencing high rates. It would appear that civil insecurity is most prevalent in middle-income countries, where inequalities are most marked, but this finding may have to be qualified if more valid and reliable indicators became available.

The most extreme level of *economic insecurity* as an unmet need can be approximated by calculating the numbers of people falling below an 'absolute' poverty level (row 16), usually defined as that income below which a minimally nutritious adequate diet plus essential non-food items is not affordable. Around one half the population of India and other low-income countries (excluding China, for which data is not available) do not achieve this absolute minimum. Even in middle-income countries, which have on average a real per capita income over three times greater, one third may be faced with chronic economic insecurity, and the rate in, for example, Ecuador and Malaysia, is higher still (UNICEF, 1987, Table 6; Bigsten, 1987). At this below-subsistence standard, effective planning for the future is dauntingly difficult and both health and autonomy are thereby impaired. The same occurs when previously low, but adjusted-to, standards of living are drastically reduced, as has happened for many groups in the Third World in the deep recession of the 1980s. Things look no brighter for the 1990s.

Reasonably consistent data on access to formal *education* are now available for most countries. Despite some improvement, the opportunities to receive secondary schooling are limited in the Third World and only in the First World do opportunities for advanced education reach more than a small minority. The present effect of such past patterns is revealed in rows 17 and 18, showing the educational status of adults in groups of countries. There is an association with income per head, especially for higher education, but there are many exceptions. China and India have a more educated population than their income level would predict. Several middle-income nations reveal highly unequal (past) patterns of educational access, with relatively low proportions having any secondary education, yet with relatively large numbers benefiting from higher education. The citizens of the state socialist nations of the Second World enjoy the widest access to basic education, and fall not far short of the West in terms of higher education. Of course, such data on inputs of formal education can never supplant direct measures of learning – whether from formal or informal sources.

Lastly, Table 12.1 presents two indicators pertaining to biological reproduction and the specific threats to the health and autonomy of women stemming from pregnancy and childbirth. Ideally information is desired on the availability of contraceptive knowledge and of the opportunities to women to avail themselves of birth control appliances, sterilisation and abortion. Indicators of contraceptive use (row 21) derived from the *World Fertility Survey* provide a useful proxy, though the data may underestimate contraceptive prevalence and more crucially take no account of the relative safety of the contraceptive techniques available. They show a steady growth in contraceptive practices over the last two decades, but vast gaps particularly in low-income nations (excluding India, China and some others).

This data needs complementing with another important indicator of reproductive choice – access to legal abortion. Comparisons of *de jure* rights to abortion (a necessary but not a sufficient condition reasonable access) show that it is most liberal in China and parts of the Soviet bloc, with most Western countries close behind. Throughout much of the rest of the Third World, however, it remains either illegal or inaccessible (Dixon-Mueller, 1990). We may safely conclude that threats to health and autonomy stemming from a lack of reproductive choice remain profound in much of the Third World and are much diminished in the First and Second Worlds. But an important qualification should be made in the case of some state socialist nations. The USSR places excessive reliance on abortions as a method of fertility control, which poses a threat to women's health, while others, notably China, operate birth control policies in ways that curtail other aspects of women's autonomy (Hillier, 1988).

The net effect of these and related deficiencies in reproductive rights is illustrated in comparative levels of maternal mortality (line 22). They show that it has been all but eliminated in the economically developed world, but maternal deaths are still prevalent throughout much of the Third World, particularly Africa. In Ethiopia two women are estimated to die for every 100 births. On the other hand some nations, notably China, have made tremendous strides in reducing maternal deaths. Two factors, out of several, influencing this are the number of babies per mother and the time span between births. One measure of the former – the total fertility rate – has fallen substantially over the last two decades in China and India and many middle-income countries. However, it remains very high in the majority of the poorest countries (World Bank, 1988, Table 33).

For our other groups of intermediate need, reliable comparative data are sparse or non-existent. For *environmental quality*, there is no uniform monitoring but a considerable amount of non-systematic data on which to draw (UN, 1987). For example, data on air pollution show that the concentration of sulphur dioxide and smoke fell at the majority of monitoring stations between 1973 and 1980, but that this decline was more marked in cities in the North than the South. Indeed, in a significant number of Third World cities, air pollution continued to worsen over this period. However, the range of variation within both North and South is great: for example both Rome and several East European cities suffer high levels of pollution. Human exposure to lead is another significant threat to health: environmental data are limited but they suggest that Mexico City has the highest levels (outside areas close to smelters), while levels in the UK and Belgium are, for example, significantly higher than in Sweden and Japan. When river, lake and ground water pollution is introduced, a simple measure of environmental quality is difficult to construct. However the broad picture suggests that overall pollution levels are generally most threatening in the state socialist countries of the Second World, that they are falling from a high level in much, but not all, of the First World and that they are rising rapidly in many of the most populated parts of the Third World. We return to this issue below.

For most of the remaining areas of intermediate need contemporary global indicators are inadequate for charting objective welfare. Improvements in social reporting are urgently required for morbidity rates and the prevalence of disability, for mental illness, for opportunities to acquire socially relevant skills and to participate in significant social activities, for the extent of free time, for the quality of work environments, for the extent of child neglect, abuse and ill-treatment, for the presence or absence of primary support groups and for economic insecurity. At the same time we must recognise the inadequacy even of many of the statistics in Table 12.1 as accurate indicators of what we really want to measure. For example, we need improved indicators of learning, such as the proportion of people with or lacking specified types of knowledge: mathematical, scientific, historical and comparative cultural.

Nevertheless, these defects do not mean that any statement on the world social situation is unfounded (let alone unfoundable). Our ignorance is not as great as the relativists would have us believe. We can draw together the evidence that is available for the major groups of nations and establish certain conclusions about individual, substantive need-satisfaction in the aggregate. It is possible to compare the levels of objective welfare of people in very different social, economic, religious and political settings.

Societal preconditions

However sensitively it is measured, the satisfaction of substantive needs is insufficient to document the potential in any social group to improve and optimise need-satisfactions. It must be complemented by indicators of those material and procedural preconditions which enable groups rationally and democratically to improve their capacity for social participation and choice. Information on the satisfaction of some of these societal needs is even more scarce than that relating to substantive needs, so the reality of any audit falls woefully short of what is necessary. However, Table 12.3 brings together just six indicators which are reasonably robust and comparable.

Table 12.3 *Societal preconditions for optimal need-satisfaction in the Three Worlds*

	Third world				Second world	First World world	
	China	India	Other low income	Medium income			
Civil/political							
1 Human rights, 1984	23	60	(38)	56	24	91	50
2 Democracy, 1985	0	3.0	0.7	1.8	0.3	4.0	1.7
Material							
3 Basics output, 1975		—0.4—		[0.6]	0.8	1.6	3.4
4 Income of poorest 20% c. 1980	–	201	(189)	(582)	–	3113	(1353)
Sustainability							
5 Energy consumption p.c., 1985	532	208	88	767	4661	4952	1498
6 Carbon emissions, 1987	0.36	0.29	–	(1.82)	2.47	3.00	–

cont. p. 262

Notes and sources (by row numbers)

Weighted (by population) averages for same country groups as Table 12.1, except where stated. Numbers in brackets refer to country groups for which data available on fewer than half the countries.

1   Humana's index of human rights performance, 1984 (Humana, 1986, pp. xiv–xv).
2   Wesson's classification of political systems, 1985. Scores: stable democracies = 4, insecure democracies = 3, partial democracies = 2, limited authoritarianisms = 1, absolutisms = 0. Unweighted averages (Wesson, 1987)
3   Cole and Miles' calculations of aggregate output of basic need-satisfiers in 1975, US$ trillion. The country groups do not correspond exactly with those used in the rest of the table. 'First World': OECD nations, plus South Africa, minus Greece, Portugal, Spain, Turkey. These are included in 'NICs + OPEC' alongside Argentina, Brazil, Chile, Columbia, Hong Kong, Israel, South Korea, Mexico, Puerto Rico, Singapore, Taiwan and the OPEC members. China and India are not distinguished from the remaining low and middle-income countries (Cole and Miles, 1984, Table 5.16)
4   'Rawlsian' index of real incomes of worst off, $US 1980. It is the product of per capita income at purchasing power parities for 1980 (World Bank, 1987, Box A.2) and the income share of the lowest quintile of households (varying dates between 1970 and 1986) (World Bank, 1988, Table 26), divided by 20.
5   Energy consumption per capita (kg of oil equivalent), 1985 (World Bank, 1988, Table 9)
6   Greenhouse gas emissions (carbon dioxide, methane and CFCs) per head, tonnes of carbon in 1987 (World Resources Institute, reported in *Guardian*, 15 June 1990).

Humana's composite index of human rights has already been introduced; his results for 1984 are summarised in row 1 of the table. It shows that Western nations do best in respecting the civil and political rights of their peoples, and that China and the (preglasnost) Soviet bloc do worst. Low-income nations also tend to show poor or very poor respect for individual rights, as do many medium-income nations. However, India scores relatively highly in the low-income group, along with such countries as Sierra Leone, Senegal, Zambia and Sri Lanka, while among the medium-income countries, Costa Rica, Uruguay and Papua New Guinea score better than some Western nations.

Indicators of political participation are also required if the procedural preconditions for improving need-satisfaction are to be charted. Table 12.3 draws on a recent survey which allocates political systems to one of five categories, which can be crudely ranked according to the scope they afford citizens to influence state policy. Representative democracy was securely established by the mid-1980s in the First World, non-existent in the Soviet bloc and China and fragile or non-existent in much of the Third World. However, India and some middle income countries are again notable exceptions. Roughly the same pattern is found by Kurian (1979, Table 43) and Derbyshire and Derbyshire (1989, ch. 3). By 1988, according to Sivard (1989, p. 21), 64 governments, well over half of Third World countries, were under military control, the largest number for at least a decade.

Turning to the material preconditions for effective *social and economic rights*, Table 12.3 presents two measures which go some way to capturing the material potential for high levels of need-satisfaction. Row 3 offers a measure of the effectiveness of the production stage of our economic model, using Cole and Miles's estimate of the output of 'basics', a concept akin to our need satisfiers. The country groupings are not identical to those used in the rest of the table and should therefore be regarded as illustrative only. Nevertheless they graphically illustrate the gross disparity in the material foundations of need-satisfaction in the contemporary world. Global inequity in the consumption of 'luxuries' (not shown) is of course wider still.

Incorporating the distribution stage, there is no monetary measure available of the consumption of basics by different income groups and we must make do with the measure of real income discussed in Chapter 11. Available data on the income shares of the poorest 20 per cent of populations show that it is among middle-income Third World countries that inequalities in income and need-satisfaction are greatest. This lends support to Kuznets' widely debated hypothesis of an inverted U-shaped relation between level of economic development and income inequality (1955; Bigsten, 1987; Ram, 1988). There is also a regional effect revealing the Latin American countries as the most inegalitarian (Selowsky, 1981). Row 4 uses this and the data on GDP per head at purchasing power parities to calculate a 'Rawlsian measure' of the real incomes of the worst off (based on selected nations within each group).

Of course, the material resources of the poorest people vary enormously between countries of the Third and First worlds. For example, in 1980, the $200 average annual income of the poor in

India amounts to less than 5 per cent of Sweden's $4400. But there are also significant disparities within the high-income group – between the USA and Sweden, for example (see Table 13.1). To overcome the discrepancies due to stages of development, in Chapter 11 we identified high-achievement countries at lower levels of aggregate income. These comparisons show for example that the average real income of the poorest fifth of the population in Kenya ($83) was less than a quarter of that in Sri Lanka ($355 in 1980). In the middle-income category, disparities were just as wide – the real income of the worst off in Brazil ($336) is even lower than in much-poorer Sri Lanka and amounts to only one quarter of that received by their equivalents in Yugoslavia. Where production is effective and distribution is not too inegalitarian, then the worst off will do best; and vice versa. Thus redistribution towards the poor *can* have some effect in compensating for a low aggregate output (Stewart, 1984, pp. 98–9; cf. Ram, 1985).

We have observed that a crucial determinant of the effectiveness of the next stage of our economic model – the need-transformation process – is the division of income within the household. A general finding throughout the world is that women's incomes are often used almost exclusively to meet collective household needs, whereas men tend to retain a considerable portion of their incomes for personal spending (Elson, 1990). We are still no closer to having reliable comparative information on the similarities and differences in intra-household inequality across societies. However, it is likely that this inequality has grown in response to the 'structural adjustment policies' pursued throughout much of the Third World and parts of the First World in the 1980s which cut social services and raised food prices. This is interfering with the reproduction and maintenance of children and other weaker members of the household, since according to a UNICEF study women's unpaid labour has not been able to absorb all the costs of such policies (Cornia *et al.*, 1987). A poignant study of an urban, low-income community in Guayaquil, Ecuador, found that in about 55 per cent of households women were just managing to cope with the effects of such policies, whereas about 15 per cent were going under. They 'were exhausted, their families disintegrating, their children dropping out of school and roaming the streets, becoming involved in street gangs and exposed to drugs' (Elson, 1990, p. 24). But such evidence remains patchy and we cannot in our present state of knowledge ascertain levels of effectiveness of the need-transformation process.

Lastly, we need to consider the material reproduction process and the global ecological constraints on production to meet needs. Rows 5 and 6 of Table 12.3 present two indices to monitor this. The first uses energy consumption per head as an indicator of the resource costs of satisfying needs in the different groups of countries. It displays enormous variations in resource use in the contemporary world. There is a sharp division here between the industrialised world – both West and East – and the whole of the Third World. The second indicator uses the World Resources Institute calculations of per capita emissions of greenhouse gases. The industrialised nations of West and East emerge as the major contributors to this particular threat to global environmental equilibrium. The advanced Western nations for example emit ten times the carbon per capita that India does. These material reproduction indicators thus qualify our earlier findings about substantive need-satisfaction. They reveal the global cost, and the cost to the world's poor, of present Northern policies, notwithstanding their contribution to present-day Northern living standards.

Gender differences in need-satisfaction

Let us complete this brief global audit of need-satisfaction by illustrating how the need-satisfaction levels of specific groups might be assessed employing the same theory of need and the same methodology. We shall focus on the needs of women. Levels of satisfaction of the reproductive needs of women have already been addressed in Table 12.1. Table 12.4 on the other hand disaggregates by gender a small number of the indicators of universal need.

Beginning with survival/health, Seager and Olson summarise the situation as follows:

> Women are biologically stronger than men. But where girls' and women's health is neglected, that edge is lost. In poor countries and in rural settings, constant childbearing, lack of village-level health care, and the neglect of infant girls in favour of boys, all make living more hazardous for women. Working harder and longer, eating less and worse, earning less and having little

control over resources – all while giving birth and nursing – make women more vulnerable to disease ... particularly in poor countries (1986, p. 26).

Sen (1990) argues that the ratio of women to men in a population provides a good index of the relative deprivation of women's health. He notes that when given the same care as males, females tend to have better survival rates, yielding an overall ratio of women to men of about 1.05 to 1. Significantly lower ratios than this indicate severe disadvantages faced by women stemming from a variety of cultural and economic factors. The data from which row 1 of the table is drawn show that South and West Asia do worst, with a ratio of 100.3 in India and as low as 0.90 in Pakistan. The highest ratios are found in the First and Second Worlds, yet they are also relatively high in sub-Saharan Africa, indicating that economic development alone is an inadequate explanation.

Turning to autonomy, international data on illiteracy are unambiguous: female literacy, despite global improvements, is still remarkably limited in the poorest nations, with some exceptions such as Sri Lanka and Vietnam. Though women are less likely to be literate than men in almost every country, the gap is especially wide in India and Pakistan. Clearly this gender inequality does not apply in those nations with universal literacy. However, more sophisticated data on functional illiteracy shows that women are somewhat more disadvantaged than men in the USA, and possibly elsewhere (Seager and Olson, 1986, p. 112). Of course much more subtle indicators are required to say much more about gender differences in autonomy. As an example, data on the prevalence of marriages among young girls suggest that, in relation to sexuality, the autonomy of women is extensively constrained in parts of Africa, the Middle East, India, Pakistan and Bangladesh (Seager and Olson, 1986, Section 2).

Gender differences in the opportunity to participate in socially significant activities are charted in Table 12.4 for employment and political representation. Both reveal less variation between the 'three worlds' than for other measures of need-satisfaction. Women's employment opportunities and participation in the paid labour force have risen almost everywhere, but measures of the sex ratio of 'gainful employment' (all work outside the home, possibly but not necessarily for a wage) show a much higher rate in sub-Saharan

Africa than in much of Asia for example (Sen, 1990, p. 64). However, this index alone ignores women's unpaid household work and needs complementing with detailed time budget studies. Data collated by Seager and Olson (1986, Section 13) confirm that women's 'double burden' persists in all parts of the world. Indeed some trends which contribute to enhancing well-being in the aggregate impose additional duties and fatigue on women. In all countries women work longer hours than men, but the absolute extent of the work is greater in poorer countries (Lesley Doyal, 1990a; 1990b).

Though women have won the vote in all but a handful of nations, Table 12.4 shows that they remain effectively excluded from participation in the exercise of political authority. Only in Scandinavia, Eastern Europe and China do women have significant representation in the legislature. Their power in executive branches of government is still more curtailed; for example, tiny numbers hold cabinet-level positions in most Western countries. This is one dimension of need-satisfaction where no significant differences appear between the 'three worlds'. Women are disadvantaged everywhere.

Table 12.4 *Gender differences in need-satisfaction*

	Third world				Second world	First World world
	China	India	Other low income	Medium income		
Figures for females in relation to males (= 100):						
Health						
Life expectancy, 1988	104.3	100.3	104.5	108.8	109.0	105.7
Learning						
Literacy, 1985	68	51	46	83	98	69
Opportunities to participate						
Employment, 1988	76	34	48	54	61	56
Legislature, 1988	21	8	9	14	8	13
Education						
Primary, 1986–88	89	72	79	93	99	86
Secondary, 1986–88	74	54	58	96	102	77

Sources:
UNDP (1990) Tables 9, 11, 20, 23, 24.

As regards access to education, marked progress has been made over the last two decades in giving girls access to primary and secondary schooling throughout most countries. In the First, Second and much of the middle-income Third World, formal equality has almost been reached. However, in many low-income countries and in most Islamic countries, gender discrimination remains. In the Yemen Arab Republic, for instance, only 11 per cent as many girls as boys receive secondary schooling (World Bank, 1988, Table 33). Moreover, 'structural adjustment' policies in recent years are undermining this progress in some countries due to the introduction of charges for education.

Turning to our other intermediate needs, there is some evidence that the nutritional status of girls is poorer than boys in several low-income countries (Sen, 1984, ch. 15). We have already referred, too, to the trends in the 1980s towards worse nutrition for women and some children in certain Third World countries. Circumstantial support for this is also found in the *World Fertility Survey* on families' preferences for sons over daughters. In some countries in Asia and the Near East in particular there is a strong preference for a male child, which can mean that girls are given less to eat (Seager and Olson, 1986, §3). There is much indirect evidence that the economic security of women is qualitatively lower than that of men in the aggregate (UNDP, 1990, pp. 22, 110–11). Violence by men against women constitutes another universal dimension of gendered difference in need-satisfaction. Comparative data on rape are compiled by the UN and Interpol, but both sets are fraught with problems of methodology and measurement. They imply that one of the richest nations – the USA – has the highest incidence of rape (US Bureau of Justice, 1988, Table 6).

Lastly, gender inequalities in the procedural and material preconditions for improving need-satisfaction can also be monitored. The *United Nations Review of the Decade for Women 1975–85* concluded that substantial progress had been made in securing *de jure* equality for women, in terms of rights to nationality, legal capacity, property ownership, freedom of movement and choice of surname (UN, 1985). Against this must be set two important facts. First, there are still many nations where these improvements in civil rights have not occured. For instance, throughout much of North and Central Africa, the Middle East and the Indian subcontinent women do not have the same rights as men to inherit wealth (Seager and Olson, §21). Second, *de jure* rights do not entail *de facto* rights while the gendered division of labour, the sexual contract and patriarchal power persist. Even in the First World it can be argued that the 'double burden' of work coupled with the 'feminisation of poverty' and rising marriage breakdown have in practice severely curtailed the ability of women to take advantage of improved legal rights (Scott, 1984; Norris, 1987, pp. 1–4).

Conclusion: global patterns of welfare

We hope to have demonstrated by now that the satisfaction of basic needs, and their material and procedural preconditions, can be compared and evaluated across broad populations espousing very different beliefs and living in varied political and social systems. Relativists are wrong: objective welfare *can* be compared and evaluated over space and over time. Of course much of this analysis has relied on statistics whose defects are only too well known. Yet these problems do not invalidate cautious use of the best statistical material to hand. In the case of open and acknowledged human need we have a duty to do the best we can rather than seek perfection. 'If a thing is worth doing,' wrote Chesterton, 'it is worth doing badly'! Moreover, the regular compilation of such social audits will reveal the weaknesses and gaps in the data and augment pressures to improve them. Let us summarise our findings for the Three Worlds.

The low-income countries including China and India

Setting aside the two giants for the moment, levels of need-satisfaction are lowest in the low-income countries in every domain of substantive need-satisfaction for which we have records. More-over procedural and material preconditions for improved need-satisfaction are extremely underdeveloped. Women in particular are most disadvantaged in the poorest countries, though there are some significant differences between nations. On all counts the blocks to human flourishing are daunting in the poorest sector of the Third World. Yet the much better record of countries such as Sri Lanka (at least until recent years) upholds the view of those who argue that the relationship between need-satisfaction and income per head is certainly not simple or linear. It is logically possible that in those domains for which there is little or no information, for example child care, standards are better (relatively or absolutely) in the Third World. But in the absence of hard data it would be foolish to contend that this invalidates the overwhelming import of such knowledge as we have.

China remains one of the star performers among the low-income nations in meeting basic needs; and performs relatively well in many measures of gender inequality. On the other hand it is one of the worst abusers of human rights and other procedural needs.

Though India does better in terms of access to certain universal satisfier characteristics than other poor countries, such as clean water, health services and education, its record in other areas is equally poor. The general level of basic need satisfaction among women in India is among the very worst. Paradoxically however its record in upholding civil and political rights is relatively good.

Middle-income countries

These exhibit a wide variation in income per head and in need-satisfaction, but generally speaking levels of need-satisfaction lie in between those of the West and the low-income countries, though usually closer to the latter. Survival chances are more akin to those in the poorest countries, and in most, people are worse off than in China, though average health status may be better than mortality rates suggest. An average calorie consumption of 110 per cent of requirements suggests that undernutrition is avoidable, but the still-high incidence of absolute poverty indicates that maldistribution generates malnutrition on a wide scale. Access to water and health services remains poor in most of these countries, and the housing conditions of the masses are very low – much closer to poor Third World than to First World standards. Physical and economic insecurity are also rife, particularly in certain Latin American countries where human rights are in general poorly protected. Indicators of access to education and literacy are intermediate between the poorest and richest nations. Access to birth control and safe child-bearing are often little better than in the low-income nations. However, the access of women to education and literacy, and average autonomy levels according to some other indicators, is better generally (except in the Middle East). The data suggests that some countries in this group achieve high levels of overall welfare, for example Costa Rica.

The Second World

Despite their lower per capita income, the state socialist countries appear to achieve comparable levels of substantive need-satisfaction to the First World as regards nutrition, physical and economic security and, most notably, education opportunities. They do less well, however, in terms of physical health, and notably less well in providing adequate housing. Women enjoy good access to education, but suffer from the same deprivations as Western women, plus possibly others besides, such as a heavier dual burden on their time. For the period up to the mid-1980s, of course, respect for civil and political rights was minimal and achievements as regards all other aspects of our social preconditions were equally poor. No doubt, after the events of 1989, some parts of this picture will begin to change, but the outcome of these changes remains indeterminate for the present.

The First World

Levels of substantive need-satisfaction are highest in the West in almost all domains for which we have data and it is here where material/ procedural preconditions for improved performance in meeting needs are most securely in place. Many (but not all) aspects of women's welfare for which we have information are highest in the nations of the First World, despite the entrenched gender-based disadvantages which persist. However the advanced capitalist world (and the state socialist bloc to a lesser extent) lay claim to a disparate share of planetary resources, in a fashion which is neither generalisable over space nor sustainable through time. In this sense its performance in the domain of material reproduction is inferior.

The higher levels of substantive and procedural need-satisfaction enjoyed in the North may be bought at the expense of lower levels in the South in other ways too. It is most likely that the poorer performance of the Third World has *some* connection with its political and economic dependence on the North, though dispute rages about the nature of that connection. The effect of United States 'predatory democracy' in limiting the rights of nations within its sphere of influence, such as Nicaragua, El Salvador and Guatemala should not be forgotten, though good indicators of such restrictions on national autonomy are not yet available (cf. Chomsky and Herman, 1979). In this way the West may well repress the rights of some Third World countries while at the same time protecting those of its own citizens. Similarly the Soviet Union has in the past actively used its national autonomy to deny that of others. However, none of this either lends support to nor disproves any particular explanation of these global disparities, nor any particular strategy for improving welfare across the globe. These contentious issues must be the subject of a separate study.

Of course our audit still leaves open the practical problem of combining disparate indices into an overall index of human welfare, a conundrum which we passed over in Chapter 8. How, for example, can we compare more education with greater infant mortality? In practice, however, the dilemma appears to be less pressing, since often the same ranking applies for different dimensions of need and for different universal satisfier characteristics. Here Sen's principle of 'dominance partial ordering' can come into play (Sen 1987, p. 4): if X has more of some object of value and no less of any others than Y, then X has a higher standard of living than Y. In the case of many, but not all, of our basic and intermediate needs this is the case when comparing the First World and the low-income Third World today. But there are some significant exceptions, and existing statistics may obscure other domains of life where the ordering is different. Where dominance partial ordering is not applicable, there is a case for ranking a person, group or nation according to their most serious domain of need-deprivation, irrespective of how well off they are in other domains. As we argued in Chapter 8, the latter cannot compensate for the former (Penz, 1986, p. 171; after Rescher, 1972, pp. 4–5).

The global audit above is not original, drawing as it does on a host of currently available statistics. What we believe is original is the linkage between measurement and theory. We have tried to show, gaps in the existing data notwithstanding, how our theory can select and order existing statistical information to give a picture of individual need-satisfactions in the modern world, albeit in a highly aggregated form for groups of people numbering in the hundreds of millions. Relativist arguments to the contrary, we can make perfectly valid comparisons between countries which embrace

Catholicism and Confucianism, Communism and Capitalism in ways which identify the preconditions for human liberation which are common to them all.

IV

The Politics of Human Need

13

Towards a Political Economy of Need-Satisfaction

Chapter 12 provides a description of need-satisfaction in the contemporary world: it does not explain what we observe. Such findings raise questions for each of the 'Three Worlds'. What, if any, is the contribution of economic growth, as conventionally defined and measured, to the level and distribution of need-satisfaction? What other political and social institutions and processes are at work? Why have the more developed state socialist societies failed to live up to their explicit goals to raise levels of need-satisfaction above those in the West? What explains the widely different achievements of nations within the First and Third worlds? These questions raise profound issues of politics and economics which cannot be tackled thoroughly here. What we shall attempt in this chapter is an outline of some of the components of a political economy of need-satisfaction for each of the 'Three Worlds' as well as an agenda for future research.

Economic development and need-satisfaction in the Third World

It is apparent from the material in Chapter 12 that in many domains of human need, levels of satisfaction are associated with national income per head. Figure 13.1, for instance, shows a non-linear relationship between life expectancy and per capita income. According to Stewart (1985, p. 62) about 70 per cent of country variation in the former can be explained by differences in the latter. Similarly Moon and Dixon (1985) have found an extremely strong association between the Physical Quality of Life Index and per capita income.[1] Such correlations appear to lend powerful support for the view that (conventionally defined) economic growth is a necessary condition for improved objective welfare. Such a relationship would have major implications for the political economy of development and for strategies of modernisation. However all the available evidence suggests that no such simple conclusion about the relationship between economic development and welfare can be drawn. This is the case for several reasons.

Figure 13.1   *The relationship between life expectancy and per capita incomes, 1979*

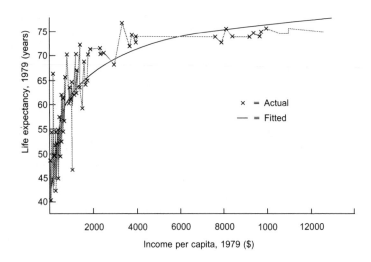

Source: Stewart (1985), Figure 4.2, p. 61.

First, the statistical association in Figure 13.1 is based on an indicator tapping only one aspect of human need. We have noted that for some domains of need-satisfaction no information is available, and in most of the others better indicators are required. It is conceivable that if these were developed, the association between objective welfare and economic growth would be non-existent or even negative. For example, we might find that the social isolation of elderly people and 'idiosyncratic' child abuse were both prevalent among high-income nations and nations undergoing rapid economic development. This is one reason for caution in reaching conclusions about the association between economic and social development.

Second, the observed associations can be explained by different directions of causality. On the one hand, all things being equal, higher incomes will permit higher food consumption, better shelter, and more extensive public goods – especially water, sanitation, health care and education programmes. On the other hand, the reduction of disease, malnutrition and illiteracy may directly improve the productivity of labour, the production of need-satisfiers and the effectiveness with which these are transformed into need-satisfactions, via improved patterns of consumption and child-rearing (see Stewart, 1985; Streeten, 1981, pp. 348–51). When other variables are introduced, such as the extent of democratic processes or the external vulnerability of national economies, the problems of disentangling causality become still more complex.

Above all, even with those indicators strongly associated with *per capita* income there are puzzling anomalies. Countries with similar levels of development have very different success rates in meeting basic needs. Some low-income countries do much better than their income level would lead us to expect, and some medium- and high-income countries do much worse. For example, South Africa has an average life expectancy of only 61 years – well below Sri Lanka's 70 years despite an average income level four and a half times higher. That rapid growth *per se* is insufficient for improved human welfare is glaringly obvious when the 'poor performers' are analysed. In Nigeria, for example, a middle-income nation with rapid growth rates from the early 1970s, life expectancy remains very low (49 years in 1985); infant mortality very high (182 deaths per 1000); female literacy is only 31 per cent; there is extensive undernutrition and malnutrition, and polluted water supplies are common even in urban areas. Matters are similar in Brazil despite the 'economic miracle' of the 1960s and 1970s and its upper-middle average income level. It is one of the most inegalitarian economies in the world: the income share of the richest fifth in 1972 was 67 per cent – some thirty times greater than that of the poorest fifth. Even in the wealthiest provinces under- and malnutrition are rife. In Sao Paulo, for example, over one half of the population has insufficient calories for a minimally healthy diet in a city of extravagant luxury. Both nations are also poor respecters of human rights.

A politics of need has most to learn from those nations which achieve substantially higher levels of need-satisfaction than their income per head would predict. On the basis of life expectancy and literacy, Stewart argues that the 'good performers' fall into three categories (1985, ch. 4). First, there are developing state socialist countries such as China and Cuba. These have succeeded in raising levels of basic need-satisfaction for the masses by 'planning production to meet basic needs, by egalitarian income distribution and by rationing/allocating basic-need goods to reach all people irrespective of income' (Stewart, 1985, p. 71). The second category includes the capitalist 'success stories' of East Asia such as Taiwan and South Korea. Though this group may appear to support the view that high conventional growth rates are in themselves the surest path to basic need-satisfaction, in fact these nations are distinguished by a substantial level of state economic intervention, such as land reform or investment in human capital, which prioritises some of our intermediate needs (cf. Sen, 1984, pp. 102–3). A third group comprises market economies with extensive state social intervention which accord a certain priority to meeting basic needs, often via state control over the price or allocation of basic foodstuffs. Examples include Sri Lanka (until the switch to market reforms in 1977) and Costa Rica. Each of these groups of countries can contribute to the construction of models for human development. There appears to be a variety of 'basic-needs strategies' to choose from (Streeten, 1981, pp. 348–51), but generally speaking the most successful countries all exhibit extensive state 'steering' of the economy guided by goals which prioritise at least some aspects of what we have called basic need-satisfaction.

Consideration of all the available indicators leads us to single out *Costa Rica* as a model of need-satisfaction in the Third World. Its purchasing power per head in 1984 amounted to 24 per cent of that of the USA – slightly below the average for middle-income countries of the Third World – and its energy consumption per head is only 11 per cent of the First World average. Costa Rica is the world's poorest country to have approximated Western levels of objective welfare across a wide range of need indicators: life expectancy, infant mortality, nutrition, access to clean water, health care, literacy, higher education enrolment, respect for human rights, maternal mortality, access to contraception, and certain measures of gender equality. Its success provides a yardstick with which to assess need-satisfaction in the Third World. Sri Lanka, up to 1977, provided a similar example for the lowest-income nations. However, since then the IMF-inspired growth strategy has eroded both the welfare system and political democracy, the twin pillars upon which its high standard of basic needs was erected, with the result that in several respects need-satisfaction there had begun to deteriorate by the early 1980s (Rupesinghe, 1986) – a deteriation no doubt exaculated by the ongoing conflict. We shall discuss below the role these exemplar countries can play in defining a 'constrained optimum' for need-satisfaction.

Of course the fact that appropriate planning for need-satisfaction has been successful in some countries in the Third World does not entail that this will or can always be the case. Such a conclusion would beg major questions about global power, inequality and justice and the strategies realistically available to optimise need-satisfaction on a global scale. While we have argued for the morality of the goal of optimum need-satisfaction for everyone, subject to ecological constraints, this alone cannot determine which strategy, if any, might achieve it. We live within a global order of sovereign states without a world government or federation. The resulting *modus vivendi* generates an unstable system where inequalities in economic and political power are crucial in determining outcomes (Pogge, 1989, §19). A political dependency has followed which denies the most elementary human rights and need-satisfactions to millions in the post-war period – witness the interventions in Czechoslovakia and Nicaragua, for instance. The vast disparities in income and wealth in the contemporary world also generate economic dependence, though the mechanisms which bring this about are hotly contested. If state capacities are a necessary, though not sufficient, condition for improved welfare in the present global market economy, then constraints on such capacities stemming from the global order of unequal states are also relevant in accounting for some Third World differences in need-satisfaction (Moon and Dixon, 1985, pp. 665–9).

At this point we encounter complex issues and fierce debates. The dominant perspective on development in the early post-war period was modernisation theory, holding out the possibility of a ladder of growth to all societies who determinedly broke their traditional bonds. In the later 1960s and 1970s this view was attacked by the dependency school, which argued that the structure of the world political economy imposed systemic blocks to development in the Third World (Brewer, 1980). Despite their differences, both approaches analysed underdevelopment at a holistic and global level. This contrasted with the emphasis of comparative historical approaches on the role and capacities of states and/or mass mobilisations within specific Third World societies. Evans and Stephens (1988) argue that out of this encounter is emerging a new comparative political economy which combines the themes of global economic integration and the specificity of different states, societies and regions.

It is apparent that such a framework offers some hope of understanding the similarities and differences which we observe in need-satisfaction in the Third World. It synthesises the modernisation and dependency accounts of the global economy, while simultaneously relating them to the political and social structural factors which enable or prevent each nation from utilising international economic ties to its benefit. The evidence is accumulating that successful development in the Third World requires a combination of state direction and market orientation. Furthermore, there is no clear support for the view that accumulation and distribution are in conflict – that economic growth requires or entails worsening inequality. The trade-off between the two, and hence the degree of *social* development, will also be affected by such factors as the nature of agrarian property rights, the extent of working-class organisation and the orientation and policies of the state. The same sorts of factors appear to explain the existence or absence of democracy within the Third World, alongside the geopolitical nature of relations between core countries, especially the USA, and the periphery. [2]

Thus the new comparative political economy of the Third World can begin to throw light on the findings presented in Chapter 12. A future research agenda would need to investigate issues such as: do correlates of crude indices of basic need-satisfaction, such as the PQLI, hold up when a broader range of indicators is used? What explains the differing economic and geo-political constraints on the capacities of Third World states to meet the needs of their populations? What socio-economic institutions and forms of political mobilisation internal to Third World countries account for examples of success and failure in satisfying basic needs? What contemporary features of the world economy are driving some Third World economies into deeper penury and desperation, and why?

State socialism and need-satisfaction in the Second World

Following the October revolution, the new Soviet society proclaimed Marx's vision of communism – 'To each according to his needs' – as its ultimate goal. Planned production to meet needs was to replace market-determined production for profit. We might therefore expect the state socialist societies to do better than capitalist societies (at least at any given level of economic development) in meeting human needs. The 1980s, however, ended with the collapse of all of the political systems of Eastern Europe and the beginning of their economic transformation towards more capitalist or mixed forms. Some have suggested that socialism is dead and that the history of ideas has reached its terminus with the worldwide hegemony of democratic capitalism (Fukuyama, 1989). Whatever the outcome of this debate, it is clear that a chasm has opened up between the ideal and the reality of socialism in the twentieth century. Though we cannot offer a systematic explanation of this failure, we can contribute to the debate with an assessment of how well or badly state socialist systems met the needs of their population up to the mid-1980s.

Let us distinguish here between developing and developed state socialist societies. We have already observed that China has achieved some impressive results in meeting basic needs such as health and literacy, most of its relative improvement having occurred under collectivist planning since 1949. Other developing state socialist nations such as Cuba and Vietnam have also succeeded in raising life expectancy and literacy for the mass of their population (relative to their per capita incomes) (Stewart, 1985). Cereseto and Waitzkin (1986) show that socialist countries have more favourable levels of need-satisfaction (at equivalent levels of economic development) on a wider range of indicators – including calorie supply and access to education. Socialist revolution and subsequent social transformation *can* therefore provide a successful route to enhanced welfare. However this favourable verdict is subject to two important qualifications. First, all such nations perform very badly in respecting human rights and in meeting some other procedural preconditions for improving need-satisfaction in so far as we can measure them. Second, other post-revolutionary countries have an appalling record in denying people's most basic needs, notably Cambodia under the Khmer Rouge and, in a different way, Ethiopia. State socialism has achieved real human liberation from the lowest levels of deprivation for many, but there are clearly counter-costs as well as counter-examples to be understood. The events since 1989 in no way obviate the importance of trying to do so.

What are the findings for the industrialised, economically advanced state socialist countries of Eastern Europe? Chapter 12 provided some answers, though the statistics are very patchy and there is a problem in assessing their per capita income and therefore in allowing for this when comparing them with other nations.[3] They reveal a mixed picture. The Eastern bloc countries do relatively well in meeting a few substantive needs, notably in providing access to education for men and women. For example, the general level of education is higher than in Western countries with a similar *per capita* income and it has continued to improve up to the early 1980s. However, these positive achievements are outweighed by the negative outcomes.

First, and most important, survival chances have *fallen* in the Soviet Union, and to a lesser extent Poland, since the late 1960s. The USSR has suffered an absolute decline in life expectancy without parallel in the industrialised world. Around 1960, the average Soviet citizen could expect to outlive his/her American counterpart, and infant mortality was approaching West European levels. By the mid-1980s, however, the picture was reversed. The crude mortality rate rose from 7.3 deaths per 1000 in 1965 to a peak of 10.8 in 1984 – an increase of 48 per cent. The infant mortality rate also increased from 22.9 deaths per 1000 live births in 1971 to an estimated 31.1 in 1976 – a rise of 36 per cent (Davis, 1988; cf. Cooper, 1987). While the other East European countries, except for Poland (Cooper *et al.*, 1984), are not known to have suffered an absolute rise in overall mortality, they have marked time while life expectancy in the West has surged ahead by another five years.

This unprecedented decline must reflect deficiencies in several intermediate needs. Davis (1988, p. 315), writing about the period since 1970, summarises a series of studies of health in the USSR as follows:

> There were several positive developments in consumption, exemplified by . . . improvements in the diet and educational standards of Soviet citizens. On the negative side, there was a substantial growth of consumption of alcohol and tobacco products and the intake of dietary cholesterol . . . the average citizen suffered from a 30–40 per cent vitamin deficit. Problems in the health environment contributed to illness as well. These included inadequate housing provision, low standards of public sanitation, the break-up of the extended family, excessively rapid mechanisation and chemicalisation of industry, increases in road traffic without adequate safety programs, growth in air and water pollution . . . As a result, the negative developments in health conditions generated growth in all four major categories of illness: degenerative, accidents, infections and nutritional.

Absolute standards fell well behind Western and some middle income nations as regards housing. For example, 17 per cent of families in the Soviet Union still have no separate house or flat but must share. Average urban living space in 1980 amounted to 8.6 sq.m. compared with the 'rational norm' of 15–18 sq.m. per capita (Aganbegyan, 1988, p. 90; Matthews, 1986, pp. 67–75). Nor has poverty been abolished, even according to the old Khrushchev budget poverty line (worth in the early 1980s about 67 roubles per head per month). Various studies report between 12 per cent and 57 per cent with family incomes below this line, with a minimum plausible figure around 40 per cent (Matthews, 1986, ch. 1). Thus the incidence of socially unacceptable income levels is higher than in any Western nation – only the USA approaches this degree of social poverty, but average standards there are of course much higher. Lastly, Soviet health care services are beset by shortages and inefficiencies. Shortages are a general phenomenon of state socialist economies, but were exacerbated in the Soviet Union which has accorded low priority to investment in health since 1970. The provision of medical services and sanitation, the supply of appropriate medical and pharmaceutical goods and the maintenance of staffing levels have all been adversely affected. As a result, the average quality of medical services in the USSR has remained low relative to prevailing Western standards (Davis, 1988, p. 317).

Vital components of individual autonomy, such as opportunities to participate in social roles, are also greatly circumscribed. One indicator here is well-known – the lack of many political and civic rights to discuss, organise and act. Yet alongside this are the extra restrictions upon free time, particularly for women. Women face a combination of paid work for relatively long hours and the persistence of the traditional gender division of labour within the home, with the result that many of them suffer a double burden greater even than that in the West (Badrova and Anker, 1985). While there is relatively generous provision of child care facilities, this must be set against the time spent queuing for necessities. A Polish survey showed that the average time spent queuing per household rose from 63 minutes to 98 minutes *a day* between 1966 and 1976 (*Economist*, 25 June 1988). The depressing impact of these factors on human autonomy was well captured by the samizdat document published by the Movement for Socialist Renewal in the USSR in 1986 (*Guardian*, 22 July 1986): 'The constant disappearance from the shops of first one series of goods and foodstuffs then another, the eternal hunt for the most basic goods and small everyday things, forces people to limit their range of interests to one ever-lasting search, leaving them neither the time nor the physical strength to satisfy their spiritual and cultural needs, and killing their human dignity.'

Our final verdict on state socialism as an economic system for meeting basic human needs is, therefore, a mixed one, with the negative elements predominating at higher stages of economic development. If it bears little resemblance to the official pre-Gorbachev Soviet ideology, neither does it really live down to the 'brutal dictatorship over needs' proclaimed by Feher *et al.* (1983). State socialism was and is an effective economic mechanism for bringing about a *transitional* improvement in substantive need-satisfaction, and for laying the material basis for further improvements. But, for reasons which need deeper exploration, it has failed to establish the procedural or material preconditions for improving need-satisfaction further and as a result now does serious harm to the health, autonomy and self-development of its citizens. The Second World is open not only to familiar Western criticisms concerning the democratic deficit, but to accusations of failure according to its own internal standards of meeting the basic needs of its people. This double failure – failure according to the lights of both liberalism and socialism – must play a part in explaining the rapid collapse of these regimes in 1989.

The reasons for this failure can be sketched in broad outline. They stem from the lack of democracy and the inefficiencies of centralised planning (Nove, 1983, Part 2; Devine, 1988, ch. 3). At the most basic level, the absence of channels of democratic representation and participation inhibits the rational identification of needs and universal satisfier characteristics by the political elite. Using the model of material production outlined in Chapter 11, we can then account for the failure of the state socialist model to provide the satisfiers to meet needs at all four stages. At the production stage, need-satisfiers are prioritised to reflect the interests of the relatively unconstrained planning apparatus in retaining power (Feher *et al.*, 1983, p. 65). Lower down the administrative hierarchy, the translation of policy goals into satisfiers is hindered, beyond low levels of development, by the efficiency and motivation problems of a centralised system of directives (Nove, 1983, pp. 32–45). The distribution and need-transformation domains are distorted by the blocks to autonomy in consumption and self-organised unions in production. Lastly, material reproduction is threatened by the fragmentation of interests again stemming from the absence of representative democracy and autonomous civil society. Need-satisfaction, though upheld in ideology, is thwarted in practice precisely by the absence of liberal rights and decentralised economic decision-making.

Advanced capitalism and need-satisfaction in the First World

The story told in the previous chapter is unambiguous: levels of individual and societal need-satisfaction are highest on average in the nations of the 'West'. This is of course a conclusion of some moment, which raises further questions in turn. Is it the sheer level of economic development of these nations which accounts for their relative privilege? Or is it the widespread existence of democratic forms and other examples of our procedural preconditions which are relevant? Are these standards of well-being parasitic on poverty and oppression elsewhere and for this and other reasons ungeneralisable? It is obvious that such questions introduce major issues in political philosophy and political economy. All we can do here is to try to establish an initial framework and database for finding the answers.

Table 13.1   *Comparative need-satisfaction in three Western countries*

	UK	USA	Sweden
Basic and intermediate need satisfaction			
1 Health: life expectancy, 1980	74	75	76
2 Infant mortality, 1980	10	11	6
3 Econ. participn: paid emp. 1985 (%)	65	68	80
4 Housing: overcrowding, 1970s (%)	0	1	2
5 Environment: water, 1985 (%)	83	74	99
6 Health services: hospital access, 1984	99	22	100
7 Econ security: income maintenance, 1989	23.4	13.8	39.1
8 Poverty, c. 1981 (%)	8.8	16.9	5.0
9 Physical security: homicide	1.0	9.0	1.4
10 Education: students in h.e.22 1980 (%)	57	38	
11 Use of contraception, 1988 (%)	83	68	78
Societal preconditions			
12 Human rights, 1984	94	90	98
13 Real income of worst-off, c.1979	3300	3300	4400
14 Electoral participation, 1965–80 (%)	76	56	90
15 Energy consumption p.c., 1986	3.8	7.2	6.4
Selected indicators of women's need satisfaction			
16 Female participn, 1987 (%)	63	66	79
17 Single mothers in poverty, c.1980 (%)	32	54	7
18 Women in higher education, 1987 (%)	37	51	47
19 Women in nat. legislature (%)	4	5	28

Notes and sources (by row numbers)

1   Life expectancy at birth, 1980. Source as Table 12.1.
2   Infant mortality rate, 1980. Ibid.
3   % working age population (15–64 years) in labour force, 1985. (OECD, 1989, pp. 10–11).

4   % population living at density of more than 1.5 persons per room, 1970s. (OECD 1986) Table 22.2.
5   Proportion of population served by waste water treatment plants (primary plus secondary and/or tertiary), 1985 or latest year. (OECD, 1987) Table 3.2.
6   % population eligible for public funding of hospital costs * % of average costs met, 1984. (OECD, 1985) Tables C1 and C4.
7   Index of 'de-commodification' – the extent to which income is independent of labour market participation and income in old age, sickness and unemployment (Esping-Andersen, 1990) Table 2.2.
8   % population with incomes less than 50% of that nation's median income, c.1981. (OECD, 1988) Table 4.2.
9   Homicides per 100000 population, 1987. Source as Table 12.1.
10 % 20–24 year age-group in higher education, 1980. Source as Table 12.1.
11 Percentage of women of childbearing age practising, or whose husbands are practising, any form of birth contraception (World Bank, 1988) Table 28.
12 Index of human rights, 1984. Source as Table 12.2.
13 An estimate of the real income of the bottom 20% in $US at purchasing power parities, c.1979. It is the product of average GDP per head at purchasing power parities and the % income received by the lowest quintile, divided by 20. GDP figures from OECD (1987a) Table 13. Income distribution data from O'Higgins *et al.*, 1985.
14 Electoral participation rate in elections 1965–80 (Korpi, 1983) p. 56.
15 Energy consumption per head in kg of oil equivalent, 1986. Source as in Table 12.3.
16 Female activity rates: participation in paid labour force (including unemployed) as percentage of total female population, 1987. (OECD, 1989, pp. 10–11).
17 Percentage of families with solo mothers and 2 + children with adjusted incomes less than 50% of the median, c.1980. (Buhmann *et al.*, 1987) Table 12.
18 Percentage of students in tertiary education who are women. (UN-ESCO, 1989) Table 1.4.
19 Proportion of women in lower house national legislatures, early 1980s. (Norris, 1987) p. 116.

Despite their high average scores there are of course notable differences in objective welfare between advanced capitalist countries. Table 13.1 sets out some indicators of need-satisfaction for just three – Britain, the USA and Sweden. Some of these indicators are the same as those in Tables 12.1, 12.3 and 12.4, but others draw on the greater wealth and variety of statistical information available for the OECD countries.

These countries have been chosen because they represent three different patterns of need-satisfaction: the United States exhibits low scores for many domains, Sweden very high scores and the UK often lies somewhere in between. This conclusion is derived from Table 13.1 and also a comparison of all the member nations of the OECD, excluding the less developed Mediterranean nations and countries with very small populations. Within this group of 18 nations, the USA is almost always found in the bottom three, if not the lowest, in terms of need-indicators, and Sweden among the top three achievers, if not the leader. Moreover the absolute differences in levels of need-satisfactions are quite substantial in many areas.

In certain fields for which indicators are shown in Table 13.1 the USA records high levels of welfare: notably housing, opportunities for higher education and female participation in education and paid employment. However levels of substantive need-satisfaction are among the lowest, across a wide range of other needs, including health, access to health services, income security and physical security. In some domains standards are at or below those found in middle income countries. For example, a black child born in Washington DC has less chance of surviving to her first birthday than one born in Kingston, Jamaica, while physical insecurity as measured by the risk of homicide is one of the highest in the world. Under- and malnutrition, poverty and homelessness are also spreading (e.g. Brown, 1989). Moreover, the USA exhibits relatively low standards of procedural need-satisfaction (respect for human rights, economic equality and political participation) and is the second most wasteful nation in terms of energy consumption. Its record in meeting women's needs is more mixed, though women are more at risk from poverty and more excluded from political participation than in most other Western countries. Its failure is therefore rather comprehensive and, given its economic wealth, initially puzzling.

Sweden provides a polar contrast – indeed it emerges as the global leader, the country most closely approximating optimum need-satisfaction at the present time. Levels of individual well-being are highest, or among the world's highest, in health, housing, water quality, access to and utilisation of health services and income security. Given the fame of the Swedish welfare state this much may be expected. However, far from being Hayek's *Road to Serfdom* (Hayek, 1944), it also achieves high scores in respect for human rights and democratic political participation as well as in securing a high basic income for the worst off. As regards the basic need of specific groups, it has dramatically reduced inequalities – in, for example, economic and political participation, education and access to economic resources. Sweden, together with its other Nordic neighbours, provides the best available yardstick with which to assess objective welfare in today's world. Of course this is not to claim that there are no inadequacies, injustices or cases of outright suffering there; merely that they do better on average than any other societies.[4]

These wide variations exist between countries with much in common: high per capita incomes, representative democracy, private ownership of the means of production, market processes, state regulation, corporate forms of organisation. Hence while one may reason that advanced democratic capitalism is a *necessary* condition for enhanced objective welfare, we obviously cannot argue that it is a *sufficient* one. Once again therefore new questions are posed. What other factors – political mobilisation, inherited state capacities, economic institutions – explain the wide variations in need-satisfaction between otherwise similar political economies? And what are the lessons for those who wish to enhance need-satisfactions not only in the West but throughout the world?

To explain patterns of need-satisfaction in advanced capitalism, we need to understand first, their generally high standards of welfare, but second, the wide variations in welfare between countries. Let us look at each in turn. Capitalist success is frequently attributed to the information and incentive mechanisms of markets. A market economy utilises the dispersed knowledge of millions of citizens, and it is the continual process of discovery which they are thus free and able to make which engenders the restless innovation and productivity of capitalism. Yet while the ability of advanced capitalism to produce a plentitude of commodities to satisfy wants is indisputable, can the same be said about needs? There are many reasons for believing that an unregulated capitalism will fail this test.

Despite the efficiency of markets as mechanisms for co-ordinating the pre-given preferences of households and firms, they are far less efficient as a source of *knowledge*. This plus the very individualisation of interests under market capitalism hinders the ability of people to perceive the generalisable interests which underly human needs. For example, the very opportunities open to people with money to 'exit' from public provision can reduce their willingness to exert their 'voice' within the democratic arena. Unregulated markets also pose problems at each stage of our model in Chapter 11. At the production stage, satisfiers of the appropriate quantity, nature and quality will not necessarily be produced due to the emergence of monopoly, to the inability of markets adequately to supply public goods or to satisfy demand for positional goods, and to the self-negating effects of some self-seeking activities (the 'prisoners' dilemma' class of problems). At the distribution stage many people are left with no entitlement to basic need satisfiers while others can satisfy their desires for every luxury. The effectiveness of the need transformation process can be undermined by the inadequate knowledge many consumers have of the properties of the constantly changing kaleidoscope of commodities. Furthermore, gender inequalities are reproduced via an interaction of unequal domestic labour with labour market power. At the stage of material reproduction unregulated capitalism appears unable to avoid macro-economic instability, and cannot make effective choices to safeguard the environment.[5]

Such deficiencies can only be overcome through public regulation. The pursuit of private interest can never secure the common good in the terms we have theorised it. Some central agency, which means in practice the state, must exist to counteract the tunnel vision and unintended consequences which markets entail. The case for a 'mixed economy', or a regulated capitalism is both theoretical and practical. *Inter alia*, state intervention is required to underwrite market exchange mechanisms, to constrain the actions of pre-capitalist elites, to overcome or replace the defects in market signals noted above, to redistribute income, to steer the accumulation process and to manage economic relations with other states. As writers from Adam Smith to Durkheim to Polanyi have recognised, a market society is a contradiction in terms – the market requires a strong set of normative underpinnings. Empirically, the evidence is growing that some form of developmental state or corporatist state is a necessary precondition for competitive success in the modern world.[6]

Second, however, states can steer societies in many different directions, not all of them by any means consistent with the goals identified in this book. The optimisation of need-satisfaction will only prevail when the state is constrained to act to pursue need-related goals. We hypothesise that such goals will only be pursued via the consistent mobilisation of citizens within broad social movements which prioritise optimal need-satisfaction. Without civic mobilisation *and* state action, any attempts to improve the need-satisfactions of the mass of people will meet with hostility from corporate interests pursuing sectional goals. Since they will normally have the power to thwart progressive policies, the power of the state must be utilised to combat them. But this will not occur without the effective mobilisation of social movements within civil society. In the case of Sweden it has been the organised labour movement which has performed this mobilising role over the last six decades (Korpi, 1983, chs 3, 9). To a lesser extent, the same can be said about the labour movement in Britain in relation to the origins of its welfare state (Gough, 1979, ch. 4). Elsewhere, other movements may perform this role. But whichever it is, some subjective agency must emerge which is capable of effective strategies to dislodge the structures which block the paths to human progress (Anderson, 1983, pp. 105–6). A future research agenda should try to identify the most effective forms of mobilisation, investigating their links with existing welfare states and the level of need-satisfaction of related populations.

Global dilemmas

This survey of the Three Worlds leaves unresolved one major question which returns our attention to the global and generational aspects of optimising human well-being. Are the best Western levels of need-satisfaction generalisable over space and time? If they are not then, according to the argument in Chapter 7, they cannot be counted as universal human needs.

For such strategies to be generalisable over *space*, there should be no social structural obstacles to the worldwide extension of the best Western standards. This raises questions about the nature of the global economic system and the extent to which the high living standards of the 'core' regions are parasitic upon the poverty and oppression in the 'periphery', rather than representing a further advance along a succession of stages of development. The route taken by some core western countries to high levels of need-satisfaction may well be closed off to the rest of the world, East as well as South. Generalisability over *time* asks whether the best achievable global standards of well-being today can be enjoyed by future generations. It poses questions about the level and patterns of material production which are sustainable and which of these would yield higher levels of need-satisfaction now and in different futures.

Both questions raise extremely complex issues which we cannot explore in detail here. However, two points are worth making. First, there is a firm moral case for a global conception of need and of just ways of meeting need – a case which is buttressed by the growing and probably irreversible interdependencies in the modern world. We agree with Pogge when he argues: 'Taken seriously, Rawls's conception of justice will make the social position of the *globally* least advantaged the touchstone for assessing our basic institutions' (1989, p. 242, our italics). In other words, politico-economic arrangements should be morally evaluated according to how they affect the need-satisfactions of the world's poorest.

Second, some pointers can be established about what this entails in practice. Optimising need-satisfaction on a world scale ultimately entails some system of global authority to enforce global rights to need-satisfaction. But transitional to this it must require a *value-based world order*, wherein states hold in common some ultimate values which are embodied in institutions regulating international relations. And transitional to this, there must be an awareness among the citizens of the privileged parts of the world that we have some responsibility for the global order, 'given that we are advantaged participants in this order, who help maintain and are (collectively) capable of changing it' (Pogge, 1989, p. 239). Those of us in the First World therefore have a strict duty to participate in some way in organisations with feasible strategies for challenging those world politico-economic structures which deny millions their most basic needs.

Towards a political economy of need-satisfaction

In this chapter we have discovered certain patterns and themes. First, average levels of need-satisfaction and the quality of societal preconditions vary, in broad terms, with per capita incomes and levels of development. However, second, there are a number of exceptions to this generalisation, indicating that a complex set of social, political and cultural factors also affect levels of need-satisfaction. Third, variations in objective welfare between capitalist and developed state socialist countries reveal the latter to be generally and on average inferior. However, fourth, there also exist substantial differences in need-satisfaction between Western nations, indicating once again that factors other than democratic capitalism *per se* are relevant.

All these conclusions raise intriguing issues which *prima facie*, sustain our earlier perspective. If the records of the USSR and the USA are anything to go by, it is apparent that neither centrally planned state socialism nor an unregulated 'casino capitalism' are effective social frameworks within which to optimise the satisfaction of basic needs. Democratic capitalism is superior in procedural justice and – in the advanced world – in generating the productive wherewithal for improved need-satisfaction. Yet in its unregulated forms it cannot guarantee those minimal levels of need-satisfaction in the absence of which liberal freedoms are for many meaningless. State socialism, on the other hand, often aims to improve the basic needs of the masses and – usually, initially and minimally – succeeds. But it denies people the democratic and other procedural preconditions for critical autonomy and thus prevents them building on this foundation and, through learning and collaboration, improving human welfare further.

If both systems have their faults, it is apparent that they are on the whole opposite and complementary ones. The findings presented in this chapter suggest that a *combination* of institutions and principles assures the best chance of optimising human welfare.[7] Such a welfare-oriented society could be termed 'liberal democratic socialism'. It is liberal because it espouses the claims of individual autonomy and it recognises, as we have seen, the contribution which (regulated) markets can make to this end. It is socialist because the organisation of economy, society and the state prioritises the optimum need-satisfaction of all people. It is democratic because citizen participation lies at the heart of the procedural processes for determining policies within these two constraints. The most successful such combination of principles in the world today is the 'democratic welfare capitalism' of Sweden and some other north European countries. This harnesses the economic dynamism and political freedoms of advanced democratic capitalism with a form of effective public regulation guided by social mobilisation which prioritises need-related goals. The evidence appears to suggest that such a combination is also most successful in achieving a constrained optimum in the Third World.

Yet we have suggested that Swedish-style welfare capitalism faces severe problems of generalisability and sustainability, and is not necessarily the best conceivable model. This raises further issues. Is the welfare state compatible in the long run with private ownership of major productive assets? Are there necesssary limits to representative democracy within capitalism? Is liberal democratic socialism in fact an unstable compound, as Anderson (1988, p. 35) suggests? Or is there a feasible alternative social framework, a genuine 'third way' between capitalism and socialism? These are issues we leave to the reader and to future research and social exploration.[8]

14

A Dual Political Strategy

Just as the economic organisation of a society which accords a high priority to optimising need-satisfaction must consist of a duality, so too must its political organisation. If human needs have strict priority over other political goals, then all people have the right to optimal need-satisfaction based on the best available knowledge. Such a view might seem to support the authority of experts. However, we have seen that appropriate and effective understanding of needs can only be obtained through informed communication between all those with relevant experience – communication which is carefully structured to optimise the rationality of its outcome. Experts constitute just one group of participants in such a debate. Here, we shall argue that central planning *and* democratic participation are both necessary components of social policy formation if it is to succeed in optimising need-satisfaction. In short, what is required for the optimisation of need-satisfaction is a 'dual strategy' incorporating both the generality of the state and the particularity of civil society.

As we shall see, the appropriate mix will vary depending on the problem to be solved and the socio-economic environment in which the solution is sought. Unlike previous chapters, our discussion of the political duality of need-satisfaction is more focused on the developed world. This retreat from universality is no accident. Some of the best approximations of the vision of the good which we have tried to develop in this book are contained within the welfare states of the developed nations and most of the relevant literature with which we are familiar is based on these experiences. Therefore, the applicability of our conception of a politics of need to the Third World must for now be based primarily on the general merit of our arguments.

The dual strategy in theory

Throughout, we have stressed the importance of individuals being able to explore their intellectual and emotional capabilites in optimal ways. To do so, they must have the right to as much self-determination as is consistent with their not violating the basic needs of others. But this means that the domain of the private must be regulated in some way by public authority. Individuals are not always the best judges of their own needs, either because of poor education and lack of relevant expertise or because their ability to diffentiate between needs and wants has been distorted by a range of external influences. A variety of public services has to be collectively planned and organised if citizens are to have access to needed satisfiers. Moreover, laws have to be enforced to ensure secure and safe access to these satisfiers. In short, the state must help individuals to look after their generalisable interests to the degree that their own short-term individual concerns are incompatible with this aim.

We have argued that for the individual's right to optimal need-satisfaction to be taken seriously there must be an agency which is responsible for ensuring that it is respected – an agency which can enforce a Constitution and a Bill of Rights which conform to our interpretation of Rawls's principles of justice. Positively, this means guaranteeing universal access to the necessary satisfiers. Negatively it involves ensuring that the procedural preconditions necessary for full participation in civil life in its broadest sense are also met. No institutional body other than a state has the power and resources to do either, though this does not imply that the geographical territory over which this public authority exerts jurisdiction should be coterminous with present-day nation states.

The case for positive social rights provides the justification for state responsibility for health, education, income maintenance and a host of other public services. (Whether or not this entails direct state provision of such services is another matter.) Similarly, protecting the negative right of individuals to go about their private lives unhampered by arbitrary constraints involves institutions such as the judiciary and the police. The implementation of such a democratic social contract – the right to optimal need-satisfaction in return for the duty of the citizen to do what is necessary for the state to achieve this goal – will meet with resistance from those with vested interests in maintaining the status quo. Again, in many instances, the power of such interests can only be resisted by the economic, legislative and judicial power of the state.

But of course such a powerful state must be democratic if needs are to be satisfied optimally. Since political power will always carry with it the temptation and opportunity for abuse, it must be regulated via democratic processes. In practice, this means a parliamentary or congressional legislature with a system of checks and balances sufficient to ensure that unregulated power does not become overly concentrated, along with a competitive party system and other mechanisms to enable citizens to organize politically around issues which they think important. It also requires an independent and representative judiciary. Further, individual autonomy cannot be optimised without the opportunity for participation not just in the polity but in the economy and other aspects of civil society as well. Constitutional guarantees of the right to such participation must exist and be enforced. Otherwise, individuals will not be in a position to exercise choice over the institutional rules which constitute their social environment and will not be able to protect themselves against the power of the state. Similarly, minorities will also be without protection from uncaring majorities.

Yet, persuasive as these general arguments for a strong and democratic welfare state might be, they still open the doors to the many bureaucratic abuses – the same potential 'dictatorship over need' – referred to in Part I. Whatever the need for centralisation, there is a corresponding requirement for the opposite – a radical decentralisation and democratisation of life on a scale that no modern society has yet witnessed. Need-satisfaction is more than the top-down application of technical knowledge and the bureau-cratic delivery of state services (even where these have been approved within an effectively democratic parlimentary system). There is another domain of understanding to be tapped – the experiential knowledge of people in their everyday lives: as workers, residents of a community, patients, pupils, older citizens, parents, immigrants, etc.

Any legislative approach to improving, let alone optimising, need-satisfaction must utilise this understanding, something which traditional electoral processess rarely do. If it does not, the arbitrary foibles of bureaucracy and the uncaring routines of professionals which are the stock in trade of life for many in today's welfare states will become still more intrusive and oppressive. This is why critiques of the welfare state advanced by feminists, anti-racists, libertarians, greens and others must be taken so seriously. Moreover, certain universal satisfier characteristics will themselves be enhanced within intimate relationships, within the family and within the community. In some domains of need-satisfaction these are more salient than state social services so that alternative forms of provision outside the market and the state must be given their due recognition.

Our position, therefore, is that a policy to improve human need satisfactions must move simultaneously in the direction of *both* centralisation and decentralisation! The role of the 'welfare state' must expand, yet at the same time co-operation and communication within civil society must be nurtured. Neither 'leg' of this duality can stand properly without the other. Rather than abolishing the division between state and civil society, as Marx envisaged under communism, it should be more clearly and appropriately defined. As Keane has argued: 'democratization...would mean attempting to maintain and to redefine the boundaries between civil society and the state through two interdependent and simultaneous processes: the expansion of social equality and liberty, and the restructuring and democratizing of state institutions' (1988, p. 14).

The argument for centralisation

If human needs are generalisable to all people, then, as we have seen, individuals should be regarded as having a right to as much need-satisfaction as is practically possible. Two alternative sources of provision are the market and unilateral charity (cf. Polanyi, 1957, chs 4, 6; Titmuss, 1970). But neither offers any guarantee that the needs of all will be satisfied even to minimal – much less optimal – levels (Plant *et al.*, 1980, ch. 4). Only the state has this capacity, though its potential has not been fully realised even in the most developed welfare states. Since any further extension of the power of the state is an understandable anathema to many people, we need to specify further why its existence is so crucial to our vision of the necessary conditions for human liberation.

Rights emerged in liberal societies as a means of protecting individuals *against* the power of the state. This was after prolonged – often revolutionary – struggle between classes and nationalist groups and often followed the mass mobilising effects of modern war. Initially, the focus was on civil rights – to freedom of speech, religion, movement and trial by jury. Around the late nineteenth and early twentieth century, attention shifted to political rights – to the vote and participation in elected government. In most developed polities – with the notable exception of the UK – such rights have now been enshrined in a constitution which can only be amended by due political process, usually by a two-thirds or still more overwhelming majority.

Yet as we have seen, when civil liberties and the negative freedoms which they embody are conceived in these ways, they risk ignoring the importance of positive freedoms – of the comprehensive social or welfare rights which are required for equal opportunity to participate in civil life. This was the subject of the next wave of struggle to extend citizenship rights in many Western societies – the right to welfare, including a minimum income, security when livelihood is threatened and access to those collective services deemed central to human flourishing and social participation. The routes towards modern welfare provision are many and varied, but by the late 1960s certain social rights had become well established in many but not all capitalist democracies.[1]

Our theory of human need propels us toward a radical extension, plus a codification, of the citizenship-based welfare entitlements presently found in Western welfare states. We believe that it provides a convincing and desirable justification for, and specification of, welfare rights. Identifying *A* as a right means that its provision is removed from the vagaries of political ideology, official discretion or individual charity. In a different context – a treatise on democracy – Held arrives at a similar conclusion:

A constitution and bill of rights which enshrined the principle of autonomy would ... involve not only equal rights to cast a vote, but also equal rights to enjoy the conditions for effective participation, enlightened understanding and the setting of the political agenda. Such broad 'state' rights would, in turn, entail a broad bundle of social rights linked to reproduction, childcare, health and education, as well as economic rights to ensure adequate economic and financial resources for democratic autonomy (1987, p. 285).

But what would such an agenda look like in practice?

The right to optimise health and autonomy entails access to the satisfaction of intermediate needs at 'minopt' levels, as defined in Chapter 8. Our taxonomy dictates minopt levels of nutrition, housing, work conditions, physical environment, health services, childhood security, primary relationships, physical security, economic security, education and childbirth. The precise specification of such levels must in principle be the democratic task of legislative institutions formulating policy in the light of the availability of resources and competing priorities (cf. Pogge, 1989, p. 144). To ensure that citizens can realise these opportunities requires specific rights to those satisfiers which are agreed to be prerequisites for optimal basic need-satisfaction. These welfare rights are redeemed in two key domains: the market and the state itself.

To purchase those satisfiers delivered through market processes, people will need a right to a sufficient minimum *income*. The level at which this is set will depend on (a) the set of satisfiers which should be made available in the form of commodities, (b) the cost of these satisfiers, and (c) the minimum amount of extra discretionary income which it is agreed should be provided to all citizens to satisfy their wants. In Chapter 8 we briefly discussed the democratic communicational form which will best ensure that a rational decision is arrived at on all these issues. In this way an income for basic need can be agreed in any particular society at any particular time. It will have to be disaggregated to distinguish households of different sizes and composition and the extra satisfier characteristics of certain groups, such as people with disabilities. As we have seen, much poverty research in recent years reflects this approach.

Once this income for basic need has been agreed, it must be delivered. This can be done in two main ways in modern economies: by providing a basic income as of right to all citizens or by guaranteeing employment for all in certain categories at wages which do not fall below an appropriate minimum, coupled with social security income for all of those who cannot or should not participate in paid labour. Proponents of the former, a basic income guarantee (BIG), take the politics of need to one logical conclusion by proposing that all social security benefits and tax allowances be scrapped and replaced by an entitlement to a regular state income for all adults, with additional benefits for all children. It has been criticised on the grounds that to offer a right to income with no countervailing obligation to work is ethically dubious, economically debilitating and politically incoherent. Advocates of guaranteed employment support something like the Swedish approach of linking state transfer benefits with a policy of full employment. However, this has in turn been criticised on the grounds that traditional male full employment is no longer feasible or desirable. In our view, both arguments serve to underline the *compatibility* of income and employment guarantees in a strategy to optimise need-satisfaction.[2]

A second category of rights would ensure that people have access to those satisfiers which are best provided collectively by the state or some other public body in a non-commodified form. In many cases, this will necessarily entail direct provision by state agencies. Since more can always be spent to improve levels of need-satisfaction and since conflicts about priorities will be inevitable, how should they be decided in practice? This important decision is again ultimately the task of legislative and executive processes, but would need to operate within certain constitutional guidelines.

Focusing, for example, on health care, one approach is to specify a core set of activities, such as physician services, inpatient and outpatient hospital services, emergency services, mental health provision, laboratory and X-ray services and give everyone an entitlement to access to them when they are in need (Plant, 1990, p. 27, citing Enthoven). The quality of such provision can be monitored and ensured through various systems of audit and appeals tribunals. An alternative is to specify the money cost of a group's standard level of health protection in relation to its 'average medical history'. 'Standard medical care' could then be defined in terms of some (above-the-mean) level of expected lifetime cost of needed medical care. Pogge suggests that citizens should have a right to minimally adequate health protection defined as some (relatively high) percentage of this figure (Pogge, 1989, pp. 178–9, 185–6). Plant (1990, p. 28) also suggests that the level at which positive rights are guaranteed in Western societies should lie somewhere between the average and the highest level achieved by any individual in that society. *Apropos* rights to health care, for example, he advocates entitlements to average 'middle-class' consumption of health care.[3]

In one form or the other similar entitlements could be drawn up for other public services. Parents should possess enforceable rights to child-care services; disabled people to aids, assistance and community services; parents and students to access to all levels of education from which they can benefit, and to certain curricula and standards of provision; all households to adequate housing to ensure their health, privacy and personal autonomy...and so on. To the degree that it is deemed appropriate for the state sector to assume responsibility for direct provision, agencies must be established for planning and resource allocation at national, regional and local levels. They will be unable to work effectively without a coherent set of social indicators of need-satisfaction along the lines suggested in Part III (Walker, 1984, ch. 9).

Yet even if such need-satisfaction is formally guaranteed as a matter of right, it will still be necessary to ensure that purchased or provided satisfiers are not hazardous and that when rights are abused, significant legal redress is available. Only the central state will have the power and resources to undertake the primary role of such regulation. The control of hazardous satisfiers at work, in the home and within the physical environment will require legislation. This may be 'statutory' or 'enabling', either banning specific hazards altogether or stipulating the guidelines within which relevant state inspectorates should work with potential offenders to try to reduce hazards through a process of negotiation. In general the scope of such regulatory legislation could and should cover the prevention of serious harm in all aspects of public and private life.

Ignatieff makes a powerful plea that there are some needs which cannot be expressed in the form of legal entitlements: 'It is because fraternity, love, belonging, dignity and respect cannot be specified as rights that we ought to specify them as needs and seek, with the blunt institutional procedures at our disposal, to make their satisfaction a routine human practice' (1984, pp. 13–14). Yet this position appears contradictory. For it implies that relevant statutory rights are appropriate when such 'routine' practice fails to come up to the mark. In other words, codification underlines the importance placed by democracies on the prevention of serious harm even in the most private domains of life (Held, 1987, pp. 292–3). The fact that it is widely regarded as an outrage that in many countries husbands cannot be convicted of raping their wifes illustrates the plausibility of legislating for private life. Similar points may be made about the treatment of children – even animals – by adults and underlines the moral rationale and importance of relevant legislation and judicial backup.

An effective judiciary is crucial in ensuring that all statutes and associated guidelines concerning basic need-satisfaction are observed by public officials and the public. How this is achieved will vary from country to country. The general link between effective regulation and judicial review, however, will remain much the same – the fair and accountable arbitration of dispute about whether or not legislative rules have been appropriately applied and the allocation of institutionally prescribed penalties and/ or damages when it is agreed that they have not. The importance of this link cannot be overestimated and is illustrated when the judicial process does not perform its functions adequately. Rights on paper are, as all lawyers know, no more than that. There can be no question that judiciaries are often biased in favour of wealth and privilege, but this does nothing to obviate the necessity for state judicial activity. Instead it implies various measures of reform in the recruitment of legal personnel and in free access to the law (cf. Dworkin, 1985, ch. 1).

All of the rights and associated areas of state activity which we have mentioned must be complemented by a programme of equal opportunities, something which again can only be effectively enforced by a strong central authority. In isolation, both positive and negative rights are insufficient to deal with the constraints and sources of serious harm which face oppressed groups, and hence their need for specific satisfiers. The fact that many women, black people and members of other disadvantaged groups suffer continuing and debilitating discrimination necessitates the existence of statutes which make clear the dictates of procedural justice and enforcement authorities which both seek out violations and ensure that penalities are adhered to. To the degree that this entails policies of positive discrimination then the role of the state again becomes crucial. The delicate issues of fairness which this sometimes poses makes it all the more important to have judicial bodies of arbitration which themselves operate neutrally and are perceived to do so.[4]

The argument for decentralisation

Yet the ability of traditional welfare states to optimise need-satisfaction has been severely criticised in recent years, from quarters other than the New Right. These provide the foundation for a countervailing argument in favour of decentralisation and participation.

First, there are well-established critiques of professionalism and bureaucracy. Illich and other anti-statists have argued that needs are in grave danger of being defined by those professionals who then purport to meet them: 'Today, doctors and social workers – as formerly only priests and jurists – gain legal power to create the need that, by law, they alone will be allowed to satisfy' (Illich, 1977, pp. 14–16). This 'disables' ordinary people and sets up a cumulative chain of increasing dependence upon the state and its agencies – a descent into 'technofascism'. Others argue that it is bureaucracy itself which is at fault. Hadley and Hatch (1981) explain the 'failure of the welfare state' in terms of its centralisation, bureaucratisation and monopoly power. Social services are organised in large, hierarchical units to deliver predetermined services to passive clients. For Ferguson, both clients and bureaucrats see themselves and each other as objects of administration with little or no scope for creative action (1984, p. 14; Pollitt, 1986). It is against the background of such inflexibility that bureaucratic power is exercised and abuse becomes almost inevitable. Where bureaucrats are not accountable and do not have to obtain consistent, coherent and representative feedback from clients then the rational evaluation and subsequent improvement of the services which they are supposed to provide becomes impossible (Plant *et al.*, 1980, pp. 107–13; cf. Bachrach and Baratz, 1970).

Second, feminism has demonstrated that the post-war welfare state in Britain and elsewhere was premised on a sharp gender division between man as breadwinner-worker and woman as dependant-wife-carer (e.g. Pateman, 1989). The operation of specific services can enforce particular roles for women. The professionalisation of health care has gone hand in hand with its masculination – witness, for example, the domination by men of hospital medicine, including obstetrics and gynaecology. It is claimed that a consequence of this can be the control of female sexuality and reproduction in ways which reinforce a particular self-image among women that pepetuates their subordination (Dale and Foster, 1986). More generally if 'difference' is ignored then citizenship can enforce privilege. 'In a society marred by group oppression and subordination, [ideas of universal citizenship] end up confirming the dominance of privileged groups' (Phillips, 1991, p. 83; cf. Young, 1989).

Following on from this, Pateman questions whether the formal freedoms assumed by liberal theory apply in the real world of class, gender and race inequality; and whether the liberal conception of a clear separation between civil society and the state can be upheld in the corporatist states of modern capitalism. Answering 'no', she advocates additional arenas for direct participation of citizens in those key institutions where people live out their lives, notably the workplace and the community (Pateman, 1970, chs 2, 6). The New Left has also objected to bureaucratic abuses of overly centralised state powers, stressing the importance of participation, community and group autonomy. Following in the footsteps of Morris, Cole and Tawney, many socialists in the late 60's attempted to generate a new 'politics of empowerment' (Harris, 1987, chs 3–4; Gutmann, 1980, ch. 3).

All this amounts to a powerful critique of 'top-down' welfare statism and a call for an alternative approach to the formation and implementation of economic and social policy. Two policy implications follow: political decentralisation from national to regional, local and neighbourhood government and new forms of citizen participation. Decentralised welfare can take a variety forms, including for-profit private provision, non-profit voluntary provision and less structured forms of community self-help. It can also entail devolved forms of delivery of government services, via 'neighbourhood offices' and community forums. There are also many examples of participatory democracy in welfare provision, such as the participation of parents in the governing of schools, although their exact form varies between countries. Similar, and frequently more far-reaching, developments have been pioneered in the Third World, such as self-help movements and rural community development schemes.[5]

Effective programmes along these lines would help tap the experientially-grounded knowledge of people in their everyday lives and utilise their energies, thus improving knowledge of deprivation and contributing to the creation of new and better need satisfiers. Existing moves towards decentralisation and participation should be encouraged, where necessary (paradoxically) by central government legislation and funding. Steps in these directions would render welfare services – and the need satisfiers delivered – more sensitive to the rich variety of cultural, social and material environments which people inhabit. Our theory of need clearly endorses much of this bottom-up critique of the welfare state and the alternatives which it proposes, such as, for example, a statutory 'right to participate' in all social services and development schemes involved in the provision of need satisfiers. The theory is not incompatible with the acceptable face of relativism – the encouragement of flourishing cultural diversity.

Yet despite these arguments, the case for centralisation still retains much force. Taken in isolation, the participatory, community-oriented approach to welfare politics has serious limitations and the need remains for a strong and representative central authority. The dangers are well-known. In a society of pervasive inequality and unmet needs, greater participation can at best act as a figleaf to cover the powerlessness of the poor. At worst, it aggravates their deprivation and limits their power still further. Too great an emphasis on 'prefigurative forms' can mean a failure to challenge the existing structure of national politics and international dependency. In the face of the growing internationalisation of the global economy, for example, local economic policies are often quite inadequate (Jones, 1990, ch. 10). 'Welfare pluralism' can also obscure the inequalities of privatisation, enabling the better-off to 'exit' from collective provision and to buy better services than those commonly available. Furthermore, 'community provision' in the context of the existing sexual division of labour is all too often a metaphor for the reliance on the unpaid labour of women. Plans based on the 'community' care of elderly infirm people, for example, even when backed up by generous local services, can condemn women carers to years of near-servitude and can inhibit the autonomy of the person being cared for.

More generally, any local, community-based, small-scale form of need-satisfaction can foster 'insider' conceptions of human need and inhibit the growth of generalisable notions based on a wider collective identity. The politics of empowerment can mean accepting a variety of racist and sexist policies, or schemes which discriminate against outsiders. Provision by and for different communities can blind people to the common needs they share with others and monitoring is needed to ensure that serious harm does not result from too much emphasis being placed on the perceptions and preferences of particular groups. The dream of a community politics which could unite groups with different specific interests and bring about mutual political action cannot be realised in the absence of precisely such a cross-cultural and cross-group source of identity as human need.[6]

The dual strategy in practice

It follows from our theory that all of the preceding critiques of state welfare contain true and false elements. The element of truth is that top-down statist approaches to need, as exemplified in the traditional Eastern Bloc, often ignore and devalue the experientially-grounded knowledge of people themselves. In Habermas's terms they usurp the system of power over the lifeworld. If need-satisfaction is to be optimised, all groups must have the ability to participate in research into need satisfiers and to contribute to policy-making. For example, a policy on racial harassment which black people have played no part in framing will probably be a poor one.

The critiques are false, however, when they argue that conceptions of individual or group interests should, whatever their source, be able to trump the best available codified knowledge concerning need-satisfaction. To accept this would be to succumb to the relativism against which we have argued throughout this book. Human need can never be automatically equated with individual wants or particular group interests. The specification of need must always appeal to a higher objective standard. While participation and the expression of preference have an indispensible role to play in determining specific *need satisfiers*, group interests cannot overide the best available knowledge about *basic and intermediate needs per se*. These are central to everyone's ability to participate in their form of life and as such their satisfaction must be guaranteed as of right by a central public authority.

We keep returning to the same dilemma: initiatives to utilise experientially-grounded knowledge, to recognise the special importance of the lifeworld, to empower the powerless, to democratise the state and civil society, all have a great contribution to make to the democratic and rational satisfaction of human needs. But taken in isolation they carry the danger that individual, group, sectional and short-term interests will undermine the identification of human need with longer-term generalisable interests. Yet this danger must always be understood in the shadow of another. While constitutional rights buttressed by the social and economic interventions of a strong state are indispensible to ensure improved need satisfaction, they run the converse risks of uniformity, inflexibility, disempowerment and paternalism which threaten cultural integrity and individual autonomy. It is clear that any adequate political strategy to optimise human need-satisfaction must embrace both of the positions advanced above.

Where there are fundamental conflicts over the definition of need itself, or the basic forms of provision to satisfy need, then we have seen that their rational evaluation will entail democratic debate in the light of the best technical and practical understanding available. If the dispute is specifically technical in nature, then scientific assessment and experiment are in order, employing established methodological principles. If it concerns the subjective impact of proposed or implemented policies on the individuals concerned, attention will focus on effective communication through opinion surveys, consultation with consumer groups and other strategies designed to elicit their accurate self-perception. Where, as is often the case, both forms of understanding are at issue then a dialogue involving both 'experts' and those in need is essential and in a forum as close to Habermas' ideal speech situation as is practically possible. Of course, the success of such dialogue will not usually mean that every party is satisfied with the outcome. Compromise will very often be the order of the day. Yet precisely because it will so often be the case, what is crucial is for all participants to perceive the outcome as the most rational and democratic possible.[7]

We have argued that our theory of need points to a dual polity, just as it does to a dual economy. The dual strategy flows from a concept of need which is rational and consensual, dynamic and open-ended. It is responsive to that very process of progress through learning which it seeks to encourage. While an idealisation, the dual strategy is rooted in what we have argued are the new practices throughout the world.

How universalisable the dual strategy itself is must remain an open question, since powerful global forces remain opposed to its goals. Its limitations are particularly obvious in the countries of the Third World given the enormity and complexity of their economic and political problems. In the North, the development of social citizenship could worsen the need satisfaction of outsiders at the same time that it improves welfare among insiders. Citizenship entails exclusion as a necessary counterpart to membership, and can exacerbate sentiments of nationalism and racism (Taylor, 1989). This threat applies to supra-national visions of citizenship such as that which some see emerging in the European Community (Meehan, 1991).

Moreover, to agree on the broad outlines of the dual strategy is by no means to agree on the specific political strategies offering the best hope of improving need satisfaction. No single 'politics of need' follows from our theory, and we do not purport to develop such a politics here. Readers may in consequence feel frustrated: where are the specific historical actors and social practices engaged in national and global struggles to achieve – or to block – the moral goals advocated here? Where, for example, are class and gender, property and privilege, power and oppression, conflict and war?

We are only too well aware of these gaps. Their relative absence from our account by no means entails an idealist view of historical change. On the contrary, the role of hardship and struggle in bringing about social progress – the paradoxical stunting of need satisfaction in order to improve need satisfaction – is an unfortunate constant of human history. However we also concur with those who believe that socialism and allied movements have in recent years sacrificed too much to short-term advantage and sectional interests and have devoted too little attention to the direction in which we should be heading. Without a universalisable conception of human need, along with accompanying rights and duties to give it effect, the political coalitions necessary to bring about sustained human progress cannot be forged.

Notwithstanding these complexities, we contend that the dual strategy constitutes a feasible, as well as desirable, model for the optimisation of need satisfaction even if it must be tempered by practical constraints. Such constraints do not negate the vision of the good which we have outlined in this book. They merely underline the importance of a commitment to overcome them and to dream of and struggle for new and more effective ways of doing so.

Notes

1 Who Needs Human Needs?

1 Belief in such 'equality of passions' is not meant to suggest that everyone responds to the same stimulus for pleasure in the same way. Those who are already wealthy, for example, will derive less pleasure than those who are poor. Programmes of redistribution not based on market principles might, therefore, seem to be suggested by the demand that happiness be maximised and by the calculation of related marginal utilities. Classic utilitarians – such as Bentham, for example – who support the free market argue against this conclusion on the grounds that without the incentives which it provides there would be much less wealth and consequently much less happiness for everyone (Gutmann, 1980, pp. 20–7).

2 See on this: Springborg (1981) ch. 6; Elster (1985) pp. 71–4. Soper (1980) chs 2–8 illustrates the range of ways in which Marx appears to reject ideas of objective need but argues that this is only one side of the story. Geras, (1983, pp. 49–54) summarises a range of other commentators who maintain that it is the only side.

3 For an example of such white feminist critiques under attack, see: Lees (1986) pp. 92–101. Such critiques are not confined to white feminists. For example, see Ghoussoub (1987) pp. 16–18 and Kabeer (1988) pp. 100–108. For a recent example of radical anti–racism in relation to feminism and social work see Shah (1989) pp. 178–191. A useful bibliography and sympathetic summary of similar arguments is in Williams (1987) pp. 4–29. We are not, of course, suggesting that all criticisms of racism are of the holistic and radical nature outlined here.

4 For guides to radical feminist thinking of this variety, see Grimshaw (1986) and Segal (1987). As with radical anti–racism, we are doing no more here than underlining extreme tendencies which are more or less explicit in some, but by no means all, radical feminist writing.

5 This said, Walzer is unclear about how these constraints can be conceptualised because he also places much emphasis on the fact that conceptualisation itself occurs within normative structures (Walzer, 1983, ch. 3).

6 This is not to reject Keane's other arguments in *Democracy and Civil Society*. Indeed the other chapters in his book have contributed towards our ideas here.

2 The Inevitability of Human Needs

1 Dworkin makes the same point apropos the law in a pluralist society:

'It makes no sense for our society to establish the right not to be convicted when known to be innocent as absolute, unless that society recognizes moral harm as a distinct kind of harm against which people must be specially protected. But the utilitarian calculus that the cost-efficient society uses to fix criminal procedures is a calculus that can make no place for moral harm... For moral harm is an objective notion, and if someone is morally harmed [through being] punished though innocent, then this moral harm occurs even when no one knows or suspects it, and even when – perhaps especially when – very few people very much care (Dworkin, 1985, p. 81; cf pp. 81–9; cf. Gewirth, 1982, ch. 5).

2 The degree to which Feyerabend actually subscribes to relativism in these terms is hard to estimate from the wonderfully colourful dance of his writing. For evidence that he comes close, see Feyerabend (1978) pp. 138–40.

3 The Grammar of 'Need'

1 A biologist or botanist would similarly argue that if the physical needs of an animal or plant went unmet then they too would be damaged (Anscombe, 1969, pp. 193–4; cf. Bay, 1968, pp. 242–3).
2 It would be a mistake to suggest that relativism has only one philosophical face. Two classic statements in recent years have been Herskovits (1972) and Barnes and Bloor (1982). Arrington (1989, ch. 5) gives a fine summary of more recent formulations. For good examples from anthropology, see Douglas (1975) and several of the articles in Overing (1985), especially her introduction. Renteln (1990, ch. 3) compares philosophy and anthropology. Hirst and Woolley (1982) Parts I–II do the same for sociology and psychology. Finally, MacIntyre (1988) provides a fascinating relativistic journey through the evolution of Western theories of justice and rationality, although he would not wish it described in quite these terms – see Chapters XVIII–XX.

4 Health and Autonomy: the Basic Needs of Persons

1 Thus conceived, lack of basic need satisfaction constitutes the sort of damage to the individual which Townsend defines as deprivation: 'if they do not have, at all or sufficiently, the conditions of life... which allow them to play the roles, participate in the relationships and follow the customary behaviour which is expected of them by virtue of their membership of society' (Townsend, 1987, p. 130). The serious harm which results in such fundamental and long term deprivation will ensue

irrespective of the values of the specific culture or of the perceptions, beliefs or actual choices of any individual actor (Plant, *et al.*, 1980, pp. 37–8; cf. Wiggens, 1985, pp. 157–9).

2 Here it is unclear how *that* action is *your* action. On the one hand, you will still be acting intentionally to the degree that it is your reasons – however misconceived – which inform your choice of what you do. On the other hand, you can hardly be called the author of, and be held responsible for, your actions. For, given the deception, you are not doing what you think that your are, as is evidenced by the different meaning which others place on what you do. It does seem correct to say that the author of the action which you carry out – as opposed to the one which you think that you have executed – is the person who deceives you (Faden and Beauchamp, 1986 ch. 10, pp. 256–62). This, of course, presupposes that there is no good reason to think that either you did or should have understood the socially accepted meaning of the action(s) in question. In short, to the extent that it is controlled by others, the intentional link between you and your action is reduced, resulting in a corresponding diminution of autonomy at its most basic.

3 Thompson defines 'interest' in the following terms:

> The primary goods we are deprived of when we are harmed (by lacking what we need) are good and worthwhile because they answer our interests, and not because they are desired. The notion of an interest defines the range and type of activities and experiences that partly constitute a meaningful and worth while life, and it defines the nature of their worth. These types of activities are primary goods and because they are good something which deprives us of them is bad and harmful (Thompson, 1987, p. 76; cf. ch. 4).

Contrast this notion of human interests with that of Feinberg (1984, p. 45) which is much the same as our conception of basic needs:

> our ultimate interests characteristically resemble what C. L. Stevenson has called 'focal aims,' ends (not *the* end) which are also means to many other divergent ends. Our more important (in the sense of 'ultimate') ends satisfy Stevenson's formal definition of a focal aim: 'an end which is also such an exceptionally important means to so many divergent ends that if anything else is not, in its turn, a means to this, it will be without predominating value.'

Feinberg (p. 47) goes on to define an undesirable thing as harmful 'only when its presence is sufficient to impede an interest' or, in other words, when it impedes basic need-satisfaction.

4 Two qualifications must be entered here. First, an individual may have a physical disease and not feel ill. However, the identification of the disease will still have depended upon the earlier recognition of the link between it and the experience of illness in others. Second, one can be physically diseased without one's ability to participate being impaired. This will depend on access to the appropriate social environment, aids and support networks.

5 Reiser (1981) chs 1–7. Curative medicine is not, of course, unproblematic and there can be no doubt that it has been widely abused in violation of individual health needs. These issues are discussed further in Chapter 10.

6 In opposition, it is sometimes argued that poor physical health can actually enhance creativity· and therefore autonomy. For example, Miller (1976, p. 131) and Harris (1987, p. 132) refer to the philosopher Brentano who suggested that he was better off having lost his sight because it enabled him more effectively to concentrate on his academic pursuits. Such arguments ignore the fact that Brentano had to possess enough physical health to acquire the conceptual tools necessary to respond to his disablement in the enhanced way he claimed.

7 Boorse provides an interesting evolutionary foundation for this approach. Drawing on Darwin and Freud, he argues that certain types of mental processes – for example, perceptual processing, memory, intelligence, pain signals and language – are invariant across the human species, and have developed in accord with standard evolutionary theory. Mental illnesses thus refer to unnatural obstructions to these functions – whatever the cultural specificity of their origin (Boorse, 1982). Fulford further maintains that cross-cultural objectivity derives from the recognition of impaired action and interaction, which cannot be reduced to some form of physical disfunction, whatever the value-system of the actors. It is this recognition which leads to the imputation of mental, rather than physical, illness and not simply the violation of any given set of social norms (Fulford, 1989, chs 8, 9).

8 The conditions for minimal rationality which we have outlined are designed to differentiate those who are capable of sustained autonomous action (as defined above) from those are not. To this extent, they are neutral as regards the degree to which actors conform to dominant norms and laws. The actions of the most radical deviants, in other words, can still reflect high levels of autonomy provided that they satisfy these conditions. The literature on rationality divides itself between those which focus on the psyche or on models of decision making. For the former, see Culver and Gert (1982) chs 2–6. For the latter, Haworth (1986) chs 2, 5.

9 Returning to our previous distinction between disease and illness, we do not use the expression 'mental disease' unless the physical pathology of the illness has been identified.

10 The danger posed by a totally relativist approach to serious mental illness is that it questions the objectivity of such disability and risks legitimating the denial of appropriate care for for those who suffer from it. As Sedgwick has powerfully argued:

> In trying to remove and reduce the concept of mental illness, the revisionist theories have made it that bit harder for a powerful campaign of reform in the mental health services to get off the ground. The revisionists have thought themselves, and their public,

into a state of complete inertia...But the tragic stance of labelling
theory and anti-psychiatric sociology cannot be taken seriously as a
posture which is above the battle...It is *in* the battle, on the wrong
side; the side of those who want to close down intensive psychiatric
units and throw victims of mental illness on to the streets, with the
occasional shot of tranquiliser injected in them to assure the public
that something medical is still happening (1982, p. 41; cf. Fulford,
1989, ch. 10).

11 Many thanks to Bernard Burgoyne for this point.
12 For an excellent introduction to recent feminist debates about the
politics of difference, see Lovell, 1990, Part III; cf. Soper, 1990.

5 Societal Preconditions for the Satisfaction of Basic Needs

1 Emphasising the importance of rules – especially those of language – in
the individuation of cultures is amply illustrated by the articles in
Douglas (1973). This is not meant to undervalue the practical and
material links between cultures which are differentiated in these terms.
See Doyal and Harris (1983) pp. 59–78; cf. Harris (1979) chs 2–4.

6 Human Liberation and the Right to Need-Satisfaction

1 Individuals who have a duty to do something do not necessarily
themselves have the right to do so (e.g. the contract killer). Further,
rights are not entailed when individuals have a duty (e.g. to try to
escape as a prisoner or war) which is not to someone in particular. And
finally, even when the duty is to someone, it must be morally binding –
a strict or 'perfect' duty in Mill's sense – if it carries with it any specific
entitlement. We may have a morally weaker duty to be charitable
without this entailing a right to charity (White, 1984, pp. 60–1).
2 White (1984, pp. 64–5) argues that it is possible to have rights without
the existence of corresponding duties. However, his examples all
presuppose the existence of *some* correlative duty even if not the one
ostensibly signified by the stated right – the right to a second throw in a
game, to criticise the actions of another or to 'look at my neighbour
across our common fence'. This said, we agree with his view that it is
misleading to conceptualise the relationship between duties and rights
as a purely logical one. Far better to regard the existence of strict duties
and correlative rights as the most important empirical indicator of the
seriousness of moral belief and commitment (Renteln, 1990, pp. 41–5).
We will argue shortly that even if seen in these terms, duties and rights
which are thus culturally bounded can still be made to yield universal
duties and rights which are not. For a good introduction to the
analytical literature on the relationship between rights, duties and
culture, see Waldron (1984) pp. 1–20.

3   Harris rejects this view through arguing that we may well believe that *A* has a duty to do *Y* (e.g. to repay a debt) without imputing to anyone the obligation to provide *A* with the means (e.g. a loan of the money) to do so and therefore any corresponding right to it (Harris, 1987, pp. 137–8). Yet his argument is unconvincing. If we really believe that *A* has a specific duty (e.g. of repayment), that he will do so if he can and that we are the *only* means by which his duty can be fulfilled, then we are correspondingly obligated to loan *A* the money.

4   Conceptualising virtue in these terms is grounded in the ethical theories of classical Greece, especially Aristotle's. 'To be a good man will on every Greek view be at least closely allied to being a good citizen' (MacIntyre, 1985, p. 135). Yet however much later moral theory has diverged from this emphasis on successful social participation in an accepted form of life – everything from the 'unhappy consciousness' of the Augustinian hereafter to the individual pursuit of preference of various types of egoism – the ethical importance of the individual's duty to the collective has always remained implicit in the doctrines espoused. To this extent, as the social embodiment of right, adherence to the rules of membership of a community is a thread weaving though otherwise divergent visions of the good. For example, it is no accident that Augustine's *City of God* had implications for the social organisation of the here and now, and we have seen that even classical liberalism implicitly presupposes an ideal community dominated by respect for law and participation in the competitive market, one in which, say, the classic Greek virtue of courage is of obvious relevance. In what is otherwise a *tour de force* of historical scholarship and philosophical argument and imagination, MacIntyre's flirtation with relativism has led him to neglect the potential which such conceptual links offer for a modicum of commensurability between different moral traditions. For further argument to this effect, see Bernstein (1986) ch. 4.

5   The moral force of this argument does not depend on our accepting the moral aims of the strangers to whom we attribute the right to need-satisfaction. The value which we impute to these conditions will vary in proportion to the value which we attach to our own vision of the good, one which, to be consistent, we must wish that all others will pursue and, therefore, be able to do so. This counters Goodin's argument that 'merely showing that something is presupposed by morality does not serve to show that it is necessarily desirable, morally' (Goodin, 1989, p. 49). For if anything specific is believed to be morally desirable – as opposed to morality itself – then the moral desirability of basic need-satisfaction must follow for the reasons outlined.

6   Again, these views are rooted in classical Greek moral theory and are outlined by MacIntyre:

> What these socially embodied agreements which are partially con-
> stitutive of a *polis* succeed in integrating and ordering are all those
> goods specific to the forms of activity in which post-Homeric Greeks
> had come to recognize impersonal and objective standards of

excellence: warfare and combat, athletic and gymnastic performance, poetry of various kinds, rhetoric, architecture, and sculp-
ture, farming and a variety of other *technai*, and the organization and
sustaining of the *polis* itself. So the goodness of a citizen is in key part
constituted by his goodness qua horseman or qua soldier or qua
dramatic poet, and the goodness of someone who is a craftsman is in
key part his goodness qua flutemaker or bridlemaker (MacIntyre,
1988, p. 107).

7 This is not due to the fact that through their omission to help, those
who might have helped can be said to have *caused* the death of the
child. The question of causality here is complex, since if we say that
omissions cause any specific thing to happen, it seems to follow that
they cause everything to happen. Do you, for example, cause all the
trees in Kew Gardens to grow because you don't take an axe to them?
This said, we can still make good sense of our capacity to interrupt
causal processes and of our moral responsibility to do so when they
impinge on the basic need satisfaction of others. In the case of our
beach, if the child drowns, everyone who has done nothing to help and
who had a 'reasonable opportunity' to do so is morally culpable
(Feinberg, 1984, pp. 165–86).

8 None of this is to deny the duties of the inhabitants of the poor nation
states themselves, which are identical to those of people in richer
countries. Even the poorest underdeveloped countries have social
inequalities which suggest that a minority are disregarding their duty
toward the majority (Sandbrook, 1985, ch. 5). While they may not have
sole responsibility for meeting the need-satisfaction of their members, it
does seem reasonable to suggest that they have a special obligation to
act to this end. They have the closest contact with and knowledge of the
deprivation in question and are in the best position to intervene to do
something to try to improve it.

9 Melrose gives the following example of how such relativist arguments
can be employed to justify abuses in need satisfaction:

> But Glaxo did respond to an earlier query we raised about their
> promotion of Calci-Ostelin syrup as a general tonic in another
> developing country, when not only does Glaxo not do this in
> Britain, but the British National Formulary describes this use as
> having no justification. Glaxo's Senior Medical Advisor responded
> by stressing that different countries have very 'different concepts of
> medical practice' (1982, p. 80).

10 This appendix was written before the recent war in Iraq which we do
not have the space to discuss here. However, it is worth pointing out
that *if* it is argued that the war was just for the reasons we have
outlined, it must follow that the foreign policy of the United States
stands condemned for similar reasons – the persistent immoral intervention in the domestic affairs of other nation states to serve its own
interests. One can only hope that the success of the war, and the moral

argument surrounding it, will make it more difficult for this to occur in the future.

7 Optimising Need-Satisfaction in Theory

1 Some have argued against such a 'use/abuse' model of science and technology, claiming that both can be so rooted in the exploitative social relations within which they have evolved that they will never be appropriate for truly liberational purposes: RSJ Collective (1981) pp. 38–44. The wheel probably evolved against the background of highly suspect social relations – patriarchy, slavery. Who knows... or cares?

2 According to Arrow's impossibility theorem, the possibility of such a reconciliation of rationality and democracy is remote (Arrow, 1963). However, the problems which his theorem appears to pose begin to dissolve once the focus shifts from preferences to needs. First, as Sen (1984, pp. 421–2) argues, his conclusion is dependent upon very strict informational limitations including a rejection of non-subjective information about social states. Once the existence of common human needs is conceded, such limits begin to recede. Second, as Miller (1989, p. 299, fn. 3) argues, a 'dialogue form of democracy' will enable participants – assuming good faith – to choose an appropriate formal method of resolving differences and thus avoid the indeterminacy resulting from the existence of conflicting methods of aggregating preferences. Again, this will only be so provided that the focus of deliberation is on more than the comparative weighting of such preferences. It is apparent therefore, that an objective theory of human need coupled with the model of communication endorsed above can contribute to overcoming the conceptual block Arrow's theorem has placed in the way of reconciling rationality and democracy. Also see: Pettit (1980, pp. 145–7).

3 White rejects the link for which we have argued between Habermas's theory of rational and democratic discourse and optimised need-satisfaction in our terms. Focusing on what he calls 'biological needs', he dismisses attempts to talk of improvements in such discourse leading to universalisable improvements in their satisfaction across cultures. To do so skirts over important differences in the ways in which needs are conceptualised and prioritised within different cultures (White, 1988, pp. 69–73). We have already assessed the difficulties with this view. No doubt, powerful exploitative groups could articulate their interests and act more effectively if their members communicated more along the lines that Habermas outlines. Yet to be consistent, when he talks of liberation and of the increased choices for *everyone* which it can bring, he must draw on a theory of common interests and needs. That he does not always do so – and White is right about this – simply puts him in other good company, including Marx. Some of Habermas's own

recent attacks on the relativism of post-modernism serve to underline this point (Habermas, 1988).

4 The individualism which seems implicit in Rawls's conceptualisation of his original position has been criticised by a number of writers. For useful summaries, see Pogge (1988, ch. 2); Kukathas and Pettit (1990, ch. 6).

5 Pogge (1988, pp. 174–5) similarly maintains that: 'Inequalities in index goods are governed by the difference principle, subject to the condition...that there must be formal equality of opportunity and rough equality of actual opportunity (that is, participants must have roughly equivalent access to education and the like).'

6 'Thoughts without content are empty, (sensory) intuitions without concepts are blind. It is, therefore, just as necessary to make our concepts sensible, that is, to add the object to them in intuition, as to make our intuitions intelligible, that is, to bring them under concepts' (Kant, 1964, p. 93).

7 Many thanks to Roger Harris for this point.

8 Measuring Need-Satisfaction

1 Among the voluminous literature here, see Streeten (1981, ch. 18); Streeten *et al.* (1981) ch. 1; Miles (1985) ch. 2; Hillhorst and Klatter (1985); Leeson and Nixson (1988) ch. 2.

2 Weigel (1986) is exempt from these criticisms, but he appears to base his case on sociobiological arguments which, while interesting, are fundamentally flawed for the reasons developed in Chapter 3.

3 Braybrooke (1987) ch. 2.2. For comparisons of some of these taxonomies see Miles (1985) ch. 6; Baster (1985), Johansson (1976).

4 Exemplified in Britain by the work of Townsend (1979). On poverty research, see also Mack and Lansley (1985), and, for a survey of many of the methodological issues, the contributions to a special issue of the *Journal of Social Policy* 16, 2 (1987). On 'social audits' see Policy Research Unit (1990).

5 Carr-Hill (1986) pp. 305–6. The third alternative is to disaggregate between groups appropriate to the domain of need-satisfaction under discussion. For example gender would be crucial when charting total work load, but not for physical environment.

6 Though see the interesting work by Desai, Sen and Boltvinik (1990).

9 Physical Health and Autonomy

1 Some of the ideas and text which follow in Chapters 9 and 10 were originally developed in Len Doyal (1988).

2 Some organisations of disabled people have rejected these definitions and distinctions, arguing that they reify, individualise and medicalise the nature of disability (Oliver, 1990, ch. 1). First, the idea of 'normality' at the centre of the WHO definition of disability ignores

the influences of sub-cultures, gender, ethnicity and other factors on what is perceived to be normal. Second, they take the social environment for granted and thus ignore the way in which physical and social patterns contribute to disability. Third, and following on from this, they explain disability solely in terms of biological pathology. The second and third criticisms are indubitably true as an account of much past research and practice, yet they are not necessarily entailed by the WHO definitions. On the contrary, the social concept of handicap permits the ways that policies and practices restrict the social participation of people with disabilities to be identified and rectified. (It goes without saying that this will in all probability not occur in practice without the active mobilisation of people with disabilities alongside other groups). The first criticism however, simply echoes relativist arguments concerning any conception of common human need, and is to be rejected for the reasons already outlined.

3 An attempt to combine 'distress' (a broader concept than pain) with disability into an overall metric of 'quality of life' has been made by some (see Williams, 1985). While this is desirable if impaired capacity to participate is to be fully operationalised, it cannot be said that present efforts have addressed the issue of cultural variation in the experience of distress.

4 Almost all the commonly available cross-cultural indicators are invalid and/or unreliable, whether they be mental hospital data and consultations with medical practitioners, or hypothesised proxy indicators such as suicide rates. See Murphy (1982) for a careful survey of the comparative incidence of mental illness, but which concludes that some firm conclusions can be drawn even on the basis of available data.

5 Hoffman eloquently makes a similar point:

> Linguistic dispossession is a sufficient motive for violence, for it is close to the dispossession of one's own self. Blind rage, helpless rage is a rage that has no words – rage that overwhelms one with darkness. And if one is perpetually without words, if one exists in the entropy of inarticulateness, that condition itself is bound to be an enraging frustration... If all therapy is speaking therapy – a talking one – then perhaps all neurosis is a speech disease (Hoffman, 1989, p. 124).

10 Intermediate Needs

1 For a useful summary of further aspects of Brown and Harris, see Gilbert (1984, pp. 176–83). Two critiques of their work are: Tennant and Bebbington (1978) and Davies and Roche (1980). Brown and Harris reply to the former in (1978b).

2 Some cross-national statistical studies have found rather weak relationships between calorific adequacy and measures of survival chances, for example with infant mortality, once income per head is introduced into the regression (Cumper, 1984, pp. 52–62). However, this may reflect the measurement problems referred to above as well as other aspects of

malnutrition not captured by this measure of undernutrition. It is clear that the relation between nutrition and health is in any case a complex one mediated by several other factors, such as stature and (possibly) genetic selection, in addition to some of our other intermediate needs.

3 There is a third factor: housing may be safe, warm and uncrowded yet so inaccessible that its occupants are unable to utilise or consume satisfiers for other human needs (e.g. access to local markets). This illustrates the interdependence between intermediate needs discussed in Chapter 8. Since the effects of this should however show up elsewhere, we shall not propose separate indicators to monitor this aspect of housing conditions.

4 Sea and air pollution are areas where the nation state is peculiarly limited as a statistical site. In many West European countries, for example, over half of the depositions of sulphur each year are emitted by foreign sources (UN, 1987, Table 1.16)

5 There are two main approaches to defining and assessing the bundle of commodities the consumption of which will permit such participation. The first, 'budget study' approach lets various experts define the basic bundle of goods and activities and the necessary minimum levels, while the second, 'consensus' or 'majoritarian' approach leaves this task to a sample of the population concerned. It is clear that both approaches have advantages, but that taken in isolation both are unsatisfactory. Our theory points to a resolution of the dilemma they pose, along the lines developed in Chapter 8 and below in Chapter 14. As Walker (1987) also argues, informed consensus on such matters can only arise from a dialogue between experts and the public – in our terms, between codified and experiential knowledge. (This is to simplify several issues. For a recent discussion of the problems in defining and measuring poverty see Townsend (1987); Veit-Wilson (1987); Piachaud (1987); Bradshaw *et al.* (1987); Walker (1987).)

If a matrix of minimum activities and practices, and the minimum economic resources necessary to enable people to achieve them, can be agreed, then relative poverty can be defined as a quantum of resources falling below this level. A process of informed consent could in principle overcome many of the disagreements over poverty lines which have bedevilled past analysis. If in practice such agreement cannot be achieved, then a number of separate poverty lines could be constructed and ordinal, though not cardinal, comparisons of populations could be made using whatever agreement on partial ordering emerges when the criteria are taken together (see Sen (1979); Atkinson (1989) chs 1–2).

6 Headcount measures have been criticised on the grounds, among others, that they are indifferent to the degree by which people's incomes fall short of the poverty line. To correct for this over-simplification these 'poverty deficits' can be calculated, summed and expressed as a proportion of total incomes.

7 Gramsci (1971), especially selections 1.1 and 1.2. For a superb account of the importance and contemporary relevance of Gramsci's views on education, see Entwistle (1979) Part I. Also Ireland (1985).

11 Societal Preconditions For Optimising Need-Satisfaction

1 These issues are aired in Vincent (1986) Part I and by several contributors in Cingranelli (1988). For a recent statement of this view, see Renteln (1990) chs 2–3. However, she rejects the argument that descriptive relativism entails moral relativism, and goes on to try to extract certain universal moral principles from cross-cultural empirical research.

2 Stewart (1985) ch. 2; cf. Cole and Miles (1984) ch. 5. There are many simplifications introduced into this model. In particular it is – quite deliberately – institution-neutral. We abstract from the overall type of economic system (for example, capitalist or state socialist) and from the institutional domains of production within them (such as market, public sector or household production).

3 Any product can be divided into its basic and non-basic components by comparing the consumption of an item X by a particular group with its consumption by the richest groups in the richest societies. Fitting an exponential curve to the consumption of agricultural goods, Cole and Miles estimate that 78 per cent of agricultural consumption by the poor majority in the low-income countries can be described as basic – compared with only 13.5 per cent of that by upper-income groups in the most advanced economies. On this basis they can, making dramatic simplifications, calculate the aggregate production and consumption of need satisfiers for different economies. This suggests that the global value of luxuries produced *exceeds* that of basics, as their estimates for 1975 indicate (Cole and Miles, 1984, pp. 135–9):

Basics	$3.4 trillion
Luxuries	$5.3 trillion
Capital goods	$2.1 trillion
Total output	$10.8 trillion

4 The problems multiply when many goods and services other than basic foodstuffs are considered. For example, a car or a telephone may constitute a satisfier – a necessary pre-requisite for successful social participation – in some societies and not in others. To devise and agree on a basket of such satisfiers in any society returns us to some of the methodological problems confronted by the poverty research discussed in the previous chapter.

5 Cf. Pogge (1989) §13.1. We leave to one side here another problem identified by Sen. Different groups of people in different circumstances will require varying amounts of universal satisfier characteristics to achieve optimum levels of health and autonomy. For example, active workers require more food than passive ones, people living in a harsh climate require more shelter, and so on. The rate at which satisfiers are converted into need-satisfaction varies, hence equality of need satisfaction does not necessarily require equality of access to satisfiers (Sen, 1984, pp. 280–2).

6 For a survey of techniques for assessing income distribution see Atkinson (1983) ch. 3; also (1989), ch. 2 for measures of poverty. For a discussion of comparative data on income distribution, see Kakwani (1980). The World Bank (1988) Table 26 and the UNDP (1990) summarise what data is available, though information on certain Western nations is more plentiful via the Luxembourg Income Study (O'Higgins *et al.*, 1985).

12 Charting Human Welfare: Need-Satisfaction in the Three Worlds

1 This chapter was collated and written before the appearance of the UN's *Human Development Report 1990* and lack of time has prevented the incorporation of some new data presented there. However we have used it to compile Table 12.4. The parallels between it and our own project are obvious, in part reflecting Sen's influence on both. The Report represents the first attempt by an international body to provide a social audit of human development fully informed by a coherent theory of human development, and as such is a landmark in the mapping of human need. The parallels and contrasts between our approach and Sen's are briefly explored in Chapter 8.

13 Towards a Political Economy of Need-Satisfaction

1 There is a large literature on the association of economic growth, indices of industrialisation and some measures of basic need-satisfaction (usually the PQLI or its separate components). See, for example, Hicks (1982); Ram (1985). For a survey see Stewart (1985) chs 4, 5. Several contributors to Cingranelli and Wright (1988) have extended this analysis to include measures of political and civil rights.
2 This passage is based on the excellent analysis provided by Evans and Stephens (1988) of the development debates, which surveys the work of global theorists such as Rostow, Gunder Frank and Amin, alongside the state approaches of Skocpol and others.
3 The state socialist economies are on average, and in most individual cases, much poorer than their Western counterparts. Thus the East European nations including the USSR should be compared with upper-middle income capitalist countries, not with the advanced capitalist democracies (Cereseto and Waitzkin, 1986, Appendix 1). This clearly refutes the earlier view that the state socialist economies would soon 'catch up' with the West. The capitalist world has recovered its economic dynamism in the 1980s, whereas corrections to state socialist statistics, not least from soviet economists such as Aganbegyan (1989, p. 89), have revised official growth rates downwards. It is now believed that the annual increase in the national income of the USSR declined steadily from 8 per cent p.a. in the late 1960s to zero in 1981–5 – a real fall in income per head once population growth is taken into account.

4 The literature on the 'Swedish model' is extensive. For an analysis of the economic and social aspects see Therborn (1991), and for a qualified critique see Gould (1988).

5 This paragraph draws on the following references among others: Hodgson (1984); Bowles and Gintis (1986), ch. 5; Ellis and Heath (1983); Crouch (1983); Hindess (1987, chs 2, 8, 9); Sen (1984, ch. 3; 1981); Elster (1979). We hope to address these issues in more detail in another paper.

6 On the case for 'bringing the state back in' see the book of that name, in particular the essay by Rueschemeyer and Evans (1985). The empirical case for democratic corporatism and a coherent industrial policy is made by Katzenstein (1985). See also the case studies in Pfaller *et al.* (1991). A good comparative and theoretical analysis of state social intervention is by Esping-Andersen (1990), a work influenced by Polanyi's classic text (1957, Part 2).

7 This is consistent with Hodgson's 'impurity principle', which states that any actual socio-economic system must contain at least one other economic structure based on different principles within it in order for the whole to function (Hodgson, 1984, pp. 85–9; 104–9).

8 For persuasive arguments and social models drawing on both liberal and socialist antecedents, see Bowles and Gintis (1986); Held (1987) ch. 9; Bobbio (1987a and 1987b); and for a critique, Anderson (1988). For some recent economic 'third alternatives' to capitalism and state socialism, see Devine (1988), Elson (1988) and Meade (1990).

14 A Dual Political Strategy

1 The literature on the historical development of citizenship rights is extensive. The classic statement of the progressive evolution of civil, political and social rights in Britain is Marshall (1963). Many critiques have been offered of this as a generalisable historical account (Mann, 1987). See Flora and Heidenheimer (1981) for a comparative historical account of the evolution of social insurance. For a comparative history of the struggles for political rights in the Western world see Therborn (1977) and on the open relationship between rights and capitalism, see Turner (1986) and Bowles and Gintis (1986). Both argue that the relationship between capitalism and social citizenship is ambiguous and that social rights in practice can contract as well as expand. The different forms of welfare capitalism, and some of their welfare outcomes, are explored by Esping-Andersen (1990). De Swann (1988) provides a sophisticated interpretation of the rise of the welfare state as the collectivisation of care, drawing on welfare economics and historical sociology, partly premised on the account of market failures adumbrated above.

2 There is now a large literature on basic income. Purdy (1988) chs 9–11, provides one of the clearest introductions together with as fair a summary of the pros and cons as could be expected from a committed

supporter. The case for a statutory right to work is advocated in Rustin (1985) ch. 7. These two positions are debated between Keane and Owens (1987, 1988) and Rustin (1987). See also the contributions by Purdy and Lister in Alcock *et al.* (1989). For an argument and a proposal that utilises both approaches see Alcock (1985), cf. Atkinson (1989, pp. 92–5). A paper by van Parijs and van der Veen (1985), which situates thinking on basic income within a broader system-theoretical and philosophical perspective, has stimulated a wide-ranging discussion, published in the same issue of *Theory and Society*.

3 Again the desirability and feasibility of justiciable rights to welfare is much disputed, not only by neo-liberal critics mentioned earlier on (see N. Barry, 1990, for a nuanced summary of these). Both Titmuss (1971) and Marshall (1981, ch. 5) have argued that shortfalls in need satisfaction are better met, and excessive litigation avoided, if certain services are allocated on a discretionary basis. However, Marshall himself provides a later critique and qualification of this viewpoint (1981, ch. 5 Afterthought).

4 See Dworkin (1985, Part 5) and Richards (1984). On the relationship between 'difference' and citizenship, see Pateman (1989) and Phillips (1991).

5 This paragraph draws on material and debates in Britain in Hadley and Hatch (1981), Johnson (1987, 1990), Fabian Society (1984). See also Gough and Doyal *et al.* (1989, pp. 269–71). A good collection which airs many of the issues is edited by Held and Pollitt (1986) – see especially Pollitt himself (1986). For the Third World, see Ruttan (1984), Mehta (1984) and Jones (1990, ch. 10).

6 These arguments are to be found *inter alia* in: Gutmann (1980, ch. 7); Fabian Society (1984); Cochrane (1986); Rowbotham (1986); Johnson (1990); Finch and Groves (1980), Finch (1990).

7 The justification for a dual strategy requires more attention than we have been able to attempt here. Elsewhere, we and others have outlined a detailed social policy diagnosis and manifesto for Britain (Gough and Doyal, 1989; Alcock *et al.* (1989). Also of interest, as examples of how it can inform a research strategy at the local level are the 'needs audits' such as those undertaken in Leeds (PRU, 1990). We hope to expand on the theory and practice of the dual strategy in a future book.

Bibliography

(Place of publication London unless otherwise stated.)

Åberg, R. (1987) 'Working conditions', in R. Erikson and R. Åberg (eds), *Welfare in Transition: A Survey of Living Conditions in Sweden 1968–81* (Oxford, Clarendon Press).

Aganbegyan, A. (1988) 'New directions in Soviet economics', *New Left Review*, 169.

Agarwal, A. *et al.* (1981) *Water, Sanitation, Health-For-All?* (Earthscan).

Alcock, P. (1985) 'Socialist security', *Critical Social Policy*, 13.

Alcock, P. Gamble, A., Gough, I., Lee, P. and Walker, A. (eds) (1989) *The Social Economy and the Democratic State: A New Policy Agenda* (Lawrence and Wishart).

Allardt, E. (1973) 'About dimensions of welfare', *Research Group for Comparative Sociology* (Helsinki, Finland).

Allsebrook, A. and Swift, A. (1989) *Broken Promise: the World of Endangered Children* (Hodder and Stoughton).

Amnesty International (1983) *Political Killings by Governments* (Amnesty Publications).

Amnesty International (1984) *Torture in the Eighties* (Martin Robertson).

Anderson, P. (1983) *In The Tracks of Historical Materialism* (Verso).

Anderson, P. (1988) 'The affinities of Norberto Bobbio', *New Left Review*, 170, 3–36.

Anscombe, G.E.M. (1957) *Intention* (Oxford, Blackwell).

Anscombe, G.E.M. (1969) 'Modern moral philosophy', in W. Hudson (ed.), *The Is – Ought Question* (Macmillan).

Archer, M. (1988) *Culture and Agency* (Cambridge University Press).

Arkes, H. (1986) *First Things* (Princeton University Press).

Armstrong, D. (1983) *Political Anatomy of the Body* (Cambridge University Press).

Aronowitz, S. (1988) *Science as Power* (Macmillan).

Arrington, R. (1989) *Rationalism, Realism and Relativism* (Ithaca, Cornell University Press).

Arrow, K. (1963) *Social Choice and Individual Values* (New Haven, Yale University Press).

Atkinson, A.B. (1983) *The Economics of Inequality* (Oxford University Press).

Atkinson, A.B. (1989) *Poverty and Social Security* (Harvester Wheatsheaf).

Avineri, S. (1972) *Hegel's Theory of the Modern State* (Cambridge University Press).

Axelsson, C. (1987) 'Family and social integration', in R. Erikson and R. Åberg (eds), *Welfare in Transition: A Survey of Living Conditions in Sweden 1968–81* (Oxford, Clarendon Press).

Bachrach, P. and Baratz, M. (1970) *The Theory of Democratic Elitism* (Boston, Little, Brown).

Badrova, V. and Anker, R. (1985) *Working Women in Socialist Countries: the Fertility Connection* (Geneva, ILO).

Barnes, B. and Bloor, D. (1982) 'Relativism, rationalism and the sociology of knowledge', in M. Hollis and S. Lukes (eds), *Rationality and Relativism* (Oxford, Blackwell).

Barrington Moore, J. (1978) *Injustice* (Macmillan).

Barry, B. (1965) *Political Argument* (Routledge).

Barry, B. (1990) *Political Argument: A Reissue* (Harvester Wheatsheaf).

Barry, N. (1990) *Citizenship and Rights in Thatcher's Britain: Two Views* (IEA).

Baster, N. (1985) 'Social indicator research: some issues and debates', in J. Hillhorst and M. Klatter (eds), *Social Development in the Third World: Level of Living Indicators and Social Planning* (Croom Helm).

Baudrillard, J. (1983) *In the Shadow of Silent Majorities . . . or the End of the Social* (New York, Semiotexte).

Bay, C. (1968) 'Needs, wants and political legitimacy', *Canadian Journal of Political Science*, 1, 241–60.

Beck, A. (1967) *Depression: Clinical, Experimental and Theoretical Aspects* (Staples Press).

Beiser, M. (1985) 'A study of depression among traditional Africans, urban North Americans and Southeast Asian refugees', in A. Kleinman and B. Good (eds), *Culture and Depression: Studies in the Anthropology and Cross-Cultural Psychiatry of Affect and Disorder* (Berkeley: University of California Press).

Bell, J. and Mendus, S. (eds) (1988) *Philosophy and Medical Welfare* (Cambridge University Press).

Benton, T. (1988) 'Marx, humanism and speciesism', *Radical Philosophy*, 50 (Autumn).

Bentovim, A. and Vizard, E. (1988) 'Sexual abuse, sexuality and childhood', in A. Bentovim *et al.* (eds), *Child Sexual Abuse within the Family* (Butterworth).

Berlin, I. (1969) 'Two concepts of liberty', in I. Berlin, *Four Essays on Liberty* (Oxford University Press).

Bernstein, R. (1969) *Philosophical Profiles* (Cambridge, Polity).

Bettelheim, B. (1986) *The Informed Heart* (Penguin).

Bhat, A., Carr-Hill, R. and Ohri, S. (eds) (1988) *Britain's Black Population*, 2nd edn (Gower).

Bigsten, A. (1987) 'Poverty, inequality and development', in N. Gemmell (ed.), *Surveys in Development Economics* (Basil Blackwell).

Blaxter, M. (1983) 'Longitudinal studies in Britain relevant to inequalities in health', in R. G. Wilkinson (ed.), *Class and Health: Research and Longitudinal Data* (Tavistock).

Bobbio, N. (1987a) *The Future of Democracy* (Cambridge, Polity).

Bobbio, N. (1987b) *Which Socialism?* (Cambridge, Polity).

Boorse, C. (1975) 'On the distinction between disease and illness', *Philosophy and Public Affairs*, 5.

Boorse, C. (1982) 'What a theory of mental health should be', in R. E. Edwards (ed.), *Psychiatry and Ethics* (Buffalo, NY, Prometheus Books).

Bottomley, K. and Pease, K. (1986) *Crime and Punishment: Interpreting the Data* (Open University Press).

Bowles, S. and Gintis, H. (1986) *Democracy and Capitalism* (Routledge).

Bradshaw, J. (1972) 'The concept of social need', *New Society* (30 March).

Bradshaw, J., Mitchell, D. and Morgan, J. (1987) 'Evaluating adequacy: the potential of budget standards', *Journal of Social Policy*, 16, 2.

Brandt Report (Commission on International Development Issues) (1980) *North–South: A Programme for Survival*.

Braybrooke, D. (1987) *Meeting Needs* (Princeton University Press).

Brewer, A. (1980) *Marxist Theories of Imperialism: A Critical Survey* (Routledge).

Brown, A. (1986) *Modern Political Philosophy* (Harmondsworth, Penguin).

Brown, G. W. and Harris, T. (1978a) *Social Origins of Depression* (Tavistock).

Brown, G. W. and Harris, T. (1978b) 'Social origins of depression: a reply', *Psychological Medicine*, 8, 577–88.

Brown, J. L. (1989) 'The paradox of hunger in the world's wealthiest democracy', *International Journal of Health Services*, 19, 2.

Brundtland Report (World Commission on Environment and Development) (1987) *Our Common Future* (Oxford University Press).

Bryman, Alan (1988) *Quantity and Quality in Social Research* (Unwin Hyman).

Buchanan, A. (1982) *Marx and Justice: the Radical Critique of Liberalism* (Methuen).

Buhmann, B. *et al.* (1987) 'Equivalence scales, well-being, inequality and poverty', *Review of Income and Wealth*, 115–42.

Bull, D. (1982) *A Growing Problem: Pesticides and the Third World* (Oxfam).

Burki, S. J. and Ul Haq, M. (1981), 'Meeting basic needs: an overview', *World Development*, 9, 2.

Busfield, J. (1986) *Managing Madness* (Unwin Hyman).

Callinicos, A. (1990) *Against Post Modernism* (Oxford, Polity).

Cammack, P., Pool, D. and Tordoff, W. (1988) *Third World Politics: A Comparative Introduction* (Macmillan).

Campbell, T. (1983) *The Left and Rights* (Routledge).

Caplan, A. *et al.* (1981) *Concepts of Health and Disease* (Reading, Mass, Addison-Wesley).

Carley, M. (1981) *Social Measurement and Social Indicators: Issues of Policy and Theory* (Allen and Unwin).

Carr, M. (ed.) (1989) *The Barefoot Book: Economically Appropriate Services for the Rural Poor* (Intermediate Publications).

Carr-Hill, R. (1984) 'The political choice of social indicators', *Quantity and Quality*, 18, 173–91.

Carr-Hill, R. (1986) 'An approach to monitoring social welfare', in P. Nolan and S. Paine (eds), *Rethinking Socialist Economics* (Cambridge, Polity).

Carr-Hill, R. (1987) 'The inequalities in health debate: a critical review of the issues', *Journal of Social Policy*, 16, 4.

Cartwright, A. (1983) *Health Surveys in Practice and in Potential* (King's Fund).

Cereseto, S. and Waitzkin, H. (1986) 'Capitalism, socialism and the physical quality of life', *International Journal of Health Services*, 16, 4.

Channer, Y. and Parton, N. (1990) 'Racism. cultural relativism and child protection', in Violence Against Children Study Group, *Taking Child Abuse Seriously* (Unwin Hyman).

Chomsky, N. and Herman, E. (1979) *The Washington Connection and Third World Fascism: The Political Economy of Human Rights, Volume 1* (Nottingham, Spokesman).

Cingranelli, D. (ed.) (1988) *Human Rights: Theory and Measurement* (Macmillan).

Cingranelli, D. and Wright, K. (1988) 'Correlates of due process', in D. Cingranelli (ed.), *Human Rights: Theory and Measurement* (Macmillan).

Clare, A. (1980) *Psychiatry in Dissent* (Tavistock).

Clutterbuck, C. and Lang, T. (1982) *More Than We Can Chew* (Pluto).

Cochrane, A. (1986) 'Community politics and democracy', in D. Held and C. Pollitt (eds), *New Forms of Democracy* (Sage).

Cochrane, S. (1977) *Can Education Reduce Fertility?* (Washington DC, World Bank).

Cohen, D. (1988) *Forgotten Millions: the Treatment of the Mentally Ill: A Global Perspective* (Paladin).

Cohen, I. (1989) *Structuration Theory* (Macmillan).

Coimbra, M. (1984) *Welfare Policies and Peripheral Capitalism: The Case of Nutritional Policy in Brazil*, Ph.D, Manchester University.

Cole, S. and Miles, I. (1984) *Worlds Apart* (Brighton, Wheatsheaf Books).

Coles, R. (1967) *Children of Crisis: a Study of Courage and Fear* (Faber).

Commoner, B. (1980) 'How poverty breeds overpopulation', in R. Arditti, P. Brennan and S. Cavrak (eds.), *Science and Liberation* (Boston, South End Press).

Cooley, M. (1980) *Architect or Bee?* (Slough, Langley Technical Services).

Coombs, P. (1985) *The World Crisis in Education* (Oxford University Press).

Cooper, R. (1987) 'Has the period of rising mortality in the Soviet Union come to an end?', *International Journal of Health Services*, 17, 3.

Cooper, R., Schatzkin, A. and Sempos, C. (1984) 'Rising death rates among Polish men', *International Journal of Health Services*, 14, 2.

Cornia, G., Jolly, R. and Stewart, F. (eds) (1987) *Adjustment with a Human Face* (Oxford, Clarendon Press).

Cox, J. (ed.) (1986) *Transcultural Psychiatry* (Croom Helm).

Cranston, M. (1973) *What are Human Rights?* (Bodley Head).

Crouch, C. (1983) 'Market failure: Fred Hirsch and the case for social democracy', in A. Ellis and K. Kumar (eds), *Dilemmas of Liberal Democracies* (Tavistock).

Crystal, D. (1987) *The Cambridge Encyclopedia of Language* (Cambridge University Press).

CSO (1987) *Social Trends* 17 (HMSO).

CSO (1989) *Social Trends* 19 (HMSO).

Culver C. and Gert, B. (1982) *Psychology in Medicine* (New York, Oxford University Press).

Culyer, A., Lavers, R. and Williams, A. (1972) 'Health indicators', in A. Shonfield and S. Shaw (eds), *Social Indicators and Social Policy* (Heinemann).

Cumper, G. (1984) *Determinants of Health Levels in Developing Countries* (Letchworth: Research Studies Press).

Cutler, P. (1984) 'The measurement of poverty', *World Development*, 12, 11/12.

Dale, J. and Foster, P. (1986) *Feminists and State Welfare* (Routledge).

Daly, M. (1984) *Pure Lust* (The Women's Press).

Daniels, N. (1985) *Just Health Care* (Cambridge University Press).

Dasen, P. (1977) 'Are cognitive processes universal?', in N.Warren (ed.), *Studies in Cross-Cultural Psychology, Volume 1* (New York, Academic Press).

Davies, C. and Roche, S. (1980) 'The place of methodology', *Sociological Review*, 28, 3.

Davis, C. M. (1988) 'Developments in the health sector of the Soviet economy, 1970–90' paper presented at a conference on Social Policy and Socialism, Leeds Polytechnic.

Derbyshire, J. D. and I. (1989) *Political Systems of the World* (Chambers).

De Swann, A. (1988) *In Care of the State* (Cambridge, Polity).

Desai, M., Sen, A. and Boltvinik, J. (1990) *Social Progress Index: A Proposal*, Preliminary version (Bogota, UNDP).

Devine, P. (1988) *Democracy and Economic Planning* (Cambridge, Polity).

Dixon-Mueller, R. (1990) 'Abortion policy and women's health in developing countries', *International Journal of Health Studies*, 20, 2.

Douglas, I. (1983) *The Urban Environment* (Edward Arnold).

Douglas, M. (1966) *Purity and Danger: An Analysis of Concepts of Pollution and Taboo* (London, Routledge).

Douglas, M. (1966) *Purity and Danger* (Routledge).

Douglas, M. (ed.) (1973) *Rules and Meanings* (Harmondsworth, Penguin).

Douglas, M. (1975) *Implicit Meanings* (Routledge).

Doyal, Len (1987) 'Health, underdevelopment and traditional medicine', *Holistic Medicine*, 2, 1.

Doyal, Len (1988) 'Basic human needs and objective well-being', *Revue de Sociologie Internationale*, 2, 133–89.

Doyal, Len (1990) 'Medical ethics and moral indeterminacy', *Journal of Law and Society*, 17, 1.

Doyal, Len and Lesley (1984), 'Western scientific medicine: a philosophical and political prognosis', in L. Birke and J. Silvertown (eds), *More Than the Parts: the Politics of Biology* (Pluto).

Doyal, Len and Gough, I. (1984) 'A theory of human need', *Critical Social Policy*, 4, 1, no.10.

Doyal, Len and Harris, R. (1983) 'The practical foundations of human understanding', *New Left Review*, 139, May-June.

Doyal, Len and Harris, R. (1986) *Empiricism, Explanation and Rationality* (Routledge).

Doyal, Lesley (1979) *The Political Economy of Health* (Pluto).

Doyal, Lesley and Epstein, S. (1983) *Cancer in Great Britain: the Politics of Prevention* (Pluto).

Doyal, Lesley (1985) *Women and Health in the European region: the Social and Economic Context* (Copenhagen: WHO).

Doyal, Lesley (1990a) 'Hazards of hearth and home', *Women's Studies International Forum*, 13, 5.

Doyal, Lesley (1990b) 'Waged work and women's well-being', *Women's Studies International Forum*, 13, 6.

Drakakis-Smith, D. (1979) 'Low-cost housing provision in the Third World: some theoretical and practical alternatives', in H. G. Murison and J. P. Lea (eds), *Housing in Third World Countries* (Macmillan).

Dworkin, A. (1980) 'Taking action', in L. Lederer (ed.), *Take Back the Night* (New York, William Morrow).

Dworkin, G. (1988) *The Theory and Practice of Autonomy* (Cambridge University Press).

Dworkin, R. (1981) 'What is equality?', Part II, *Philosophy and Public Affairs*, 10.

Dworkin, R. (1985) *A Matter of Principle* (Oxford University Press).

Eckholm, E. (1982) *Down to Earth* (Pluto).

Edwards, R. E. (1982) 'Mental health as rational autonomy', in R. E. Edwards (ed.), *Psychiatry and Ethics* (Buffalo, NY, Prometheus Books).

Eisenstein, Z. (1979) 'Some notes on the relations of capitalist patriarchy', in Z. Eisenstein (ed.), *Capitalist Patriarchy and the Case for Socialist Feminism* (New York, Monthly Review Press).

Ellis, A. and Heath, A. (1983) 'Positional competition', in A. Ellis and K. Kumar (eds), *Dilemmas of Liberal Democracies* (Tavistock).

Elson, D. (1988) 'Market socialism or socialisation of the market?', *New Left Review*, 172, 3–44.

Elson, D. (1991) 'Male bias in macroeconomics: the case of structural adjustment', in D. Elson (ed.), *Male Bias in the Development Process* (Manchester University Press).

Elster, J. (1979) *Ulysses and the Sirens* (Cambridge University Press).

Elster, J. (1985) *Making Sense of Marx* (Cambridge University Press).

Engelhardt, H. T. (1982) 'Psychotherapy as meta-ethics', in R. E. Edwards (ed.), *Psychiatry and Ethics* (Buffalo, NY, Prometheus Books).

Entwistle, H. (1979) *Antonio Gramsci* (Routledge).

Enzensberger, H. (1976) *Raids and Reconstructions* (New Left Books).

Erikson, R. and Åberg, R. (eds) (1987) *Welfare in Transition: A Survey of Living Conditions in Sweden 1968–1981* (Oxford, Clarendon Press).

Esping-Andersen, G. (1989) *The Three Worlds of Welfare Capitalism* (Oxford, Polity Press).

Estes, R. (1984) *The Social Progress of Nations* (New York, Praeger)

Evans, P. B. and Stephens, J. D. (1988) 'Development and the world economy', in N. J. Smelser (ed.), *Handbook of Sociology* (Sage)

FAO/WHO Expert Committee (1973) *Energy and Protein Requirements* (Rome, FAO).

Fabian Society (1984) *Socialism and Decentralisation*, Tract 496 (Fabian Society).

Faden, R. and Beauchamp, T. (1986) *A History and Theory of Informed Consent* (New York, Oxford University Press).

Feher, F., Heller, A. and Markus, G. (1983) *Dictatorship over Needs* (Blackwell, University Press).

Feinberg, J. (1973) *Social Philosophy* (Englewood Cliffs, Prentice Hall).

Feinberg, J. (1980) *Rights, Justice and the Bounds of Liberty* (Princeton, Princeton University Press).

Ferguson, K. (1984) *The Feminist Case Against Bureaucracy* (Philadelphia, Temple University Press).

Feyerabend, P. (1978) *Science in a Free Society* (New Left Books).

Finch, J. and Groves, D. (1980) 'Community care and the family: a case for equal opportunities?', *Journal of Social Policy*, 9, 4.

Finch, J. (1989) 'Kinship and friendship', in R. Jowell, S. Witherspoon and L. Brook (eds), *British Social Attitudes: Special International Report* (Aldershot, Gower).

Finegold, D. and Soskice, D. (1988) 'The failure of training in Britain: analysis and prescription', *Oxford Review of Economic Policy*, 4, 3.

Fishkin, J. (1982) *The Limits of Obligation* (New Haven, Yale University Press).

Fitzgerald, R. (1977) 'Abraham Maslow's hierarchy of needs - an exposition and evaluation', in R. Fitzgerald (ed.), *Human Needs and Politics* (NSW, Rushcutters Bay, Pergamon).

Flew, A. (1977) 'Wants or needs, choices or commands', in R. Fitzgerald (ed.), *Human Needs and Politics* (NSW, Rushcutters Bay, Pergamon).

Flora, P. and Alber, J. (1981) 'Modernisation, democratisation and the development of welfare states in Western Europe', in Flora P. and Heidenheimer, A. J., *The Development of Welfare States in Europe and America* (Transaction Books).

Foster, G. and Anderson, B. (1978) *Medical Anthropology* (New York, Wiley).

Foster, P. (1983) *Access to Welfare* (Macmillan).

Freden, L. (1982) *Psychosocial Aspects of Depression* (Wiley).

Freire, P. (1985) *The Politics of Education* (Macmillan).

Freud, S. (1961) *Civilisation and its Discontents*. The Standard Edition of the Complete Works of Freud, vol. 21, trans. J. Strachey (Hogarth).

Frosh, S. (1987) *The Politics of Psychoanalysis* (Macmillan).

Fukuyama, F. (1989) 'The end of history?', *The National Interest*, 16.

Fulford, K. (1989) *Moral Theory in Medical Practice* (Cambridge University Press).

Galtung, J. (1980), 'The basic needs approach', in K. Lederer (ed.), *Human Needs* (Cambridge, Mass, Oelgeschlager, Gunn and Hain).

Galtung, J. (1982) 'Why the concern with ways of life?', in I. Miles and J. Irvine (eds), *The Poverty of Progress* (Oxford, Pergamon Press).

Gastil, R. (1978) *Freedom in the World: Political Rights and Civil Liberties* (New York, Freedom House).

Geras, N. (1983) *Marx and Human Nature* (Verso).

Geras, N. (1988) 'Post Marxism', *New Left Review*, 169.

Geras, N. (1989) 'Our morals: the ethics of revolution', in R. Miliband *et al.* (eds), *Socialist Register 1989* (Merlin Press).

Gewith, A. (1978) *Reason and Morality* (University of Chicago Press).

Gewirth, A. (1982) *Human Rights* (University of Chicago Press).

Ghoussoub, M. (1987) 'Feminism – or the eternal masculine – in the Arab World', *New Left Review*, 161.

Giddens, A. (1979) *Central Problems in Social Theory* (Macmillan).

Giddens, A. (1984) *The Constitution of Society* (Cambridge, Polity).

Giddens, A. (1982) *Profiles and Critiques in Social Theory* (Macmillan).

Gilbert, P. (1984) *Depression* (Lawrence Erlbaum).

Gilbert, A. and Ward, P. (1984) 'Community action by the urban poor', *World Development*, 12, 769–82.

Godfrey, E. M. (1986) *Global Unemployment: the New Challenge* (Brighton, Wheatsheaf).

Goldstein, J. (1985) 'Basic human needs: the plateau curve', *World Development*, 13, 5.

Goodin, R. (1985) *Protecting the Vulnerable* (University of Chicago Press).

Goodin, R. (1988) *Reasons for Welfare* (Princeton University Press).

Gorovitz, S. (1982) *Doctor's Dilemmas* (Oxford University Press).

Gough, I. (1979) *The Political Economy of the Welfare State* (Macmillan).

Gough, I. and Doyal, L., with the Sheffield Group (1989) 'Socialism, democracy and human needs', in P. Alcock *et al.* (eds), *The Social Economy and the Democratic State: A New Policy Agenda* (Lawrence and Wishart).

Gould, A. (1988) *Conflict and Control in Welfare Politics: the Swedish Experience* (Longman).

Gouldner, A. (1971) *The Coming Crisis of Western Sociology* (New York, Basic Books).

Gramsci, A. (1971) *Selections from the Prison Notebooks*, trans. Q. Hoare and G. Nowell Smith (Lawrence and Wishart).

Gray, J. (1983) 'Classical liberalism, positional goals and the politicisation of poverty', in A. Ellis and K. Kumar (eds), *Dilemmas of Liberal Democracies* (Tavistock).

Green, D. (1987) *The New Right* (Brighton, Wheatsheaf).

Griffin, J. (1986) *Well-Being* (Oxford University Press).

Grimshaw, J. (1986) *Feminist Philosophers* (Brighton, Wheatsheaf).

Grundy, S. (1987) *Curriculum: Product or Praxis* (Lewes, Falmer).

Guntrip, H. (1968) *Schizoid Phenomena, Object Relations and the Self* (Hogarth).

Gutmann, A. (1980) *Liberal Equality* (New York, Cambridge University Press).

Gutmann, A. (1982) 'What's the use of going to school?', in A. Sen and B. Williams (eds), *Utilitarianism and Beyond* (Cambridge University Press).

Habermas, J. (1970a) 'Towards a theory of communicative competence', *Inquiry*, 13.

Habermas, J. (1970b) *Towards a Rational Society* (Boston, Beacon Press).

Habermas, J. (1971) *Knowledge and Human Interests* (Boston, Beacon).

Habermas, J. (1974) *Theory and Practice* (Heinemann).

Habermas, J. (1976) *Legitimation Crisis* (Boston, Beacon).

Habermas, J. (1981) *The Theory of Communicative Action*, Volume 1, trans. T. McCarthy (Boston, Beacon).

Habermas, J. (1981) 'New social movements', *Telos*, 49 (Fall).

Habermas, J. (1988) *The Philosophical Discourse of Modernity*, trans. F. Lawrence (Oxford, Polity).

Hadley, R. and Hatch, S. (1981) *Social Welfare and the Failure of the State: Centralised Social Services and Participatory Alternatives* (Allen and Unwin).

Hardiman, M. and Midgley, J. (1982) *The Social Dimension of Development* (Wiley).

Hardin, G. (1977) 'Lifeboat ethics: the case against helping the poor', in W. Aiken and H. LaFollette (eds), *World Hunger and Moral Obligation* (Englewood Cliffs, NJ, Prentice Hall).

Harris, D. (1987) *Justifying State Welfare* (Oxford, Blackwell).

Harris, M. (1979) *Cultural Materialism* (New York, Vintage Books).

Harris, R. (1987) 'Socialism and democracy: beyond state and civil society', *Radical Philosophy*, 45 (Spring).

Haworth, L. (1986) *Autonomy* (New Haven, Yale University Press).

Hayek, F. (1944) *The Road to Serfdom* (Routledge).

Hayek, F. (1960) *The Constitution of Liberty* (Routledge).

Hedstrom, P and Ringen, S. (1987) 'Age and income in contemporary society', *Journal of Social Policy*, 16, 2.

Hegel, G. W. F. (1977) *Phenomenology of Spirit*, trans. A. Miller (Oxford University Press).

Held, D. (1987) *Models of Democracy* (Cambridge, Polity).

Held, D. and Pollitt, C. (eds) (1986) *New Forms of Democracy* (Sage).

Heller, A. (1976) *The Theory of Need in Marx* (Allison and Busby).

Helman, C. (1990) *Culture, Health and Illness* (Wright).

Herskovits, M. (1972) *Cultural Relativism* (New York, Vintage Books).

Hicks, N. (1982) 'Sector priorities in meeting basic needs: some statistical evidence', *World Development*, 10, 6.

Hicks W. and Streeten, P. (1979) 'Indicators of development: the search for a basic needs yardstick', *World Developments*, 7, 6.

Hillhorst, J. and Klatter, M. (eds) (1985) *Social Development in the Third World: Level of Living Indicators and Social Planning* (Croom Helm)

Hillier, S. (1988) 'Women and population control in China: issues of sexuality, power and control', *Feminist Review*, 29.

Hindess, B. (1977) *Philosophy and Methodology in the Social Sciences* (Brighton, Harvester).

Hindess, B. (1987) *Freedom, Equality and the Market: Arguments on Social Policy* (Tavistock)

Hirst, P. and Woolley, P. (1982) *Social Relations and Human Attributes* (Tavistock).

Hodgson, G. (1984) *The Democratic Economy* (Penguin).

Hoffman, E. (1989) *Lost in Translation* (New York, Minerva).

Hollis, M. (1987) *The Cunning of Reason* (Cambridge University Press).

Humana, C. (1986) *World Human Rights Guide* (Pan).

Hume, D. (1963) *Enquiries* (Oxford University Press).

Ignatieff, M. (1984) *The Needs of Strangers* (Chatto and Windus).

Illich, I. *et al.* (1977) *Disabling Professions* (Marion Boyars).

International Assessment of Educational Progress (1988) *A World of Differences: an International Assessment of Mathematics and Science* (Educational Testing Service).

International Association for the Evaluation of Educational Achievement (1988) *Science Achievement in Seventeen Countries: a Preliminary Report* (Oxford, Pergamon).

International Labour Organisation (1976) *Employment, Growth and Basic Needs: A One-World Problem* (Geneva).

Ireland, T. (1985) 'Antonio Gramsci and popular education: reflections on the Brazilian experience' (unpublished).

Jacobs, M. (1989) 'What is "sustainability"?', Paper presented to Green Policies Seminar, Nottingham, UK (May).

Jacobs, M. (1990) *Sustainable Development* (Fabian Society, Tract 538).

Jaggar, A. (1983) *Feminist Politics and Human Nature* (Brighton, Harvester).

Jahoda, M. (1958) *Current Concepts of Positive Mental Health* (New York, Basic Books).

Jahoda, M. (1982) *Employment and Unemployment: a Social-Psychological Analysis* (Cambridge University Press).

Johansson, S. (1976) 'Towards a theory of social reporting', Swedish Institute for Social Research paper.

Johnson, C. (1982) *Revolutionary Change* (Longman).

Johnson, N. (1987) *The Welfare State in Transition: The Theory and Practice of Welfare Pluralism* (Brighton, Wheatsheaf)

Johnson, N. (1990) 'Problems for the mixed economy of welfare', in A. Ware and R. Goodin (eds), *Needs and Welfare* (Sage).

Jones, H. (1990) *Social Welfare in Third World Development* (Macmillan).

Jones, P. (1990) 'Universal and particular claims: from welfare rights to welfare states', in A. Ware and R. Goodin (eds), *Needs and Welfare* (Sage).

Judge, A. (1980) 'Needs communication: viable needs patterns and their identification', in K. Lederer (ed.), *Human Needs* (Cambridge, Mass, Oelgeschlager, Gunn and Hain).

Kabeer, N. (1988) 'Subordination and struggle: women in Bangladesh', *New Left Review*, 168.

Kakwani, N. (1980) *Income Inequality and Poverty* (Oxford University Press).

Kant, I. (1964) *Critique of Pure Reason*, trans. N.K.Smith (Macmillan).

Kamenetzky, M. (1981) 'The economics of the satisfaction of needs', *Human Systems Management*, 2.

Katzenstein, P. (1985) *Small States in World Markets: Industrial Policy in Europe* (Cornell University Press).

Keane, J. (1988) *Democracy and Civil Society* (Verso).

Keane, J. and Owens, J. (1986) *After Full Employment* (Hutchinson).

Keane, J. and Owens, J. (1987) 'Reply to Mike Rustin', *Critical Social Policy*, 18.

Keat, R. (1981) *The Politics of Social Theory* (Oxford).

Kellmer-Pringle, M. (1980) *The Needs of Children*, 2nd edn (Hutchinson).

Kennedy, I. and Grubb, A. (1989) *Medical Law: Text and Materials* (Butterworths).

Kleinman, A. (1984) 'Indigenous systems of healing: questions for professional, popular and folk care', in W. Salmon (ed.), *Alternative Medicines* (Tavistock).

Kleinman, A. and Good, B. (eds) (1985) *Culture and Depression: Studies in the Anthropology and Cross-Cultural Psychiatry of Affect and Disorder* (Berkeley, University of California Press).

Korbin, J. (ed.) (1981) *Child Abuse and Neglect: Cross-cultural Perspectives* (Berkeley, University of California Press).

Korpi, W. (1983) *The Democratic Class Struggle* (Routledge).

Kuhn, T. (1962) *The Structure of Scientific Revolutions* (Chicago University Press).

Kukathas, C. and Pettit, P. (1990) *Rawls* (Oxford, Polity).

Kurian, G. (1984) *Book of World Rankings* (New York, Facts on File Inc.).

Kuznets, S. (1955) 'Economic growth and income inequality', *American Economic Review*, 45, 1.

La Fontaine, J. (1985) 'Person and individual: some anthropological reflections', in M. Carrithers, S. Collins and S. Lukes (eds), *The Category of the Person* (Cambridge University Press).

Laclau, E. and Mouffe, C. (1985) *Hegemony and Socialist Strategy: Towards a Radical Democratic Politics* (Verso).

Laclau, E. and Mouffe, C. (1987) 'Post Marxism without apologies', *New Left Review*, 166.

Lancaster, K. (1966) 'A new approach to consumer theory', *Journal of Political Economy*, 74.

Lane, J.-E. and Ersson, S. (1987) *Politics and Society in Western Europe* (Sage).

Lash, S. and Urry, J. (1987) *The End of Organised Capitalism* (Cambridge, Polity).

Laurence, J. (1988) 'Statistics of a taboo', *New Statesman and Society* (1 July)

Lawson, H. (1985) *Reflexivity: The Post-Modern Predicament* (Hutchinson).

Lebowitz, M. (1979) 'Heller on Mart's concept of needs', *Science and Society* 43, 349–55.

Lederer, K. (1980) 'Introduction', in K.Lederer (ed.), *Human Needs* (Cambridge, Mass., Oelgeschlager, Gunn and Hain).

Lee, P. and Raban, C. (1988) *Welfare Theory and Social Policy* (Sage).

Lees, S. (1986) 'Sex, race and culture', *Feminist Review*, 22 (Spring).

Leeson, P. and Nixson, F. (eds) (1988) *Perspectives on Development* (Manchester University Press).

LeGrand, J. (1987) 'An international comparison of inequalities in health', LSE Research Paper.

Leiss, W. (1976) *The Limits to Satisfaction: An Essay on the Problem of Needs and Commodities* (University of Toronto Press).

Lerner, G. (1986) *The Creation of Patriarchy* (New York, Oxford University Press).

Lessnoff, N. (1986) *Social Contract* (Macmillan).

Levinson, D. (1989) *Family Violence in Cross-Cultural Perspective* (Sage).

Lieven, E. (1989) 'The psychological basis of co-operation and caring', in R. Hinde and P. Bateson (eds), *Education for Peace* (Nottingham, Spokesman).

Lindley, R. (1986) *Autonomy* (Macmillan).

Lovell, T. (ed.) (1990) *British Feminist Thought* (Oxford, Blackwell).

Lukes, S. (1974) *Power: A Radical View* (Macmillan).

Lukes, S. (1982) 'Of gods and demons: Habermas and practical reason', in J. Thompson and D. Held (eds), *Habermas* (Macmillan).

Lukes, S. (1985) *Marxism and Morality* (Oxford University Press).

McCarthy, T. (1978) *The Critical Theory of Jürgen Habermas* (Hutchinson).

McInnes, N. (1977) 'The politics of needs – or, who needs politics?' in R. Fitzgerald (ed.), *Human Needs and Politics* (NSW, Rushcutters Bay, Pergamon).

MacIntyre, A. (1983) *After Virtue* (Duckworth).

MacIntyre, A. (1988) *Whose Justice? Which Rationality?* (Duckworth).

McKeown, T. (1976) *The Modern Rise of Population* (Edward Arnold).

MacPherson, C. B. (1962) *The Political Theory of Possessive Individualism* (Oxford University Press).

MacPherson, C. B. (1973) *Democratic Theory: Essays in Retrieval* (Oxford, Clarendon Press).

MacPherson, S. (1987) *Five Hundred Million Children: Poverty and Child Welfare in the Third World* (Brighton, Wheatsheaf).

Mack, J. and Lansley, S. (1985) *Poor Britain* (George Allen and Unwin).

Mallmann, C. and Marcus, S. (1980), 'Logical clarification in the study of needs', in K. Lederer (ed.), *Human Needs* (Cambridge, Mass, Oelgeschlager, Gunn and Hain).

Mann, M. (1987) 'Ruling class strategies and citizenship', *Sociology*, 21, 2.

Marsalla, A., Sartorius, N., Jablensky, A. and Fenton, F. (1985) 'Cross-cultural studies of depressive disorders: an overview', in A. Kleinman and B. Good (eds), *Culture and Depression: Studies in the Anthropology and Cross-Cultural Psychiatry of Affect and Disorder* (Berkeley, University of California Press).

Marshall, T. H. (1963) 'Citizenship and social class', in *Sociology at the Crossroads and Other Essays* (Heinemann).

Marshall, T. H. (1981) *The Right to Welfare and Other Essays* (Heinemann).

Marx, K. (1961) *Capital*, volume 1 (Moscow, Foreign Languages Publishing House).

Marx, K. (1973) *Grundrisse*, trans. M.Nicolaus (Penguin).

Maslow, A. (1943) 'A theory of human motivation', *Psychological Review*, 50, pp. 370–96.

Maslow, A. (1954) *Motivation and Personality*, 2nd edn (Harper and Row).

Mason, J. and McCall Smith, R. (1987) *Law and Medical Ethics* (Butterworths).

Matthews, M. (1986) *Poverty in the Soviet Union* (Cambridge University Press).

Mauss, M. (1985) 'A category of the human mind: the notion of person; the notion of self', in M. Carrithers, S. Collins, S. Lukes (eds), *The Category of the Person* (Cambridge University Press).

Meade, J. E. (1990) 'Can we learn a " third way " from the Agathotopians?', *The Royal Bank of Scotland Review*, 167, 15–28.

Meehan, E. (1991) 'European citizenship and social policies', in M. Moran and U. Vogel (eds), *The Frontiers of Citizenship* (Macmillan).

Mehan, H. and Wood, H. (1975) *The Reality of Ethnomethodology* (New York, Krieger).

Mehta, S. (1984) *Rural Development: Policies and Programmes* (New Delhi, Sage).

Meillassoux, C. (1972) 'From reproduction to production: a Marxist approach to economic anthropology', *Economy and Society*, 1.

Melrose, D. (1982) *Bitter Pills* (Oxford, Blackwell).

Meyers, D. (1985) *Inalienable Rights: a Defense* (New York, Columbia University Press).

Mezzicch, J. and Berganza, C. (eds) (1984) *Culture and Psychopathology* (New York, Columbia University Press).

Midgley, M. (1979) *Beast and Man* (Methuen).

Miles, I. and Irvine, J. (eds) (1982) *The Poverty of Progress* (Oxford, Pergamon Press).

Miles, I. (1985) *Social Indicators for Human Development* (Frances Pinter).

Miller, D. (1976) *Social Justice* (Oxford, Clarendon).

Miller, D. (1989) *Market, State and Community: Theoretical Foundations of Market Socialism* (Oxford, Clarendon Press)

Miller, R. (1975) 'Rawls and Marxism', in N. Daniels (ed.), *Reading Rawls* (Oxford, Blackwell).

Moon, B. and Dixon, W. (1985) 'Politics, the state and basic human needs: a cross-national study', *American Journal of Political Science*, 29, 661–94.

Moore, H. (1988) *Feminism and Anthropology* (Cambridge, Polity).

Morgan, M., Calnon, M., and Manning, N. (1985) *Sociological Approaches to Health and Illness* (Croom Helm).

Morris, M. D. (1979) *Measuring the Condition of the World's Poor* (Oxford, Pergamon Press).

Murie, A. (1983) *Housing Inequality and Deprivation* (Heinemann).

Murphy, H. B. M. (1982) *Comparative Psychiatry: the International and Intercultural Distribution of Mental Illness* (Berlin, Springer-Verlag).

Myrdal, G. (1960) *Beyond the Welfare State* (New Haven, Yale University Press).

Nagel, T. (1971–2) 'War and massacre', *Philosophy and Public Affairs*, 1.

Nagel, T. (1979) *Mortal Questions* (New York, Cambridge University Press).
Nagel, T. (1978) *The Possibility of Altruism* (Princeton, Princeton University Press).
Naroll, R. (1983) *The Moral Order: an Introduction to the Human Situation* (Sage).
Nevitt, D. (1977) 'Demand and need', in H. Heisler (ed.), *Foundations of Social Administration* (Macmillan).
Nickel, J. (1987) *Making Sense of Human Rights* (Berkeley, University of California Press).
Nordic Conference on Environment and Development (1991) *Towards Sustainable Development: Reports on 14 Nordic Supported Projects* (Panos Institute).
Norman, R. (1976) *Hegel's Phenomenology* (University of Sussex Press).
Norman, R. (1983) *The Moral Philosophers* (Oxford, Clarendon).
Norris, P. (1987) *Politics and Sexual Equality: the Comparative Position of Women in Western Democracies* (Brighton, Wheatsheaf).
Nove, A. (1983) *The Economics of Feasible Socialism* (Allen and Unwin).
Nozick, R. (1974) *Anarchy, State and Utopia* (Oxford, Blackwell).
Obeyesekere, G. (1985) 'Depression, Buddhism and the work of culture in Sri Lanka', in A. Kleinman and B. Good (eds), *Culture and Depression: Studies in the Anthropology and Cross-Cultural Psychiatry of Affect and Disorder* (Berkeley, University of California Press).
O'Brien, M. (1981) *The Politics of Reproduction* (Routledge).
O'Higgins, M., Schmaus, G. and Stephenson, G. (1985) 'Income distribution and redistribution: a microdata analysis for seven countries', *LIS-CEPS Working Paper* 3.
Oliver, M. (1990) *The Politics of Disablement* (Macmillan).
O'Neill, O. (1981) 'Nozick's entitlements', in J. Paul (ed.), *Reading Nozick* (Oxford, Blackwell).
O'Neill, O. (1986) *Faces of Hunger* (Allen and Unwin).
OECD (1976) *Measuring Social Well-Being* (Paris).
OECD (1985) *Measuring Health Care 1960–83: Expenditure, Costs and Performance* (Paris).
OECD (1986) *Living Conditions in OECD Countries* (Paris).
OECD (1987) *OECD Environmental Data: Compendium 1987* (Paris).
OECD (1987a) *National Accounts: Main Aggregates: Supplement* (Paris).
OECD (1988) *Reforming Public Pensions* (Paris).
OECD (1989) *OECD in Figures* (Paris).
OPCS (1986) *Occupational Mortality*, Series DS, no. 2 (HMSO).
OPCS (1988a) *The Prevalence of Disability among Adults* (HMSO).
OPCS (1988b) *The Prevalence of Disability among Children* (HMSO).
Open University U205 Course Team (1985) *The Health of Nations* (Open University Press).
Osborne, P. 'Radicalism without limit?', in P. Osborne (ed.), *Socialism and the Limits of Liberalism* (Verso).
Overing, J. (ed.) (1985) *Reason and Morality* (Tavistock).
Pahl, J. (1980) 'Patterns of money management within marriage', *Journal of Social Policy*, 9, 3.

Pahl, J. (1989) *Money and Marriage* (Macmillan).

Parfitt, D. (1984) *Reasons and Persons* (Oxford, Clarendon Press).

Parsons, T. (1958) 'Definitions of health and illness in the light of American values and social structures', in E. Jago (ed.) *Patients, Physicians, and Illness* (New York, Free Press).

Partridge, E. (1981) 'Posthumous interests and posthumous respect', *Ethics*, 91, 243–64.

Pateman, C. (1970) *Participation and Democratic Theory* (Cambridge University Press).

Pateman, C. (1988) *The Sexual Contract* (Cambridge, Polity).

Pateman, C. (1989) 'The patriarchal welfare state', in C. Pateman (ed.), *The Disorder of Women* (Cambridge, Polity).

Penz, P. (1986) *Consumer Sovereignty and Human Interests* (Cambridge University Press).

Petchesky, R. (1984) *Abortion and Women's Choice* (Longman).

Pettit, P. (1980) *Judging Justice* (Routledge).

Pfaller, A., Gough, I. and Therborn, G. (eds) (1991) *Can the Welfare State Compete? A Comparative Study of Five Advanced Capitalist Countries* (Macmillan).

Phares, E. (1976) *Locus of Control in Personality* (Morristown, NJ, General Learning Press).

Phillips, A. (1991) 'Citizenship and feminist politics', in G. Andrews (ed.), *Citizenship* (Lawrence and Wishart).

Piachaud, D. (1987) 'Problems in the definition and measurement of poverty', *Journal of Social Policy*, 16, 2.

Piaget, J. (1952) *The Origins of Intelligence in Children* (New York, International Universities Press).

Plant, R. (1971) *Hegel* (Allen and Unwin).

Plant, R., Lesser, H. and Taylor-Gooby, P. (1980) *Political Philosophy and Social Welfare* (Routledge).

Plant, R. (1986) 'Needs, agency and rights', in C. Sampford and J. Law (eds), *Law, Rights and the Welfare State* (Croom Helm).

Plant, R. (1989) 'The neo-liberal social vision', in J. Elliott and I. Swanson (eds) *,The Renewal of Social Vision* (University of Edinburgh Centre for Theology and Public Issues, Occasional Paper 17).

Plant, R. (1990) 'Citizenship and rights', in IEA (ed.), *Citizenship and Rights in Thatcher's Britain: Two Views* (Institute of Economic Affairs).

Platts, M. (1979) *Ways of Meaning* (Routledge).

Pogge, T. (1989) *Realizing Rawls* (Ithaca, Cornell University Press).

Polanyi, K. (1957) *The Great Transformation* (Boston, Beacon Press).

Policy Research Unit (1990) *Finding Out About Your Community: How to do a Social Audit* (Leeds Polytechnic, Policy Research Unit).

Pollack, S. (1985) 'Sex and the contraceptive art', in H. Homans (ed.), *The Sexual Politics of Reproduction* (Gower).

Pollitt, C. (1986) 'Democracy and bureaucracy', in D. Held and C. Pollitt (eds), *New Forms of Democracy* (Sage).

Prais, S. J. and Wagner, K. (1985) 'Schooling standards in England and Germany', *National Institute Economic Review* (May).

Pritchard, K. (1988) 'Comparative human rights: promise and practice', in D. Cingranelli (ed.), *Human Rights: Theory and Measurement* (Macmillan).

Purdy, D. (1988) *Social Power and the Labour Market* (Macmillan).

Radical Science Journal Collective (1981) 'Science, technology, medicine and the socialist movement', *Radical Science Journal*, 11.

Ram, R. (1985) 'The role of real income level and income distribution in the fulfilment of basic needs', *World Development*, 13, 5.

Ram, R. (1988) 'Economic development and income inequality', *World Development*, 16, 11.

Rawls, J. (1972) *A Theory of Justice* (Oxford University Press).

Rawls, J. (1982) 'The basic liberties and their priority', in S. McMurrin (ed.), *The Tanner Lectures on Human Value*, 3 (Salt Lake City, University of Utah Press).

Raz, J. (1986) *The Morality of Freedom* (Oxford University Press).

Reiser, S. (1981) *Medicine and the Reign of Technology* (Cambridge University Press).

Renner, C. and Navarro, V. (1989) 'Why is our population of uninsured and underinsured persons growing?', *International Journal of Health Services*, 19, 3.

Renshon, S. (1977) 'Human needs and political analysis: an examination of a framework', in R. Fitzgerald (ed.), *Human Needs and Politics* (NSW, Rushcutters Bay, Pergamon).

Renteln, A. (1990) *International Human Rights: Universalism versus Relativism* (Sage).

Rescher, N. (1972) *Welfare: the Social Issues in Philosophical Perspective* (Pittsburgh: University of Pittsburgh Press).

Richards, J. R. (1984) *The Sceptical Feminist* (Penguin).

Rist, G. (1980), 'Basic questions about basic human needs', in K. Lederer (ed.), *Human Needs* (Cambridge, Mass, Oelgeschlager, Gunn and Hain).

Roderick, R. (1986) *Habermas and the Foundations of Critical Theory* (Macmillan).

Rorty, R. (1980) 'Pragmatism, relativism, and irrationalism', *Proceedings and Addresses of the American Philosophical Association*, 53.

Rose, S., Lewontin, R. and Kamin, L. (1984) *Not in Our Genes: Biology and Human Nature* (Penguin).

Rowbotham, S. (1979) 'The Women's Movement and organizing for socialism', in S. Rowbotham, L. Segal and H. Wainwright, *Beyond The Fragments* (Merlin Press).

Rowbotham, S. (1986) 'Feminism and democracy', in D. Held and C. Pollitt (eds), *New Forms of Democracy* (Sage).

Rueschemeyer, D. and Evans, P. B. (1985) 'The state and economic transformation: towards an analysis of the conditions underlying effective intervention', in P. B. Evans, D. Rueschemeyer and T. Skocpol (eds), *Bringing the State Back In* (Cambridge University Press).

Runciman, W. (1966) *Relative Deprivation and Social Justice* (Routledge).

Rupesinghe, K. (1986) 'The welfare state in Sri Lanka', in E. Øyen (ed.), *Comparing Welfare States and their Futures* (Gower).

Rustin, M. (1985) *For A Pluralist Socialism* (Verso).

Rustin, M. (1987) 'The non-obsolescence of the right to work', *Critical Social Policy*, 18.

Rustin, M. (1989) 'Post-Kleinian psychoanalysis and the post-modern', *New Left Review*, 173.

Ruttan, W. (1984) 'Integrated rural development programmes: a historical perspective', *World Development*, 12, 393–401.

Sahlins, M. (1974) *Stone Age Economics* (Tavistock).

Salmon, J. (ed.) (1984) *Alternative Medicines* (Tavistock).

Sandbrook, R. (1985) *The Politics of Africa's Economic Stagnation* (Cambridge University Press).

Schutz, A. (1965) 'The social world and the theory of social action', in D. Braybrooke (ed.), *Philosophical Problems of the Social Sciences* (New York, Macmillan).

Scott, H. (1984) *Working Your Way to the Bottom: the Feminisation of Poverty* (Pandora).

Seager, J. and Olson, A. (1986) *Women in the World: an International Atlas* (Pluto).

Sedgwick, P. (1982) *Psychopolitics* (Pluto).

Segal, L. (1987) *Is the Future Female?* (Virago).

Seligman, M. (1975) *Helplessness* (New York, Freeman).

Selowsky, M. (1981) 'Income distribution, basic needs and trade-offs with growth', *World Development*, 9, 1.

Sen, A. (1970) *Collective Choice and Social Welfare* (San Francisco, Holden-Day).

Sen, A. (1981) *Poverty and Famines* (Oxford, Clarendon Press).

Sen, A. (1984) *Resources, Values and Development* (Oxford, Blackwell).

Sen, A. (1985) *Commodities and Capabilities* (Amsterdam, Elsevier).

Sen, A. (1987) *The Standard of Living: the Tanner Lectures*, ed. G. Hawthorn (Cambridge University Press).

Sen, A. (1990) 'More than 100 million women are missing', *New York Review of Books* (20 December).

Shah, N. (1989) 'It's up to you sisters: black women and radical social work', in M. Langan and P. Lee (eds), *Radical Social Work Today* (Unwin Hyman).

Silber, J. (1983) 'ELL (the equivalent length of life) or another attempt at measuring development', *World Development*, 11, 1.

Singer, P. (1979) 'Famine, affluence and morality', in P. Laslett and J. Fishkin (eds), *Philosophy, Politics and Society* (Oxford, Blackwell).

Sivard, R. L. (1989) *World Military and Social Expenditures 1989* (Washington DC, World Priorities Inc.).

Smith, B. and B. (1983) 'Across the kitchen table: a sister to sister dialogue', in C. Moraga and G. Anzaldua (eds), *This Bridge Called My Back: Writings by Radical Women of Color* (New York, Kitchen Table Press).

Smith, D. (1983) *Barrington Moore* (Macmillan).

Smith, G. (1980) *Social Need: Policy, Practice and Research* (Routledge).

Smith, R. (1987) *Unemployment and Health* (Oxford University Press).

Soper, K. (1981) *On Human Needs* (Brighton, Harvester).

Soper, K. (1990) 'Feminism, humanism and post-modernism', *Radical Philosophy* (Summer).

Spearitt, D. (1990) 'Evaluation of national comparisons', in H. Walberg and G. Haertel (eds), *The International Encyclopedia of Educational Evaluation* (Oxford, Pergamon).

Springborg, P. (1981) *The Problem of Human Needs and the Critique of Civilisation* (Allen and Unwin).

Stacey, M. (1988) *The Sociology of Health and Healing* (Unwin Hyman).

Stankiewicz, W. (1980) *Approaches to Democracy* (Arnold).

Stanley, L. and Wise, S. (1983) *Breaking Out: Feminist Consciousness and Feminist Research* (Routledge).

Stark, E. (1982) 'What is medicine?', *Radical Science Journal*, 12.

Steedman, I. (1989) *From Exploitation to Altruism* (Cambridge, Polity).

Stern, A. *et al.* (1984) *Fundamentals of Air Pollution* (Academic Press).

Stewart, F. (1985) *Planning to Meet Basic Needs* (Macmillan).

Streeten, P. (1981) *Development Perspectives* (Macmillan).

Streeten, P. (1984) 'Basic needs: some unsettled questions', *World Development*, 12, 90.

Streeten, P. and associates (1981) *First Things First: Meeting Basic Human Needs in Developing Countries* (Oxford University Press).

Szasz, T. (1961) *The Myth of Mental Illness* (New York, Harper and Row).

Szulkin, R. (1987) 'Political resources', in R. Erikson and R. Åberg (eds), *Welfare in Transition: A Survey of Living Conditions in Sweden 1968–1981* (Oxford, Clarendon Press).

Tang Nain, G. (1991) 'Black women, sexism and racism: black or anti-racist feminism?', *Feminist Review*, 37.

Taylor, C. (1975) *Hegel* (Cambridge University Press).

Taylor, D. (1989) 'Citizenship and social power', *Critical Social Policy*, 26.

Taylor, P. (1986) *Respect for Nature* (Princeton University Press).

Tennant, C. and Bebbington, P. (1978) 'The social causation of depression: a critique of the work of Brown and his colleagues', *Psychological Medicine* 8, 565–75.

Therborn, G. (1977) 'The rule of capital and the rise of democracy', *New Left Review*, 103, 3–41.

Therborn, G. (1991) 'Sweden', in A. Pfaller, I. Gough and G. Therborn (eds), *Can the Welfare State Compete? A Comparative Study of Five Advanced Capitalist Countries* (Macmillan).

Thirlwall, A. (1983) *Growth and Development*, 3rd edn (Macmillan).

Thompson, G. (1987) *Needs* (Routledge).

Timpanaro, S. (1975) *On Materialism* (New Left Books).

Tinker, A. (1981) *The Elderly in Modern Society* (Longman)

Titmuss, R. (1970) *The Gift Relationship* (Allen and Unwin).

Titmuss, R. (1971) 'Welfare "rights", law and discretion', *Political Quarterly* (April-June).

Townsend, P. (1962) 'The meaning of poverty', *British Journal of Sociology*, 18, 3.

Townsend, P. (1972) 'The needs of the elderly and the planning of hospitals', in R. Canvin and N. Pearson (eds), *Needs of the Elderly for Health and Welfare Services* (University of Exeter).

Townsend, P. (1979a) *Poverty in the United Kingdom* (Penguin).

Townsend, P. (1979b) 'The Development of Research on Poverty', in Department of Health and Social Security, Social Security Research, *The Definition of Poverty* (HMSO).

Townsend, P. (1981) 'An alternative concept of poverty', *Division for the Study of Development* (Paris, UNESCO).

Townsend, P. (1985) 'A sociological approach to the measurement of poverty – a rejoinder to Professor Amartya Sen', *Oxford Economic Papers*, 37, 659–668.

Townsend, P. (1987) 'Deprivation', *Journal of Social Policy*, 16, 2.

Trigg, R. (1984) 'The sociobiological view of man', in S. Brown (ed.), *Objectivity and Cultural Divergence* (Cambridge University Press).

Trigg, R. (1985) *Understanding Social Science* (Oxford, Blackwell).

Turner, B. (1986) *Citizenship and Capitalism* (Allen and Unwin).

Turner, J. (1972) 'Housing issues and the standards problem', *Ekistics*, 33.

United Nations (1975) *The Status of Women and Family Planning* (New York, UN).

United Nations (1977) *The Social Impact of Housing* (New York, UN).

United Nations (1984) *Recent Levels and Trends of Contraceptive Use as Assessed in 1983* (New York, UN).

United Nations (1984a) *Improving Concepts and Methods for Statistics and Indicators on the Situation of Women* (New York, UN).

United Nations (1985) *Selected Statistics and Indicators on the Status of Women*, Report of the Secretary-General (Nairobi A/CONF. 116/10).

United Nations (1987) *Environmental Data Report* (New York, UN).

UNDP (1990) *Human Development Report 1990* (Oxford University Press).

UNESCO (1974) *International Standard Classification of Education* (Paris, UNESCO).

UNESCO (1989) *Statistical Yearbook 1989* (Paris, UNESCO).

UNICEF (1987) *The State of the World's Children* (Oxford University Press).

US Bureau of Justice (1988) 'International Crime Rates', *Bureau of Justice Statistics: Special Report* (May).

Van der Veen, R. and van Parijs, P. (1987) 'A capitalist road to communism', *Theory and Society* 15.

Veit-Wilson, J. H. (1987) 'Consensual approaches to poverty lines and social security', *Journal of Social Policy* 16, 2.

Vincent, R. (1986) *Human Rights and International Relations* (Cambridge University Press).

Von Wright, G. H. (1963) *Varieties of Goodness* (Routledge).

Waldron, J. (ed.) (1984) *Theories of Rights* (Oxford University Press).

Walker, A. (1984) *Social Planning: A Strategy for Socialist Welfare* (Oxford, Blackwell).

Walker, R. (1987) 'Consensual approaches to the definition of poverty: towards an alternative methodology', *Journal of Social Policy* 16, 2.

Wall, G. (1975) 'The concept of interest in politics', *Politics and Society*, 5, pp. 487–510.

Wallace, A. (1986) *Homicide: the Social Reality* (Sydney, NSW, Bureau of Crime Statistics and Research).

Walsh, A. and Warren, K. (1979) 'Selective primary health care', *New England Journal of Medicine* 301, 967–74.

Walzer, M. (1977) *Just and Unjust Wars* (New York, Basic Books).

Walzer, M. (1983) *Spheres of Justice* (Oxford, Blackwell).

Warr, P. (1987) *Work, Unemployment and Mental Health* (Oxford, Clarendon Press).

Weale, A. (1983) *Political Theory and Social Policy* (Macmillan).

Weigel, V. (1986) 'The basic needs approach: overcoming the poverty of *homo oeconomicus*', *World Development* 14, 2.

Wesson, R. (ed.) (1987) *Democracy: A Worldwide Survey* (New York, Praeger).

White, A. (1971) *Modal Thinking* (Oxford, Blackwell).

White, A. (1984) *Rights* (Oxford University Press).

White, S. (1988) *The Recent Work of Jürgen Habermas* (Cambridge University Press).

Whitehead, M. (1988) *The Health Divide* (Penguin).

Wiggens, D. (1985) 'Claims of need', in T. Honderich (ed.), *Morality and Objectivity* (Routledge).

Williams, A. (1974) '"Need" as a demand concept', in A. J. Culyer (ed.), *Economic Policies and Social Goals* (Martin Robertson).

Williams, A. (1985) 'The value of QALYs', *Health and Social Service Journal*, Supplement (18 July).

Williams, F. (1987) 'Racism and the discipline of social policy: a critique of welfare theory', *Critical Social Policy*, (20 Autumn).

Williams, R. (1965) *The Long Revolution* (Penguin).

Williams, R. (1973) *Communications* (Penguin).

Williams, R. (1979) *Politics and Letters* (Verso).

Winch, P. (1974) 'Understanding a primitive society', in B. Wilson (ed.), *Rationality* (Oxford, Blackwell).

Wisner, B. (1988) *Power and Need in Africa: Basic Human Needs and Development* (Earthscan).

Wittgenstein, L. (1973) *Philosophical Investigations* (Oxford, Blackwell).

Wolff, R. (1970) *In Defense of Anarchism* (New York, Harper and Row).

Wong, D. (1984) *Moral Relativity* (Berkeley, University of California Press).

World Bank (1985) *World Development Report 1985* (Oxford University Press).

World Bank (1987) *World Development Report 1987* (Oxford University Press).

World Bank (1988) *World Development Report 1988* (Oxford University Press).

World Commission on Environment and Development (1987) *Our Common Future (the Brundtland Report)* (Oxford University Press).

World Health Organisation (1973) *The International Pilot Study of Schizophrenia* (Geneva, Switzerland, WHO).

World Health Organisation (1978) *Primary Health Care* (Geneva, Switzerland, WHO).

World Health Organisation (1980) *International Classification of Impairments, Disabilities and Handicaps* (Geneva, Switzerland, WHO).

World Health Organisation (1982) *Manuals on Child Mental Health and Psychosocial Development* (Geneva, Switzerland, WHO).

World Health Organisation (1983a) *Traditional Medicine and Health Care Coverage* (Geneva, Switzerland, WHO).

World Health Organisation (1983b) *Depressive Disorders in Different Cultures* (Geneva, Switzerland, WHO).

World Health Organisation (1987) *Evaluation of the Strategy for Health for All by the Year 2000: Seventh Report on the World Health Situation* (Geneva, Switzerland, WHO).

World Health Organisation (1989) *World Health Statistics Annual 1989* (Geneva, Switzerland, WHO).

World Resources Institute (1987) *World Resources 1987* (New York, Basic Books).

Wright, P and Treacher, A. (eds) (1982) *The Problem of Medical Knowledge* (Edinburgh University Press).

Young, I. M. (1989) 'Polity and group difference: a critique of the ideal of universal citizenship', *Ethics*, 99.

Young, R. (1977) 'Science is social relations', *Radical Science Journal*, 5.

Yoxen, E. (1983) *The Gene Business* (Pan).

Index